# Power, Performance and Ethics

# Power, Performance and Ethics

Key articles from *Director*
Britain's leading boardroom
magazine

Edited by
Stuart Rock and Carol Kennedy

Butterworth-Heinemann Ltd
Linacre House, Jordan Hill, Oxford OX2 8DP

 PART OF REED INTERNATIONAL BOOKS

OXFORD   LONDON   BOSTON
MUNICH   NEW DELHI   SINGAPORE   SYDNEY
TOKYO   TORONTO   WELLINGTON

First published 1991

**British Library Cataloguing in Publication Data**
Power performance and ethics in the boardroom:
  Key articles from 'Director'.
  I. Rock, Stuart   II. Kennedy, Carol
  658.001

ISBN 0 7506 0104 3

Printed and bound in Great Britain by
Redwood Press Limited, Melksham, Wiltshire

# Contents

**Section Ten  Predictions**

# Foreword

*Director* is unique among the world's business magazines in the range and diversity of the information it provides for its influential boardroom readership. Published exclusively for the Institute of Directors (IOD), with 48,000 members around the world, its principal aim is to help its readers run their businesses more effectively with its comprehensive coverage of boardroom issues. But in keeping with the individual, rather than corporate, nature of IOD membership, the magazine also views its readers as having a wide range of interests beyond the strict confines of the executive desk – interests in such areas as politics, religion, ethics, social trends, national and international developments.

In few other business magazines would one be likely to read, in the same issue, an analysis of management at American Airlines, an article on the business activities of TV celebrities, the reflections of a leading management educator and an interview with the Archbishop of Canterbury which became headline news on the national media after Dr Robert Runcie warned of Britain becoming a 'Pharisee' society in which the wealthy and successful felt superior to the poor and unsuccessful.

A year earlier, in a 1988 issue containing major business and political interviews and an in-depth study of Nikko, the Japanese financial giant, *Director* published a wide-ranging investigation of Britain's changing social goals and culture since 1950. It reflected some important aspects of the national mood at the end of the acquisitive 1980s, and its theme was carried through a subsequent series of interviews with church leaders in Britain, culminating in the much-reported Runcie comments.

These 'social' studies can all be found in this book in Section Five, Ethics and Values, an area that increasingly concerns business leaders who must consider the responsibilities of business to its community and its environment, and who have the problem of attracting the brightest and best of a diminishing pool of young talent in the decade ahead.

Connected with this, and the values that young people can bring to a business career in the 1990s, is the whole subject of 'company culture' and how it can be changed and managed. This is covered in Section Three, The Art of Management, a section that also includes Sir Adrian Cadbury's 'Rules for a responsible board', the leading international management guru Peter Drucker on managing innovation, insights into how Nissan gets the best from its workforce and the qualities needed in 'tomorrow's chairmen'.

One of *Director*'s strengths is its ability to get inside companies and watch their chief executives in action. In September 1985 the magazine published a 'fly-on-the-wall' study of Lucas Industries' new strategy for out-performing the best of its competitors. This 'Competitiveness Achievement Plan' proved the bedrock of Lucas' revival in a testing period for the British engineering industry. Section Four, Inside Companies, reveals how it was done, along with other illuminating glimpses of top management at work.

In Section Two, Power and Leadership, readers will also be able to watch such powerful figures at work as Lord King of British Airways, Sir Jeffrey (now Lord) Sterling of P & O, the Cadbury brothers, Sir Simon Hornby, chairman of W. H. Smith, and, across the Atlantic, Ken Olsen, the austere chief executive of DEC.

In Section Eight, The Ultimate Enterprise Culture, we chart the heady rise of Hong Kong as a business and financial centre for the Pacific Rim, and watch it plan for its future after 1997 under a new 'head office' – China. Finally, in Section Nine, The European Dimension, we look at some of the companies and institutions in the vast market for which all business people will need to plan by 1992.

*Director* has been in business in its present form since 1947, publishing hundreds of influential articles over the years and interviewing many of the leading figures of the past five decades. This book represents the pick of the issues published from 1980 to 1991, providing many insights into the business achievements of the decade and ideas that have shaped the age, starting with Friedrich Hayek's vision of a monetarist economic miracle and ending with the predictions of four of Britain's top industrialists for the challenges facing business in the 1990s.

We believe it will prove stimulating, informative and lively reading for anyone interested in the arts of management, the encouragement of enterprise and an understanding of the wider issues which will increasingly affect all types and sizes of company as we approach the twenty-first century.

*John Nicholas*
Chairman, Director Publications Ltd and Deputy Director-General of the
Institute of Directors

Section One

---

# Introduction: How the Eighties Looked Then

---

# 1

# Britain and business in the next ten years

January 1980

## Four chairmen predict

On Monday 3 December 1979, as my Transatlantic flight from New York approached Prestwick Airport, I saw to my left the Arran hills looming through the early morning mist. We banked steeply prior to landing and below us the small farms of Ayrshire looked particularly bleak. An American in the seat behind, sighting the land of his fathers for the first time, said to his wife, 'Gee, Scotland sure is a gutsy country!' I thought of this remark as I drove through the industrial wasteland that forms so much of the west of Scotland. On I drove to Edinburgh where I passed the house in which Sir Walter Scott had lived and I remembered how he had blamed no one for his financial disaster and had so bravely written his way out of crippling bankruptcy; and on I drove past the houses in which Bell of the telephone and Simpson of chloroform had been born, and as I entered Charlotte Square I thought of the great entrepreneurs in the latter part of the nineteenth century who had started the many investment trusts which are today my business neighbours. And so I reached the pile of arrears on my desk.

'Please let me have a 500 word article on your hopes for the 1980s' wrote George Bull, 'and let me have it in two days' time.' My first reaction was that there was insufficient time. Perhaps I would write a brief note about the control of inflation, improved employee relationships, the sort of thing that every sensible businessman would comment upon. But I had come from the United States where people do find time and so I determined to produce my 500 words.

So what do I hope for the 1980s? I hope that the Scottish people of that decade will be, as my co-passenger stated, 'gutsy' people and that like Sir Walter Scott they will not blame others for their misfortunes. Rather will they, by their own energies and commitment, cure the problems which I saw on my homeward journey through Clydeside.

I hope that my countrymen in the 1980s will show the inventiveness (dare

I ask for a little of the genius?) that was found in Bell and Simpson and so many other Scots of an earlier age.

I hope that a generation of entrepreneurs will emerge to build businesses like the innovators who founded our investment trusts. With North Sea oil and the many science-based companies already operating in Scotland, there are such great opportunities.

I hope that when I fly into Prestwick in December 1989 I will be as proud of the Scotsmen of the decade that will have then passed as I am today of the remarkable Scotsmen of history who have so influenced the world.

And above all, I hope that all who live North of the Border during the next ten years will have as much fun and fulfilment as I have enjoyed in the last ten years.

*Charles Fraser, W & J Burness and Chairman of the IOD Scottish Division*

My hopes for Britain and business in the 1980s centre on the need for a radical change in corporate objectives and in the style and content of management to bring it about. This change is the responsibility of both management and the investment community. It has the advantage that it is unlikely to be broadly opposed by the trade union movement.

Of the changes foreshadowed under the heading of corporate change, the most critical to me is that we should recognize the finite size of the world and the nearness of each area of its surface to every other, brought about by the revolution in communications and telecommunications.

Britain is not the home market to be fought over with cut-throat ferocity. Win 100 per cent of it and you are still small in the world today. Do not just export but translate into other markets all round the world before it is too late. Preoccupation with the home market is the surest way to stay small enough not to be able to resist the competition of imports.

Of course there will be a shift in emphasis from manufacturing to service industries, but the same principles apply. Already other nations are catching up or overtaking us in the service areas too.

Our pre-occupation with the home market is matched only by our preoccupation with obsolete products and industries. We have lost out entirely in the development of consumer durables – not a typewriter, a binocular, a camera; not a transistor radio or portable tape recorder, a watch or a calculator of consequence is made in this country, and television and private cars are going the same way.

The next revolution, the technological revolution leading to the information society, is just round the corner. Positions have already been taken by the leading industrial countries: in microprocessors and computers, in data handling, transmission and storage, in word and text processors, in transaction terminals and in voice recognition and response robots.

We must ask ourselves squarely what position we have taken. How can technology management and finance find a common language in a society in which they scarcely have a common meeting ground? And unless this is done, who is to finance the vast investment which will be needed to get Britain into just a handful of products, systems and services which relate to the future.

Do not expect it from government directly – the investment in Concorde alone would have put the UK in the forefront of the microprocessor business.

For the same reason do not say we cannot afford it – the investment resource is there but it needs massive re-direction.

The critical decisions for Britain in taking stock of the technology revolution are in education and in investment. Both need, in differing ways, co-operation with the state, with government. They will not be effected by market forces alone – because we are no longer an island. It is the world market forces that we are talking about and they are large and they are against us.

We have more material and energy resources than Japan or Germany. We have a fund of human talent better educated than most. We need some good management decisions backed by adequate financial resources to survive and grow.

*Sir Kenneth Corfield, Chairman and Chief Executive, Standard Telephones and Cables Limited*

In looking to the future for Britain and particularly business, it is my hope that in the 1980s we can start by accentuating the positive rather than the negative.

There is a lot in British industry which is good but we rarely hear about it and instead we seem to spend time finding out what is wrong and highlighting it rather than highlighting what is good and quietly correcting what is not.

I hope to see this positive attitude from people in all parts of industry, whether they be white or blue collar, managers or managed, unionized or non-unionized, and by stating it in this way I emphasize something which I hope can be gradually eliminated from companies – the concept of the two sides of industry, the 'we' and 'them'. Our companies cannot compete effectively and thereby generate the cash flow which produces investment, which produces jobs, unless there is a genuine desire on the part of all people in the company to keep the company in business and work together for a common aim rather than in opposite directions.

If we can eliminate, or at least reduce, the amount of conflict, those who produce can produce more at a lower cost and those who plan and develop for the future can have more time to get their plans right and ensure the investment takes place. So I hope for more stability and less conflict.

This does not mean less change. It probably means more change, but positive change which is itself exciting and which generates the enthusiasm which produces results.

In the industrial and commercial world which produces the wealth on which we all depend, it is the results which count and results come from positive action. I want to hear of more people approaching a problem by saying, 'That's a good idea – how do I apply it and how do I make it work?' Then, when the results come in, I want us to be proud of what we have done and not be apologetic because I believe there are the native resources in Britain to revive the nation's fortunes if we decide that is what we want, and then take a determined and positive approach to achieve it.

*Dr A. W. Pearce, Chairman and Chief Executive, Esso Petroleum Ltd*

I have high hopes for Britain and business in the 1980s. I have written previously, 'I do not believe that this island race which has been breeding courage, stamina, determination and native genius for a thousand years, can go into the same backwaters as Eastern Europe after thirty-five years of soft living on borrowed money and lack of dynamic, outspoken leadership'.

Since 1946 Britain has gone backwards: six years of socialist borrowing, the débâcle of Suez, Macmillan's salesmanship 'You've never had it so good,' opportunist Wilson, indecisive Heath; and finally, last winter, when Callaghan showed himself less able to deal with the situation than an average Rural District Councillor.

Nevertheless, last winter was our turning point. People saw through the vicious Left Wing minority and recorded this on 3 May. We elected a new type of leader, a woman with brains, drive and integrity who has shown that no Prime Minister in peace time in this century has matched her courage and determination in fighting for Britain, regardless of personal popularity. Her belief in private enterprise, individual freedom and fair reward is not offered as a quick solution but much has been achieved in six months.

Writing in December it is encouraging to see light coming from many directions. British Leyland workers voted seven to one to accept a re-organization plan. The miners have voted not to strike. I believe we will see a further reduction in public expenditure of at least £2,000m a year. Civil Service staff will probably be cut another 50,000, making a saving of £250m a year. Cuts in our over-manned Local Government staff can save £350m a year. Several per cent of hospital administrators are surplus and will probably go.

Five years ago Monty Finniston reported that British Steel would not be viable unless over-manning of 50,000 or 60,000 was eliminated. This will now take effect. Failure to take action previously has cost us over £2,000m.

I believe that by the time you read this we will again be closer to our Rhodesian friends who voluntarily fought side-by-side with us in the last war.

We are the only industrial country in the world which will be self-supporting for oil. On current world prices that is a bonus of £7,500m a year. We have vast reserves of coal. We deep-mined 285m tonnes of coal manually in 1913 – three times our present output. We can and must double our present output with new techniques in our newly-found thick seams.

More people now realize that we will only get what we work for and they must be encouraged. Management at all levels has failed to communicate with workers. We must tell everybody that the production time of a Mini is double what it was twenty years ago; production time of a Volkswagen is half what it was and the man hours in a Honda are a third of what they were twenty years ago. Their quality is constantly improving – ours is deteriorating. Real earnings in Germany, France and Japan are much higher than ours but British workers must understand that, as these people produce more, their costs are lower. Enlightened management realizes that we must accept a high degree of responsibility for our failure because we have allowed the 'Red Robbies' to do all the talking. Managers are learning that their first priority is the ability to lead their own work people.

Perhaps the greatest asset of the British people is that when they are told what faces them, when they are appealed to in the right way and called on to exploit what they have – British character – they always respond. History has proved this again and again, but people must be told the facts and properly led. Employers and management must roll up their sleeves to show what can be done, clearly spell out the truth and stand firm. Then I believe we will again see Britain a leading country in the world. There is a little more light showing every day; we have slowly started to come back. In 1980 we must ensure that everybody is encouraged to quicken the pace.

*Howard Hicks, Chairman of the IDC Group Ltd and Chairman, IOD Midlands Branch*

# 2

# Britain's economic miracle: is it still within grasp?

February 1982

## Edmund Goldberger discusses with Friedrich Hayek

Professor Hayek is one of the intellectual giants of this century. Awarded the 1974 Nobel Prize in Economics, he was Professor of Economics for some twenty years – including the war years – at London University, afterwards at Chicago University and finally at Freiburg, Germany, where, now retired from teaching, he continues to enrich the world with his writings and lectures.

He showed his eminence in the practical field as well as the co-architect and co-author of the Erhard-led 'Social Market economy', which brought about the German 'economic miracle' after the war, an event unique in our or other times.

In his *Constitution of Liberty* he re-formulates the great aspirations of man, the conditions for liberty and freedom so indispensable to the dignity of the individual. People are individuals and not abstractions: not objects for organized compassion or political effusions, but persons who act and react.

The work which exerted most influence is his *Road to Serfdom*, first published in 1944. Even Keynes, whose 'Keynesianism' was criticized in the book, found himself in 'deeply moved agreement'. In classical and closely argued logical form, Professor Hayek exposes the true face of socialism and its consequences for the fibre of society and the hard-won elementary freedoms of the individual.

Professor Hayek took up the battle against authoritarian and totalitarian attitudes from whatever quarters they originated. He clinically exposed the origins and concepts, which the tyrants of the Left and the Right had in common.

Inspired by the great humanist tradition and true-humanitarian aspirations, he has persevered through his long life and courageously emphasized the classical verities that spring from within, the essential values of civilization and its foundations, which should not be manipulated by expediencies and desires for political popularity.

*Professor Hayek, you once said that 'to aim for heaven makes life hell'. What did you mean?*

Yes, this was in the context of my belief that high-minded social justice concepts make the state behave in a way which results in the opposite of its best intentions. Ideals cannot be enforced by coercive government. Here lies the fallacy of socialism and of its superficial attraction. Socialism requires a completely planned economy. To operate this, it must in practice be totalitarian, however much this may be rejected in theory. So it obliterates the freedom which we take so much for granted.

The tragedy is that people realize what freedom really means only after it is lost. The mild authoritarians in our midst are incapable of foreseeing what is in store for them – their elimination by more determined and rigorous totalitarians.

Another intellectual trap for the gullible innocent (or the semi-marxist, the *salon* marxist) has been to condone the brutal horrors of Stalin as regrettable means to an ideal end. Or to hold the strange belief that if socialist power is achieved by democratic process, by voting, it will then not be coercive. Well, Hitler was democratically elected. There are socialists of the Right as well as of the Left. . . .

Socialism equates society with the state. From this it follows that the state is automatically assumed always to act in the interest of society. When the whole economy is nationalized and exclusively in the hands of the state, the individual becomes a cog in the economic machine. Coercion of all his activities – economic and non-economic – is deemed to be for the public good.

As socialists demand the dominance of politics over economics, their ruling group – that socialist élite which represents the reality of inequality in an ideology of equality – has to control all human action. Individual conduct is destroyed by collectivism. An individual is absolved from all responsibility – economic and moral.

The advertised freedoms of socialism are a false prospectus. By the time the fraud is discovered, the non-guilty party, the gullible citizen, is enslaved. Political promise is not enforceable by statute. It should at least be morally mandatory, but moral sense itself becomes a manipulative instrument of a socialist state.

There is a shadowy counterpart of this process in the Western democracies when politics prevail over policies and when politicians knowingly sacrifice essential economic policies for political expediency. We have seen in our times how many governments have regularly abandoned disinflationary policies, whenever any unpleasant side-effects have become visible.

Spending is always more popular than prudent housekeeping. To debauch the currency internally has appeared to be a lesser crime than to please the uninformed gallery. Alas, this popularity-seeking bending of essential objectives has resulted, particularly in Britian, in the decline of standards of living, and the decline of the British economy.

You have been vehemently attacked in one of your books by Sir Ian Gilmour, who is now also a leading critic of Mrs Thatcher and his own Conservative Government. What is your reaction?

This raises wider issues. I once quoted Harold Nicolson to the effect that some conservative parliamentarians were socialists at heart.

Sir Ian seems to be against competition and to feel that it is not compatible with the true conservatism he espouses. Here he is in good company with socialism. Socialism condemns competition (though there are now indications that Soviet Russia tries to introduce competition to improve the performance of its unproductive economy). Sir Ian favours state direction – benevolent state direction of course – somehow following a paternalistic tradition. Sir Ian also questions the profit motive. He seems to be prepared to modify economic processes to make them acceptable to the electorate.

This kind of false pragmatism, in someone as highminded as Sir Ian, is not to be equated with opportunism. But, if one is prepared to bow to prevailing tendencies or to sail with the wind of discomforted opinion, then logically one may be prepared in practice to accept the notion of socialism in the name of what is claimed to be part of a populist conservative tradition. Adherence to paternalistic customs may mean opposition to a free or market economy.

There is a kind of anti-libertarian alliance between socialist conservatism and conservative socialism. The one is marked by, however wrongly perceived, pragmatical expediency and intervention, the other by the perception that full-blooded socialism would not win an election.

But a mere prejudice against socialism is damaging. Active and resolute opposition against socialism, which is aggressive by concept is needed, because every successive step in that direction leads to more of the totalitarian medicine. The enemy is at the door and not, as in the eighteenth century, centuries away.

Invoking a pre-Disraeli Tory tradition of protection and paternalistic welfare invites the danger of its transference to a modern non-benevolent state. In the hands of such a state, populist attitudes become tentacles. The much spoken of 'middle way' is a compromise with middle socialism. It compromises only to be indecisive: half of one; half of the other.

Neither Burke nor Disraeli were men of indecision. Yet their patrimony is always claimed by the indecisive. Disraeli may have desired one nation, united in a common purpose and progress of accepted principles. Could he possibly have advocated a middle way of compromise with socialism? Or a 'consensus' with Gladstone?

Would you describe the middle way, to use Byron's words, as 'not quite adultery, only adulteration'?

Oh no. Once you compromise with socialism and destroy the economic bastions against it, retreat becomes increasingly difficult. Through seemingly cosy beginnings the totalitarian embrace tightens. You fall from the consensus handshake into the unshakeable grip of society's enemy.

Is there a middle way with inflation? Either you counter it or you get more and more of it.

You were the co-author of the social market policies adopted in Germany in 1948 which led to the economic miracle and which transformed a defeated and destroyed country, which had lost part of its territory, into the most prosperous in Europe and one of the strongest economies in the world. How did this gaping difference arise between Germany's spectacular advance and Britain's greatest economic decline relative to all other industrialized and even some developing countries?

There are many reasons. Some stand out as especially important.

I hold, unhesitatingly, that excessive union power is the foremost factor in the lower living standards of and the lower wealth creation in Britain, and also the main cause of its relatively higher unemployment. The foremost factor, because any economic policies may have been ineffective with trade unions placed above the law and endowed with privileges which no other institution or group has ever enjoyed in British history. This began with the 1906 Trade Disputes Act, which exempted the unions from the provisions of the ordinary law and absolved them from any civil liability. Their position was strengthened further by various governments.

The temptation to use these powers was too great. As a result, we saw intimidation by pickets coupled with excessive wage demands, the misuse of the strike weapon, disregard for agreements, closed shop, restrictive and demarcation practices, and over-manning. Such privileges conferred on the unions do not exist in other countries.

It looked as if a blanket of lead was overhanging British industry. Rigid differentials boxing in relative wages in a straitjacket of conformity and inflexibility contributed to the loss of productivity which made industry uncompetitive. This led to a low wage economy. It affected investment.

The trade union leaders can take the credit for this lamentable result, or be blamed for it. In fact, their union members did not benefit.

This preponderant power of the unions has been most effectively and more ruthlessly exercised in the monopoly areas of nationalized industries, or those on which essential services depend (however unskilled a function they perform) such as hospital cleaners, porters and ancillary workers. Public sector cost inflation led private sector inflation, unless it was government subsidized, and this meant suppressed inflation.

As unions can, among other things, enforce excessive wage demands, the socially most disruptive yet least recognized consequence is unemployment. Trade unions are responsible for unemployment in Britain being relatively higher than in other comparable countries. As unions have caused more unemployment than market conditions would have brought about, the burden to undo this damage is placed on the government. It is called upon and urged to create additional demand, to stimulate the economy so that the unemployment and the threat of more unemployment are reduced.

As wage and overmanning excesses caused a rise in unit costs and prices to uncompetitive levels, more money and so more inflation was created to mitigate and adjust the damaging consequences of union power.

Such disastrous sequences result in accelerating inflation and protected jobs only last as long as ever increasing inflation continues to protect them.

Create new jobs or protect existing ones? Once existing jobs require government or union protection, they would appear to be at risk. Artificial protection does not solve the problem. The centrepiece of the British trade unions' thinking is to protect jobs in the first place. Essentially this means protection of many otherwise not viable jobs. I emphasize the role of the British unions because this was not the aim of trade unions in any of the more prosperous countries. Their principal purpose has been to improve their members' standards of living.

No system can exist profitably with dominating union power of this kind, because only efficient allocation of labour, as of all other resources, can create employment and wealth: more so and more effectively than any stimulation. Union power inhibits planning as well. This is why collectivist socialist systems cannot function with free unions. In the totalitarian Soviet Union, they disappear altogether.

It is interesting how many misconceptions have entered economic folklore when communist countries are discussed. For instance, it is said that there is no unemployment in the totalitarian paradise. Officially there is not, but there is considerable concealed unemployment. Then there is the impression that inflation does not exist. But subsidies have hidden a lot of it.

Events in Poland have given us a glimpse of socialist reality – the state's fight against free unions and the lid covering inflation, subsidies, overmanning shortages, maldistribution and inefficiency being slightly lifted.

After all, the upheaval in Poland was triggered off by inflation. Inflation's social disruption is in evidence everywhere. Solidarity was a protest against price rises as well as against the enforced economic inefficiencies inherent in the 'socialist' system.

Next to union power the blame for economic decline has to rest on policies. In Britain the neo-Keynesians were dominant in all parties and throughout the establishment. The fear of unemployment dominated their thinking. They thought that by stimulating demand whenever there were signs of reduced employment, unemployment would be prevented. This was the policy of full employment.

These policies brought about inflation. As each stimulation produced diminishing results, the pursuit of demand policies resulted in accumulating inflation. It is no coincidence that the countries under greater neo-Keynesian influence suffered more inflation and had less productivity and lower growth. The UK is the prime example. The excessive creation of money unrelated to higher output was encouraged and not resisted as it was in European countries, which remembered the savagery of hyperinflation and tried to avoid a repetition of the inevitable social collapse which followed the pursuit of inflation.

The neo-Keynesians adopted Keynes as their patron saint, but they distorted his intentions. From my many conversations with Keynes in his last years in the 1940s I know that he would never have supported or tolerated their self-created road to inflationary destruction. Keynes himself always highlighted the devastating dangers of high inflation. He always stressed the need for stability, the opposite of the instability inherent in inflation.

When Keynes wrote his major opus in the 1930s, prices were actually falling, there was no inflation. At that time the money supply was severely restricted, in the US most severely. With no inflation and large unemployment, there was a valid case for monetary expansion and for demand stimulation. A new balance had to be created. Inflation would not necessarily be created.

The circumstances were entirely different when Keynes' epigones in Britain applied demand stimulation. There was 'over-full' employment as well as rising prices. So the consequences would also be different. They contributed to de-stabilization, to more inflation.

Keynes was fully aware of the fact that if real wages unrelated to productivity were too high, unemployment resulted. This happens if the money supply is not increased but kept under control. If the money supply is increased to counteract the effects of wage rises, and thereby to avoid the resultant unemployment, then this results in inflation.

The responsibility for avoiding both inflation and unemployment rests in the first place on wage demands not being relatively excessive. So one comes back to the unions.

However, as the neo-Keynesian establishment accepted the full employment concept, it became easier for the unions to behave irresponsibly. The burden of acting responsibly was taken away from the unions' shoulders and transferred to the Government, which then accommodated excessive wage rises by expanding the money supply. This promoted inflation, but had the Government not acted there would have been more unemployment. Boxed in between the unions' power and its self-imposed prescription of full employment, the Government inflated. Once it rejected any other prescription the result was also clear.

It was politically easier not to fight the strongly entrenched unions to retain competitive wages. So the neo-Keynesian establishment achieved this by stealth. By demand stimulation, continuing and rising inflation, they devalued the higher money wages the unions had enforced. Nobody was better off, but the unions retained the illusion of 'higher' wages and the pleasure of exercising their excessive power, while the epigones were pleased to put their theories into practice – and perhaps with having cheated the earners with inflation money, without increasing unemployment.

Inflation is not a gift from heaven, nor a curse from hell. It is man made. It does not happen without cause. The Government can reduce, halt, or increase inflation.

In the end, a point is always reached when inflationary illusion is exhausted. It all depends when this point is reached – after hyper-inflation has undermined the social and political system, or before; after only little, or maximum, damage has been inflicted.

When a consensus in indecision is aimed at, incomes policies are wheeled out. They retard needed counter-inflationary measures while creating temporary illusions. Income policies are repressed inflation covering up the real thing, and they are a special evil. As history over centuries has clearly shown, they have always failed. Yet many intelligent people expect some kind of magic when they promote or adopt such obvious and well-tried losers.

A combination of privileged trade unions, inflationary policies considered to be an antidote to unemployment used even in times of over-full employment, political indecisiveness, the pursuit of what looks like easier options, have caused the economic decline in Britain. It was self-inflicted. Different policies could have produced different results.

By contrast, most European countries which had reached 50 to 100 per cent higher living standards than the British over the last twenty-five years had freed market forces, allocated resources more efficiently, adopted proper monetary policies with appropriate fiscal action/support, and above all had trade unions, which, though strong and effective, were not privileged and did not misuse their power in consequence.

This is not a pretty or encouraging picture. What should be done to make Britain as prosperous as others are? As we want to avoid the Road to Serfdom, which is the right road to take?

After Mrs Thatcher won the election for the Conservative Party in 1979, I advocated as a matter of urgency that the excessive power of the trade unions be curbed. Their statutory privileges should be cancelled or substantially reduced. Their position above the law and their privileges have in the main brought about more inflation, overmanning, low productivity, low investment, low relative wages and growth and uncompetitiveness of industry. A catalogue of sins. They were the greatest hindrance to economic progress and they cause a sense of frustration and despondency in others. This is the root of the matter.

Governments, since the 1930s, have hesitated or refrained from reducing the unions' excessive power because of fear that by their resistance the economy could be completely wrecked, not just wrecked piecemeal as happened in practice over the years. I thought an opportunity presented itself after the election following the winter of discontent, when the unions had become deservedly unpopular. I suggested then that a referendum be held, which I thought would receive overwhelming support, cancelling the 1906 Trade Disputes Act. Thus the grip of the country's economic jugular would be relaxed. Then and only then could new policies succeed, inflationary habits changed, economic processes made to function more freely and effectively. As long as privileged union power was preserved, the road to recovery would be more painful and more prolonged. It would mean more unemployment over a longer period of time than otherwise would have occurred.

When faced with unpopularity resulting from increased unemployment, no post-war government has maintained its course. They all reflated with disastrous results. A slow reduction of inflation over years, the gradual process advocated by my friend Milton Friedman, is a very difficult process for democratic governments. The pressure of unpopularity and electoral prospects is too great for any politician.

Without fighting and reducing inflation, government can achieve no lasting and real recovery. This government was quite right in making this its principal objective. The means to do this is to control the money supply. In my view both monetary and fiscal policies should be used to reduce government spending and to redress the balance between the public and private sectors. Equally an impetus should be given to push back the frontiers of the state, a release of market forces, dismantling of state interference, its intervention, its directives. That would invigorate energies latent in the economy. More freedom all round, less encroachment by the state.

An educational campaign in depth to explain the reality and implications of the issues, to counter facile and futile opposition, to redress an inflationary mentality, is as much needed as specific economic measures. As it is, more and more people begin to see through the sham of socialism even if they still pay some tribute to its many false faces.

In the end the market is supreme in the economy – sooner or later. This also applies to the socialist–communist Soviet empire, though it will take longer there to become more visible. All people are market participants. In practice and individually they express themselves by their activity in the market. What is more, the greater army of consumers has taken over power from the producers. To see inflation as the primary enemy and be conscious of it is the victory of the consumer over the producer.

This shift is significant. It weakens Marx's appeal to transfer power to the state *via* the fiction of giving it to the worker in the form of nationalization. It is the consumer who becomes the dominant factor in social equations cutting across all strata of society. This new power of the consumer, who daily experiences the threat of inflation, should be mobilized.

What is your opinion now of Mrs Thatcher and what more could or should she do?

One should not underrate the very considerable change of outlook which Mrs Thatcher represents. A rather radical departure from past attitudes. Her government gives Britain the first chance in decades to bring the country back to the forefront of the world economic league, reversing its economic decline.

The obstacles are immense, because new policies, new perceptions and a change of outlook are required, and this will be resentfully opposed. The interventionists in her own party, presumably also in her government, the half socialists, the timid, those steeped in the ideas of the last thirty years, the non-believers in a market economy, all those who grew up in fear of the unions will continue to frustrate her efforts. The excessive wage increases in the first year, especially in the public sector, contributed to unemployment and retarded recovery. They resulted from the preceding voluntary wage restrictions, which I had called 'repressed' inflation and which are more damaging than open inflation.

Mrs Thatcher is fighting an uphill battle. She can still reduce some union privileges. This will help. She will have to reduce the total of government expenditure by monetary and/or fiscal means, part of which is to see public sector wages at lowest levels. Her principal objective must remain the reduction of inflation. If she manages that to a meaningful degree, the worst may be over.

It appears that overmanning is being considerably reduced. If that is so, productivity could rise quite substantially, and coupled with wage restraint and low inflation, could achieve a radical recovery. The timing will be influenced by the world cycle of events. The US economy will be a major guide.

What do you make of the agitation and criticism of senior conservatives such as Mr Heath, Sir Ian Gilmour as well as some younger ones? They all advocate reflation of one kind or another.

Well, if their concern is unemployment, reflation will not help anyway. The kinds of reflation which they seem to advocate will have no tangible affect. But it will be devastating on the inflation front. Inflationary expectations, which are now beginning to be subdued, would soar and inflationary habits would be resumed. Interest rates are then more likely to rise, the exchange rate reflecting inflation could fall, wage demands will increase, hopes for productivity may suffer. It is very difficult indeed to believe that they do not understand these implications. What are the motives of these reflationists, who urge what will be distinctly inflationary consequences? If it is wrongly conceived compassion, reflation now will not help the disadvantaged. On the contrary. Or is at the heart of all this a penchant for intervention and *dirigisme* and *approchement* to semi-socialist attitudes? They do not seem to believe in a market economy. Or could it be that these same politicians are actually against growth, against higher living standards, as the pursuit of something which is not in accord with their philosophy and political outlook?

It strikes me vividly that if, for instance, people of similar views had had any influence in 1948, they would have prevented the social market economy which was the foundation for Germany's good fortune and its rise to unprecedented prosperity. Everybody nowadays professes to represent the true conservatism; they all adopt Disraeli as their godfather, and they are all entitled to do so as Disraeli has said many very different and even contradictory things in his lifetime.

May I ask the question which I wanted to put before you from the beginning of our conversation: can you as a confirmed pessimist about the world's inflationary future and the resulting anarchy see an economic miracle happening in Britain?

Of course I can. I have sketched out the needed direction and the policies and actions which could, in my opinion, make it possible. Whether they will or can be pursued I am unable to judge, because this is a matter of political will and also of circumstances.

However, let me tell you, before parting, that whereas I have indeed been sceptical and rather pessimistic for fifty years about the future, I now feel for the first time more optimistic. More optimistic about the Western world, and that includes Britain.

# Section Two

## Power and Leadership

# 3

# King of the airways

April 1986

## Carol Kennedy

Lord King was steaming with suppressed anger, exuding banked-down power like one of his own Babcock boilers. The cause was a newspaper story speculating that the British Airways (BA) chairman, who also heads the board of Babcock International and is playing a key role in preparing Royal Ordnance for the private sector, was 'ready to quit' BA if the airline's flotation was delayed beyond the summer. It also suggested, none too subtly, that BA's chief executive Colin Marshall was 'tired of playing second fiddle' to his chairman. In fact, the two men have a highly effective working relationship and King, who spent eighteen months searching for the right candidate to pilot BA into private enterprise, considers Marshall 'an outstanding businessman' of quite unusual qualities.

From his second-floor office in the Babcock headquarters overlooking St James's Square – the BA head office sits diagonally opposite – King had just despatched a blistering letter to the editor of the offending paper, copy to his proprietor. He was genuinely upset, because news of the article had travelled fast round the airline; in his hand was a letter from a 747 purser, asking King not to resign at a time when, in his view, BA was at last well managed and led.

King has no intention of leaving before seeing the job through. The float was delayed first by legal action in the United States arising from the demise of Laker, but had been expected this summer until Transport Secretary, Nicholas Ridley, announced a further setback – uncertainty over renegotiation of transatlantic routes under the Bermuda II Agreement. Against BA's strongest advice, the float was again postponed – speculation is that it may not find a slot until early next year – but the Government has reaffirmed its commitment to a freemarket BA. As for King, he remains determined, an associate said, 'to see this airline privatized' (plans for a management buyout were quickly tabled when Ridley stalled take-off). He expects, subject to the board's and the shareholders' approval, to continue as chairman for a few years, in order to deliver what we're promising. Otherwise, I would feel I had not made a success of the operation as a whole, after taking it on to sort out and take into the private sector. I would want to demonstrate to the private sector that I had done it. You could say there is a little bit of vanity mixed in. . .

Vanity or not, King has a big reputation riding on the world's largest airline privatization, a venture which will be watched keenly as a model for other countries. Margaret Thatcher and her former defence secretary Michael Heseltine both chose him as the man to prepare state industries for the lean, mean world of private enterprise. King was once offered and declined the chairmanship of British Steel. He also 'managed to avoid', as he puts it, the hot seat at British Rail, a job he views as 'not do-able' in the sense of being able to provide the desired, all-round level of customer service. 'British Airways had all the ingredients, all the goodies were there.'

It is easy to see why King enjoyed the esteem of the Prime Minister, to whom he is reputedly close despite the mid-March alterations. He gets things done, turns businesses around and picks the right managers to direct them in new directions, shares Mrs Thatcher's faith in simple home economics applied to corporate balance sheets.

His connections are legendary; close friends include Lord Hanson of Hanson Trust and the Princess of Wales's family. In the office, photographs of Presidents Reagan and Carter mingle with those of horses and dogs. In the international markets in which Babcock as well as BA must earn its living King's well-informed influence 'can open doors for me,' says Babcock group managing director Michael Hoffman.

King's great talent is for finding talent. In Marshall and Hoffman, both appointed in 1983, he has exceptionally vigorous, decisive managers of whom he has said that, in essence, each could do the other's job. The fact that both had American management experience is coincidental, King says (Marshall had run important marketing operations for Hertz and Avis in Europe as well as for Hertz in America), but a key common denominator was that both came from outside.

Babcock's home-grown management has been steeped in power engineering; BA's in the flying of planes. In both cases, says King, 'I needed a fresh eye on the company.' Babcock was battening down its boiler side to expand into new markets which required active selling, and BA, going private required urgent attention not only to its debt-swollen balance sheet but to its function as a service industry.

'Aeroplanes happen to be the vehicle, but what we are selling is service,' says King firmly. 'It costs a certain amount of money to get a customer for British Airways and a hell of a lot more to get him back if you lose him, so you have to keep him through service. Colin Marshall understands that. He has a fantastic capacity for detail but, like Hoffman, he can also see the broad scene as well.'

Even with such experienced drivers at the reins, King manages a powerful pair of horses in Babcock and BA, working around 80 hours a week yet still retaining enough energy at sixty-seven to hunt at a punishing pace in Leicestershire at weekends: he is reputed to have, and clearly relishes the accolade, 'the fastest man ever to ride to hounds'. Two days before we met, he had been thrown twice within 15 minutes from a nervous young Irish horse, Star, but stoutly maintained 'it had been a marvellous day'.

John King's career has been marked by a 'can-do' attitude since he set up in 1945, with no formal engineering qualifications, his own engineering business in a depressed area of Yorkshire making components for the ball-bearing industry, then dominated by three giant firms.

He is typically reticent about the beginnings of the venture and its financing: 'Borrowed it. Had a little bit, borrowed the rest. The giants provided the opportunity. There's a vulgar expression that says there's room for lice on the belly of a hog. I looked for gaps, for one or two places where they were not really paying attention, or where they had something of a monopoly. Ford Motor Company was tremendously helpful to me: I went to them and said, "you're paying too much for that, I can do that".'

By 1969 King's company, Ferrybridge Industries (later the Pollard Ball and Roller Bearing Co. Ltd), had grown to the point that he received the proverbial offer he could not refuse, though he tried hard enough. It came from Tony Benn and George Brown, who through the Industrial Reorganization Corporation were attempting to rationalize the British ball-bearing industry to compete with the international giants. They asked him to continue running the company, but he told them, unanswerably: 'Not if you pay me what I'm going to charge you.'

At that point he was asked to take over the chair at Babcock, whose old-established business of manufacturing steam boilers had run into near-terminal problems through a series of loss-making contracts, a declining world market, inefficient production methods and lack of proper financial control.

Under King, the company was streamlined, its German subsidiary, Deutsche Babcock, hived off and the proceeds invested in US acquisitions; financial controls introduced and a team of shop-floor officials sent to Japan to study the methods used by Babcock Hitachi in the use of manpower and machine tools, quality circles and other techniques.

Severe pruning of labour – a third of the workforce – followed in the late 1970s, and in 1983, under the aggressive direction of Mike Hoffman, Babcock began to grow into a conglomerate of cash-generating businesses capable of trebling the profit levels of old, steam-boiler Babcock.

Hoffman, who doctored Massey-Ferguson out of its worst period of debt crisis, was hired, as he says himself, primarily as an acquisitions man. Acquisitions strategy certainly forms a large part of his daily 8.15 a.m. telephone conferences with King, which last half an hour and are preceded by King's 7.30 a.m. talks with Colin Marshall. There is also a permanent acquisitions review team at the St James's head office.

The company is moving more into the defence area – it already makes submarine hull sections at Renfrew, Trident missile tubes and components for the Harpoon, and hopes to get the management contract for Rosyth dockyard in a joint venture with Thorn EMI. 'We believe that we should have a much stronger share of our manufacturing turnover in defence-related equipment,' says King.

A UK acquisition in a defence-related area is likely to be announced later this year. Before that, probably in the spring, there will certainly be another major acquisition in the US, linked to the group's existing interests there in lighter, high-volume products like plastics to balance the heavy engineering side, which now provides only one-fifth of Babcock's business.

At British Airways, which in five years has moved from a loss of £136.8m to profits of £168.1m before tax, King had identified a number of overgrown departments before bringing in Marshall as chief executive. He had also severely pruned the board that had 'grown like Topsy at the behest of successive Secretaries of State. One of the things nationalized industries suffer from is too many ideas on how the board should be put together by people who have never run a company themselves. The chairman presides over something someone else has created. I preside over something *I've* created'.

Talents he has brought into the BA board from outside include, as deputy chairman, Robert Henderson of Kleinwort Benson; Basil Collins, chairman of Nabisco, and Henry Lambert, former chairman of Barclays International. Captain Jack Jessop, director of safety services on the executive side, is the sole survivor of the old BA board.

The hardest task was taking out 22,000 of the workforce, which cut between £200m and £300m off the wage bill; savings which could be applied to reduce the borrowings government had allowed to inflate. 'We set up machinery to examine the jobs that everyone did. There were all kinds of departments that had been born out of the desire to maintain size. I think the workpeople knew what was wrong with the airline. Mind you, we were quite generous as well. Government said we were spending too much and I said, "You tell me how much you should give a man when he hasn't got a job."'

At Royal Ordnance, Europe's largest producer of ammunition and Britain's principal manufacturer of armoured vehicles, King was brought in by Heseltine last year to carry out a get-fit programme for privatization (due in late 1986). He found the same 'town hall syndrome' – his phrase for bloated bureaucracy – as he had done at BA. With the deceptively anodyne title of non-executive deputy chairman, he set to work to find an executive team to put the historic defence contractor (dating from 1560) on commercial tracks. This team, headed by chairman Bryan Basset, a former investment banker, and chief executive Bill Meakin, a Royal Ordnance manager of thirty-five years' experience, is now in place.

King's reputation as an axeman sits oddly with his own conviction that a prime attribute of good management is to be 'interested in people's well-being and to let them know they are wanted. Most people perform very well, if you give them the opportunity. I like to reward people who do things properly. It is essential that you have a good team, and that takes time. If you have more successes than failures, they say you are a good picker.'

'Companies are best run from the top, and you have to make sure you first have objectives in management and then communicate them. You should not give management down the line shocks if you can help it.'

Able to stand back somewhat now from Babcock, King is determined that BA will show a clean pair of wings to the rest of the airline business in looking after the customer better 'either side of the aircraft door' as well as in finding new routes to fly profitably (South America is one major area in view) and in improving the productivity of each aircraft. He is not worried by problems of size such as those attributed to Pan Am – that airline's troubles, he believes, stemmed from other reasons, a decline in service among them. 'Size in itself is nothing to worry about. Your ability and the capacity of your management and board to understand size is what counts.'

'Leasing aircraft will be a large part of our future programme, and I do not think the spend we have in mind on re-equipping the fleet is dis-proportionate to the company or its profits or its capital base, whatever that is decided to be. As far as finding new routes is concerned, there is still a bit of room on the planet to earn a living.'

Ultimately, in King's view, BA's success in the private marketplace starts and finishes with the customer. 'What else do you have to sell but service? It is like friendship – you have to keep on mending it.'

# 4

## Partners in success

November 1988

Carol Kennedy

Corporate duopolies, where a pair of senior managers work so closely together that they are virtually two halves of one person, appear in many different guises and roles, but most dynamic companies have at least one of them, although they are not always visible to the outside eye. Companies rated highly for their strategic skills frequently have such a partnership at the top. When predators move in, they are often a company's best defence. As management consultant Barry Curnow of MSL Group puts it, they are 'the people who give companies their competitive edge.'

At the top of a company they are typically pairings of executive chairman and managing director, or non-executive chairman and chief executive. Less visible partnerships may be between chairman or chief executive and finance director.

At this sort of level, when the chemistry works well, they can be true power partnerships. They could even be described as corporate marriages, because, for all the complementary skills that provide classic fits – strategist and administrator, marketing genius and financial superbrain – ultimately they depend for their success on what Bob Meadows of international search consultants Heidrick and Struggles calls 'the personal spark.'

Such marriages can be 'made in heaven' – happening spontaneously during two individuals' careers – or created by the matchmakers of the executive recruitment industry.

Meadows believes that external pressures on a business – whether from shareholders, the city, the competition, technology or sheer pace of change – are so intense today that without partnerships, precious time may be 'focused on the wrong goals.' And he adds warningly: 'You need a partnership for successfully rebutting a takeover bid.'

One does not have to look far to see the logic in this. Rowntree's Kenneth Dixon, for example, had to carry the whole external burden to fighting off Nestlé – ultimately no avail – as well as managing the company from day to day. At Cadbury-Schweppes, by contrast, the formidable duopoly of the Cadbury brothers has been better placed to handle the twin tasks of marshalling external opinion and beefing up financial performance against unwelcome stake-building by US conglomerate General Cinema.

While there is nothing surprising about partnerships at the beginning of a business – 'after all, companies get set up because people get together,' says Jan Szydlowski of consultants PA Management – the critical factor is durability. Some of the most successful duopolies have worked in tandem for around twenty years, either climbing together up a single corporation or moving from company to company.

Take, for example, Lord Hanson and Sir Gordon White at Hanson Trust and Hanson Industries respectively; Sir Jeffrey Sterling and Bruce Mac-Phail at P & O; Sir Simon Hornby and Malcolm Field at WH Smith; the original Argyll Foods partnership of James Gulliver and Alistair Grant; the Dixons duo of Stanley Kalms and Mark Souhami; the brothers' Charles and Maurice Saatchi.

Others are working partnerships of comparatively recent development. The high-profile Richard Branson brought in his 'power partner', managing director Don Cruickshank, only in 1984, at a comparatively late stage in the development of the Virgin Group. The Cadbury brothers' partnership also dates only from 1984, when Dominic Cadbury was appointed group chief executive. Elder brother Sir Adrian had been chairman from 1975; at that time Dominic was a management trainee with the Cadbury company.

Companies can experience a loss of dynamism if a duopoly splits up, and attempts to replace the lost partner are rarely as successful second time around. One leading industrialist who knows GEC's Lord Weinstock well senses a 'loneliness' in him since the departure of finance director Sir Kenneth Bond.

Hi-tech companies founded by entrepreneurs are particularly vulnerable if complementary skills are absent as the company develops. Sir Clive Sinclair is the prime example, and the mystery is why none of his financial backers pushed him hard enough on it. MSL's Curnow, however, believes the providers of venture capital can be 'singularly unimaginative about specifying the people requirement. With institutions, too, the level of debate about management skills is often very naive – it is all done on financials.'

Duopolies differ in fascinating ways when put under the microscope. Some have an element of the mentor or 'wise man' in them – Virgin's solid, steady Cruickshank is said to be almost a father-figure to the flamboyant Branson. Others require their partner to be essentially subservient, what Curnow calls 'the Lone Ranger and Tonto syndrome.'

Still others convey a combination of 'hard' and 'soft' personalities, which may be particularly effective in acquisitions or relationships with suppliers. Many are driven by the needs of a particular business for an outward-looking and inward-looking double act at the top – in industries like shipping or broadcasting, for example, where international or regulatory requirements mean that a chairman needs to spend a lot of time on outside meetings.

In all cases, functional roles are paramount. And partnerships do not work well if those roles are not clearly defined or there is too much overlap. Yet, if the chemistry is right, there may be a creative sharing in strategy that would, in functional terms alone, normally be the domain of the chairman. Dominic Cadbury, for one, believes that a chief executive should share strategy-making with his chairman.

'When the relationship is a very good one, you do share in strategy,' he asserts. 'You contribute different things to it, but it is terribly important that you both do share in the formulation.'

Whether the partnership is equal within its functional roles or not – and MSL's Curnow maintains that, however equal a partnership looks, 'one will always have the edge' – there is usually a genuine principle of inter-dependence at work, and therefore an element of dependence. 'You can be critically dependent on someone even if you are in a superior role,' says Curnow.

So what makes power partnerships tick? *Director* asked three highly successful pairs at the head of large international companies to analyse their relationships and roles – a novel experience for one or two of the individuals concerned.

A classic example of a long-established duopoly working intimately on functional and personal levels is that between Sir Jeffrey Sterling, the gregarious chairman of P & O, and group managing director Bruce Mac-Phail, a quiet and somewhat buttoned-up personality.

The pair of them dominate corporate direction of the highly decentral-ized transport-to-housebuilding group, where eight of the ten main board executive directors are managing individual businesses, several equivalent to sizeable plcs in their own right – Bovis, for example, is one of Europe's biggest construction businesses with an order book currently standing at £4bn. (The remaining two main board directors, finance director Andrew Robb and corporate affairs director Peter Thomas, complete the small corporate management core at P & O, but very much in a supporting role to Sterling and MacPhail.)

At the annual long-term strategy meetings in P & O's elegant first-floor boardroom, flanked by oil paintings of the shipping line's founders and overlooking a quiet courtyard at the back of Pall Mall, Sterling and Mac-Phail operate a formidable double act. Their differences of style are charac-terized by one insider as the natural contrast between, respectively, a master chess-player and former student of the violin and an Oxford mathematics graduate and boxing blue.

Sterling, who prides himself on his instinctive negotiating skills, will draw out a 'feel' on how his managing directors are approaching their objectives. MacPhail, the clinical, direct intellectual, will move in to probe the detail and logic of those objectives.

'You need a clear grasp of your subject or Bruce will grasp it for you, analyse it, define its weakness and demolish it before you can blink an eye,' says one P & O director, but without rancour. MacPhail's art is to leave no bruises.

Chairman and managing director are by no means always at one during strategy meetings. 'Creative tension ... a very open dialogue' is how one board member describes it. Yet MacPhail is essentially less competitive than his chairman; no duopoly would work otherwise with the volatile Sterling who comments that 'ultimately, no one competes with me.'

Sterling is a highly visible head of the company, and during his chairmanship has transformed motivation within it. In his first week he issued a credo to all his managers stating that he intended to 'lead P & O from the front.' As chairman, he believes 'in the ultimate, you are alone.'

He was never more alone in his business life than during the first, shattering trauma of the Zeebrugge disaster in March last year, a matter of days after P & O had completed its purchase of the Townsend Thorensen ferry company, previous owners of the *Herald of Free Enterprise*.

'It is quite a testing ground,' says Sterling. 'When you go through the fire together, it makes an even tighter team than before. I think we are a much stronger group at the centre than we were a year-and-a-half ago.'

Throughout his career, he has made a point of knowing his close colleagues before a working relationship begins, believing that you find the essence of a person when they are 'up against it' or 'going through the fire' in their own lives.

Sterling and MacPhail first encountered each other in the early 1970s in the corporate finance department of Hill Samuel, where MacPhail helped put a venture together for Sterling. They began working as a team when Sterling set up his property company Sterling Guarantee Trust, in the mid-1970s. For some time, however, it remained a team of four, in which, as Sterling recalls, 'the ideas, which way we should move, came from Oliver Marriott, a brilliant analyst of real estate, and the implementation, carrying them out financially, was done by Bruce. Gradually, through the years, Bruce emerged naturally as having the best overall mind, and being very financially strong indeed.'

When Sterling, as a non-executive director and then deputy chairman of P & O, was appointed chairman in succession to Lord Inchcape in 1983, there was no doubt in his mind that MacPhail would assume an important role on the board with him. The company was then fighting off a hostile bid from Sir Nigel Broackes's Trafalgar House group. Sterling used the financial muscle of his property company to establish a stake in P & O that provided the firepower to see off the Trafalgar bid. The two companies later merged together completely.

'The personal chemistry is such that we travel a lot together, fly a lot together,' says a shirt-sleeved Sterling, thinking aloud about the factors that make his long-standing relationship with MacPhail the formidable working tool it is. From the company's point of view, flying together might seem risky, but, maintains Sterling: 'Some of the best things we've ever thought through have been on long flights.

'Some of our interests are different, and in education, Bruce has had a vastly superior experience to me,' he goes on. (Sterling went to grammar schools in Reigate and Preston, followed by the Guildhall School of Music; MacPhail to Haileybury and Balliol.) 'He has an extraordinary financial brain and an extraordinary capacity for work; his concentration is phenomenal, and he has a great capacity for detail, where I would have none whatsoever.

'But in the sense of having a vision, or an horizon, I suppose that is more me. I set the parameters.'

Sterling is a great believer in the virtue of the outside opinion that can stand back from a company and see the broad overview. He has one or two 'guru' friends outside the company, Lord Goodman among them, whom he will occasionally use as sounding boards, even after lengthy discussions with MacPhail.

But if he had to define one quality he would most miss should he find himself without his corporate partner, he says it would be 'the day-to-day friendship, the batting backwards and forwards of everything we talk about, intellectually as equals.'

Sir Adrian Cadbury is in no doubt about the primary factor in his partnership with Dominic, who at 48 is 11 years his junior.

'I suppose the big thing about having a blood relationship is that you have absolute, total trust,' he says.

'That isn't to say that you don't have trust in other people, but that obviously has to be built up over time working with them. Clearly, I start with Dominic knowing there is complete trust and confidence between us and, equally, no political element. I don't have the least concern that he's going to want my job or I his.'

Sir Adrian is a convinced believer in separating the roles of chairman and chief executive; Dominic is a late convert to the principle. ('If you had asked me ten years ago if I thought there was room for both, I would have said probably not,' he comments.)

'I do see the roles of chairman and chief executive as separate but complementary, in a sense one,' says Sir Adrian, shaping a circle in the air. 'Within that, I believe there are two distinct roles, but they are complementary and they depend on the two people concerned not being in competition with each other. The essential thing is to use the strengths of both participants, and these will be affected by the experience of the two people.'

In the case of his previous managing director, Basil Collins, a Schweppes' career executive, 'we each had a deep understanding of one half of the business and we were much closer in age than I am with Dominic. We had both been MDs and worked together in that role, so operationally it was a slightly different mix, divided slightly more on background and experience than on the functional split. I would have had more of a say in decisions affecting the confectionery division, for example, than I would wish to now.

'With Dominic, I have had a longer time in the business and I have known the people in it over a longer period. So the area in which I would feel able to offer advice is over people.'

Sir Adrian's route to the board was largely on the personnel side, whereas Dominic's has been in marketing and international business management, both academically (he has a Stanford MBA) and operationally in the company's overseas subsidiaries.

Sir Adrian sees Dominic's strengths as 'operational with a strong marketing angle to them.' His own, he describes as 'conceptual and analytical, the ability to look at the direction in which the company is going and the continuity of the business over a fairly long time horizon.'

He likes to 'put thoughts down on paper.' About the time Dominic became chief executive, Sir Adrian brought out a six-page statement of company values that was the distillation of his business lifetime in the company founded by the brothers' great-grandfather, a Birmingham tea and cocoa merchant.

Talking individually to both, it is clear that any disagreements between them are likely to be tactical rather than strategic, and mainly a matter of timing. Sir Adrian refers obliquely to 'a new generation's view on the running of businesses,' but adds 'there has been no issue of any importance on which we have found ourselves arguing at board meetings from different points of view.'

Dominic, dark, craggy and conveying a sense of taut energy, dismisses any notion that his elder brother is a mentor.

'If there were an elder/younger relationship in that way, that might inhibit the development of strategy: you've got to feel you can talk to each other on absolutely equal terms,' he insists.

That said, he admits to having learned a thing or two about pacing the implementation of policy.

'I think he is an absolutely outstanding chairman and I would be short-sighted not to be picking up lessons,' he comments. 'I have learned a great deal, for example, over the time, care and trouble we took in selling off the

foods business and Jeyes; not jumping the gun, not doing things too fast in
order to produce a result.

'Timing can make the difference between a business decision being right
or wrong, and I have learned from Adrian on timing. We got things right
when we could have got them wrong.'

Watching Sir Adrian in action on the General Cinema challenge, he was
impressed by the way the chairman detected potentially hostile intentions
from day one.

'He got the response absolutely right because he had considered all the
issues and where it might lead,' he says. 'That is something I would have
found very difficult to get right if I had been working on my own.'

Strategy on General Cinema was discussed between them, and there is a
standing 'defence committee,' chaired usually by finance director David
Nash, occasionally by Dominic. But the chairman's response as public voice
of the company was all-important.

'Had we made the wrong response initially it would have weakened
everything we did thereafter. The way you handle that sort of pressure says
a lot about a company,' says Dominic emphatically.

The brothers differ oddly when it comes to discussing how much time
they spend talking business outside the office. They both play keenly
competitive golf, but Sir Adrian says it would ruin his game to talk business
on the links whereas Dominic claims it is often the best place to grab his
attention in a working life spent largely on the move.

When it comes to the question of shared business values – vital for duos,
say management consultants – it is obvious that those come naturally to a
pair bearing the Cadbury name, synonymous for generations with the
caring Quaker ethos.

A mile or so south of the Cadburys' London headquarters at Marble
Arch, however, a duopoly without any such links has forged a strong
company ethos and culture at WH Smith.

Here, chairman Sir Simon Hornby has a family connection with the
196-year-old business – CH St John Hornby was a partner at the turn of the
century – but group managing director Malcolm Field joined the company
in the early 1960s after a spell with ICI. The two always got on well, and
moved steadily together up the company, Field 'one step behind,' as he likes
to say. Both experienced senior management on the retail side, Field has
wholesale under his belt as well.

On the same day in 1982, Hornby was appointed chairman and Field his
operational chief. Before that, Hornby had done a four-year stint as chief
executive but clearly prefers his present role as 'public face of the company'
and chief strategic planner.

'He is definitely better than me – he is stronger,' says Hornby of Field in
the chief executive role. 'He is enormously fair, enormously upright, leads

by example, absolutely incorruptible with people. But his great thing is to be able to get to the nub of something and say "these are the things that really matter".'

The tight complementary fit of the two roles and temperaments has markedly improved City perceptions of the company.

Field has a considerable input on the strategy side – 'together we agree the strategy, I execute it,' he says – and the pair devote most of one day a month to strategy discussions.

From the start, they discussed how they would manage the company and split the responsibilities.

'I never believed that you could build organizations around people, but I was quite wrong,' says Field, a large, genial man whose relaxed air belies a huge work load and congested diary. 'You can, because it suits people's strengths and weaknesses. We decided that we never wanted too much power vested in one person.'

One result is that Field reports not to Hornby but to the board. ('Who gets rid of you? It is always worth finding out!', he jokes.) There have been differences of opinion between the two, but Hornby believes strongly that they should never take issue publicly 'unless it really matters.'

In his view, the chairman's business is 'to pose questions, just as a board should, but ultimately to support the management. If you have a chairman who is stopping the MD from doing what he wants to do, as long as he is making a success of it, it won't be a good relationship.'

'To some extent, I think people see Malcolm and me as setting the tone,' says Hornby. He regards himself as *primus inter pares* – finance director Brian Jamieson has been to a degree part of a triumvirate – and the absence of a hierarchical feel at the top of WH Smith is something no visitor can fail to pick up. Although, as Hornby says, 'there can only be one public figurehead in a business,' the WH Smith duopoly comes very close to an interdependence of equals.

On the other hand, there can be few 'public figureheads' who would disarmingly volunteer, as Sir Adrian Cadbury does: 'If you ask which of us is the company most dependent on, I would see it being more dependent on Dominic than on me. I am more easily replaced than he is.'

# 5

# Programming the puritan work ethic

August 1989

## Tom Nash

In 1986, Ken Olsen was described by *Fortune* magazine as 'arguably the most successful entrepreneur in the history of American business.' Three years on – and some 32 years since Olsen founded Digital Equipment Corporation (DEC) – the only change to that analysis might be to remove the word 'arguably.'

*Fortune* pointed out that DEC's 1986 turnover of $7.6bn made it 'bigger, even adjusting for inflation, than Ford Motor Co when death claimed Henry Ford, than US Steel when Andrew Carnegie sold out, than Standard Oil when John D Rockefeller stepped aside.'

Today, Olsen is still president and chief executive, and in 1988 DEC's revenue was $11.5bn, maintaining its reputation as one of the world's fastest-growing companies – generally doubling in size every three years.

DEC is the world's second-largest computer manufacturer – IBM's most serious competitor – and the 38th largest American industrial corporation. It has some 130,000 employees doing business in 65 countries and manufacturing in 11 of them.

Ironically though, growth was never the company's prime objective. 'We specifically said in our original plans that growth was not a goal,' said Olsen. 'We said that we would only grow because of demand. Growth came about because we concentrated on the product.'

Despite success, wealth and a growing mythology surrounding him, 63-year-old Olsen remains remarkably unaffected. He is a shy, practical man and there is no hint of grandeur in his modestly furnished office in the converted woollen mill in Maynard, Massachusetts, that has been DEC's home since its inception.

Although he shuns the trappings of power, Olsen is held in awe by his employees. It is easy to see why. He is intimidatingly large and has the steely features of his Scandinavian forebears.

While Olsen's image has not been helped by his formidable looks or his introverted, unpredictable nature, behind the determined jaw and cold blue eyes lies a deeply religious, disciplined and friendly character. He learned his first management lessons not in business school but running a church Sunday school. He brings the same paternalistic attitude to management.

'I am always conscious of weaknesses in the company – places where entrepreneurial spirit is lacking,' he says. 'But I keep on correcting it. It's like raising children. You don't ever get to the point where you succeed. You can always improve.'

This philosophy may go some way to explaining DEC's remarkable and relentless expansion. But Olsen and Harlan Anderson, a fellow researcher at Massachusetts Institute of Technology (MIT), were engineers first and foremost when they started the company in 1957 and it is no surprise that Olsen homes in on the technological impetus for DEC's birth.

'We had developed a transistor computer at MIT, but the industry was not interested,' says Olsen. 'They said it was academic and not of any use. But computers then cost $3m each and we could build one for $100,000. So we had to show them.'

The biggest problem Olsen and Anderson faced in 1957 was finding the finance to start the venture. They eventually managed to raise $70,000 from a Boston venture capitalist in exchange for three-quarters of the stock. It was an expensive deal by today's standards – the stake was sold for $400m in 1972 – but risk capital was hard to come by in the fifties, and in any case, the two engineers were not sufficiently financially sophisticated then to shop around.

Olsen, the undisputed leader, Anderson and just two other employees, rented a corner of the Maynard mill and set about manufacturing logic modules – low cost, digital logic circuits on a single board. These made DEC a $3,000 profit in its first year, but they represented only a cautious first step towards producing a working computer.

Not that computers were new. By 1957 IBM had sales of $1bn for its room-sized number-crunching mainframes. But Olsen had a different vision. His aim was to make machines that were not only less expensive but easier to use – 'interactive' computers that could be linked together to share information and provide a range of non-technical uses.

In 1960 the vision materialized in the form of the first programmable data processor (PDP-1). Although it was the world's first small interactive computer, the word 'computer' was deliberately not used to describe it – computers were still mistrusted and difficult for small companies to sell to sceptical industrialists.

Costing just $125,000, PDP-1 was greeted enthusiastically and new products followed thick and fast throughout the sixties, spurred on by the world's first minicomputer in 1962 and the first mass-produced mini in 1965.

Simultaneously, worldwide markets opened up. The first European office was established in Munich in 1962 and was soon followed by operations in Australia, France and the UK. Flotation in 1966 provided finance for further expansion, but Olsen has never considered the company's growth to have been exceptionally fast.

'At any one time it looked like we were growing slowly,' he says. 'We often lost people because they couldn't stand how slow we were moving. And there was always somebody growing faster. But if you keep growing at 25 per cent it adds up.'

In the early seventies, DEC's goal of interactive computing changed with the realization that small computers could be built by many companies. 'We specifically planned not to play an important part in the personal computer business,' says Olsen. 'It was too easy for our expensive research-oriented environment.'

But this explanation of the loss of the personal computer market to IBM and Apple is a little too cosy for some. It is difficult to disagree with a recent biography of Olsen and DEC, *The Ultimate Entrepreneur* by Glenn Rifkin and George Harrar, which suggests that 'Olsen's recollections gloss over the wounds that DEC has suffered along the way to becoming an $11bn company.'

Olsen refused to co-operate with the book, a fact that highlights his continuing desire not to be singled out, despite his achievements. Rifkin and Harrar describe him as 'that rare business leader who avoids, rather than seeks, the spotlight. He feels towards his computer company like a father to his family. Words that question or perhaps disparage DEC's performance hurt him personally.'

At the time, DEC's failure to compete in the personal computer market was a crisis. And there have been others in its history, such as an exodus of key engineers to form rival Data General in 1967 and a slowdown in sales in the early 1980s that led to calls from Wall Street for the removal of Olsen himself.

But Olsen has survived the turbulences and, characteristically, plays it down, preferring to talk about DEC's technical progress. The priority here, as it has been for the last fifteen years, is networking – the complex and expensive task of linking up information technology systems within and between whole organizations.

'That is where our expertise lies,' says Olsen. 'We were the only ones interested in interactive computing at the start and very few people set out with the intention of sharing computing around the world. That has been unique to DEC.'

Another subject that Olsen makes light of is that of DEC's competitors, particularly IBM, a company that he once described as being like a communist state – 'they knew nothing about the rest of the world, and the world knew nothing about what went on inside.'

However, he does acknowledge that IBM has always had a different approach to computing. 'Their approach is organized the way business is organized. Everything is hierarchical. Everything goes from the top down,' he says.

'They are evolving towards a more open system, but they still have a tendency towards centralizing. Their networking is still concentrated on headquarters.

'Our approach is more like a telephone network, where everyone can call everyone else. You have freedom and it is easy to make changes – you just plug in like a telephone.'

Although DEC has always invested heavily in research and development – more than $1bn last year – Olsen rejects as simplistic the common assertion that DEC is a technology-driven company, while IBM is market-driven. 'Reporters dream up these things,' he says. 'It is nonsense.'

Nevertheless, there have been countless tales of lost contracts because of marketing that has supposedly been slothful by comparison with the company's engineering excellence. While DEC has been more marketing aware in recent years – in 1987 it spent more than $30m on a conference-cum-extravaganza called DECworld – Olsen himself remains no salesman. His introverted personality apart, his puritan ethics allow for clean-living, hard work and honesty as the route to business success rather than expensive advertising campaigns and promotions.

'We refuse to sell bad products or to persuade a customer to buy a product that he does not really want,' he says. 'The computer industry has been very guilty of that.

'We do do marketing, but it just does not appear that way to a reporter. For example, we are involved in manufacturing products for a business market rather than a consumer market. So we do not advertise to consumers, but we do produce technical books that explain all our products to our business customers. That is a form of marketing.'

Olsen is scathing about the media, partly, one suspects, because of his dislike of publicity, but also, he claims, because of inaccuracies they have spread about his company. He cites the example of reporters who have accused DEC of never attaching much importance to software.

'But software has always been important to us. The reason our computers sell is because of the software and it is because of software that the Russians try to steal our products,' he says.

Olsen's views on management also combine traces of the puritan emphasis on hard work and a paternal instinct to protect. His refusal to be drawn into detail about DEC's problems and mistakes stands out most.

'There are always times when some things are not going well in an organization,' he says blandly. 'There are times when the economy is not going well and there have been times when we have done dumb things, but nothing particularly memorable.'

According to Olsen, the 'memorable' aspects of DEC's development have been its periodic organizational changes. But in many ways, he says, managing a start-up, then a small fast-growing company and now a major multinational is the same.

'Encouraging creativity and product development and the marketing of it is the same at all times,' he says. 'People need to be trusted to set their goals and to have resources that will not be taken away from them for no good reason. This is true when you are small and when you are big.

'The one thing that destroys innovation is the risk of having resources taken away, perhaps because someone more politically capable has another project. In a small company it may be the boss who changes his mind and in a large one it may be committees or controllers. But either way, it destroys motivation.

'The thing that gets more difficult as you get bigger is an increase in the number of people who want to control everything.'

Olsen's analogy between IBM and a communist state takes on a greater significance when he ridicules communism, 'which does not work because they do not take risks. They do not give freedom to people to set goals and accomplish things.

'Yet we have an enormous tendency in companies to think that we have to control everything for efficiency. Control, control – people are always talking about control: do not allow duplications, do not allow risk taking. But this is what destroys creativity. Innovation means trying many things in the hope that some of them will succeed.'

DEC's first major organizational change took place in 1965 when it introduced a management structure that later became known as the 'matrix' and won praise in Tom Peters and Robert Waterman's *In Search of Excellence*. Olsen dislikes and does not use the term 'matrix', but the idea was essentially very simple: the company was broken up into product lines, each with its own manager, business plan and budget.

Innovation was fostered by each product line manager having freedom to set his own goals and a budget that, once approved, could not be taken away. There were no barriers between product lines, so that a free exchange of knowledge could take place. Often described as a form of 'organized chaos,' it allowed each manager to be genuinely entrepreneurial within the company – or 'intrapreneurial' to use the management jargon.

'It revolutionized the company,' says Olsen. 'We grew enormously because product line managers took responsibility for their own plans and made them work. The plan may not have been perfect, but they corrected it because it was theirs.'

He cites DEC's overseas subsidiaries as examples of the way the company spread responsibility downwards through the organization. 'We gave all our European operations their head. We gave them freedom to play out their plans. But Europeans were not quite used to this and did not understand it. They were used to having a boss.

'So when our English group wanted to manufacture in England, we said yes. Halfway through the year they said: "Maynard did not give us enough. Hewlett Packard is doing more and they are hurting us." We said: "but we gave you exactly what you asked for. You did not ask enough." They still could not come to terms with that – they were so used to having the boss make the mistakes. But they learned and after a while they did very well.'

So well, in fact, that Reading-based DEC UK is now the company's largest and most successful subsidiary, employing more than 8000 people and turning over more than $1bn (£737m) last year.

But weaknesses developed in the matrix structure. Olsen admits that, just as he had frustrated people by initially being slow to devolve responsibility, so too did the leaders of the product groups.

'They did not see the need to pass on the freedom that I gave to them. They were so much smarter than I was,' he says sarcastically and with more than a touch of bitterness. 'They were better educated, spoke better, understood things better – even when I could not control something of $14m without breaking it up, they could control something of $1bn because they were so much smarter.'

Olsen's enthusiasm for the matrix structure had all but withered away by the early 1980s and in 1983 he announced a new management philosophy – one company working towards one set of goals. Nevertheless, he still claims not to control the plans and activities of his subordinates.

As a result of the 1980s reorganization virtually all the product line managers left. 'I did not fire them,' says Olsen. 'I asked them to stay. But they were so confident, so experienced, so important, working together was too humbling for them. They quit and very few of them have done well.'

Olsen has never been afraid to get tough with individuals and groups of managers who become obstructive, but his benevolence still shows through. Getting tough is, he says 'the hardest part of being the boss because they are all good people with good intentions.'

To him the only way to run a business is to run it ethically. 'We automatically do what we think is right and figure out ways to justify it afterwards,' he says.

An example of DEC's benevolence-tempered-with-commonsense approach is the 'single status' treatment of employees. Although the principle is firmly established, it is not taken to ridiculous extremes. While all members of staff share the same dining and car parking facilities, Olsen has a reserved parking space for himself, because it would not make sense for him to arrive late for meetings.

'We make adjustments because none of these things is black and white,' he says. 'Honesty is the critical thing. If you want your employees to be honest, and you want your customers to trust you, you have got to be honest yourself.'

Olsen's management methods, though based on a haphazard mixture of theory, ethics and necessity, continue to bring results. Since the redefinition of priorities in 1983, the company has surged into second place in the computer league, simultaneously clawing large chunks of business away from IBM and others.

The industry remains volatile, however, and in the US DEC is currently among a growing list of computer and software companies that are experiencing a slowdown. Marc Schulman, Wall Street analyst for broker Union Bank of Switzerland (UBS), expects around $1.45bn profit for 1988–89 on turnover of $12.7bn – slightly less than earlier estimates, but significant continued growth nevertheless.

After thirty-two years in charge of DEC, twenty-three of them while it has been a public company, Olsen is unlikely to lose any sleep over results in this range, or indeed worse. 'The theory that the boss looks at the financial figures and then *does* things is usually nonsense,' he says. 'It is the people doing the work who are motivated by them and who learn from them.

'Right now things are going very well in Europe. They are a little slow in this country, but that is just something we have to live with for a while.'

UBS's Schulman agrees. 'I have followed the company for seventeen years, he says. 'Throughout that period – and longer – it has achieved compound growth of more than 25 per cent. No other technology company has grown so fast for so long.

'It has had several difficult periods, but it has always come back stronger than before. I think the same thing will happen again.'

'The primary reason is flexibility,' continues Schulman. 'When the market has changed, the company has been able to change too.'

While Schulman reckons future growth must be slower than in the past, he still predicts a long-term growth rate of 15 per cent – twice what he forecasts for IBM.

Of all the questions that Olsen skilfully circumvents – and there are many – the one he most often brushes aside concerns his own retirement. He clings to the position at the top, never mentioning a successor.

'Up to now he has even prevented any operating officer from joining the board of directors,' comments another Wall Street analyst, SF Bernstein's Barry Willman. 'He is not motivated by money. He just is not tired of running the company.'

In the meantime, although he refers to others 'doing the work,' Olsen still gets personally and heavily involved in important projects. 'There is nothing I will not do if it is important,' he says. 'There is nothing below my status.'

# 6

# Creating tomorrow's chairmen

April 1990

## Hugh Parker

As recently as twenty or so years ago it was probably safe to say that in this country there was little thought given to, and even less discussion about, the role and responsibilities of public company chairmen. The titles and functions of the chairman were more or less taken for granted: it was generally understood that he presided at board meetings and at the annual general meeting; that he entertained important customers and shareholders; that he spoke for the company in the city and elsewhere; and when appropriate, conducted high-level negotiations with governments and major customers. It was also accepted that the title of chairman was accompanied by considerable prestige and privileges.

In the 1950s and 1960s, UK public company chairmen came in many shapes and sizes: there were the visionary founders, the autocratic but effective builders of great companies, the distinguished technologists, and the colourful eccentrics. There were a fair proportion of relatively ineffectual but harmless office-holders; and probably quite a few out-and-out incompetents.

Today, the convergence of several forces, notably the successful penetration of traditional British markets by foreign competitors, the effects of Margaret Thatcher's free market policies, and the rising tide of so-called 'financial re-structuring' through leveraged buy-outs, buy-ins and acquisitions have changed and continue to change the role of the 'chairman of the board'.

But some clarification of terms is needed, especially of the titles of chairman, chief executive, and managing director.

In the US, the title of 'chairman of the board' usually connotes what in this country is often called a 'non-executive chairman'. The most common usage in the US is to combine the titles of chairman and chief executive which implies a chairman who, in the UK, is often called an 'executive chairman', that is, a chairman with full executive powers which he may share by delegation with another officer who, until a few years ago, was usually called managing director. The relatively recent importation into this country of the title chief executive – which has no roots in British tradition or law – has created a great deal of confusion about the dividing line between the roles, powers and accountabilities of the chairman and the chief operating executive. This is an important issue.

Under the present Companies Acts of this country, the board of directors of a public company is appointed by its owners (shareholders) to direct and manage the affairs of the company for the benefit of and in the best interests of those shareholders. In that sense, the board of directors is the trustee of the shareholders' investment with a fiduciary responsibility to them for protecting and enhancing the value of their investment.

Under the articles of association of most UK companies there is a provision for the election of a chairman by the board. This provision recognizes the need for some individual to act as a focal point for the board's deliberations, that is, by acting as the chairman of its meetings. But these articles usually make it clear that a chairman, elected by his peers, has *per se* no executive powers greater than those of any other director. Executive powers, like its decision-making powers, are vested in the board as a whole. From this it follows that, if the board intends its decisions to be implemented, it must delegate some of its executive powers to an individual to do so.

In American companies today, the chairman is usually also called the chief executive officer. This means that the chairman/CEO is not only the leader of the board, but also has the delegated power to execute its decisions. He, in turn, usually delegates some of these powers to a president or executive vice president who may also be called the chief operating officer. In general, this system is well understood in the US, and on the whole it works well.

It is in this matter of titles, and the powers implicit in those titles, that things have gone wrong in some UK companies. Perhaps without understanding the power-shift implications of titles, some UK boards and chairmen have allowed the title – and with it the powers – of a 'chief executive' to be conferred on an officer who previously was known as a 'managing director' and whose real job is to manage the existing businesses to achieve budgeted results. With this change of title the chairman – by subtraction – now becomes, in effect, that paradox called a 'non-executive chairman'.

There has been a good deal of debate in this country lately about the pros and cons of separating the roles of chairman and managing director. But there are two virtually full-time jobs to be done: the chairman's outward-orientated and forward-looking role of planning the company's longer-term strategy, setting its standards and priorities, directing the formulation of its policies, representing and speaking for the company to the outside world; and the role of chief operating officer (US) or managing director (UK) for managing the company's operations on a day-to-day basis, accountable to the chairman and through him to the board for doing so effectively. In other words, responsibility for corporate governance and executive action are divided between the chairman and the managing director.

In my view the most successful public companies in this country today are those that are led by a strong chairman (who may or may not have the title of chief executive) and a strong managing director with clearly defined responsibility and authority for managing the company's operations – in US parlance a chief operating officer.

Other arrangements may be workable, given the right combination of individuals, and at any given time there will be companies operating successfully with different models. As a general rule however, I strongly favour the chairman/CEO and managing director/COO model for managing not only today's business but ensuring the timely development of tomorrow's. And it is usually desirable that their respective roles and powers – and the relationship between them – be clearly defined and clearly understood. In the absence of such clarity there will be confusion and, potentially, serious trouble.

There is a distinction often not clearly understood between corporate governance and strategic direction on the one hand, and strategy development and implementation on the other. The former is primarily the function of the chairman and his board, the latter the job of the managing director and his management team. This distinction is essential to what I term the 'corporate renewal' process, defined so well by Sir John Harvey-Jones in his book 'Making it Happen' as 'creating tomorrow's company out of today's.'

Corporate renewal is one continuous iterative process. It is not a one-time event, a five-year plan, or even a series of five-year plans. But the process can be broken down into a number of specific actions. It is the chairman's role to:

- Create and work with a board that is capable of helping and supporting him in the overall direction and governance of the enterprise.
- Create a strategic vision for the business that derives realistically from the company's existing strengths, and that builds on its distinctive competitive advantages.
- Establish the basic priorities, ethical values, policies and attitudes within the company that will transform it from being a 'repeating' culture into a 'learning' culture.
- Set standards of performance in terms of such criteria as product quality, customer service, technological leadership, market share, and financial measures that will ensure an above-average p/e ratio.
- Appoint a managing director with a clear mandate to achieve established standards of operating and financial performance. Monitor the

managing director's performance against these standards, help and support him. But if and when necessary, replace him.

At the level of strategy development and implementation, it is the job of the managing director and his top management team to:

- Develop business strategies and operating plans that reflect the longer-term corporate objectives and priorities established by the board. Maintain an ongoing conversation with the chairman and board to ensure that these objectives and priorities are constantly adjusted to reflect changes in the external environment.
- Restructure the business portfolio in line with the board's decisions that determine the future shape and strategy of the business. Redraw the management organization structure to reflect the restructured business.
- Undertake a programme for systematically strengthening management at all levels – but especially at the higher levels – by training, retraining, development, delegation, motivation, recruitment and replacement.
- Ensure that operational planning and financial control systems are in place, appropriate to the new management organization structures of each business unit.
- Ensure that operating objectives and standards of performance are not only understood but also 'owned' at all levels of the enterprise – ie seen to be challenging, but realistic and attainable.
- Closely monitor operating and financial results of each business unit against agreed plans and budgets. Take remedial action where necessary.

What are the personal qualities that distinguish the leader-chairmen? I have found that the most effective chairmen share a number of basic beliefs and qualities. These naturally vary in degree among individuals, but I believe it is true to say that successful contemporary chairmen share these: strong basic convictions, clear strategic vision, intellectual capacity, management experience and political skills.

All leader-chairmen seem to hold a number of strong convictions about the kind of company they want to lead – not just about its formal structure and systems, but about its values and standards; what is sometimes called its 'culture'.

In defining strategic vision I cannot improve on Harvey-Jones' 'creating tomorrow's company out of today's.' If the chairman and his board are constantly asking themselves the question 'what do we want this company to be in X years from now?' they will, in time, hammer out a set of goals, standards and priorities that will guide all their future decisions and actions to the achievement of those goals. Imperfect and changeable as such goals must always be, the very process of formulating and promulgating them will give strategically led companies a great competitive advantage over other companies that have no such clearly-defined goals.

The corporate renewal process in which public companies must be constantly engaged is a process of extraordinary complexity – like playing a gigantic game of three-dimensional chess – requiring the most sophisticated analytical and decision-making techniques. The need for a high order of intellectual capacity in the leadership of such companies is clear. However, this by itself is not enough: it needs to be tempered by common sense.

There is a Spanish saying that 'el sentido commun es el menos commun de los sentidos' (common sense is the least common of the senses) and in an odd way this often seems to apply among the more sophisticated students of management, especially among academics and management consultants. In developing elaborate theories for, say, better decision-making or more precise financial analysis, some of these thinkers seem to lose sight of the realities of business life. No chairman can afford to do that.

A sound grasp of the business and how it is managed – ie how it is organized and controlled, and above all how it actually makes money – is an essential element in the make-up of a corporate leader. This may seem self-evident, yet there are some substantial companies still in this country in which the chairman lacks such a background. This is often the case with so-called non-executive chairmen which, as I have tried to make clear, are in my view not the kind of leader-chairmen that today's and tomorrow's conditions require.

It may be an old-fashioned notion, but I still believe that the best way to learn the fundamentals of a business is to work in it 'up through the ranks.' John Loudon, who deserves much credit for the present strength of the Royal Dutch/Shell Group, is a good example. I remember him telling me of his own experiences as a young trainee in the company, manhandling oil drums on the docks in East Boston before the war. He went on to become one of the great chairmen of Royal Dutch Shell, and one of the most impressive business leaders I have ever been privileged to know.

That said, however, there have been some notably successful appointments of chairmen from outside the company and even outside the industry. Perhaps one reason why such outsiders often prove so effective is contained in the word 'innovation'. New leadership with new ideas is often what is needed to trigger the corporate renewal process.

By political skill I mean the use of power and persuasion within an organization by which leaders get people to do what they want them to do. The classic exposition of the uses of power is, of course, Machiavelli's *The Prince* which every chairman should re-read occasionally. After all, the chairman of a large multinational corporation today is, in many ways, the equivalent – though often on a much larger scale – of the prince of a city-state like Florence 500 years ago, or for that matter Athens 2500 years ago. Human nature does not change and in that sense the practice of politics is still an important part of leadership.

I would go so far as to say that effective boardroom management is, to a large degree, an exercise in politics: using persuasion, motivation, inter-personal relations, even threats to get agreement on decisions or actions necessary to achieve desired objectives.

But what are the specific tasks and priorities that the chairman must address in the execution of that role? What does an effective chairman actually have to *do*? There are, I believe, five elements of corporate gover-nance with which the chairman must be constantly concerned and per-sonally involved.

The first priority for the chairman's attention should be the board itself. On this point again, I cannot do better than to quote Sir John Harvey-Jones: 'the job of corporate governance today is too great for any chairman to do alone. That is why you need a board. The primary job of the chairman is to run the board. This means that he must decide on its composition, ensure that it is balanced, set out its agenda, organize its work efficiently, and guide its deliberations to reach sound strategic and policy decisions. *It is through the board that the company takes its drumbeat from the chair-man.*' (my italics.)

This 'drumbeat of the chairman' will however only be audible and credible to his board if he himself makes sure that the process for setting strategy includes the full input of his colleagues before plans are finalized; that those priorities and standards are seen to be reflected in his own actions; and that the selection and appointment of the managing director (and when necessary his replacement) is seen to be consistent with estab-lished standards of performance and conduct.

It is not enough just to have a vision. This must be translated into all the specific statements of long-term objectives, strategic options, detailed busi-ness plans, action programmes and budgets that are necessary to make the vision a living reality which is 'owned' at every level of the business.

This strategic planning process is done differently in every company and, in large multiproduct multinational companies it is an immensely complex and time-consuming process involving managers at every level of the organ-ization. But it is the chairman and his board who must be the architects and mainspring of this process.

The chairman must ensure that the culture, which every company has, is robust and adaptive. For it is an intangible quality that reflects the com-pany's customs and values, and draws its inspiration from the characters and personalities and successes of its past and present leaders. Thomas Watson and his successors at IBM imprinted on that company its very distinct culture. Culture in this sense is sometimes epitomized as 'the way we do things around here.' But its reality is much broader. It is also 'the way we think around here, what we value, how we reward people and whom we promote.'

Culture in this wider sense reflects the personality of the company, and there are two basically contrasting kinds of culture: on the one hand, a culture that tends to enshrine the past, to discourage the non-conformist, to see the future as an extrapolation of the past – in short, a 'repeating' culture. On the other hand, a culture that encourages innovation, that challenges 'the way we do things around here,' a culture always seeking and moving towards 'tomorrow's company.' These are the hallmarks of a 'learning' culture.

In any corporate culture, priority tends to be given to those aspects of the business in which the chairman himself is seen to take a close personal interest. Marks & Spencer, for example, has a long tradition – started by its founders and continued by its successors – of emphasizing the equal importance of supplier relations, customer service, value for money and employee welfare. Other companies have other priorities: strict financial discipline at BTR, GEC and Hanson; technology at Hawker Siddeley and British Aerospace; R & D at Glaxo and other pharmaceutical industries. But whatever the company's priorities, they need to be clearly established and constantly promulgated.

Therefore it is important for the chairman to be an effective communicator, both inside and outside the company. He must find ways to ensure that his strategic vision for the company, that his priorities, that the values and standards he wants imprinted on the company, are made known not only to his colleagues in the boardroom but to all managers and employees throughout the organization, as well as to its constituents outside the organization – its customers, suppliers, shareholders and the city. And, above all, that they are seen to be acted on.

If it is accepted that *every* organization depends for its success on the excellence of its people and how well they are organized, motivated and developed, then the human resources of any organization must be – and must be seen to be – high on the list of the chairman's priorities. Who gets promoted expresses the standards and the culture of the organization more powerfully than any vision statement or chairman's message to the staff. If there is seen to be inconsistency between policy and management practice, leadership will be perceived to speak with 'forked tongues'.

Finally, there is today a whole new dimension to the chairman's traditional role. Today, any public company chairman must be capable of leading his own company on the acquisition trail, and of defending it against other acquirers. Chairmen today must therefore be capable of clear and innovative strategic thinking, sophisticated financial and legal negotiation, and the credible presentation to their shareholders and the city of their companies' strategies and performance to a degree that was quite unheard of even a few years ago. In this new financial climate the chairman and his board must always think and occasionally act like predators.

Chairmanship is a highly subjective activity, not an exact science subject to any fixed rule or laws. Every successful chairman 'does it their way.' It is not possible to prescribe in anything but the broadest generalizations just how the chairman's role should be performed.

However, every successful chairman is by definition a leader. Without this quality of personal leadership, however that is defined, the vital process of corporate renewal – making tomorrow's company out of today's – is unlikely to occur. Indeed, it almost certainly will not, and the company will sooner or later fail or be taken over. The 'financial restructuring' factor, referred to earlier, will almost certainly continue, and the pressures and demands on the chairman will continue to increase accordingly.

The only way that any chairman can hope to cope with these future conditions is through teamwork. Sir John Harvey-Jones' observation that 'the job of corporate governance today is too great for any chairman to do alone,' suggests the key to this dilemma. A wise chairman will not attempt to be a one-man band, for all the obvious reasons: it is too risky for the company; it is unfair to himself and his colleagues; and in today's world it is simply impossible. He must create and use his board wisely because it is the board as a whole that must ultimately bear the full weight of corporate governance and renewal. That is the true meaning of the title 'chairman of the board'.

# 7

# Rules for a responsible company

July 1990

## Sir Adrian Cadbury

Chairmen and companies do not want for advice on their responsibilites to society. Yet these responsibilities are difficult to define. In addition, they do not stand still; they are continually evolving. Social responsibility is a woolly term; it is, therefore, important for boards to decide what social policy their companies should follow, and companies do have social policies, whether or not they are thought through deliberately. In the absence of a positive lead from the chairman and the board, the company's attitude towards its social responsibilities will appear confused to those inside and outside the company.

It would be simple if there were just two ways of recognizing this social dimension. The first would be for companies to concentrate on running efficiently, and then allocating a proportion of the profits to some agency which would make the social judgements for them or distribute as much as possible to the shareholders, who would make the social judgements for themselves. The alternative would be for the board to regard social aims as inseparable from business aims. Most companies plan to steer a middle course between these two extremes.

There are a number of reasons why social responsibility has become such a live issue for boards. Business has proved remarkably successful at meeting society's material needs in the developed world. But now much more is being learnt about the side-effects of economic growth and development on the environment. Just as companies have to balance the demands of the future against those of the present, so does society, and communities are becoming more conscious of their responsibilities to future generations.

Another reason is the apparent increase in the power of companies. They are seen as being capable of changing the societies in which they carry on their business. And there has also been a general rise in the expectations of society. The traditional view of companies being simply providers of goods and services is being challenged.

The broadest way of defining social responsibility is to say that the continued existence of companies is based on an implied agreement

between business and society. The freedom of operation of companies is
dependent on their delivering whatever balance of economic and social
benefits society currently expects of them. The essence of the contract
between society and business is that companies shall not pursue their
immediate profit objectives at the expense of the longer-term interests of the
community.

The company has to meet its material obligations to shareholders,
employees, customers, suppliers and creditors, to pay its taxes and to meet
its statutory duties. Companies should be attempting to minimize any
adverse effects of their actions, rather than adhering to the lowest acceptable standard.

Beyond these two levels, how far has business a responsibility to maintain
the framework of the society in which it operates, and how far should
business reflect social priorities rather than its own commercial ones?
Companies have to look outwards at the changing terms on which society
will license them to carry on their own activities. Business decisions are like
stones thrown into a pool, which is society, and companies are asked to take
account of the ripples they cause.

Chairmen and boards have to come to their own individual conclusions
on what constitutes social responsibility in the particular circumstances of
their own company. Boards must ensure that there is no confusion down the
line over aims and keep a check on their progress towards these aims.

It is by its decisions and actions that a company's policy on social
responsibility is ultimately defined. It is helpful to everyone concerned if
the board agrees a written social policy, to which ready reference can be
made. The test, however, which managers will apply to board statements
on social responsibility, is how far adherence to them is recognized in
decisions on their pay and promotion.

The board has the task of balancing the different interests which
companies have to take into account in arriving at such policy decisions.
Managers in their turn have to balance the social objectives of their
companies with meeting their budgets. The dilemma is the same at the
policy level and at the level of implementation: that is, what weight should
be given to which business and social pressures?

A key issue for companies is to be clear on what terms they are prepared to
become involved in fields for which government is responsible.

First, the choice of social goals has to be a political decision, which should
not be delegated to business. Second, companies should not undertake
governmental obligations for which they do not have matching authority.
Lastly, the state should not be attempting to transfer its responsibilities to
companies.

The argument for companies to take on the responsibilities which society
expects of them is largely one of self-interest. If a company invests in

training its own employees, the costs are known and the return is direct to the company. If, however, a company gives managerial time to an educational partnership with the local school from which it recruits, the returns are indirect and do not accrue solely to the company. This means that the board's decision on the amount of effort to put behind community initiatives has to be more a matter of judgement than of calculation.

Boards have to choose from a formidable list of worthwhile social causes. I have mentioned links with schools. Companies are being asked to find appropriate work experience places for pupils and teachers, to provide teaching materials and equipment, to fund city technology colleges, to back enterprise schemes in schools and to sponsor students. All of these initiatives depend for their success on the active support of companies.

There are other causes, such as the regeneration of inner-city areas, the encouragement of new enterprises and the raising of standards of training.

This could give the impression that the issues of how best to respond mainly face larger companies. In fact, companies of any size can make a useful contribution to the community, thus businesses big and small need to decide what their policies are in this regard.

Some of the most effective education/business partnerships have been between one- and two-man businesses and their local schools. A small business can often give children a better insight into the world of work than a large company, because its activities are on a more human scale. The cost of this kind of social initiative to the one-man business is the time of its owner/manager, which is its main resource. The balance between the interests of the business and the interests of society has, therefore, to be as carefully struck by an owner/manager as by the board of a large corporation.

Large companies in their turn, particularly those with locations right across the country, are already involved to a greater or lesser extent in most of the social initiatives which have been mentioned. They have a particular need to establish clear social priorities, because the execution of those policies will be local and therefore the responsibility of a site or branch manager. For companies to obtain the best value for their efforts on behalf of the community, it is essential that local management decisions should be made within the context of a well-defined company policy.

The lead has to come from the top and it is for chairmen and their boards to draw up the company's community affairs policy and to communicate it throughout the enterprise. They also have to ensure that there is an organizational structure in place for putting the policy into effect. Unless this is done, the response to the policy will depend on the public-spiritedness of individual managers and there will be no reliable means of monitoring its progress or of modifying it in the light of experience.

What criteria might boards use to decide on the level of support which they put behind their companies' social objectives? The main resources that companies have to offer to the community are people and money; on the whole, management skills are in even shorter supply in the social field than funds. Loaning experienced and committed managers to the community can achieve what donations of cash on their own cannot.

It may be helpful to say something about the way in which Cadbury Schweppes has approached the matter, by way of illustrating.

The board began by defining the kinds of community activity which it thought that the company should support. The first test was that the organizations concerned should be working in fields that were relevant to the company's long-term strategic objectives. Within that category, a further test was the degree of common interest between the aims of the organization and those of the company. In addition to common aims, the board was also looking for shared values, for bodies which had the same kind of outlook as the company on people and on priorities. Two further points to be taken into account were the capacity of the organizations concerned to become self-sustaining and the closeness of their links with any of the company's sites.

The company also gave its support to business in the community, an organization set up and funded by companies to put new heart into Britain's older industrial areas. They did this on the basis that many community problems were best tackled by companies working together in a co-ordinated way, rather than on their own. By working through a collective body, companies encourage others to join it. One of the ways in which established companies can help new local initiatives is by backing them at the outset and thereby giving them their seal of approval.

In dealing with charitable appeals, the company worked to six main headings, between which a rough split of the charitable budget had been agreed in advance. The headings were:

- Job/wealth creation and youth employment.
- Environment.
- Education/business links.
- Health and welfare.
- Clubs and societies in local communities.
- Industry-related causes.

Other companies would choose different headings and allocate their funds in different proportions between them. The main point is that by having clear guidelines, the difficult task of discriminating between the many worthy causes that come across the chairman's desk is made manageable. A clear policy focus means that the company's support is targeted, and therefore more effective than if it were spread thinner and more widely. It also enables a brief statement of the company's policy to be sent to those whose appeals fall outside the guidelines.

Secondments come naturally to mind when thinking of the ways in which companies can help the community through people. Secondments are indeed valuable and can achieve what part-time help cannot. But the sheer scale of part-time help that people from business give to the community is impressive. Some of it is in working hours, most of it is not. By sitting on a school governing body, by being a committee member of a voluntary organization or by belonging to one, employees are putting business experience to work in the community. Most of this volunteer help will be the result of individual initiative, rather than being organized through the community. Where the community can play its part is by letting employees know what kind of help is needed by local organizations and by making it as easy as possible for employees to serve the community in this way.

The active involvement of employees in a cause is a strong argument for giving it company support. The company could match charitable donations made by its employees. This ensures that the company's contributions go to causes which the workforce has identified as worthwhile; it also helps to raise the level of charitable giving in general.

What has been the record of British companies to date in carrying out their responsibilities to the community? I would suggest that business' main failure has been its slowness to pick up society's signals and to see the direction in which companies were bound to move. Over such issues as pollution or consumerism, the first reaction of business has been one of opposition. As a consequence of taking up this position, later attempts to modify proposals for controls in a practical way have been seen as a change of tactics, not of heart. In other instances, companies have lain low and hoped that the pressures for action would prove ephemeral.

The lesson is that companies should pay attention to forecasting social changes in the same way that they do to changes in their own markets. This will guide them as to which social trends are relevant to their type of business and help them to identify appropriate social objectives; these may well be different from the ones which are being pressed on them most stridently.

Companies have to pick up the signals as to the pace and direction of society's expectations of business, in order that they can play an active part in shaping the rules, whether it be statutory or voluntary, within which they will have to work.

A readiness by companies to provide more information about their policies and actions in fields of social concern is an important element in encouraging this dialogue. Disclosure is not in itself a panacea for improving the relationship between business and society, but it does represent a willingness to operate an open system which should be the foundation of that relationship. Companies need to be open to the views of society and open, in return, about their own activities. This is a necessary condition for the establishment of trust and for the sensible resolution of conflicts of interest.

Companies, then, certainly have to be prepared to become more involved in the political process through which governments respond to social pressures, so that they can play their part in that particular process more effectively. One way is to encourage employees at all levels to play their full part in social and political affairs.

The ability to manage is a rare resource and the lack of management experience is at least as much of a handicap to most social institutions as is the lack of money. Successful secondments benefit everyone concerned: the giving and receiving institutions and the individual secondees. The best work of reference on secondments that I have come across is the one published by IBM describing the secondment policies and practices of its UK company.

The loan of managerial talent to help achieve community goals is a working example of the way in which business and society interact. By contributing to the solution of some of society's pressing problems, companies improve their own environment and therefore their own chances of success.

The defensive argument is that any failure by business to keep in touch with society's views of its responsibilities will lead to increase in rules and regulations, with all their attendant inefficiencies. Alternatively, society will attempt to reduce the power of the business community, if it thinks that power is being used to the detriment of the community at large.

Finally, an important positive reason for companies to be seen to be meeting society's expectations of them is the vital need to attract able young people into industry and commerce. Companies will win the commitment of people of the calibre they need, only if they are seen to be making a worthwhile contribution to society.

# Section Three

## The Art of Management

# 8

# Culture club: companies with a mission to change

December 1989

## Carol Kennedy

'When I hear the word "culture",' Hermann Goering is reputed to have said, 'I reach for my revolver.' Culture, however, is very much the word of the moment in its business sense, and the concept of a company's culture – how you identify it, build on it, or if necessary change it – is fast becoming one of these rare academic theories that catch on with the people who actually run businesses and manage change.

Having gone through the often painful structural changes of the 1980s, companies are increasingly being persuaded to look more deeply into their essential cultures – broadly definable as those underlying beliefs and values in an organization that have always been treated as unchallengeable – as part of the far-reaching corporate and social changes going on around them.

Barry Curnow of MSL Group International, the newly elected president of the Institute of Personnel Management, believes that culture began to move out of the province of behavioural scientists and into the world of financial analysts with the arrival of the M & A boom. 'The making or breaking of mergers is all about chemistry,' he observes. 'The financial implications were what got the CEOs and the corporate finance people interested, with two-thirds of all mergers coming unbundled within ten years.'

The other trigger, in Curnow's view, is demographic change and the skills shortage. Those whose managerial or professional skills are now in a seller's market are paying more attention to the culture of potential employers and testing the assumptions they like to present to outsiders – that they are truly participative, for example, or truly international, or truly committed to pay for performance. In the world of headhunting, companies will increasingly need to 'market' themselves through their culture, having realized, as Curnow told a Paris conference in late 1987, that 'the human edge is what actually makes for achievement, performance and competitive advantage, once all the financial and technological structures have been put in place.'

Bill Critchley of Ashridge Management College, who heads a small specialist team working with companies to help them discover their culture, identifies three mainsprings that can move chief executives to cultural change:

- Becoming aware that the prevailing management style is going to change dramatically in the next few years, away from that of control and command towards that of coach and educator.
- Attempting to solve problems through changes in structures and finding that nothing happens, particularly in areas like moving towards a more customer-service culture, because the underlying culture has become a resisting force.
- Responding to the changes in people's aspirations; a recognition of the need to develop people as assets rather than overheads.

Critchley is technically a 'process consultant,' but he trained as a psychotherapist after a business career and believes there are many analogies between an organization's culture and an individual's personality, even to the extent of a company unconsciously adopting individual traits recognized by psychotherapists – persistent fear and mistrust, passivity/aggression, hysteria and so on.

'How we become the people we are, our beliefs about ourselves, how we relate to the world and to others, our patterns of behaviour, whether we are successful or not – with individuals and companies alike, these seem to be a matter of early conditioning,' says Critchley. 'Many beliefs operate almost at an unconscious level, and in a company they tend to be carried along and not examined unless there is a crisis.'

All companies, Critchley believes, have a culture, though in some cases it can be confused with the aura of a powerful chief executive. It is said, for example, that a visitor to the Holborn Circus headquarters of the Mirror Group can tell whether Robert Maxwell is in or out of the building just by sensing the atmosphere. Curnow believes a culture can be read in all sorts of ways – on noticeboards, in employee handbooks, in recruitment ads, in the way staff talk to each other, in the atmosphere of the canteen. . . .

Conglomerates may have a corporate culture harbouring individual cultures in their subsidiaries, while the latter may or may not share one or more threads of the corporate culture. Derek Birkin of RTZ, for example, insists that all the mining group's subsidiaries have their own style and that there is no attempt to impose a corporate culture, though the 'agreed strategy, finance and ethics' central to the group could be said to contribute towards a shared set of goals and values.

ICI always had a powerful, proud culture, both corporate and divisional: the old Mond Division at Runcorn regarded itself as the innovative cutting-edge of the company. The enormous changes wrought by chairman Sir

John Harvey-Jones between 1981 and 1986 are seen by some as a truly cultural as well as an organizational shift, which took the company away from a focus on the laboratory to a focus on the marketplace. Others, however, including Curnow, see Harvey-Jones' achievement as proof of ICI's existing strong culture: the capability of the company to produce leaders being such that the hour brought forth the charismatic man needed.

'He is a rare example of someone who did it from the top,' says Critchley, who believes that in general, cultural changes imposed from the chairman's office are bound to fail; they need to be organically grown.

'There is an assumption in many organizations, for instance, that you have to control people to get them to work hard, to produce quality. The notion that you can change that by writing a mission statement enumerating a set of values such as "From tomorrow we will treat people as human beings and not costs," or "From tomorrow we will become more customer service oriented," is a bit like saying "From tomorrow, I am going to become a thoroughly nice, warm, caring person".'

Not only will that not work; it also runs the risk of exposing to employees the gap between what the company professes and what it actually practises, as perceived by the people who work in it.

Examples abound of organizations that fail in such top-down attempts to establish or improve a set of values. In the same way, the Ashridge team resists imposing or suggesting solutions to the companies it works with. 'If you walk in with a solution and the old culture resists it, it will not take,' says Critchley.

'The trick is to get a critical mass involved – enough people wanting to change. For this you need to get all senior managers involved, at the start of the exercise and also supervisory or junior management. In newer organizations a lot of those old middle management layers have gone: they can be a force for resistance otherwise. But you have to work at all those levels – you can't pick one and ignore the others.'

Critchley illustrates his point by recalling the head of a public authority (shortly to be privatized) who, when advised to broaden his decision-making by involving more of his top management, replied in genuine puzzlement: 'But what if they disagree with me?'

Which companies have demonstrated the ability to change themselves in profound ways? MSL's Curnow thinks Rank Xerox has managed to produce a strikingly distinctive culture in the UK, separate from that of either Rank or Xerox in the US. The major computer companies seem to do well: Curnow cites Digital Equipment Corporation and almost anyone who has thought about the question of successful cultures mentions the achievement of Sir Edwin Nixon at IBM UK. 'Nixon built a culture,' says Curnow.

In fact, IBM already had a powerful culture going back to the three founding principles of Thomas J. Watson Senior: respect for the individual, the best customer service, and excellence in all things. 'IBM runs on the basis that everyone in the company is of equal value as an individual,' says ex-IBM director Peter Morgan, now director-general of the IOD.

What Nixon did during his twenty years heading the British company was to buttress those beliefs to such effect that IBM employees voted 97 per cent against unionization in the collectivist late 1960s, where Kodak and others fell to the shop stewards.

Thorn EMI is an interesting example of a conglomerate that went through a culture change with a new-broom chief (another natural trigger) when Colin Southgate succeeded Peter Laister following a much-publicized boardroom coup in the mid-1980s. Several of its subsidiaries, notably Radio Rentals, have independently reassessed their basic philosophy and goals.

Inmarsat, the international satellite co-operative based in London's Euston Station complex, offers a fascinating case study of a leading-edge business working with an old and resistant management culture it is now attempting to change.

In each case, there was a direct business trigger for the change on top of an awareness of underlying problems: with Thorn EMI, it was a dire financial performance; with Radio Rentals, a gloomy future for the TV and video rental market; and with Inmarsat, the desire of a chief executive to shift a technology-based culture into the marketplace, rather like Harvey-Jones at ICI.

What happened at Thorn certainly qualifies in hindsight as a culture change, though at the time, points out group personnel director Don Young, the process presented itself as a simple question: 'What do we need to do to be successful in this business?'

Thorn EMI's performance at the time of the boardroom upheaval was a cause for concern on three fronts. 'The financial performance was dreadful and getting worse,' recalls Young. 'It was also very difficult for anyone to get a handle on what the company "meant" five years ago because its diversity was so huge. Third, most of the individual businesses were losing out in relation to the competition in their industries.'

What happened since has been dramatic in its impact. Where the Thorn EMI umbrella sheltered some 100 business entities in the mid-1980s, there are now only six major ones, following a massive disposal programme. Top management has been shaken like a pocket kaleidoscope: over 90 per cent of the top 120 people in the company have been replaced. Internal systems have been changed root and branch, particularly in information ('what they measure, how they do it, how well they do it, who they pass information to') and in rewards systems for management.

'The whole character of the company has changed from that which came out of the takeover by EMI in 1979,' says Young. Southgate, who became managing director in 1985, chief executive in 1987 and chairman as well in 1989, gave strong direction and leadership, but the fundamental changes occurred, explains Young, through the 'shared perceptions' of perhaps twenty or thirty people of what needed to be done. The key was to form a core of multi-skilled people who could lead the same kind of change processes in the group's subsidiary businesses.

'If we did not get control of the businesses we were in, then grand strategic visions were not likely to bring us to the point of success,' says Young. The core function of Thorn EMI as a group was seen as bringing 'added value' to the businesses, which henceforth would be expected to run virtually as mini plcs.

A broad set of values or convictions for the group as a whole did emerge in the early Southgate days. Keeping promises was one; confronting problems directly another. Absolutely central was 'valuing people', which, as Young points out, 'meant paying as much attention to the needs of those departing as to those coming in or staying.

'The way in which you get rid of people is noticeable to those who stay,' he observes.

The main message the top 100-odd managers were required to disseminate was that personal lives mattered, down to the 'hatch', 'match' and 'despatch' factor: births, marriages and bereavements. 'That is something we will not let go,' says Young.

The disposal programme was triggered by a far-reaching review of what businesses Thorn EMI believed it should stay in, and one of the key criteria was whether each business could become internationally successful. The goal for those remaining was to get 'an exceptional level of growth out of the mix.'

At Radio Rentals, for example, the target was to gain growth in a mature and declining market; at EMI Music, to become Number 3 in the world from Number 5; at Thorn Lighting, which had 40 per cent of the UK market, to become a global lighting business.

'There isn't a business in Thorn EMI that isn't doing something pretty bloody radical about itself,' says Young.

The impetus for change in Radio Rentals did come from the main board, specifically from Jim Maxmin, the director responsible for the group's several competing rental businesses. Maxmin joined in 1984, when Thorn's internal debate was getting under way, and proceeded to throw out some fundamental challenges on the future of the rental business. The received wisdom then was that rental, which had flourished for twenty years on TV and video hire, was set irrevocably on a downward slide. Both items of equipment had become much cheaper in real terms and were more sophisticated and less likely to break down than in the early years, when rental offered both a painless way of paying and a repairman on call.

The company had developed 'a sense of fatalism' about itself, says its personnel director Jim Donovan. Yet it remained the market leader and enjoyed a strong culture based on technical know-how and a customer-friendly image. Management was almost entirely company-bred – Donovan, who joined from another Thorn EMI company in 1984, was probably only the third senior executive to be recruited from outside.

It was a culture in which 'the technician was king' and the TV repairman 'everyone's friend.' People stayed for years, happy with the conditions of work and not aspiring to change. Unfortunately, life outside Radio Rentals' rambling old Swindon headquarters and its regional outposts was changing – and customer expectations with it. 'We were trapped in our history,' says Donovan.

The two big challenges were cheaper and better technology – thus less incentive to rent – and a change in customers' working patterns, leading to a more demanding attitude to service. People wanted service when it suited *them*. This in turn fed back to technicians feeling less appreciated and more aggrieved. Employees began to question the value and prospects of their careers.

It was at this point that Maxmin issued his challenge: how to make these businesses grow. (Thorn EMI also embraces rival rental company DER and chainstore Rumbelows, currently running a heavily anti-rental ad campaign.) The process of change at Radio Rentals was kicked into gear by new managing director Brian Coe, whose career had been spent with the company from apprentice technician upwards, but who nevertheless had the ability to stand back from its history.

Like parent group Thorn, the corporate question was: 'What sort of a company do we want to be and how do we get there?' An exhaustive process of debate got under way; endless workshops and meetings, aiming to boil down business objectives into sentences. Core objectives were clarified. Role models – such as 3M – were studied. Huge changes ensued. The Swindon head office was moved out of its Victorian warren to one floor of a blue and white tower owned by Allied Dunbar near Swindon railway station, and head office staff pared from 140 to thirty-five – most of them redeployed to other parts of the country.

Paperwork – 'we were paper-laden' – was chopped back by expedients like abolishing the statistics department. The regional network was concentrated into six operating companies, semi-autonomous business units.

These, however, were structural targets. The mission was still to come. This eventually resolved itself into achieving a level of service that, basically, no competitor could better.

The outcome has been threefold: the company's currently advertised

'24-hour service' in which it literally offers a repair service round the clock; 'customer teams' based on town areas, handling new products and offering on-the-spot technician service rather than from a remote service depot; and the new products themselves, a whole new range of rental items including white goods such as washing machines, with full service backup.

With high-tech Inmarsat, the problem was basically a microcosm of that confronting John Harvey-Jones at ICI in 1981 – not the catastrophic balance sheet of that year, but the underlying culture that first invented the product, then waited for markets to emerge. Harvey-Jones' philosophy of 'inventing into the marketplace' turned that historic old assumption on its head.

At Inmarsat – where Harvey-Jones spent a morning with the board sharing his wisdom on culture-changing – a blunt-speaking Canadian adviser on organizational development called Cheryl Young was taken on to initiate a programme of management change.

'What we had here was an expert culture – the thing that was valued was technical expertise and technical excellence. The attitude was, we will develop this brilliant technology, and if the customer doesn't like it or can't afford it, tough bananas,' says Young.

Management's attitude to time was another indicator of its resistant culture. 'There was never a meeting that started on time,' Young recalls. 'The attitude was, it's no big deal if you are fifteen, twenty or thirty minutes late for a meeting, just as it's no big deal if you are three or six months late in a project.'

There was also what Young scorns as 'management by shouldism – we should do that and we should do this and people should be able to handle things. Well that goes as far as a cast-iron boomerang. Nothing happens, there is no energy being put in.'

Inmarsat is basically a non-profit making organization, though it must make an adequate return on investment – minimum 14 per cent – for its stakeholders, a group of roughly 55 different countries represented by postal, telephone and telecommunications networks or large corporations such as British Telecom International. Its tower block at Euston is a mini United Nations, with nearly forty nationalities among its 250 employees. Hitherto it has leased satellites for onward leasing in various applications – maritime, air and land – but is now launching its own.

Its Swedish director-general, Olof Lundberg, wants it to push into new markets, but has been hampered by his own visionary, hands-off style, expecting his directors to run things while he travelled the world as an 'ambassador' for Inmarsat.

Young cheerfully admits her strategy so far has been 'ad hoc'. She started by reviving a training programme that had been cancelled within one of the company's operational groups and has proceeded to other small turnrounds by 'looking for a crack in the door and getting a foot wedged in,' believing that if even a small group begins to react differently, it can impact on others in the organization.

The board's assumptions began to change as a result of a three-day think-tank in the country organized by Young and process consultant Wendy Pritchard, but there is still, says Young with unvarnished directness, 'a high degree of cynicism among the staff, having never seen real control or real leadership in the group.' The need now, she adds, is for some formal systems to demonstrate that the organization really is changing in the way it operates – in its reward systems, for example.

After two and a half years with Inmarsat, and eighteen months of the management change programme, Young says 'some messages are getting through,' but she expects it to be another year before success is clear.

Ultimately, Young does not believe that it is possible to 'manage change' from the top in the conventional sense. 'I think that is putting nice words on an autocratic management style. I think you have got to look at what you have got with the culture and try to see how you can massage that and use its strengths, and by working with people in a fairly low-key kind of way, get them to recognize that there are different ways of operating, so that they can work together to make things happen.

'Every company has a dynamic, a source of energy that can be fanned into flames.'

# 9

# Nissan and the art of people management

March 1990

Roy Hill

Of all the manufacturing companies that have established themselves in the UK in the past decade, few have attracted as much media attention as Nissan. Few have had so many other companies beating a path to their door, eager to identify anything that may be useful to them.

But the lessons to be learned from the assembly plant the Japanese established on a greenfield site in Washington Road, Sunderland, Tyne and Wear, are not the ones you might expect. This is no factory operated in the image of Japanese car plants in Tokyo or Osaka. 'Japanese culture' is not the flavour of the month in Sunderland. Rather it is Nissan's pragmatic good sense, its willingness to tailor its policies to suit local conditions which is the keynote of its success in the UK.

True, there exist at Nissan Manufacturing (UK) some ways of working that are widely identified with Japan. For example, there is a single union agreement, with the AEU. Everyone works under the same conditions of employment and, from the managing director down, wears the same neat blue overalls. All salaries are paid monthly into bank accounts. All staff and their families may choose to be covered by private medical insurance. There is a single status subsidised canteen. Privileged parking does not exist. There is no clocking on. There are no written job descriptions. There are no salary deductions for lateness or absenteeism, which in any case is less than 3 per cent. And communications meetings are held every day (as opposed to monthly at Peugeot, for example).

But these are not exclusively Japanese ideas or attributes, any more than the idea of 'total quality' originated in Japan. Those habits that are originally Japanese, such as exercise programmes at the start of each shift or company songs and mottoes are not imposed on the Sunderland workforce. 'One of the good things about this company,' says its British managing director, Ian Gibson, 'is that it is not the sort of corporation to say "this is the way we do it". It is more a case of saying "we know that what we do in Japan is very different from what we do in Australia and also very different from what we do in the US. So what is the right thing to do here in Europe"?'

When Nissan chose the UK to set up its plant it took infinite pains to select the right top management to run it. The first British employee, Peter Wickens, who was appointed personnel and information systems director in October 1984, had been with Ford for ten years, ending up as industrial relations manager at the Dagenham body plant. But just as attractive to Nissan as his motor industry know-how was his experience as director of human resources at Continental Can Company (UK), helping to establish that company, also built on a greenfield site.

The same year Gibson, who has been managing director at Sunderland since last June, came on board, initially as director of purchasing and production control. He, too, had worked for Ford – ever since he left university with an applied physics (general engineering in today's terms) degree. He has also worked for Ford in Germany and Spain, as well as at Dagenham and Halewood.

Both Gibson and Wickens disagree with any notion that Nissan has been privileged, and its success practically guaranteed, by virtue of the fact that it started on a greenfield site and could design everything on a blank sheet of paper. As Gibson remarks, the last greenfield site in the British motor industry was Linwood: 'that opened, I guess, in the early 1970s and closed in the late 1970s. Greenfield sites guarantee you nothing in this world, other than the freedom to lay down the roads where you would like them to be.'

If Nissan UK had said that it wanted to be like Nissan US, it could have picked up all sorts or organizational manuals and pre-tested ways of doing things, and made early life much easier for itself.

Gibson and Wickens turned their backs on anything like that. 'Over the first couple of years we spent hours thrashing out the right approaches to running the company and managing its people,' says Gibson. 'Clearly we looked at what Nissan was doing in Japan; but we also looked at what was happening in excellent non-motor industry companies around the world. At IBM, for example.'

That habit has not gone away now that Nissan is well established in the UK. An interchange of plant visits with IBM continues. Nissan is also strongly interested in Marks & Spencer, which it feels has a lot to teach in terms of improved delivery and receipt systems. The important thing, Gibson says, is never to think that something that succeeds elsewhere is so different that you cannot learn anything from it.

Gibson gives the impression of absolute belief in the tenet that, generally, there are no bad employees but only bad managers and mangement systems. It is something he shares with Wickens, who says that management should never blame shop stewards or the workforce if things go wrong: 'you get the shop stewards, and the workforce, you deserve.'

## Milestones

The speed with which Nissan Motor Manufacturing (UK) has progressed is unmatched by any other motor industry start-up in Europe in recent years. Here are a few of the highlights:

**1984 February** Agreement with the Government to build a car plant in the UK.

**November** Construction begins.

**1985 April** Single union agreement with AEU.

**May** First training programme in Japan.

**December** Factory completed by Sir Robert McAlpine & Sons, on target in 62 weeks.

**1986 March** Assembly components for Nissan Bluebird arrive in the UK.

**June** Twenty-seven British component suppliers announced.

**July** First Bluebird for commercial sale produced.

**December** Phase one target of 95 cars per day achieved. Internal audit shows the quality of Sunderland produced cars is at least as good as vehicles assembled in Japan.

**1987 May** Year's production increased to 29,000.

**July** 436 acres of 'option land' purchased.

**August** Fifty-four employees leave for training in Japan.

**November** Employment levels reach 1100. Nightshift eight months ahead of schedule.

**December** Nissan announces a further £216m investment at Sunderland, bringing the total to £600m.

**1988 March** Engine plant equipment installed. Ground breaking of new body shop. Britain chosen as location for Nissan's European Technology Centre.

**September** Two hundred variants of Bluebird produced in Sunderland. Computer-aided design network links development and production centres in Japan, Europe and US.

**October** Left-hand drive exports to Europe begin.

**December** Employment reaches 1800. 56,000 cars produced. Flexible Learning Centre offering 350 training courses in Sunderland is opened.

**1989 February** 2000th employee and 100,000th Bluebird.

**May** 2500 employees and 75,000 cars a year.

**1990** 26,000 square metre body shop operational. Engine machining introduced. 80 per cent local content planned. 80,000 cars a year.

An incident at the plant illustrates Gibson's and Nissan's cool and sensible approach to problem solving. Two drums stood together, for fire safety reasons, in the same part of the plant. An employee connected the wrong drum to a pump, so that bottles awaiting windscreen washing liquid were filled with the wrong fluid. This went on for some time before the mistake was discovered. A lot of bottles had to be drained, washed out and refilled, wasting time and money.

A case, perhaps, for a reprimand to the worker from his supervisor? That is what would have happened at Ford when Gibson worked there. If a man failed to tighten a bolt says Gibson, he would be penalized. The shop steward would appeal that decision and it would end up with the plant manager inevitably backing the supervisor – a rigmarole that wasted everybody's time and generated needless ill-feeling. ('Later,' says Gibson, 'you would get to thinking that if that guy tightens four bolts on each of 500 cars a day and misses one bolt a month, that is a very high success rate, in percentage terms. How can you expect any human system to do better?')

Nissan's approach was different. Management noted that the drums containing different fluids both came from ICI, were the same size and colour and had the same label stamped on top. Only the wording of the stencilling was different. 'Now I have been known to read a road sign wrongly and turn the wrong way,' Gibson remarks. 'So we did not reprimand the man involved. What we did was to ask ICI to deliver one product in a drum twice the size of the other and make the connectors different. Then the man cannot misconnect. The mistake was management's, for permitting a system that was not fail-safe when run by a fallible human being.'

What management should aim to do, Gibson suggests, is set up an interlocking system that gives people time and a routine to check what they are doing. On critical items you have someone else perform a related operation, so that instead of relying on one man you rely on two. 'You install fail-safe modes throughout the system.'

Job flexibility also helps reduce mistakes and therefore wasted time. Gibson reckons that it takes about nine months to get a man fully skilled as a manufacturing operator – what Nissan likes to call manufacturing staff. He learns not only an assembly task but maintenance techniques that apply to his area. So if he is working alongside robots he learns how to programme them. And if he is in the paint shop, he learns to control the paint mix.

The flexible use of individuals' skills is helped by the lack of job descriptions and departmental specialization. 'Whereas, in many companies, it is the finance department that does the cost control, we expect every department to get involved in it,' explains Gibson. 'Similarly, we do not have a department formulating systems and procedures. That is done by the management group, which helps to keep everybody looking outwards, instead of inwards, and the whole company better able to cope with change.'

Above all, Nissan in the UK is a line managers' company. Its supervisors are empowered – a word that Peter Wickens uses often – to do a lot more than they would in most companies. Indeed, he asserts that there cannot be many supervisors who have more responsibilities thrust upon them.

The average supervisor at the plant has about twenty people reporting to him. He has the final say in who he takes on to his work team, personally offering that person the job – it is not done at second or third hand through the personnel staff. Thereafter he is personally responsible for the new recruit's integration and development within the work team.

He also controls the layout of the production line, line balancing and many other physical aspects of building a motor car. In return, he enjoys the same status and rewards as other valued professionals such as the personnel officer, the financial analyst, the systems analyst, the buyer. 'It is based on our conviction that the people closest to the job know best how to do it,' Wickens adds. 'The guy sitting up at head office often does not have a clue.'

He insists that he would never allow his personnel people to make an assembly line hire or fire decision, or to sort out an industrial relations problem. The personnel department's job is to select, equip, train and motivate line managers to sort out their own problems.

Wickens claims that Nissan's supervisors are the opposite of militant shop stewards and their teams identify with them. As he points out, when you have men who have selected their people, trained them, had tea and lunch breaks and played football with them, the team simply does not want to score points over the supervisor.

'Add to that our concept of continuous improvement,' Wickens says, 'and you will find that most of the suggestions for improvements come from the production staff themselves. We do not have to come along and say "we want to do this". More often it is the lads on the shop floor saying "we want to do this differently".'

It is not a suggestion scheme. It is not a quality circle. It is built into Nissan's everyday way of running the job. It is organic, not tagged on. And Nissan will pay overtime so that work groups can discuss continuous improvement without the time constraints of the normal working day. 'We built a workshop where guys on the production line can actually build the equipment they think they would like to have and give it a try,' says Gibson. 'In the last two and a half years we have made literally thousands of changes, many of them very small, in the way we build cars.'

No wonder visitors from other companies turn up on Nissan's doorstep at the rate of about one a week, not to do business but to learn. They find that what they learn is easy to assimilate but not so easy to emulate. That requires the dedication born of conviction.

# 10

# What it takes to be a woman at the top

March 1984

## Carol Kennedy

The sight of a woman in the British boardroom is rare enough; that of one in the managing director's chair almost as exotic as a pair of nesting ospreys. Even basic statistics are hard to come by: 18.8 per cent was the 1981 figure for women in senior and middle management, but at director level one is reduced to guessing at something like 2 per cent of Britain's estimated 250,000 directors, a ratio roughly reflected in the Institute of Directors' own membership.

Yet women *are* quietly advancing into the upper echelons of British management, principally in the service industries, where it is traditionally assumed women do best. To test the truth of this and other assumptions about women in management – and why there are not more of them – *The Director* sought the seasoned views of six successful women who have made it to the top levels, asking them to expound their business philosophy, how they ran their working lives and whether they felt there was any significant difference in management style between the sexes.

These were the six we interviewed:

**Eileen Cole:** managing director of Research International, Unilever's big market research subsidiary. Set up initially to monitor Unilever's own consumers, it now boasts a blue-chip list of clients including Monsanto Chemicals, Reynolds Tobacco, Allied Breweries and General Foods. From her modest office in Southwark, Miss Cole has responsibility for technical market research worldwide, and for twelve European companies with a current turnover of £26m. She works a punishing day, leaving her Hampshire farmhouse at 7 a.m. and returning around 8 p.m., always with 'half a day's reading' at weekends. She travels on business about two months of the year and is a part-time member of the Post Office Board, which takes up an average of one day a week, as well as being on the Careers Advisory Service Board at Cambridge and Reading Universities. Single and in her fifties, she is probably one of the highest paid women executives in the country but admits: 'My ambition is by no means sated.'

**Eileen Cullen:** company secretary of the National Westminster Bank since 1980 and the highest-ranking woman in British banking. She works relatively structured hours, but takes 'a case full of papers most evenings' to her South London home.

**Patricia Lamburn:** editorial director of IPC Magazines and until recently the only woman on IPC's main board, where her voice is sought on matters of general editorial judgement. She is responsible for keeping watch on the editorial content of some sixty-three varied publications within Europe's largest consumer magazine publishing group, as well as for identifying top editorial clients. Married to a West End dental surgeon, with two grown-up children, she describes herself as 'very much a self-starter' whose workload ('One is never *not* busy') accommodates membership of the IBA's General Advisory Council (of which she was elected chairman in 1982), the Royal College of Physicians' PR Committee and the Press Council.

**Maureen Smith:** managing director of Good Relations, the only PR company quoted on the stock exchange. Together with chairman and founder Tony Good, she runs a group of five autonomous subsidiaries handling corporate consumer, financial, industrial and government affairs PR. It is a young business – most main board members are in their forties – and very much a meritocracy between the sexes. She had her daughter (now aged three) in her three weeks' annual holiday, 'so I did not miss any time'.

**Dawn Mitchell:** chairman and chief executive of Research Services Ltd, Britain's fifth largest market research company and one of the two oldest. Since restructuring the board last year she has two MDs reporting to her, travels extensively lecturing on market research and now sees herself as primarily an ambassador for the company.

**Valerie Boakes:** group commodity adviser to Napier Brown, a firm of city merchants with a huge volume of sugar dealings. Her responsibilities revolve around international market forecasts, a skilled and sensitive exercise of judgement six months to a year ahead. 'If I am wrong a lot of other people will be too.' She is married to a businessman in Berkshire and has three adult step children.

All six were patently achievers by temperament; all emphasized the need for a woman executive to be a rigorous organizer of time; all, in different ways, asserted there need be no barriers to a woman determined to succeed, though the price to be paid may prove too exacting for many. 'Business is a hard life,' as Eileen Cole observed, and men at the top also have to make sacrifices – strains on marriage and other relationships, the insidious erosion of holidays and private life.

Miss Cole was one who weighed up the challenges and accepted them at the start of a career with Unilever which began thirty-five years ago after she graduated with an economics degree.

'I am a professional manager in the true, large-business sense. I came in as a trainee and went through all the stages that men do.' In her early days she found it harder as a woman to convince the company that she intended to stay: now, she says with a wry smile, 'I do not expect to keep men that long. For trainees the loss rate is the same between men and women, and the average length of stay the same – for all managers, the loss rate among men is actually 10 per cent greater.'

Small and dark, incisive of mind but with a readily communicable warmth of interest, she has forthright and considered views on women in management. 'They may get off to a slower start than men, but because there are fewer women jockeying for position, they are more noticeable.' Unilever, she says, has always had an enlightened approach to the hiring of women on equal terms – 'and if you do that, you get the pick of the crop. There still are not that many companies which do.'

Miss Cole stamps firmly on the accepted wisdom that market research is a business particularly suited to women: 'you have to be very numerate, very logical, have a good statistical background, be lucid, intellectually orderly and have a rigorous mind that does not permit half-truths – all, ironically enough, attributes men think of as untypically feminine.'

Women, she thinks, do have a different style of management – 'not better or worse, because one can't generalize about a male style of management either, it varies enormously. But I would say women perhaps have a more co-operative approach in the handling of people.' One significant factor, she feels, is that women have no traditional 'role models' of management – 'they have had to work it out for themselves.'

She does believe that, once a woman has achieved high responsibility, 'the role emulation theory works – other women in the company feel it is possible.'

Maureen Smith, in her eyrie of a Bloomsbury office reached by five flights of stairs, personifies the young, fast-moving and stylish image of PR. She studied journalism as a way in to PR and worked at Bovis, the construction group, in 1968 before joining Good Relations, then a tiny, Canterbury-based consultancy. After two other jobs in corporate and financial PR, she returned to Good Relations when it took over BBDO Public Relations, in 1971, where she was a director. As the new company grew to its present market capitalization in excess of £11m, she rose with it, becoming group MD in 1975.

'I do not like to think of myself as a woman manager, any more than I think of men managers,' she says crisply. 'You are either a good manager or you are not.' If there *is* a difference between the sexes on their way up the corporate ladder, it could be that 'women set out more ambitious than men but are often satisfied with a lower goal achievement. Men may be less passionately ambitious to start with but are driven to rise further as they go along. That is why more and more women are going into middle management – they have not got that killer instinct that takes them to the very top.'

Patricia Lamburn of IPC worked her way to the boardroom from beginning as a trainee subeditor in 1943 with the old Amalgamated Press (later Fleetway Publications, a component of the present IPC group). Although IPC Magazines derives most of its revenue from women, she is not surprised that she found herself for so long the sole female on the main board, pointing out that, historically, women have entered magazine publishing on the editorial side, and for advancement to top-level management the key tends to be in financial, publishing and advertising areas.

To succeed in business, she believes, takes a rigorous commitment for a woman. 'It means an iron self-discipline, it means remaining feminine but never using that femininity to set oneself apart from one's colleagues on the board . . . it means a dedicated sense of organization between one's private and personal life. Not many are able to cope with all that.

'But I think we can get very stereotyped in thinking a woman has approached a business problem in a different way from a man. I do not think we should be different animals in our working environment.'

Eileen Cullen, who also began her career during the war, is an unexpected figure to meet in the imposing office of the Natwest Company Secretary. Soft-spoken, unassuming in manner, she appears mildly surprised by her rise to eminence. When she started in branch banking, 'women were appreciated for their depth of knowledge but since they could not move on themselves they could only pass that expertise to the men.' It was not until the 1960s that women started to obtain senior bank appointments. Wartime shortage of male staff, however, meant 'management was always pleased to give you any job you were capable of doing. I was ambitious to do any job well and to do the most senior job available. I never refused to take on anything I was offered, perhaps to prove to myself that I *could* do it.'

On women's advancement in banking and elsewhere, she retains a certain caution. 'I would not want to rush along too quickly. I feel we may be in danger of appointing women simply because they are women – it is important that they should be chosen on merit.' Modestly, she takes the view that 'if I can do it, anyone can. The secret for women is to be ready to take the opportunities.'

Dawn Mitchell started her career abroad but after divorce in the early 1960s entered market research as a part-time job she could do while looking after her baby, and which would enable her to use her three foreign languages. After a stint at IPA, she returned to Research Services, concentrating initially on developing international business. Having come up through the staff, she felt supported by the goodwill of her colleagues when attaining the managing director's chair, 'but that would have been the same for a man as for a woman.'

Research Services Ltd has produced three high-flying women executives who have gone on to other companies, but there are no other women on its board. Mrs Mitchell was reluctant to generalize about management style but thought, perhaps surprisingly, that women were 'greater risk takers' than men. 'For women over forty, on the whole one was not brought up to expect a career, so perhaps therefore one has a greater sense of freedom.'

Valerie Boakes operates very much in a male-dominated environment but has been impressed by the number of women quietly moving into senior posts in the city. In elegant modern offices overlooking the rippling waters of St Katherine's Dock, she observed that in day-to-day management decisions 'some women's thought processes may follow a different route from those of some men, but they reach the same objective.'

Like Eileen Cole, she feels women – particularly younger ones – 'try to be co-operative in their approach to handling people: it is, after all, the way to get things done. If tempted to generalize, I would say that perhaps women are better at planning than men. If you look at women running a home, they are managers, after all: they acquire a whole range of management skills, though they may not identify them as such – forward planning, marketing, social planning, public relations.'

The emphasis on planning and time management ran like a steel thread through all our conversations. 'I've always said that what every woman manager needs is a good wife', joked Eileen Cole, pointing out more seriously that almost every senior woman in business has an added responsibility over her male peers – if not a family, then elderly parents, or at any rate a home to manage. Eileen Cullen runs her life with the aid of lists and a loyal, long-established secretary. Patricia Lamburn, riding as she said 'something of a hobby-horse', would like to see domestic work upgraded and given the dignity it has in the US (where home helps often run their own little entrepreneurial businesses) in order to release the hidden 'cream layer' of female executive talent.

Not surprisingly, all six of our successful women had mobilized their domestic lives for maximum efficiency: Miss Cole manages her farmhouse and five acres with a gardener and a battery of sophisticated equipment;

Patricia Lamburn and Maureen Smith have had or still have nannies and other staff to help run their London houses; Valerie Boakes acquired domestic help when she married, but as a single woman did everything herself and took the Institute of Marketing diploma in three years of evening study.

Even for the most dedicated of 'self starters', one fact – obvious perhaps, but significant coming from such high achievers – emerged to indicate that women in the boardroom are still going to remain a fairly rare species. 'There is no doubt', Patricia Lamburn summed it up dispassionately, 'that a woman manager has to carry a greater load, and for some the burden can become almost insupportable.'

# 11

# The secrets of innovation

July 1985

Peter Drucker

## *Is everything consistent?*

O. M. Scott & Co. is the leader among American producers of lawn care products: grass seed, fertilizer, pesticides, and so on. Though it is now a subsidiary of a large corporation (ITT), it attained leadership while a small independent company in fierce competition with firms many times its size, ranging from Sears, Roebuck to Dow Chemicals. Its products are good but so are those of the competition. Its leadership rests on a simple mechanical budget called a spreader, a small, lightweight wheelbarrow with holes that could be set to allow the proper quantities of Scott's products to pass through in an even flow. Products for the lawn all claim to be 'scientific' and are compounded on the basis of extensive tests. It prescribes in meticulous detail how much of the stuff should be applied, given soil conditions and temperatures. All try to convey to the consumer that growing a lawn is 'precise', 'controlled', if not 'scientific'. But before the Scott Spreader, no supplier of lawn-care products gave the customer a tool to control the process. And without such a tool, there was an internal incongruity in the logic of the process that upset and frustrated customers.

O. M. Scott grew from a tiny local seed retailer into a fair-sized national company because it asked dealers and customers what they missed.

Every hardware-store clerk knew about the frustration of his lawn customers – and talked about it. What was lacking, however, was someone willing to listen, somebody who took seriously what everybody proclaims: 'the purpose of a product or a service is to satisfy the customer'. If this axiom is accepted and acted upon, using incongruity as an opportunity for innovation becomes fairly easy – and highly effective.

## Can you satisfy a public need?

As late as 1965, Japan had almost no paved roads outside the big cities. But the country was rapidly shifting to the automobiles, so the government frantically paved the roads. Now automobiles could – and did – travel at high speed. But the roads were the same old ones that had been laid down by the oxcarts of the tenth century – barely wide enough for two cars to pass, full of blind corners and hidden entrances, and with junctions every few kilometers at which half a dozen roads meet at every conceivable angle. Accidents began to mount at an alarming rate; rebuilding the roads was out of the question; it would have taken twenty years anyhow. And a massive publicity campaign to make automobilists 'drive carefully' had the result that such campaigns generally have, namely, none at all.

A young Japanese, Tamon Iwasa, seized on this crisis in an innovative opportunity. He redesigned the traditional highway reflector so that the little glass beads that serve as its mirrors could be adjusted to reflect the headlights of oncoming cars from any direction on to any direction. The government rushed to install Iwasa reflectors by the hundreds of thousands. And the accident rate plummeted.

## Are you geared to changes?

Every one of the world's automobile manufacturers, large or small, has had to act or face permanent eclipse. However, three small and quite marginal companies saw in this a major opportunity to innovate: Volvo, BMW and Porsche.

Around 1960, when the automobile industry market suddenly changed, the informed betting was heavily on the disappearance of these three companies during the coming 'shakeout'. Instead, all three have done well. They have done so through an innovated strategy which, in effect, had reshaped them into different businesses. Volvo in 1965 was small, struggling and barely breaking even. For a few critical years, it did lose large amounts of money. But Volvo went to work reinventing itself, so to speak. It became an aggressive world-wide marketer – especially strong in the United States – of what one might call the 'sensible' car; not very luxurious, far from low-priced, not at all fashionable, but sturdy and radiating common sense and 'better value'. Volvo has marketed itself as the car for professionals who do not need to demonstrate how successful they are through the car they drive, but who value being known for their 'good judgement'.

## Grab the new knowledge and fly

Particularly instructive is the failure of the British to reap the harvest from their own knowledge-based innovations.

The British discovered and developed penicillin, but it was the Americans who took it over. The British scientists did a magnificent technical job. They came out with the right substances and the right uses. Yet they failed to identify the ability to manufacture the stuff as a critical knowledge factor. They could have developed the necessary knowledge of fermentation technology; they did not even try. As a result, a small American company, Pfizer, went to work on developing the knowledge of fermentation and became the world's foremost manufacturer of penicillin.

Similarly, the British conceived, designed, and built the first passenger jet plane. But de Havilland, the British company, did not analyse what was needed and therefore did not identify two key factors. One was configuration, that is, the right size with the right payload for the routes on which the jet would give an airline the greatest advantage. The other was equally mundane: how to finance the purchase of such an expensive plane by the airlines. As a result of de Havilland's failure to do the analysis, two American companies, Boeing and Douglas, took over the jet plane. And de Havilland has long since disappeared.

## Face it: people do change

One American retailer who accepted the 'baby boom' was then a small and undistinguished shoe chain, Melville. In the early 1960s just before the first cohorts of the 'baby boom' reached adolescence, Melville directed itself to this new market. It created new and different stores specifically for teenagers. It redesigned its merchandise. It advertised and promoted to the sixteen- and seventeen-year-olds. And it went beyond footwear into clothing for teenagers, both female and male. As a result, Melville became one of the fastest-growing and most profitable retailers in America. Ten years later other retailers caught on and began to cater to teenagers just as the centre of demographic gravity started to shift away from them and toward 'young adults', twenty- to twenty-five-years-old. By then Melville was already shifting its own focus to that new dominant age cohort.

## Shocked? Don't grin and bear it

The failure of the Ford Motor Company's Edsel in 1957 has become American folklore. Even people who were not born when the Edsel failed have heard about it, at least in the US.

Very few products were ever more carefully designed, more carefully introduced, more skilfully marketed. The Edsel was intended to be the final step in the most thoroughly planned strategy in American business history: a ten-year campaign during which the Ford Motor Company converted itself after the Second World War from near-bankruptcy into an aggressive competitor, a strong number two in the United States, and a few years later, a strong contender for the number one spot in the rapidly growing European market.

Ford went to extreme lengths to plan and design the Edsel, embodying the best information from market research, the best information about customer preferences.

Yet the Edsel became a total failure right away.

The reaction of the Ford Motor Company was very revealing. Instead of blaming the 'irrational consumer' the Ford people decided there must be something happening that did not go with the assumptions about reasons everyone had been making.

The result of Ford's decision to go out and investigate was the one genius innovation in the American automobile industry since Alfred P. Sloan, in the 1920s, had defined the socio-economic segmentation of the American market into 'low', 'lower-middle', 'upper-middle', and 'upper' segments, an insight on which he then built the General Motors Company. When the Ford people went out, they discovered that this segmentation was rapidly being replaced – or at least paralleled by another quite different one, the one we would now call 'lifestyle segmentation'. The result, within a short period after the Edsel's failure, was the appearance of Ford's Thunderbird, the greatest success of any American car since the Model T in 1908.

## New moods, new menus

Traditionally, the way people feed themselves was very largely a matter of income group and class. Ordinary people 'ate'; the rich 'dined'. This perception has changed within the last twenty years. Now the same people both 'eat' and 'dine'. One trend is towards 'feeding', which means getting down the necessary means of sustenance, in the easiest and simplest possible way: convenience foods, TV dinners, McDonald's hamburgers or Kentucky Fried Chicken, and so on. But then the same consumers have also become gourmet cooks. TV programmes on gourmet cooking are highly popular and achieve high ratings; gourmet cookbooks have become mass-market best-sellers; whole new chains of gourmet food stores have opened. Finally traditional supermarkets, while doing 90 per cent of their business in food stuff 'feeding', have opened 'gourmet boutiques' which in many cases are far more profitable than their ordinary processed food. In West

Germany, a young woman physician said to me recently: 'Wir es sechs tage in der woche, aber einen wollen wir doch richtig speisen (We feed six days, but one day a week we like to dine).' Not so long ago, 'essen' was what ordinary people did seven days a week and 'speisen' what the elite did, seven days a week.

(Extracted from *Innovation and Entrepreneurship*, published by Butterworth-Heinemann 1985.)

# 12

# Performance pay: cash on delivery

November 1986

## Carol Kennedy

Sir Peter Walters of BP practises it; so do Pat Sheehy of BAT Industries, Sir John Egan of Jaguar, Sir John Harvey-Jones of ICI and Sir Ralph Halpern of the Burton Group. Sir Trevor Holdsworth of GKN is one chairman who does not, but the highly paid Dick Giordano of BOC certainly does – and insists that it goes a long way down the management tree. Bob Bauman, the new American chief executive at Beecham, plans to bring it in.

It is performance-related pay, where achievers are rewarded with handsome cash bonuses amounting to as much as 50 per cent of their salary. This is a concept that comes naturally to the competitive world of US business; it was at first resisted in British boardrooms but now is sweeping through companies of all sizes this side of the Atlantic.

From a mere ripple a few years ago, incentive bonus schemes have become a wave, according to Inbucon, the management consultants who specialize in designing them. Companies ranging from giant multinationals down to those employing fewer than 250 are rushing to join the payment-by-results bandwagon; those already on it overwhelmingly endorse the effectiveness of bonus schemes in improving motivation and focusing attention on key priorities for better company performance and profitability.

More than half the UK's directors now have some performance-related element in their pay, reports consultancy group Hay-MSL, whose researchers predict that the figure will rise in 1987 by 5 to 10 per cent. Inbucon, reporting a similar ratio, finds that the level of bonus is typically 18 to 20 per cent for managing directors; 14 to 15 per cent for others. A parallel shift to cash incentives is taking place in mainland Europe (where basic management salaries are almost everywhere higher than in Britain). Along with this trend, differentials are widening dramatically. A 50 per cent gap between senior and junior management is not uncommon.

'The mood is definitely becoming one of greater selectivity,' observes a senior executive at BP, where that is very much Walters' philosophy and one that is encouraged throughout the organization. Each individual business in

BP, however, is responsible for thinking through its own remuneration needs, and not all divisional chief executives, it is fair to say, are as convinced as the chairman of the merits of incentive bonuses.

Certainly when the idea began to take root in the UK about six years ago many boards looked on it with horror. It was unnecessary (management already worked as hard as it could), complicated to devise and operate, divisive and damaging to that hallowed British concept 'team spirit'. International search consultants Spencer Stuart Associates carried out an in-depth survey at that time, and half the companies studied were firmly against bonus schemes. But among those who supported the idea, one executive took a pungent view of the team spirit argument: 'Ours is a friendly company and everybody gets on terribly well,' he commented. 'I think they get on far too well. One of the reasons for an incentive scheme would be to try and sharpen them up and make them a little less friendly.'

Bonus schemes certainly shake up the companies that apply them, often uncomfortably. 'They change people's behaviour,' says Inbucon's Ken Schwarz. 'You often find less able people tend to put up smokescreens.' Spencer Stuart's Nigel Dyckoff agrees: 'An incentive scheme completely alters a company. It reveals the areas of weakness.' And, of course, not all companies are suitable cases for treatment: some, as Dyckoff says, are perfectly happy and even successful in their own terms with a bureaucratic culture. They remain as opposed to payment by results as any trade union. But Inbucon found that of eighteen companies surveyed that had installed such schemes, 95 per cent were fully or partly satisfied that they had achieved their purpose.

Attitudes have certainly changed profoundly in six years. Striving for greater financial reward is not, it seems, so un-British after all. In its 1980 study, Spencer Stuart was forced to the conclusion that 'there is evidence to suggest that the British are simply not motivated by money – at least the acquisition of money – to the extent that their competitors are.' Today, Dyckoff observes, top executives are motivated by financial rewards and a sense of visible achievement.'

The catalyst of change was the Thatcher government's decision in 1979 to cut the top rate of tax on earned income from 83 to 60 per cent. Cash was suddenly a worthwhile incentive again after years of attempts to flesh out heavily taxed executive salaries with ever more contrived sets of perks, from school fee assistance to free suits. And cash was a very visible signal of achievement and approval – 'the most powerful signal we have around here,' one senior BP manager remarks.

One of the first big companies to apply cash incentives was BOC. In 1979 it acquired the US company Airco and with it Airco's president Richard Giordano as BOC chairman and chief executive. Giordano brought with him a vigorous American belief in orienting people to perform; a philosophy of 'good pay for good performance and out the door otherwise,' as a colleague puts it succinctly.

'Dick set out to built a performance-oriented management team with some real discipline, but the scheme developed quite cautiously over five years.'

Giordano has been very much the driving force behind it, yet his own well-publicized salary – which fluctuates with the dollar rate but is currently £883,100 – has no performance reward in it other than stock options. The committee of non-executive directors that sets his salary believes the chairman should operate on a longer view than would be implied by cash bonuses on yearly results.

The 'disciplined' approach of BOC's performance-related philosophy shows up in the detailed thoroughness with which the company's appraisal mechanism is constructed. It affects executive directors (apart from the chairman) and a number of other senior executives and managers. From September 1986 it was extended even further, and now covers between 400 and 500 people worldwide, with the heaviest concentration in the US. Around 70 UK managers are affected.

Bonuses are worked out on a 'grid' formula relating to company and individual performance. If the company has done well but the individual has not performed in a sparkling way, there will be no bonus. On the other hand, a good individual performance in a year when the company also does well will yield handsome results.

As well as cash bonuses, about 150 people worldwide (between 40 and 50 in the UK) will be on stock options. Bonuses for the most senior executives could amount to 50 per cent of salary – and this is by no means an unusual figure today.

Consultants usually advise that such schemes cease to be effective below the second line of management – heads of functions or just below – though exceptions can, and often should, be made for people who can 'influence a company's results' even if they are lower down the line. (In a retail chain, for example, it could be a store manager; in a brewery company it might be a publican.)

At BOC, 'fairly precise' pre-set goals are agreed at the beginning of each year between the executive and his superior. 'We try to remove as much subjectivity as possible,' says BOC's Nigel Rowe, adding that the system 'forces the department head to work out what that department is trying to achieve. A very important spin-off benefit is that it helps us to manage the business better.

'We do believe that it works, but it only works really well if there is discipline in setting real goals and being reasonably objective and precise,' Rowe adds.

That said, there has to be an important discretionary element even in judging performance against goals. As Rowe points out, even a modest growth in profits can be pretty good if your industry had had a generally disastrous year.

The Burton Group, which last year paid out a record £8.2m on performance-related schemes (pretax profits were up by 42 per cent, comfortably exceeding the mid-year forecast), has been in no doubt about the practice since introducing it in 1980.

'The aim of the whole incentive system is to clarify individual accountability and to relate individual performance to the achievement of overall profit figures,' chairman Halpern told shareholders in 1982. 'The results of the last two years demonstrate the effectiveness of this policy for both management and shareholders.' Each year since, the number of staff receiving bonuses has increased – in 1986 it covered 12,500 of the group's total 14,739 employees.

Ronald Utiger of TI (the former Tube Investments) is another chief executive utterly convinced of the motivating force of bonus payments tied to tough targets. The system was introduced last year as TI was labouring under an increased burden of debt. Top managers were offered a 10 per cent bonus if they could reduce overdraft interest levels. Stock-to-sales ratios were another target selected by Utiger, and in 1986, when the number of managers in TI's scheme was doubled to 200, attention was focused on profit margins. 'People watch them and see results very quickly, and that fuels their enthusiasm,' Utiger observes.

Construction group John Laing brought in cash incentives after much boardroom agonizing and has seen the principle triumphantly vindicated in the bottom line. In 1982 profitability was badly down and the company was struggling financially. Paternalistic by tradition, the Laing management style had been characterized by a tendency to 'keep heads down and not be too aggressive in business terms,' according to one executive.

'People were too comfortable,' recalls Leslie J. Holliday, who in 1982 was chief executive and chairman-designate. He reasoned that the bonus system already worked well further down the line – 'why not at the top?' But the board required a good deal of persuasion, many taking a similar view to the one Spencer Stuart's survey found so prevalent in 1980 – that management already worked to its limits and could not be tempted by cash to work any harder.

However, as everyone concerned has found, the key benefit is not so much working harder as focusing on priorities. In Laing's case, the results were dramatic. 'We just leapt forward from almost nil profit to £30m in four years,' says Holliday, who retired from the company last year. Such was the motivating force among the 70 or so individuals affected that, whereas Holliday had initially been the one to push for setting and meeting goals, 'within six months I was having to apply the reins.' The enthusiasm to achieve targets was forcing the pace in some areas faster than the chairman wanted – where there were sensitive issues of redundancies, for example.

But Holliday is in no doubt about the efficacy of such schemes, as long as they are properly thought out and applied. Laing's housing group, he says, where everybody is on some sort of incentive is 'probably the fastest-growing housing group in the UK. Everyone there just bubbles.'

Holliday is adamant, however, that incentive schemes are no substitute for good management. 'It is a tool to help good managers,' he insists. 'If management is inadequate it could do more harm than good.'

One way the doubters on Laing's board were brought round was to involve them in the target setting, and these targets, Holliday believes, 'are among the highest you will find.' The way the company applied its new philosophy was described to Holliday as 'champagne or the guillotine.' Holliday does not deny the truth of that – but results speak for themselves, he believes.

Laing's experience is unusual, however. Most consultants admit that it is difficult to establish a direct relationship between installing a bonus scheme and improved company profits. Indeed, there is *no* real evidence in the short term, says Inbucon's Schwarz. What many schemes do is focus objectives in key result areas, 'and they do that very well.'

Typical key areas might include better return on capital, reduced borrowing levels, improved cash flow. Taking the last as an example, every manager in the scheme could be asked to concentrate on ways in which his department could use less cash; in manufacturing, the focus might be on work in progress, reducing wastage, better monitoring, quality control and better energy management. A sales director might pick better forecasting as his contribution.

Whatever the targets set, it is important, says Inbucon, to relate them to outside yardsticks. This establishes credibility and avoids the temptation to set budgets that are too soft. Another way to prove the objectivity of the scheme – and all consultants stress the importance of making them 'defensible' to workforce and shareholders – is for the targets to be set by someone outside it, like the chairman or the non-executive directors.

As boardroom salaries rise – base levels have been going up by 9 to 10 per cent for the past three years and show no signs of reducing to anything ike inflation level, as Chancellor Nigel Lawson would prefer – and as more companies adopt performance-related bonuses on top of those, the principle of defensibility clearly becomes paramount.

Sir John Harvey-Jones fielded some blunt questions from ICI shareholders when his salary took a leap upwards two years ago, with a performance-related £97,261 making a total of £287,261. 'It is not for us to say if we are worth what we are paid,' was his comment then, but he invited critics to look at the 'considerable responsibility' carried by ICI directors 'and the way in which the company is now performing.' (ICI had just broken the £1bn profit barrier – the first British company to do so.) In the following year the ICI chairman received £312,991, of which basic salary was £220,000, performance-related bonuses £74,800 and the rest a variety of accumulated entitlements, including stock options.

Tony Vernon Harcourt of Monks Publications, who prepares studies on executive pay for the Charterhouse Group, says the level of basic increases is unlikely to come down while company profitability is still 'visibly going up wherever you look.' But the real test of the performance-related principle in terms of credibility will come, consultants believe, when company results begin to slow or turn down. 'The US will be a test bed,' says Nick Boulter of Hay-MSL. 'Company profitability has been falling there, but there is no evidence yet of top pay being cut.'

A study this summer by the *Sunday Times* of Britain's '100 best paid directors' against their company results suggested that comparatively few, as yet, are prepared to take substantial cuts in line with falling profits. (One exception was Bryan Christopher of BSR, whose pay took a 22 per cent dive in response to his company's 100 per cent collapse in profits.) But the survey did not differentiate between those on straight salary and those earning performance bonuses.

If UK business culture is changing towards the acceptance of high risk, high reward in management, it needs to change on both sides of the equation to be fully accepted. Hay-MSL has no doubt that the principle could be thoroughly discredited if rewards are seen to come without risk.

'It is crucial that some sort of penalties and downside should be imposed if bonuses are not to become just another expected norm,' said one of the group's recent papers on remuneration. 'There is little evidence to suggest, as yet, that UK employees are prepared to take cuts in their total remuneration packages when results are poor. However, the consequences of not doing so in the future are potentially grave; in terms of overall public reputation, in terms of present and future government pay policies and in terms of economic competitiveness.'

# 13

# Death of an entrepreneur

June 1988

## Stuart Rock

If death and taxes are the only two certain things in life, accountants are here to deal with one of them. Confronting the other in a business environment, though, is not something that can just be handled by advisers. The sudden death of a chief executive is, perhaps, the sternest task for a board to face; not only does it test an ability to respond, it also tends to expose previously unseen fragilities and puts future performance under greater scrutiny. A company that can cope will have more than proved its mettle.

When Atlantic Computers, a computer leasing company, went public in 1983, the company *was* its chairman and chief executive John Foulston, and the City institutions backed it as such. Foulston, who previously had taken only three years with Memorex UK to reach the rank of European vice-president, set up Atlantic in 1975 with a £50,000 loan. In the early 1980s he persuaded an individual businessman to inject capital of £8m into the venture and doubled that investment within three years.

1987 was no exception to Atlantic's hectic growth. A series of deals took place between April and September, fulfilling Foulston's prophecy that the once-scattered computer leasing market would become the province of one or two major players.

On September 22 last year Atlantic unveiled impressive interim figures. Pretax profits rose 32 per cent to £12.7m; turnover was up by 47 per cent to £228m. A major acquisition of CBF, an Australian computer supply and leasing company, was announced.

On September 29 Foulston was killed in a car crash. He was forty. It was not even a mundane accident. A motor racing fanatic, he died at the wheel of an 800 horsepower McLaren Indianapolis single-seater on the Silverstone racetrack.

For the management of Atlantic, it was like hearing the news of Kennedy's assassination – they can all remember vividly where they were and what they were doing when they learned of it. Derek Blackiston, marketing director of the computer systems division, was on holiday – he was phoned by one of his friends expressing personal sympathy before he himself heard what had happened.

John Tompkins, then group finance director, was negotiating new financing arrangements with the bank when one of the mechanics telephoned from the racecourse. 'My first reaction was one of disbelief,' he says. 'It could have been some sort of joke.' He returned to the office and immediately called Silverstone back. When the news was confirmed, he called an executive board meeting that convened within ninety minutes.

As the news spread through the office, staff were openly in tears. The recollection still strikes a deep emotive chord with Tompkins – 'JGF' (as Foulston was known) was a close personal friend as well as a business colleague.

The board, in conjunction with its merchant bank, acted swiftly. 'We needed to be seen to be taking positive action,' says Tompkins. He was appointed chief executive; John Gillum of Rothschilds became non-executive chairman. Corporate affairs manager Neil Ashworth, who had just unpacked his bag in an Amsterdam hotel, flew back to draft statements for staff, subsidiary companies and the press. Tompkins handled the press calls. The limelight might have been too bright for the back room boy but, as Tompkins put it, 'when you are pushed hardest, you perform best. It went pretty well, all things considered.'

Tompkins stressed that although it was a personal tragedy, it was not a business tragedy. Business was as usual.

Atlantic's management team was fired with adrenalin. All the standard office politics disappeared and teamwork came to the fore. The motivation seems to have come from two sources – the determination to prove to investors and the press that Atlantic was not just the one-man band it had been portrayed as, and the need to do it 'for JGF'. (A letter from Lloyd's Bank systems chief said: 'It is your mission to take the lead you have inherited and, through example and innovation, to power the Atlantic Group to new heights. *You owe it to John.*')

Two weeks later, and two days after Black Monday on the stock market, Atlantic convened a seminar for fund managers and analysts to meet the management team. If there had been any nervousness among the company's backers, it was swiftly dispelled. By the end of the day the share price had defied gravity, rising 17p when all around had tumbled.

The group's latest results, announced in mid-April, showed that the momentum had been maintained (although Tompkins describes them as 'satisfactory' rather than 'good'). Profits were up to £38.2m on turnover of £630.7m.

Obviously, no one at Atlantic would ever have wished to experience that traumatic September day. The management team does feel that it has learned from it, however, and has been able to use that experience positively.

'If it had happened when we had just floated then it would have been extremely difficult for me,' admits Tompkins 'But in the four years JGF made the transition from being a busy managing director to a strategically minded chairman of a quoted company; responsibilities had been devolved to competent people.'

Yet Foulston was a charismatic man who led from the front. 'If JGF and four others were at a presentation,' says Tompkins, 'he would be the only one talking. We would see that he liked doing it and so we let him get on with it. That is not a denigration of our management, but it is just the situation we slipped into. JGF had a dog but would often bark himself.'

Such a scenario no longer happens. When it came to discussing the relocation of Atlantic's administrative headquarters, the board worked as a team to identify alternative properties and space requirements. It was eventually decided to move to Staines, near Heathrow – a momentous decision for a business that had always been in the heart of London. 'If we had not felt strong as a company it could well have been disruptive,' says Tompkins. Perhaps, too, Foulston's presence would have influenced the decision.

There will be no aping of Foulston's style. Tompkins, 'a team leader and a member of the team,' is his own man. Foulston himself had started to develop a more corporate and less individual image for Atlantic. (While he held the posts of chairman and chief executive, moves were already afoot to appoint a deputy chairman. The division of responsibilities between Tompkins and Gillum after his death was merely an acceleration of Foulston's thinking.)

Perception was a crucial issue at stake for Atlantic. Tompkins and his board had to prove that they were capable of running the company without its inspirational founder. Eight months have elapsed and, to an extent, perception does remain an issue. The onus will continue to be on Atlantic, as the press and the City watch to see whether the company's inexorable growth will continue – and the press and the City can have long or short memories. The case of European Ferries, though substantially different, has enough similarities to bear out this point.

When Keith Wickenden, chairman and chief executive of European Ferries, was killed in an aeroplane crash in July 1983, his successors were supported warmly. The stock market took the news in its stride. (The share price shed 4p – Atlantic's dropped nearer 40p.) Brokers' circulars reassured investors.

'Mr Wickenden's impressive management style somewhat overshadowed what he had himself encouraged: delegation of responsibility,' wrote the shipping industry's paper *Lloyd's List*.

It took a month for a successor to be named – managing director Ken Siddle. Siddle was very much an administrator, praised for his firm and detailed grasp on the business. He was not a man for the limelight, however. 'He is known to dislike public prominence,' commented *Lloyd's List*.

Yet three and a half years later, when European Ferries was acquired by Sir Jeffrey Sterling's P & O, commentators remarked that the company had lost its sense of direction since Wickenden's death. Those who were close to the company say that this is false, but the issue is one of perception rather than necessarily of fact.

Wickenden, like Foulston, was a man of influence and immense charisma. He came into the job when his brother Roland – the architect of the company – died of a heart attack after the launch of one of the company's *Free Enterprise* ferries.

'He sat centre stage,' says Alan Kelsey, head of research at stockbrokers Kitcat & Aitken. (Kitcat was also EuroFerries' broker.) 'He *was* the company.' A gifted speaker, Wickenden spent some time as MP for Dorking – the share price fluctuated sharply when he announced his intention to stand.

Wickenden described himself as a 'happy opportunist.' If he had an idea, he acted upon it fast. At boardroom level, he carried all before him. It was these qualities that brought the port of Felixstowe into the EuroFerries portfolio – a move that was unanimously described as brilliant. The AGM was always well attended and Wickenden had shareholders 'eating out of his hand,' according to Kelsey.

EuroFerries diversified rapidly under his ambitious stewardship. Wickenden enjoyed taking chances. It pitched into US property, particularly around Denver and Houston. It bought Singer & Friedlander, a merchant bank. 'It started to go bananas,' said one broker who watched events there, 'and the acquisitions became weirder and weirder, including hotels and frozen chip producers.'

On July 9, 1983, Wickenden's light aircraft crashed at Shoreham airport in Sussex. It was the third time that aircraft had made a disastrous imprint on his life. A foray into airship production had come to nought, and, far more tragically, a party of young West Country mothers had died on an Invicta Airways flight when Invicta was owned by EuroFerries.

'Whatever the appearance, Keith was not as important to EuroFerries as Roland was when *he* died,' said Bob Bevan, who was then group public relations manager. 'I did not see it had a bearing on the company,' says broker Kelsey. In September 1983 he put out a circular recommending the company as an attractive long-term investment.

After Siddle took over, the board identified ferries, ports and property as the core business. Many of Wickenden's more idiosyncratic purchases were to be sold off. These were regarded as sensible moves. Analysts at stockbrokers Laurence Prust wrote in October 1985: 'the diversifications . . . were well suited to the previous chairman's management style . . . Following his tragic death . . . these have been sold at a considerable profit. The result is a well-defined company suited to the present management's skills.'

There were, however, problems lurking. One was the US property business; the other was presentation. As the US oil market nosedived, so the once-lucrative real estate became an albatross. It was the losses incurred that weakened EuroFerries fatally. It will always remain a point of conjecture whether Wickenden would have forseen the problems arising and, furthermore, could have dealt with them successfully.

There is probably less doubt that he would have handled some other matters better. The first AGM after his death was, according to the *Financial Times*, 'rowdy and confused.' The disorder, which was caused by proposals to curb the voting rights of those shareholders who were entitled to cheap fares on the company's ferries, gained 'absolutely no marks for presentation.' Siddle confessed that he had not found the day easy. Following that, a dissident shareholders group started, complaining about a loss of direction and the presentation of accounts, notably the arrangements for the US property business.

'There were one or two old boys who said at the time of P & O's acquisition that it would have been different, if Keith had still been around,' said Kelsey. 'There is no way that is true. No one can tell whose fault the US property fiasco was. But perhaps the dislocation that the company suffered was too great.'

PR man Bevan agrees. 'Keith's death did not contribute too much to the demise of the company,' he says. 'It was the US properties that did that. Nothing could have saved it unless those were sold. But the press and, to some extent, the staff believed in Keith as the figurehead.'

Nobody can ever plan for these bolts from the blue, but it seems that companies are thinking more seriously about how to cope with such an eventuality. The growth of the key man insurance business is an example of this.

There are no independent figures about the market but, says David Seargent of Sedgwick Personal Finance Management in some branches business is up 40 to 50 per cent on last year.

Management buy-outs and venture capitalists invest in people and their particular skills. Insurance of those talents is a prerequisite. Indeed, investment groups can often demand key man insurance well in excess of their financial backing. 'Normally, only one out of a boardroom of five will be picked,' says one venture capitalist, 'as accountants are two a penny.'

Clearly, prevention is better than cure. Strength and depth need to be nurtured. Rosalyn McIntyre of the management consultancy arm of Deloittes poses a number of questions to those companies she suspects of being overly dependent on one individual. These include: 'Are the company's values their own? What is it like when they are on holiday or sick? Are problems held over until their return? Who holds different factions within the group together?'

Atlantic's Tompkins stresses two points: 'You must keep your management structure under review to ensure that you are ready and covered. You must take considered and positive action and not leave a gap in time before announcing a successor.'

Tompkins has a framed picture of Foulston in his office – it shows him in his McLaren racer. 'The board never tries to derive inspiration from his memory,' he says, 'but I know most of the time what he would have done. He was always bold and forthright. If ever I am hesitating about something that I know should be done, I look at his picture and say "sod it, let's do it".'

# 14

# A week on the deeper matters

September 1990

Peter Hennessy

The scene is the Travellers' Club in Pall Mall, canteen of the British diplomatic and intelligence services, just down the road from IOD head-quarters. The time, the early weeks of this year. The cast, three retired members of the secret world taking tea and stock of the dramatic changes in central Europe. 'I suppose,' says a voice from one of the armchairs, 'that these days, the only good German is a live German.' Once the laughter had died down, it was judged pretty apt as one-liners go.

I sympathize with them. The world in which the old gentlemen had worked was one in which you knew your place (and everybody else's as well), as in General Ismay's celebrated job description of NATO forty years ago as existing 'to keep the Russians out, the Americans in and the Germans down.' Not even Ismay could siphon an all-explaining aphorism from the turbulent pool of nineties East–West relations.

The old spies in the Travellers' are not alone. Their modern counterparts in contemporary Whitehall were, like the rest of us, reduced to watching the *Nine O'Clock News* to find out what was going on as 1989 turned into 1990, iron curtains disintegrated, walls crumbled and secret policemen presented themselves at the East European equivalents of the job centre.

If they are confused, with all that wonderful espionage infrastructure, human and electronic, what hope is there of the rest of us making sense of a kaleidoscopic international scene which both exhilarates and terrifies us in turn? Yet it is a picture we cannot ignore, either as citizens (can it really be peace after forty years of cold war?), or professionals (international in-stability can be very bad for business).

There is a handful of people in the world to whom we can turn for a bit of help – for a kind of Cook's tour through the confusion with, at the end, a few tentative pointers to the future. (Anybody who offers you certainties or talks about the end of something, whether it be 'history' or 'ideology', is a quack of nil value.) My own favourite mentor is Paul Kennedy, an English-man, now Dilworth professor of history at Yale and author of the famed *The Rise and Fall of the Great Powers* (Fontana).

As the world unravelled and all the 'isms turned to 'wasms (to borrow the elegant phrase of the Foreign Office spokesman the day the Nazi–Soviet Pact was signed in August 1939), this quiet, thoughtful Geordie came to London to deliver the annual lecture of the Institute of Contemporary British History. He took as his text the reply the most brilliant German politician ever, Otto von Bismarck, used to give when admirers would visit him in private and ask how he had unified Germany and changed the face of history. 'Man can neither create nor direct the stream of time,' the old statesman would reply. 'He can only travel upon it and steer with more or less skill and experience; he can suffer shipwrecks and go aground, and also arrive in safe harbours.'

Professor Kennedy's theme was 'contemporary history and the future.' He warmed to Bismarck's notion of history as the stream of time because, he said, 'it reminds us that it is not static and immobile, but changing. History did not "stop" in 1945, as Sellars and Yeatman once facetiously suggested [in *1066 And All That*], or in 1961 or in 1980. History flows on, as a stream of time, and what the historian is doing, usually, is looking back up-river, at where the world has come from. This also means that we are living history, watching history today; it is flowing, unfolding, moving, in some way perhaps faster than before.'

Professor Kennedy went on to do what few historians dare – he launched himself upon the perilous rapids of forecasting. 'What will the historian of, say, the year 2040 point to as being the major changes that occurred over the past half-century, that is, since today?' he inquired.

He broke up his answer into five sections: politics, demography, environment, technology and economics. He saw further shifts away from a bipolar world dominated by a pair of superpowers to a globe of regional powers. Would it be safer? Not necessarily. Sophisticated weaponry, some of it chemical or nuclear, was now within the reach of smaller powers in troubled areas.

What will be the political consequences, Professor Kennedy wondered, of the declining proportion of the world's population housed in the industrial nations (22 per cent in 1950; 15 per cent in 1985; perhaps below 10 per cent by the early twenty-first century)? Would the have-not regions allow the haves to get away with it? What about the complicating factor of global warming as seas rose and wheat-belts shifted towards the poles?

On technology he touched on three pacemakers: the robotics revolution, a rapid surge in agricultural productivity and the communications explosion. These, he predicted, will increase dramatically the pace at which nations or regions have risen and fallen in the past. The gap between winner and loser populations will be stark.

Rightly, Professor Kennedy upbraided the media for failing to gauge these deeper streams of time and for concentrating instead on short-term ripples on the surface which flow more readily into the normal channels of current affairs reporting. Not that he was at all deterministic. He did not write individuals out of the story. In fact, he quoted Marx to the effect that 'men make their own history, but they do not make it just as they please; they do not make it under circumstances chosen by themelves, but under circumstances directly encountered, given and transmitted from the past.'

As I listened, it became plain that what he had to say about political leaders applied just as much to business leaders: 'They have to understand which way the currents are moving, and how the winds of change are blowing, and then adjust their course accordingly.' Just how businessmen can get help in fulfilling this requirement, the most exacting part of their job specification, is something that had been exercising my mind for quite a time before Kennedy brought it once more into sharp focus.

No company chairman, however buoyant his profits, can hire himself an equivalent of Whitehall's Joint Intelligence Committee, which puts patterns on chaos and calibrates uncertainty for those Cabinet ministers on the 'need to know' distribution list. There are private organizations which offer briefing services and distribute newsletters that do try to plug the gap, as do, at considerably less cost to the customer, the pages of the quality papers and the better weeklies. But all too often, the businessman's picture of the wider world is a succession of snapshots snatched on the run. Very few, unless their university specialisms were oriented that way, have, at any stage in their lives, made the kind of intellectual investment against which the uncertainties associated with rapid world change can be sifted, tested and assessed.

I am convinced that there is a place for a new course for business people which would enable them – with periodic refresher sessions – to invest in precisely this kind of personal intellectual research and development. Just as the deeper, more complicated themes which swirl around the long-term intractables leave the average newspaper or television news editor cold, it is all too easy for the hard-pressed industrialist or financier to push such thoughts into the categories of 'too difficult', 'nobody knows the answer', or, worse still, 'not relevant.' Such a course would involve spending money and deploying time and the pay-off is not easily demonstrated. Yet business people should spend and deploy. They need this extra hinterland of understanding, more so in the nineties than ever before.

Just think, for a moment, how the world has changed since your chairman joined the company in the early 1950s. Who could have – who did – predict any of today's apparent fixtures apart from one or two visionaries who thought the European Coal and Steel Community might lead to something? And they, too, were doing intellectual dances in the dark. There was nothing certain about the movement towards European integration. The old Habsburg Empire was a customs union and that produced the reverse effect – an explosion of fragmentary nationalisms with dire consequences for European stability in the inter-war period. Only a currency union is near-certain to bring some kind of political union in its wake.

My ideal course would aim to give the businessman certain maps of understanding, no more. Prior reading of the Paul Kennedy volume and associated genres would be necessary and, in terms of effort, the sessions would be demanding.

During this week-long intellectual assault course I would want to include the following experiences:

- Instruction on the uses and abuses of intelligence analysis and forecasting, with especial emphasis on the dangers of extrapolating from where we are and saying 'this is the future'.
- A day linking economic, industrial and scientific forward looks – a technology-driven twelve hours.
- A day on the political and social side – never underestimate the capacity of man-made upheaval to throw out the most careful calculations;
- A day on international and defence matters which, all too often, are left to a tiny group of specialists and acronymiacs, remote from the business world and arguing among themselves in an area where big mistakes can mean curtains for all of us.
- A wrap-up day of synthesis and serendipity which, if the week's investment of time and thought has paid off, should yield rich dividends.

If I were a chief executive (or hoped to become one), I would want a course like that, whatever the price tag and the pain in terms of tired brain cells. If I were a senior politician I would want it too – but that really is crying for the moon! For not only are all the 'isms 'wasms, but rounding up the usual standard clichés and monocausal explanations will not work (it never did in real life) even in circles where conventional wisdom passes for insight. Businessmen of the world sign up! You have nothing to lose but your preconceptions.

# Section Four

## Inside Companies

# 15

# A day in the work of Tony Gill: inside track to success

September 1985

## Carol Kennedy

7.45 a.m. on a summer morning with the promise of heat, and already the traffic is thick on Coventry's eastern ring road. Soon after 8 a.m., Tony Gill's slate-blue Daimler is parking outside the Lucas Aerospace Switchgear and Ignition Systems Group factory, a 1939 building which miraculously escaped Coventry's devastation in 1940. It was then making Spitfire parts: today it makes sophisticated systems for civil and military aircraft, supplying more than 200 customers in over forty countries. Its chief international competitors are in France and the US. In 1984–85 the factory is forecast to achieve a turnover of more than £7m, with a healthy profit margin, and growth potential in the civil aviation market looks good.

Though small, the Switchgear and Ignitions unit is one of the good financial performers within the Lucas Industries group with a consistently good return on capital employed, but as Tony Gill will make clear today, 'the whole CAP concept is about what happens if conditions that keep you in that position should change.'

The Competitiveness Achievement Plan, which every Lucas business unit – even 'service' areas like PR – is expected to develop, is built on one simple, basic requirement: find out what the best of our competitors are achieving and plan to do better. It means more than just *improving* performance in areas like productivity, quality control or delivery times. The only way to judge if you are improving *enough*, says Gill, is to measure your planned achievement rigorously against the competition – a distinction he finds is not always understood.

We are about to test whether the Switchgear and Ignition unit has the right concept. In a spartan office partitioned off from the main factory floor are Tony Bridges, the unit's general manager, and his team – finance manager, manufacturing manager, sales and marketing manager, chief engineer. Gill, fifty-five, a mechanical and production engineer by background, looks in his element here, shirtsleeved like the rest of the men. He stresses that he will not be 'negotiating' over the plan – that will be for

Dr Alan Watkins, managing director of Lucas Aerospace. Nevertheless, his assessment will obviously be of critical importance.

## Double market share by 1990

Tony Bridges kicks off the two and a half hour presentation by detailing his group's financial results and market strategy. Typically, it ranks fourth or fifth in world market share in contactors and ignition systems and aims to double that share by the end of the 1980s. Market strategy includes various time-scales for the introduction of replacement ranges and new products, developing in line with market requirements. They are reorganizing systems to reduce manufacturing cost (major aerospace customers now expect incremental reductions each year), to improve delivery lead times and to reduce inventory.

The plan has identified some promising areas for improving output per hours worked, necessary because some product prices are too high, though others are competitive. Improved product support (after-sales service) is also planned.

Bridges analyses intensively the company's chief competitors in contactors and ignition systems. (US firms hold the lion's share in both markets.) Competitors' management is assessed and their performance measured in various markets. Bridges pulls out one key finding: 'We've got to get our lead times down.'

Chief engineer Gerry Littlehales explains key actions to be taken on the engineering side. He demonstrates a new range of modular units being introduced over the next few years. Helicopters are an increasing market that everyone is studying. The trend is towards 'electronic packages', complete systems, and they have pinpointed several areas on which competitors are focusing.

More use of computer-aided design and a rethink of quality control are next on the list. Littlehales says their previous quality control system was 'Very much inspector-oriented. Now every department is made accountable – we have encouraged and trained operators to be responsible for their own work. Testers and fitters have been trained to do each other's work'.

Progress on customer returns is monitored – 'The object is to get to nil returns'. There is a new emphasis on cost control: many old products succeeded on a 'flight-approved' basis but costs were not always seen as a critical factor. Production is now being planned and controlled by a new computer system, says manufacturing manager Mike Francis.

Another key area for improvement is inventory control. Gill interjects some crisp comments here – 'Those figures are twice as high as they should be, in my book' – as he has done at intervals throughout the presentation.

The financial performance continues good, 'probably as good as or better than most of our competitors', says finance director Peter Whalley.

Meanwhile, Gill has been leafing through the plan in its ring binder: he is several jumps ahead of the presentation and perceives there could be an overmanning problem in 1986–87 if they do not face up to it in planning terms now.

## Not ambitious enough

Bridges sums up their key competitive issues: understanding the market better, market segmentation ('identifying what is best for us to have a go at'), competitive analysis of rival products. And 'Deliveries are very critical', though Lucas is generally competitive in this area.

It is time for Gill to deliver his analysis. Any criticisms, he stresses, should be taken in the context of a financial performance that is a credit to the group. Nevertheless, he identifies a familiar problem: 'Your plan is not really a CAP; it is what you can see your way to doing. A CAP should identify the level of performance achieved by your best competitor in every area of your business. Unless you know that in absolute terms you cannot measure your shortfall against it and have a plan to close the gap.'

'Your targets are not realistic or ambitious enough. We ought not, for instance, to be fixing stock to sales ratios under what we think we would be lucky to achieve, but against what our best competitor *is* achieving. That ought to be the minimum we aim for – if he can do it, we can.'

It is now 12.30 and starting at 2 p.m. in Birmingham Gill has six 20-minute meetings scheduled with executives of Lucas subsidiaries, mostly to develop points raised at the recent board meetings. The Daimler hums up the motorway to Lucas headquarters in Great King Street, Birmingham, a massive redbrick monument to the great days of Midlands engineering supremacy. During the drive, Gill muses about the CAP exercise. It takes a fair slice of his time, visiting at least one unit a week. This week alone he has three, the other two in Nottingham and Gloucester. About forty units have been closed or sold or merged following CAP assessments. On the whole, products have been found competitive: the thrust for improvement has been in manufacturing systems and Dr John Parnaby, group director of manufacturing technology, has set up a central Systems Engineering Projects facility to help.

Some businesses, Gill concedes, find it easier than others to discover what their competitors are achieving. But managers who tell him something is not possible invite the sharp retort that 'What you are saying is, you have not tried hard enough.' Gathering intelligence can be done in many ways: 'To put it very simply, if you want to find out, say, the volume of sales per employee, you can find out by taking the published sales figures and standing outside the factory counting heads.'

Turning to Lucas Industries as a whole, two-thirds of whose £1.5bn sales are outside the UK, Gill says the majority of business units are improving their performance, but 'Our overall profitability is no better than a third of where it ought to be.' In foreign markets, the US turnover is around $200m a year and has grown dramatically to be the group's second biggest market (to France) outside the UK. For the longer term 'We have to consider those territories with small sales at present but huge long-term potential. The outstanding one is China, where they now need many of the technologies which Lucas can offer.' Japan is 'already a well fished pond', but Lucas Girling has several licensees in Japan bringing in £3m a year in royalties. Sixty per cent of all cars made in Japan are fitted with braking systems incorporating Lucas Girling designs.

## Necessity breeds a new business

The afternoon sessions begin in Gill's large-windowed modern office, sun blinded against the glare. John Handslip, organization and development manager, wants approval for a revised brochure for senior management setting out the organizational structure and responsibilities within Lucas Industries. Mike Jenner, financial director of Lucas Industries Systems, discusses Duralith, a recently acquired American subsidiary, and how it is being integrated. Dr Brian Edwards, product engineering director of Lucas Girling, reviews the latest position on licensing agreements, especially with the Japanese.

Alan Gaves, director of strategic planning, has an outline report on Asia Pacific being prepared for discussion by the Lucas Executive board in a month or two.

Freddie Brown, training director, comes in to update Gill on the group's current training programmes for product engineers, manufacturing systems engineers, finance and computer systems people and, the latest, for marketing managers, a key area. They discuss selling the centrally-devised programmes to the individual companies, much as Lucas Industries' computer and research centre in Solihull markets its services commercially within the group. 'If it is worth having, it is worth paying for,' is Brown's opinion.

The last meeting before Gill turns his attention to paperwork and digesting the thick pile of documentation his visitors have left, is with Mike Stacey, operations director, Electronics Systems within Lucas Electrical. He is carrying a piece of equipment the size of a small suitcase which is basically a powerful little computer programmed to test on site the electronic fuel management systems Lucas manufactures for a range of cars. Garage service operators baffled by the sophisticated electronics tend to return the whole unit for replacement, assuming any defects in the car's performance must be due to 'the black box'. Most were proved to be perfectly all right, but the cost in reputation and warranty terms was enormous,' says Stacey.

With this mobile diagnostic unit, devised by a team of young engineers working flat out seven days a week for three months, the operator is taken through a programme which automatically checks the whole system, identifing any faulty part or connection, which can then be corrected. Once set to the appropriate car model and engine size, the system is virtually foolproof. 'We have deliberately taken all the company jargon out,' says Stacey.

## 'A positive sell'

Gill seizes on the market possibilities: 'Are you restricting it to existing customers for Lucas engine management systems, or marketing it more widely?' Stacey agrees it could be "an embryonic little business" – and besides that it should turn out 'a positive sell for these systems'.

Gill smiles with an engineer's satisfaction in technical ingenuity. 'A classic example of necessity being the mother of invention,' he says. 'Congratulate the lads.'

# 16

# Hoechst: coming out of the closet

March 1988

## Carol Kennedy

There is no mistaking the entrance to the huge industrial complex of Hoechst AG in the old suburb of Frankfurt from which the company takes its name. It is the real-life model for the Hoechst logo; a soaring tower and arch in pale brown brick built in the German Expressionist style of the early twenties. The fortress-like headquarters, however, is about the only feature of Hoechst these days not to be undergoing dynamic change.

The corporate philosophy of the 125-year-old chemical giant has been thoroughly shaken up and redirected by a younger and more internationally minded management over the past five or six years.

One result is Hoechst's own version of *glasnost* – a new willingness to make the company better known as it increasingly extends its activities beyond the borders of West Germany.

A low profile has come naturally to the big West German chemical companies for historical reasons. Like its rivals Bayer and BASF, Hoechst (which originated in 1863 as a small dyestuffs factory developing the British invention of synthetic dyes) became part of the powerful combine IG Farbenindustrie in the years between the two world wars.

By 1926 IG Farben, as it was generally known, was seriously threatening the US and British chemical industries, and ICI was formed by four British companies as a defensive strategy. Postwar, the Allies broke the combine up and in 1951 reconstituted Hoechst, Bayer and BASF (none of whose plants were severely damaged by bombing) as part of the revival of German industry.

'Five or six years later we were casting our nets around the world again,' says public affairs director Dominik von Winterfeldt, an urbane aristocrat who formerly headed Hoechst's operation in the UK.

Today, the three German giants are each bigger than IG Farben at its zenith; all regularly rank in the world's top five chemical companies. Having 'started from zero after the war,' as a senior executive puts it, the Frankfurt group is Europe's largest supplier of pharmaceuticals and second only to Merck in world-wide pharmaceutical sales. Of its 467 consolidated companies only 60 are based in Germany, though they provide jobs for around half the world-wide workforce of 200,000 and are responsible for half Hoechst's production. The remainder are spread through 120 countries, along with majority interests in a further 250 subsidiaries and associated companies.

The group sells three times as much outside its home country as within it – DM27bn (£9bn) of a total DM38bn (£13bn) in 1986 – and half those external sales come from products manufactured outside Germany.

Like ICI and other major European chemical enterprises, Hoechst has taken the rewarding road west to large-scale acquisition in the US, the world's biggest single market for chemicals. Its $2.8bn purchase of American Celanese in early 1987 (none of its previous acquisitions there had exceeded $200m) would undoubtedly have lifted its sales ranking to world number one were it not for the complications of new European Community accounting legislation affecting the way sales and profits in consolidated companies are reported.

The US Federal Trade Commission also exacted a price – divestment of Celanese's $350m polyester business. Without that, the combined Hoechst-Celanese textile fibres operation would have become number one in US polyester production, outstripping Du Pont.

Even in reduced form, however, the Celanese acquisition increases Hoechst's sales in the US to $4.5bn, raises the company's scale of production outside West Germany from 37 per cent to 50 per cent and also opens up opportunities for Hoechst to develop Japanese business through joint ventures in which Celanese is involved.

The Americanization of Hoechst may lead to some interesting cross-fertilization in management styles. Two-thirds of the new Hoechst-Celanese board are Americans, and its chairman and CEO, Juergen Dormann, who also sits on the parent group's board of management with responsibility for finance, plans to step down soon from Hoechst-Celanese in favour of a US citizen.

Management in the US subsidiary is much more informal than at Frankfurt, where executives address each other by elaborate titles, and the management board chairman, a shy and retiring chemist, is referred to as 'Professor Dr' Wolfgang Hilger. One cannot imagine a flamboyant Harvey-Jones figure at Hoechst.

As ICI did under Harvey-Jones, though, Hoechst has looked hard at itself and rewritten its priorities.

Changes in the last five years have been 'dramatic,' says deputy finance director Helmut Schnabel.

The company has restructured its product portfolio to diminish reliance on commodity chemicals and take it more into the high value-added speciality field. Hoechst directors say the company's ratio of specialities to commodities has now gone from 50:50 to nearer 60:40 (said to be higher than rival BASF).

Hoechst is stressing the new emphasis in its corporate advertising under the trademarked slogan 'Hoechst High Chem,' a play both on the company name (Hoechst means 'highest' in German) and on high technology.

The diversified portfolio of US Celanese is divided about half and half between commodities and specialities. It is a leading US player in the fast-growing market for engineering plastics or industrial resins, used widely in the aerospace industry.

The US company's 50 per cent dependence on fibres led some analysts to conclude mistakenly from the acquisition that Hoechst was swinging back towards commodities.

'Of course,' says director von Winterfeldt, 'what you really hope for is that the speciality of today becomes the commodity of tomorrow.'

(There is no generally accepted definition in the chemical industry for a speciality product. Hoechst's plastics division has invented its own definition: if there are not more than five producers, it is a speciality.)

The agrochemicals field provides a good illustration of Hoechst's changing strategy. In 1975 its sales volume in this area broke down as 42 per cent fertilizer, a classic bulk commodity product; 46 per cent plant protection chemicals and 12 per cent animal health products. By 1990, it is expected that the fertilizer share will be a mere 9 per cent – it might even be phased out entirely. Plant protection, on the other hand, will probably account for around 70 per cent and animal health for 21 per cent.

Hand-in-hand with Hoechst's growing internationalism and emphasis on higher value-added products has gone a major shift in corporate philosophy – a willingness to divest. Until 1980, says deputy finance director Schnabel, the very concept of divestment was alien to the company's thinking. Its strategy for 117 years had been to invest in new business 'and once we had it, we kept it.'

A string of hard decisions followed the company's first divestment in 1980. From 1981 to 1984 one after another lossmaking operations were closed down in plastics, refineries and fertilizers.

In 1986 the company made its biggest divestment of all, shedding the entire monostyrene and polystyrene business acquired in the 1970s from Foster Grant of the US and worth DM1.2bn (£400m) in sales. That was part of the move out of unprofitable commodity businesses.

Most recently, Hoechst UK has sold Berger Paints in a £133m deal to Williams Holdings, which already has Crown Paints under its belt and, with the sale confirmed, will become second to ICI in the UK paints market.

The other significant change in corporate strategy has been to adopt a philosophy of 'de-leveraging'. The company's borrowings were reduced by almost half over the five years prior to the Celanese purchase. (Even with that, debt is still 25 per cent below its historic peak of more than DM10bn (£3.3bn) in 1981.)

The changes have paid off handsomely. Profit after tax exceeded DM1bn (£330m) for the first time in the company's history in 1984 and in 1986 broke the billion-mark barrier for the third year running. It is expected to maintain that level in 1987. Hoechst's 330,000 shareholders saw a return on equity in 1986 of 14.1 per cent – 15 per cent in real terms after taking into account West Germany's 1 per cent negative inflation rate.

'It is a great and satisfying achievement,' says Schnabel. Yet the company remains curiously undervalued on the stock market, with a p/e of only nine against the West German industrial average of 13 (the pre-crash level in the US was 20 and in Japan a monumental 70).

It is not easy to work out why, except that adoption of the new accounting system among German companies has led to some share prices falling. Also, Germany's three big chemical companies between them command a fifth of the market value of all the Federal Republic's industrial corporations, including banks. The German market, Schnabel suggests, is just too small to create a proper valuation.

'We have to internationalize our shareholding,' he adds. But Hoechst seems unlikely on present readings to follow ICI's lead in seeking a Wall Street listing.

Since the nineteenth century the German chemical industry has always had a sharp innovatory edge, honed by the historical importance given to scientific training in the German education system. Germany led the world in the discovery of new drugs between the wars. In the 1930s, Bayer produced the first sulphonamide and the first synthetic antimalarial compound; earlier Hoechst was responsible for the first syphilis cure and the anaesthetic 'Novacain'.

(ICI owed the rapid development of its fledgling prewar pharmaceuticals division to the need to find substitutes for German drugs.)

Hoechst's pharmaceuticals research today takes about half the group's R & D budget of DM2.1bn (£700m), a total which represents between 5 and 6 per cent of group sales. Its scientists are working in many leading edge areas, notably that of recombinant DNA – the technique of altering patterns of genetic information, popularly known as genetic engineering.

Genetically programmed bacteria can already aid diabetic patients by producing a longer-acting insulin with high toleration in humans, and Hoechst is due shortly to begin large-scale production of this insulin. In co-operation with Bayer, the company's biochemists are also chasing DNA clues to that grail of the world's pharmaceutical industry, a cure for AIDS.

Of the twenty-one men on Hoechst's supervisory board, ten are elected by the employees through the central works council. (Germany's two-tier corporate system provides for a supervisory board and an executive board of management.)

The scale of the company's investment in training is formidable. At present, a total of 6500 young people (60 per cent male, 40 per cent female) are being trained all over Germany on a three-year scheme, with a number of scholarships being awarded in Britain. In 1986 90 per cent of trainees ended up being offered jobs with Hoechst.

It costs DM20,000 (£6,600) to train one apprentice, but the way upwards is then wide open. The present head of the pharmaceuticals division himself started as an Hoechst apprentice.

Trainees who land jobs with Hoechst have the opportunities to pursue higher education, perhaps an MBA equivalent, and about half of them take up this option.

Hoechst is not likely to be worrying about where to find its managers in the twenty-first century.

# 17

# Toughened glass: the rebuilding of Rockware

September 1989

## Stuart Rock

'We are different. We have different passions away from the job, different politics. But like different people, we get on together. It is a better dovetail.

'Peter's a thinker, I am a doer. He has different skills. He knows everybody and has lots of contacts in the City; when I first came to this company I knew no one in the City at all.'

Sir Peter Parker and Frank Davies, chairman and chief executive respectively, form an unlikely alliance at Rockware, the glass company that has now become a broadly-based packaging concern.

After his stewardship of British Rail, Parker is one of the public faces of British business; Davies has spent most of his career in the corporate anonymity of large US companies. Parker's political affiliations have been varied – socialism, the SDP, the SDLP; Davies describes himself as 'a true Thatcherite Tory'. They live at opposing ends of the same county, Oxfordshire.

Unlikeliness has proved effective. When Parker returned to Rockware in 1983 after a seven-year stint at BR he found it, and the glass industry, in disarray. Rockware's losses that year amounted to £18m. In September 1983 Davies was appointed group chief executive after fifteen years' work with Alcan Aluminium.

'Davies brought the business a healthy dose of realism because he was not born in a glass bottle,' says Sonia Falaschi, paper and packaging analyst at stockbrokers UBS Phillips and Drew, 'and he probably saved Rockware from going belly-up.' The rescue partnership has put a healthier glow on the balance sheet; last year's profits were a shade over £11m. And now glass accounts for only 50 per cent of Rockware's activities.

The share price may still be too low, Davies grumbles, but then adds that there is rather more to this business than the financial figures. The change and development of this particular top partnership as it coped with the problems of a traditional manufacturing industry has been central to the turnround.

'In the early days I was much more involved, and Frank was finding his feet,' says Parker. 'Now it is completely different. I am non-executive chairman, and Frank lets me have his way! When Frank arrived he concentrated on the glass business; I kept an eye on the reconstruction of the board and of the company's reputation. As soon as glass responded to treatment Frank was able to move into the group chief executive role and place a managing director for glass underneath him. And when that happened that changed my role.'

Davies arrived as a City novice. 'I came with no pretensions of experience of running a public company,' he says. 'I had worked in large companies in senior jobs but I was not a front man, just an operations man. But Peter knew that was what he was getting. So he provided me with the introductions.'

Fortunately, Parker is quick to add, 'he took to it like a duck to water. The City wants to see the man who is running the company and have direct contact with him. And Frank has a knack for exposition. Getting him in front and finding that it worked was an immense relief to me.'

From the other side of the presentational divide, Phillips and Drew's Falaschi reckons that Davies 'has got a lot more polished as he has gained experience. The difficulty for Rockware has been that the message it has had to communicate has been a problem – that the supermarkets do not want glass! But communications with the City are pretty reasonable. Parker, with his other interests, is a bit flitty-aroundy, but he is more in touch than most non-executive chairmen. Davies is always open. Maybe he is slightly prone to over-optimism – but then he has had to be.'

It is clear that Parker did not want to be the leader. He found in Davies a man with broad shoulders, someone who could not just get Rockware off the rocks but sail it away from danger as well.

The process entailed painful cutbacks. Glass-making had all the classic symptoms of manufacturing illness – large, highly unionized plants that were usually in areas of existing high unemployment. Manning was too high, quality too low.

'When you start to tighten up on these things it is painful,' says Davies. 'After all, many people had worked with us for a long time and had nowhere else to go.'

In 1979 the British glass industry employed 23,000; today it is 8000. 'Between 1980 and 1985 we paid out £18m in redundancies,' frowns Davies. 'I think that with the possible exception of coal mining we have made a greater percentage reduction in our overall workforce than anyone else.'

Wielding the axe was one thing, but Davies was also there to make the company more wieldy as well. 'I had only ever worked with big companies, and in comparison to them Rockware was small,' he says. 'But I have made

Rockware behave like a big company, particularly in its structure and planning systems.'

According to analyst Falaschi, this has been Davies' crucial contribution. 'He got costs under control,' she says, 'and also led the thrust towards higher quality. Previously, supply and demand were all over the place. It should never be worth anyone's while to import empty glass bottles from France, but that was what was happening.'

'When I came,' Davies observes, 'Rockware used to have five-year plans and ten-year plans, neither of which had any real basis. Then there was a completely separate annual plan that had no relationship to either of them. Now every year has a budget with lots and lots of targets – turnover, return on capital and so on. Then you have a three-year plan, of which the first year is budgeted. So I have brought more formal methods of setting targets, agreeing them and then working at them.

'This is something the Americans are very good at – everyone has objectives. All managers sit down with their boss every six months – often every three months – and look at how they are matching up to their targets. You see, people do sharpen up their performance if they know what they are supposed to be doing.'

The board structure at Rockware reflects Davies' big company, new world thinking. Creative tension is an oft-misapplied phrase, but the divergence of views on this subject between Davies and Parker is a genuine example.

'There is a continual bracing of each other about how a board should work,' says Parker, warming enthusiastically to the theme, 'and, after all, managing the board is part of the role of the chairman and the chief executive. Neither of us are formula people, and the challenge of managing a board means that you are continually asking: "have we got the right board?" And this is the real test of a relationship.'

There are nine members of the board; only three are executives (Davies himself, financial director Tony Hargreaves and Ken Stokes, whose printing company was acquired in 1987). The non-executives are Parker; Peter Grunwell, finance director of Pilkington; Richard Langdon, former senior partner of accountancy firm Spicer & Oppenheim; John Biffen MP; former technical director Peter Coward; and Tony Cann, formerly chairman of the two companies that now form Rockware's metals division.

For Davies, this hand gives him long suits in strategic wisdom and technical know-how. 'Take Richard Langdon,' he says. 'He is a doyen of the accounting profession and a great source of wisdom. If he asks a question, you have to have the answer right. On the other hand, I get much more close-to-the-ground stuff from Tony Cann; he does not have a full-time day-to-day management role but I would not hesitate to ask his opinion about buying a piece of machinery or whether the marketing was right or for his judgement about particular people.'

An executive committee makes day-to-day decisions, which are then approved by the board. 'It is a two-tier system, but not as formal as, say, the German system,' Davies observes.

Parker and Davies launch into the coffee, biscuits and the debate. Davies, leaning back in the sofa, implicitly expresses his preference for the North American system, where 'there are directors who see themselves as judges and management as players. In the UK directors are judges and players. I think Peter would favour more directors who are active on the board.'

But it is Parker who is the voluble one, expounding ideas and shaping phrases. The line – 'Now I am non-executive chairman and Frank lets me have his way' – rings true.

'My experience,' he says, 'is that I have gained an awful lot by the balance. Non-executives should bear a cross; they should be ready to go down into an organization in a certain area, as that always gives special insights. I like to see all of them totally committed to the total purpose of the board, because if it comes off you get a team spirit that you may not get in the two-tier board system.

'A board is there to make sure it is continually auditing the sources of talent. It is much easier to understand what is coming up if you can occasionally see the quality of your executives. Otherwise the whole thing – theoretically – channels through your chief executive. Non-executives need a span of familiarity.'

Theory gives way to practice. 'In 1983 the company was in disarray,' Davies recalls, 'and there was no point putting people on the board then.' Now the possibility of more executives is greater and the auditing of talent is under way. 'We get an executive to sell a particular idea to the board – so they can show their paces, win their spurs,' he says.

The atmosphere is affable, conversational and punctuated by chuckles from the chairman. But there is always a grip on seriousness.

'I have a well-delegated organization,' says Davies when asked how he spends his working time, 'and each division has its own managing director and complete team. I have a meeting with that team once every six or eight weeks and spend a day with them. I like to visit two factories each week and usually do. I like to meet customers – they tell you the truth more than anybody else. I probably spend only a day-and-a-half in the office each week.' Most of his days start with a journey from Oxfordshire – twenty-three factories scattered from Doncaster to South Wales to Norfolk dictate that.

The mobile office in the chauffeured car gives Davies flexibility, a much-valued asset in the relationship.

'Structured planning of time is quite effective as an exercise,' says Parker, 'but the great capacity of any enterprise is to be capable of taking the strain of surprise. You simply must not overstructure or overbureaucratize. So then if there is a sudden danger or a sudden possibility, you can rely on each other to find time. Whatever the programme, the knack is to be relaxed enough to be continually interrupted and to be adapting.'

Both stress the value of travelling together – it is one of the great welders. 'It is not the formal meetings that keep us together,' asserts Parker.

Every year the two men visit each factory together, holding what they describe as 'mini AGMs,' or open meetings with the staff about the contents of the annual report. It is always unscripted, says Parker. 'Sometimes I am on form, sometimes Frank's on form. But it is always a double gob – that is a technical term from the glass industry!'

It is at such meetings that the value of Parker's high public profile is an advantage, according to Davies. 'People feel good because they know him as a public figure. So, when we stand up in the canteen and say: "ask anything you like," they do.'

Parker likens communications to clearing the mouth of a river – you can remove the silt but it can soon silt up again.

'You are never clear of dredging if you are in a flow of activities and innovation,' he says. 'You have to take different themes to push it along; you have to refresh people's ideas of interdependence. The mini AGMs are part of that, conveying that we are all in this together. Take our recycling policy; you have to keep quickening that so people get used to responding, and responding together. The art of communications is never finished.'

There are other consonant notes. Parker calls upon his considerable knowledge of the Japanese as he talks about the old class structures in British industry. 'The quality of life between different levels in this country has been in a pickle for generations,' he says. 'The style I admire is where there is no pomp or circumstance, where you are level with one another. It is a quality we would do well to watch.' At the moment Rockware is negotiating a single-status package for its employees.

Openness of debate is another Parker passion. Managers should challenge and contradict, yet know that they are not being unfriendly in the process.

The thinker/doer divide appears again. Parker's enthusiastic Japanese anecdotes are balanced by Davies' observation that the Japanese 'started with no industrial scars, no industrial bad habits. We are on brownfield sites and are making a success of it. Ninety per cent of the people who work for us today worked for us when I joined and will be working for us when I go. Only a few change. So, when you go into somewhere like Doncaster you do not say: 'clear all this lot out.' You make the best of what you have got. And I think that our success is that we have made a success out of situations that were previously disasters. It is a different skill. I would much rather do the greenfield sites, to be honest.'

The practical man is not short of a few dreams. A central theme is how to generate job satisfaction, for therein is a key to success. He recounts one influential moment of twenty years ago, when he discovered that a man in his plant was, in his leisure time, a highly accomplished band leader.

'He had an awful bloody job – boring, boring, boring,' says Davies. 'He was a man who had worked for the company for forty years but who lived for the moment that he left the factory gates. Then he would change his whole nature, from being a bloody labourer to being a great teacher, leader and organizer. Look what we were losing. And look what he was losing – wasting eight hours every day of his life just so as to live the next six.'

There are still plenty of boring, boring, boring jobs around in Rockware; still much automation to be implemented. In the scheme of things, however, quality is the first priority. At Rexpak, Rockware's Warrington-based plastics plant, managing director Peter Collard points to a framed certificate in the reception area; it is a quality award from a client.

'A few years ago Rexpak was synonymous with poor quality,' Collard says. 'As we were seen as bad, we went to non-existing but demanding clients like Lever or Heinz. Then we had to have the quality. Total quality management? That is formalizing it. It has been a basic and bloody hard slog.'

Davies' horizons for Rockware are expansive, as expansive as the giant Lincolnshire fields of arable land where he was brought up. ('I felt that I could have gone into that kind of farming,' he says. 'It was interesting because it was all done on a magnificent scale. But I could only be a manager rather than an owner – I had no land to inherit.') Perhaps the horizons were enough to convince three men – Cann, Tony Hutchinson and Bob Watts – to sell their thriving metal-pressing businesses – Presspart and Decorpart – to Rockware.

There is a mutual admiration. Davies says that the Lancashire metal factories are 'the best I have got – lovely plants'. Ex-chairman and now non-executive director Cann thinks highly of Rockware's 'quietly impress-ive' achievement and of its 'highly devolved' style.

'Setting the budget is the start point,' he explains, 'but if we feel like making a decision we still do it. And we liked the way Frank negotiated – he was almost as good as us. Discussions were on and off over a year, but there was never any panic or any sourness.'

Just as amicable was the purchase of a 75 per cent stake in Dartington, the crystal glass maker; Dartington got the money, Rockware the consumer brand.

Such acquisitions have not completely satisfied Rockware's City moni-tors. 'I think that: "where do they go from here?" and "can they grow as effectively as they would like?" are valid questions,' says Phillips and Drew's Falaschi.

In Davies' eyes, the next goal is Europe. 'I'm very conscious that we are too British,' he says. As regards the glass business, further domestic expansion is out since the company already holds 25 per cent of the UK market. It is a source of profound irritation to Davies; he cannot bid for another British company, but a much larger European competitor can.

Environmental matters are also high on the chief executive's agenda. In some respects, greenness is a shot in the arm for the glass industry because of the material's inherent recyclability. Rockware collects 130,000 tonnes of glass each year for recycling (roughly 50 per cent of the UK's total), and Davies says that it pays its way.

'We pay the local authority whatever it would cost us to make it,' he says. 'Then we direct empty trucks that have been delivering coal to power stations to call in at central collecting points. So we get a cheap return load. Then, because we can melt broken glass at half the temperature of sand, we only use half the energy. At the moment we are only taking 16 per cent of bottles back, so it is a huge opportunity.'

Phillips and Drew's Falaschi is more cautious about the glass renaissance, particulary in the UK. 'Here the supermarkets have great influence – and they hate glass,' she says. 'In mainland Europe the food manufacturers have more sway, so there is more potential there.'

Plastics present a greater problem. The various types of plastic cannot be easily differentiated by the consumer, although the industry is considering proposals that each type is distinguished by a number, thus making bottle-bank-style disposal a possibility. (A stray container going into the wrong pile, however, can degrade the entire contents; and, as Davies points out, people can still put amber glass into a hole marked 'clear glass.')

But the issues go deeper than that. The environmental arguments inform company strategy.

'It is so important that I will not take Rockware into PET [a type of plastic] beverage bottles,' says Davies emphatically. 'It is a great product. It is very successful, with one billion unit sales per year. But it is dying on its feet for environmental reasons. I am guiding Rockware away from PET in food and drink and towards cosmetics and pharmaceutical products. A girl with some cosmetics on her dressing table will throw the containers into a wastepaper basket; the lout who drinks his beer from a PET bottle throws it on the ground and it becomes litter. So we have got to take the environment seriously.

'If we do not, we are doomed.'

# 18

# Paper tigers: the battle for London's newspaper

July 1989

Mihir Bose

Two years ago this month a newspaper died. The *London Daily News*, meant to break the evening newspaper monopoly in the capital enjoyed by the *Evening Standard*, had lived for only five months and proved one of Robert Maxwell's costliest publishing setbacks, with an estimated loss of £20m. In the process it had produced quite the most extraordinary newspaper war this country has seen, converting the rivalry for London evening papers into something like a personal duel. In one corner Maxwell, the self-made publishing millionaire; in the other Lord Rothermere, owner of the *Evening Standard* and inheritor of the very successful family publishing business centred round the *Daily Mail*. The Lord against the self-proclaimed man of the people. This is how Maxwell saw it; this is how the media pictured it.

Yet throughout the raucous battle Maxwell never managed to smoke Rothermere out. The *Standard*'s sucessful defence of its patch was led by a quiet middle-aged man who is almost the exact antithesis of Maxwell. Bert Hardy, then managing director of the *Evening Standard* (now managing director of Mail Newspapers), could not be more different from Maxwell. Where Maxwell is loud, Hardy is quiet; where Maxwell thrives on public exposure and seems to delight in making policies in the glare of television lights, Hardy is happy to be the methodical planner who will spend hours preparing his case. About the only extravagance Hardy is known to indulge in is his love for Bristols – cars that is – which he collects with great passion.

Maxwell versus Hardy may not have the same ring as Maxwell versus Rothermere, but in Hardy Maxwell had found an opponent who had been educated in the tough school of Fleet Street newspaper publishing. He had served his apprenticeship at the *Daily Mirror* under Hugh Cudlipp, then helped Rupert Murdoch create the *Sun*, an alliance that was formed just as Murdoch defeated Maxwell to acquire the *News of the World* and gain a toehold in British newspaper publishing.

Hardy himself sees that mild December day in 1968 when Rupert

Murdoch rang him as the turning point of his career. Twenty years on he can remember it as if it were yesterday. The call came at about seven in the evening, on Hardy's private line at his Long Acre office.

'It was completely out of the blue and I do not know how he got hold of my private number,' says Hardy.

But it could not have been better timed. After twenty years with the *Mirror* Hardy was eager to get away. During that time Cudlipp had built the *Mirror* into the greatest newspaper in the land with a circulation of over five million. As he did so, Hardy had worked his way up through the advertisement departments of the group. He had been a sales representative for the magazine *Reveille*, worked as group advertisement manager in Manchester and much to his relief – he is a Londoner – was brought back to the capital by Cudlipp to become advertisement manager for the *Daily Herald*.

When the ill-fated alliance between journalism and trade unions broke down, Cudlipp converted it into the *Sun* and Hardy took over as advertisement manager of the new paper. Launched in 1964 and meant to appeal to the new generation liberated by Harold Wilson's white heat of technology, it had wonderful promotions and dreadful sales. The paper quickly became known at the *Mirror* as 'King's cross', a reference to Cecil King, head of the Mirror Group, and the failure even began to cast doubts on the successful *Mirror* itself.

As deputy ad director of the *Sun* and the *People*, Hardy could feel that 'the *Mirror* was beginning to lose a bit of confidence. The group had expanded and expanded but none of the moves had been particularly good moves. The dynamic that created the expansion was lost in the mass of publications they had moved into – Fleetway, George Newnes, Odhams – in the bog of all those big magazines.' Perhaps Hardy sees more gloom than there was, but there is no doubt that, having just turned forty, he felt despondent. 'I was not getting anywhere. My career had come pretty much to a halt,' he says.

It was at that moment that the phone call from Murdoch came. Half-an-hour later they met in the near-deserted Bouverie Street offices of the *News of the World*; there seemed to be no one else around apart from Murdoch and a secretary.

'I saw him at half-past-seven. At quarter-to-eight I had signed on,' Hardy continues. 'I had broken twenty years' service with the *Mirror* in just fifteen minutes.'

Hardy was 'instantly impressed' by Murdoch's decision making. 'He was a young, confident Australian with huge energy. He was galloping when I got there and he did not stop galloping for the rest of the years I worked with him, which was ten years. I mean galloping mentally. I sensed instantly that he was going to make his way in this country.'

Indeed, Murdoch had just galloped on to the London newspaper scene from Australia as a white knight all ready to rescue the distressed Carr family from the clutches of Maxwell, who had launched a hostile bid for the *News of the World*. The chairman, Sir William Carr, could only repel Maxwell by doing a deal with Murdoch. It left Carr as chairman and made Murdoch managing director. (Within six months Carr was to realize, as Maxwell's biographer Joe Haines puts it, that the white knight was Count Dracula in disguise. Murdoch forced Carr out and completed his takeover.)

Murdoch offered Hardy the job of ad manager of the *News of the World* at a salary 40 per cent more than Hardy was getting – but 'what struck me was the man. He asked me what I wanted; I gave him a figure and he instantly agreed. The money was good, but that was not the important thing. In any case, Rupert was never a great payer. He got most of his people in those days on the basis of the enthusiasm he engendered and the obvious expertise the man had. I suppose proprietor was too big a word for Rupert then. But I could see that here was an embryo proprietor who obviously knew as much about the business as anybody on the shop floor.'

Murdoch stipulated one condition: Hardy must lift advertising revenue by £1m. The figure was of some importance. The previous ad director had told Murdoch that this figure was 'an impossible target', Murdoch had sacked him and the ad director, claiming wrongful dismissal, took the matter to court. Eventually Murdoch had to pay out some money, but, as Hardy recalls, 'we not only got the extra £1m Rupert wanted, we got an extra £3m. It was not difficult. The *News of the World* had been undersold and we succeeded in getting display ads – good Sunday lunchtime ads.'

Hardy, in turn, had got Murdoch to agree to one condition. 'I said I would take the job provided that if he bought any more newspapers he would make me ad manager of those,' he says. 'As he expanded I would expand with him, and he agreed to that.'

Within a few months Murdoch decided to buy the *Sun* from the Mirror Group. Before he did so he asked Hardy if he could guarantee advertising revenues of £20,000 a week. 'It sounds a ridiculous sum of money now, but I said we could.'

Murdoch bought the *Sun* and brought in Larry Lamb as editor with Bernard Shrimsley, who had been recommended by Hardy as editor, as deputy. Just over a year after arriving in Britain Murdoch was ready to take over the country's biggest paper – the *Mirror*.

'Everybody thought,' recalls Hardy, 'that Murdoch was a fool to buy the *Sun*. But we changed it to proper tabloid size from this "bastard" size, neither broadsheet nor tabloid, and instantly it was a success.'

Hardy's job was to provide the money while Lamb and Shrimsley re-discovered what Hardy saw 'as a return to the *Mirror* of a few years previous to that date. The *Mirror* had been brash, it had been very direct, it had been open, it had a very close relationship with its readers. The *Sun* was beginning to do all those things again.'

Though the *Sun* did not overtake the *Mirror* until the 1970s, within months of the launch, in November 1969, Hardy was totally convinced that the *Mirror*'s premiership could be conquered.

'We knew we were on our way,' he says. 'We were instantly hitting the circulation of the *Mirror*. By the spring of 1970 we knew we had something pretty sensational on our hands. Our circulation was going up in leaps and bounds and the readership figures just could not keep up.'

And as the *Sun* rose, so did Hardy in the Murdoch empire.

One journalist who knows Hardy well and still considers him a friend is convinced that 'Hardy's concept created the *Sun* for Murdoch. Murdoch valued his toughness, his reputation for knowing what he was doing and his ability to negotiate with the unions. He was a tough negotiator but a fair one. If he made a deal he stuck to it.'

Interestingly, Hardy takes no responsibility for creating what has since been called the '*Sun* generation'.

'It had,' he says, 'nothing to do with me in the sense of the editorial content. My job was to provide money. The paper then was not what it is now. It looked different, it had a totally different feel about it. It was, I think, more liberal in its approach than it is now. It was not as strident, it was not as direct as it is now. I did not then feel we were creating a '*Sun* generation' or anything like that. Clearly we had broken the barriers with bosoms, that was a clear barrier to be seen – other barriers that were being broken were, I think, less obvious.'

Murdoch also valued what another editor who has worked closely with Hardy calls 'his willingness to try anything. If something does not work he does not blame anybody, he just gets on with the next thing.'

By the mid-1970s Hardy could do no wrong in the Murdoch empire. Murdoch was expanding in all directions and Hardy was enjoying the sheer 'excitement' of working for him. There was always something new, different, challenging.

Murdoch moved into television in a big way and into radio; he launched the *National Star* in the US. Hardy played a part in all these moves, constantly finding his roles widening as Murdoch discovered new areas of expansion. By now he had become chief executive of the *Sun* and chairman of a number of Murdoch companies.

Hardy had also begun to sketch out plans for the Murdoch printing plant at Wapping in east London. Sometime in 1976 he bought the land and saw it as a giant modern plant that would house everybody and finally solve the growing printing problems the group faced. The lease in Manchester was coming to an end, Bouverie Street was running out of capacity, and Hardy began to visualize Wapping and Glasgow (where he had also put up a printing plant) as the two Murdoch printing centres in the country.

'The idea was that everybody, printers, compositors, journalists, would move to Wapping,' says Hardy. 'We didn't then plot to get rid of the unions. What we were going to do was use modern technology to sharply de-man. But we were going to maintain the presence of the unions and, indeed, we had a big office block planned there for that purpose. Rupert blew hot and cold about Wapping. In the end he regretted giving me my head over Wapping.'

They also disagreed about how the company should expand. 'I wanted to concentrate the company's efforts in the UK, and he wanted to expand overseas,' Hardy comments.

So, just as suddenly as Murdoch had summoned him from Long Acre, he banished him. In 1978 Hardy was sacked and Wapping was scaled back in size and intent. Hardy had just negotiated a pay deal with *Sun* journalists, and one journalist, who had taken part in the talks, remains convinced that Hardy got the sack 'because he was too liberal. The bargaining was tough, but we had a good deal and everytime the chapel did well Murdoch sacked the managing director. It happened to the previous managing director, it happened to Bert. I suppose he was too intelligent for Murdoch, whose idea of a good man is one who constantly says "*nyet*" to the unions.'

Hardy himself bears no grudges about the sack. Now when he meets Murdoch they meet on 'the best of terms'.

'I was sad that ten years of huge output, the time and energy I had spent in building things, was lost overnight,' he says. 'But there was no regret, no bitterness. Regret is a useless emotion. You just get on with the next job in hand.'

That, as it happened, was not far away. Though he was on the board of London Weekend as a Murdoch representative, LWT asked him to stay on as a director in his individual capacity, and he was also a director of Hutchinson.

'I was not penniless like some other executives, but in reduced circumstances,' says Hardy.

The circumstances improved dramatically within a year. In 1980 the *Standard* and the *Evening News*, exhausted by the war for the shrinking London evening market, merged. The deal between their owners, Associated Newspapers and the Express Group, gave them both 50 per cent of the merged paper but stipulated that an independent, an outsider, must manage the business. 'Luckily,' says Hardy, 'both sides selected me.' Hardy joined in October 1980 as chief executive of the *Standard*; his exile from the newspaper business had lasted just one year.

Hardy jealously guarded the independence of the *Standard* and this was to lead to a revealing moment in the months leading up to Maxwell's launch of the *London Daily News*. At a conference about the press in Paris, chaired by Hardy, the then managing director of Mail Newspapers, John Winnington-Ingram, let slip that his company still owned the title to the *Evening News*.

There had been much talk of a new evening paper being launched in London. A group of Murdoch journalists under Charles Wilson, now editor of the *Times*, was working on the *Post*, and Maxwell had long broadcast his desire to have an evening paper. Winnington-Ingram's remark was, recalls Hardy, meant 'to be a throwaway. He was trying to illustrate something but I reminded him that he did not own the *Evening News*. It was owned by the *Standard*, and the *Standard* was still an independent company at that stage and I was determined to keep it fiercely independent of both groups.'

However, six months later the *Standard* lost its independence. Lord Stevens' bid for the Express Group triggered an option that allowed Mail Newspapers to buy up the 50 per cent it did not own. Now the import of Winnington-Ingram's throwaway remark began to be appreciated by Hardy. A month before Maxwell launched his *London Daily News*, Mail Newspapers held a board meeting. Rothermere suggested that it might be a good idea to relaunch the *Evening News*. The idea was at once brilliant and nasty.

Hardy's justification is simple.

'The *Standard* was weak. There was not room for two evening papers in London. You could have two weak ones, not two strong ones,' he says. 'So we felt if there were going to be two evening papers, then the two of them might as well be ours.' His methods, however, showed how ruthless he could be.

While Maxwell was launching his paper in the full glare of publicity, Hardy conducted a secretive, cloak-and-dagger operation. Extra printing machines were organized with the *Express*, the print distribution union SOGAT was persuaded to carry the *Evening News* in *Standard* vans, and then five days before the *London Daily News* was to appear an agreement was signed with a firm in Clerkenwell to do the typesetting.

So, on the day that Maxwell, to great fanfare, launched the *London Daily News*, Hardy relaunched the *Evening News* eight years after it had merged with the *Standard*. A one evening paper town suddenly became a three evening paper town. The *Evening News* was probably the worst paper ever to be launched in this country – little more than a rag produced by a skeleton staff and reflecting the speed and secrecy with which it had been put together. But it served its purpose admirably. Its title was similar enough to the *London Daily News* to confuse some people, and, what is more significant, Maxwell fell into the trap Hardy had designed.

'He began to fight the newcomer rather than the *Standard*, says Hardy. 'It became a battle between two newcomers. The *Standard* could pretend to hover over the battle and during the period actually began to put on circulation.'

Maxwell, instead of ignoring the *Evening News*, fulminated against it. The *Evening News* had been priced at 10p. Maxwell slashed the price of his paper from 20p to 10p, confusing readers and angering advertisers. The *Evening News* retaliated by slashing it down to 5p. Punters who bought both the *Standard* and the *London Daily News*, often got the *Evening News* free.

Every move that Maxwell made saw a countermove by Hardy. 'I must say Maxwell did not play it particularly well,' says Hardy. 'But while we did wrong-foot him he often fell over himself.'

Maxwell made accusations against the *Standard* that had to be withdrawn, but Hardy still denies the widespread view that the *Standard* tried to intimidate newsagents into not stocking the *London Daily News*. 'The only ones we told were the ones employed by us,' he says. 'Those who were independent stocked the newspaper.'

Haines, biographer of Maxwell, believes that Maxwell allowed himself to be distracted by a libel action against the satirical magazine *Private Eye* and failed to control the launch of his new paper. Certainly, *London Daily News* contributed to its own downfall. While its editorial contents won plaudits, its distribution was abysmal, there was much confusion as to whether it was a 24-hour newspaper or a proper evening paper and there was never any proper control over costs.

All this would probably have doomed the paper, irrespective of what Hardy and the *Standard* did, but, significantly, Hardy got Maxwell to fight the battle for London's evening paper on his, Hardy's, terms. Maxwell had seen it as a crusade to provide Britain with a 24-hour newspaper and London with an alternative to a *Standard* grown fat and lazy through eight years of monopoly control. Hardy used the sheer 'bombast of Maxwell' to make it appear as if the *Standard* was the little boy in the corner being bullied by a big newcomer.

Even now, with the battle consigned to frayed newspaper cuttings, Hardy cannot quite forsake the little boy role that paid him such handsome dividends. 'We had been attacked both as an individual and as a group by a very powerful group,' he says.

But with the *Standard* part of the powerful Mail Newspapers, was this not more of a fight between two evenly balanced newspaper empires? Hardy's reply is revealing: 'Maxwell, sensing the public value of accusing us of being a monopoly, was trying to bring into play the traditional fear of monopolies. A monopoly existed, there was only one evening newspaper in London, but the monopoly had evolved, it was not something we had plotted. The *Standard* had lived through the years of the evening newspaper wars in London: the *Star* being merged with the *News* and then the combined *Star* and the *News* slugging it out with the *Standard*. Finally, the two old enemies having fought each other to a standstill, had come together to have some respite. But just as the people who wrote the stories and sold the ads had a breathing space along comes another competitor. In any case, what happened in London has happened all over the world – one by one they close down until only one is left.'

What made the Hardy–Maxwell duel fascinating was that while Maxwell constantly pictured it as a fight between his 'deep pockets' and the deep pockets of Lord Rothermere, in the television confrontations and newspaper interviews it was Hardy, never Rothermere, who answered Maxwell. 'Lord Rothermere was in touch with us on a daily basis. But I do not think it is his way to seek publicity,' says Hardy. 'The Maxwell way is not his way.' The result was that there was always an impression that for all his sound and fury Maxwell was chasing shadows, never able to engage the real enemy.

Before the *London Daily News* had been launched Hardy had told colleagues how important it was to strangle it at birth. It had been launched in February; by June he was predicting it would close by the summer. 'Our intelligence was pretty accurate and we knew they were sinking,' he says.

This intelligence network had kept Hardy informed about the editorial innovations the *London Daily News* was preparing. The *Standard* had made the most of this 'intelligence', poaching ideas, like a Metro section, before the *London Daily News* was launched. Now it accurately told Hardy about its disastrous sales figure – below 100,000 when it required 200,000 to survive. On July 25 Maxwell announced the closure of the *London Daily News*. Hardy had been wrong by six days. He had predicted it would close by August.

Not long after that the *Evening News* closed and London was back with just one evening paper. Hardy will not say how much was lost on the *Evening News* spoiler – 'quite a lot' is as far as he will go, but whatever it was, it was a price worth paying to stop Maxwell.

The demise of the *London Daily News* has not meant an end to the newspaper battles. Now, as managing director of Mail Newspapers, Hardy finds the enemy in his sights is his old mentor Murdoch, particularly the threat posed to the *Daily Mail* by *Today*.

What makes the *Today* threat most potent is, says Hardy, 'the ability of Murdoch to hold down prices better than other papers. His basic cost structure is substantially less than other newspaper groups because he does not recognize unions. If he uses that cost advantage to hold down prices then we might be in for new battles.'

If such battles emerge, then, as he did with Maxwell, Hardy will plan carefully and wage the fight singlehandedly. For, if he has a fault, then it is his inability to delegate. As one editor who has worked closely with him says: 'He has to know everything that is going on. At the same time he is the most open of men. He will tell you the most confidential of things. Then he will go and do outrageous deals without consulting the editor – like running weather reports from LBC in the paper.'

Yet the same journalist is willing to overlook this trait because Hardy is 'one of the rare men from the other side – advertisement and circulation – who has shown himself to be sensitive to editorial. Like all ad men who get the money, Hardy understands the commercial reality of newspapers, but it is rare for such men to show editorial judgement. Hardy is the exception.'

Yet for all his empathy with journalists, Hardy does not share the romance that journalists can so easily conjure for newspapers. This hard-headedness makes him doubt if the planned *Sunday Correspondent* newspaper can succeed. 'I would not want to invest in it,' he says. Nor does he share the view that the *Independent* is the journalistic success of a generation.

'I am not sure it has been that successful,' he says. 'To be regarded as a success one needs more than the plaudits of one's fellow journalists. One wants the acceptance of the business community.'

It is this ability to keep the romance of journalism at bay that makes Hardy such a consummate newspaperman.

# 19

# We, the accused: the Safeline saga

February 1990

## Tom Nash

At 7 a.m. one February morning last year a group of lawyers appeared outside Andrew Lock's home. He was away at the time, but they brandished a court order in front of his wife, giving them the right to search the house from top to bottom. They duly carried out the order – with scant regard for her and her children's privacy, or indeed the fact that it was too early for her to obtain advice from her own solicitor.

Lock, managing director of Safeline, a small Manchester-based electronics manufacturer, was accused of stealing trade secrets from his former employer, who had been granted an Anton Piller order – which operates much like a search warrant. At the same time as Lock's house was scoured, so too were the homes of two other Safeline employees and the company's business premises.

In the end, Lock and his colleagues were able to clear Safeline from injunctions restraining it from using alleged trade secrets and confidential information. They were also awarded costs and the right to sue for damages. But they have walked away far from unscathed. They had been able to recover only two-thirds of their costs, and remain many thousands of pounds out of pocket. They have decided that to try to recoup the rest of the money, let alone to sue for damages, would represent a further time and cost burden that they cannot afford. More important than their financial loss, however, is that the development of their young company was severely disrupted and delayed.

The misuse of the Anton Piller order against Safeline shows how, even in the small company's victory, the UK legal system can leave much of the commercial and financial benefit in the hands of a larger, more powerful opponent whose main virtue appears to be the possession of a deep pocket.

The case also highlights some disturbing infringements of individual rights in the application of the Anton Piller order, including apparent breaches of the principles of the sanctity of the home and the presumption that a person is innocent until proven guilty.

Originally, electronics manufacturer Lock International was started by

Andrew Lock's father in the early 1950s. He remained the main shareholder
until the mid-1960s when he sold the majority of the shares to a multinational. Lock International remained fairly autonomous and successful,
but there was little synergy with the rest of the group, which was chiefly
involved in manufacturing chemical additives. In due course it was sold on
to a large electronics distributor, but again the fit was not ideal so it was sold
for a third time – to the Grosvenor group.

While Lock International continued to run profitably, even winning the
Queen's award for export achievement in 1984, the Grosvenor group as a
whole made some unsuccessful investments and got into financial difficulties. It was rescued by Hollis Industries, then a vehicle being used by Robert
Maxwell to diversify his communications empire into engineering. The first
year as part of the Hollis group saw a record turnover and profits, but
non-trading problems were emerging.

'The Hollis style of management did not suit quite a number of people
within Lock International,' says Andrew Lock. He diplomatically avoids
expanding on the statement, but Hollis is well known for its tough style and
the exceptional demands it makes on its managers.

In the autumn of 1988, a previous managing director of Grosvenor raised
finance from 3i and formed a new company, Safeline. Shortly afterwards,
Andrew Lock and two of the company's directors accepted an offer to join
the venture. During the fund-raising period, the trio – though not contrac-
tually restricted – was mindful of the fact that there could be legal problems
involved in leaving Lock International to take part in a competing business.
They were advised to take legal advice on what they could and could not do.

'We were well advised,' says Lock. 'For example, we were told that we
were not permitted to use any of the technical and commercial information
that we had developed at Lock International – or to keep copies or records of
that sort of information. When we left, we walked away with nothing except
what we carried in our heads. We were told that this was absolutely crucial
and we even had to sign undertakings for 3i because obviously its investment was in jeopardy if we did something we should not have done.'

Lock and his colleagues were also warned that there was an outside
possibility that their previous employer, Lock International, would suspect
that they had taken information with them to which they were not entitled
and there was a chance that it would try to obtain an Anton Piller order. 'We
knew it could happen, but we did not really think it would,' says Lock. 'It is
like being warned a plane can crash. When it does it is a shock.'

For the first four months the company consisted of eight employees, all
technical, whose objective was to design a completely new type of machine,
independent of any trade secrets owned by Lock International. For
example, they could not use any of Lock International's marketing information, customer lists, price lists or circuit diagrams.

Nevertheless, the product developed by Safeline – a sophisticated metal detector for finding contamination in food products – was directly competitive with those of Lock International. And there was no escaping the fact that the Safeline team had themselves been responsible for Lock International's research and development for the previous twenty years.

'We did have knowledge of how these systems were made, but we were advised that we could use that knowledge quite legitimately to develop a new machine,' says Lock. Much later, this was substantiated in court when the judge said that if Safeline were prevented from using its own efforts to develop a competitive machine, it would constitute a new form of industrial slavery.

Safeline took pains to go back to first engineering principles in developing its equipment in order to ensure that no charge of copying could be levelled at it. It duly constructed a prototype, using new methods, materials and subcontractors that bore no relation to those used previously. In the meantime, however, Lock International had started to watch what was going on at Safeline.

Agents of Lock International took photographs of Safeline employees as they went to and from work, and of equipment as it was moved in and out of the factory. Later it transpired that their previous employer was trying to gather evidence of wrongdoing in order to persuade a judge to grant an Anton Piller order against Safeline. In due course it succeeded and the order was implemented.

'I was out at the time, but my wife was at home,' says Lock. 'She was told that she could contact her solicitor, but of course it was virtually impossible to get hold of a solicitor at 7 a.m. I felt that this was a deliberate tactic to deprive us of the opportunity of being fairly represented at our homes.

'As our people arrived at the office, they were told to sit in a corner. By then it was about 9 a.m. and we could contact our solicitor who came to read through the court order. Following that they searched the offices and removed volumes and volumes of documentation.

'The order was written so broadly that they were able not only to take documents that they said were theirs, but any information relating to the design, manufacture, marketing or sales of metal detectors. They took our confidential information – circuit diagrams, computer print-outs, price lists and prototypes. We felt this was most unfair and should never have been allowed.'

Lock says that the documents that were taken away were recorded in a very hurried and vague way. At the time his lawyer pointed out that there was a danger that the opposition, if unscrupulous, would have plenty of scope to plant incriminating evidence. Lock stresses that nothing like that ever happened in this case, but the fact that the possibility existed seems to highlight one of the many weaknesses in the use of Anton Piller orders.

'The second warning from our lawyer was that there would be quite a lot of psychological stress involved. Third, he said that we could be killed by a shortage of cash. He told us that it was going to cost us tens or hundreds of thousands of pounds to defend ourselves.'

The psychological pressures soon materialized. After the order was carried out, Lock says that many of Safeline's employees continued to be watched and followed by agents of a private detective company. Sometimes they were followed for several hours at a time. 'It was very sinister,' says Lock. 'We spoke to our lawyers who said it was done to unsettle us and also to see if we were visiting other premises where we might be keeping stolen items.

'We also suspected interference with our telephone lines, though we could not substantiate it. Seven employees received calls at home from someone claiming to be a telephone engineer needing to make modifications on the lines. All the calls were made in different telephone districts within half an hour of each other, but British Telecom had no record of any of their engineers making the calls. We could not pursue it, but it created more pressure on us knowing that our telephone conversations may not be private.'

In theory, the case – officially known as 'Lock International versus Beswick and others' (Beswick being a fellow director of Safeline) – was due ultimately to be heard in the High Court.

However, a court decision last April overturned the original granting of the Anton Piller order, with the plaintiff, Lock International, unable to substantiate any of its allegations of, specifically, breach of contract and copyright and passing off. The judge, Mr Justice Hoffmann, ruled that Safeline should be awarded costs and the right to sue Lock International for damages for the wrongful obtaining of the original order.

The judge criticized the granting of the Anton Piller order on the grounds that there was insufficient evidence to justify it, but he also took the view that Lock International had misled the court when applying for the order by failing to make full disclosure of its financial position. Had the rapidly deteriorating financial performance of the company's owner, Hollis group, been known, the original order might not have been made on the grounds that Hollis might have been unable to honour the cross-undertaking for damages that, as the plaintiff, it was obliged to sign.

Judge Hoffmann also commented that Lock International had made liberal accusations against Safeline of fraud, theft and perjury, but was unable to bring any evidence to support them. By discharging the original order and awarding costs to Safeline on a full indemnity basis, the judge expressed his disapproval of Lock International's conduct and made it clear that no *prima facie* case of dishonesty on the part of Safeline was shown.

Andrew Lock argues that the granting of the original Anton Piller order amounted to a presumption of guilt based on extremely flimsy evidence. 'These orders were always intended to be used when there is factual information to show wrongdoing, but clearly this was not the case in our example. The judge also made the point that these cases can sometimes be brought by companies threatened by competition to try to crush the egg before it is hatched,' he says. 'The reasoning is that it will never get to trial because the defendant will have long since run out of cash.

'We were warned that even if it was found that there was no *prima facie* case against us, there was likely to be an appeal – which would mean that we would not receive the funds that we were entitled to and it would cost us more money.'

This was exactly what happened. 'The appeal dragged on and on and on,' says Lock. 'Our funds got lower and lower and eventually an offer was made to us to settle out of court for a nominal amount – which we rejected.'

A month later, the nominal offer was increased slightly and rejected again. 'You eventually get to a point where you cannot afford to get what is due to you, says Lock. 'You have just got to settle because you've got to have some money or you will go out of business.

'Just after the raid our lawyer made the comment that whatever the outcome, we would lose – either because we had done something we should not have done or else simply in financial terms.'

Safeline also suffered severely in terms of the amount of management time spent on defending itself. Lock estimates that in the six-week period between the granting of the Anton Piller order and the lifting of injunctions against it, about half the board's time was spent compiling evidence (submitted in the form of written affidavits) or briefing counsel in London. 'Probably the other 50 per cent was spent worrying about it,' he says. 'Virtually nothing was going into the business itself and there is no doubt it delayed us by weeks.'

Fortunately, because Safeline's product had not yet reached the production stage, the legal cloud hanging over the company did not damage customer confidence. However, this has been an unwelcome side effect in similar cases where the Anton Piller order has been used. For example, Mr Justice Pain, in discharging an Anton Piller order in another recent case, commented that: 'an Anton Piller order plainly carries the suggestion that a person is not to be trusted and is likely to destroy evidence. This is a very serious thing. People who owe a defendant money, or may enter into further obligations with him, are reluctant to carry on business with him in the ordinary way while this is hanging over him.'

'Had we been in production it would have been a disaster,' says Lock. 'If we had got to a stage where we were trying to build a customer base, it would most likely have destroyed the company. When we had the order served on us we still had a fair portion of our institutional investors' funds on deposit and our outgoings were relatively low – we had about nine employees and we did have the funds to defend ourselves. That was really just luck.'

In the end, Safeline spent around £150,000 in legal fees, but actually recovered only about 60 per cent of this money. To have pursued the rest it would either have had to wait longer or go through the appeal process which would have required further funding. 'We did not have the resources, the management time or the inclination to do that,' says Lock. 'We accepted an offer that we felt was in our long term best interests to take.' For the same reasons, Safeline did not counter-sue for damages, which would have been a difficult figure to assess and one bound to involve lengthy haggling with the opposition.

In fact, after Safeline had been awarded full costs, the company's barrister noted that it is unusual for costs to be decided in an interlocutory hearing. Often, even when a defendant is seen to be wholly innocent, costs are not awarded until the ultimate trial which can be many months, even years later – thus stacking the legal odds even more heavily against small companies involved in legal wrangles with much larger opponents.

Despite the setbacks, Safeline is now back on a sound financial footing and is fast making up for lost time. For example, it has successfully established a European distribution network and a US subsidiary.

A key lesson that Andrew Lock draws from the episode is the importance of taking legal advice from the moment a company is formed. Another is to document plans and development work as thoroughly as possible.

'I feel that Lock International genuinely thought that when it raided our premises it would find a mass of confidential information that we had removed from it,' he says. 'And I think it was quite surprised when it did not find any. But we were in a no-win situation. We have settled on a cost award – but that does not mean it is acceptable.'

Least acceptable of all in Andrew Lock's eyes was the way in which the Anton Piller order was granted – presuming guilt on his and his colleagues' part – and implemented in an intrusive and intimidating way.

# 20

# What price the peace dividend?

July 1990

## Carol Kennedy

If you run one of the estimated 3000 companies in Britain connected with the defence industries, the words 'peace dividend' are unlikely to fall like music on your ears. While politicians and headline-writers speculate euphorically on the civilian bonanza that could result from the lessening of the Soviet military threat, industrialists accustomed to decades of steady profits from MoD contracts are nervously reviewing strategy in the event that, as the saying goes, 'they cancel the war.'

Defence is one of the biggest businesses in the country, the current MoD budget of £21bn representing over 4 per cent of Britain's gross domestic product. The Defence Manufacturers' Association, which has a current membership of around 500 companies, estimates that the defence industries employ 255,000 directly on MoD contracts, a further 210,000 indirectly on subcontracts and another 100,000 on defence-related exports – a total that exceeds even the jobs within the National Health Service, often described as Europe's largest employer apart from the Red Army.

Although Defence Secretary Tom King has indicated that cuts are unlikely in the short term (and Margaret Thatcher is known to take an extremely cautious view of the changes in Eastern Europe), King's procurement minister Alan Clark has been arguing for substantial cuts in the British Army of the Rhine (BAOR) and in the Navy's surface fleet, leaving Trident unscathed.

Opposition voices clamour loudly for cancelling at least the fourth, if not the third, Trident. The Navy insists it needs four to maintain the refit and operational cycle, but if the fourth were to be scrapped it could save an estimated £800m. The 'long lead' arrangement that precedes a formal contract for a Trident involves the MoD in substantial preliminary costs, but without it, the programme would fall behind.

Depending on whom you speak to, and on which side of the House, up to £5bn could theoretically be released from defence spending for hospitals, schools, tax cuts, roads or other electoral goodies. (The left of the Labour party is demanding cuts of up to £9bn.) Politically, it is an entrancing prospect for an Opposition manifesto, though history suggests that Labour in power usually takes a very different posture on defence commitments from Labour in opposition. Labour's recent policy document avoided putting a price on the peace dividend, though the party is committed to helping the industry retool for civilian work.

The future for defence contracts, however, is far from certain, and no one in the industry can see the position stabilizing for years to come. How, then, if you are chairman of a £466m turnover company whose production is 98 per cent defence-related, do you address the unknown? This is the dilemma facing Lord Chalfont and the board of VSEL (Vickers Shipbuilding and Engineering Ltd), builders of the Trident nuclear-armed submarines, nuclear and electric-powered conventional submarines and two sophisti-cated new howitzers, among much else.

VSEL has already begun to consider its strategy for the latter half of the 1990s, when the Trident programme would have come to an end, but the collapse of the Warsaw Pact threat pushed everything into a higher gear.

'I have to be coldly realistic and come to the conclusion that over the next decade, VSEL has got to revise its strategic planning,' says Chalfont. The government – any government – might be expected to have some moral responsibility for the fate of 16,000 defence-related jobs (Barrow is cur-rently a Tory marginal seat after, ironically, years of being represented by Labour's CND-supporting Albert Booth), but Chalfont is under no illu-sions that even a Thatcher administration would keep the axe away from defence.

'A very high-ranking official in the MoD told me recently that there is no piece of equipment that is now sacred. All are up for discussion. Even a beautiful piece of equipment like the AS90 howitzer cannot be said to be safe.'

The AS90, a highly sophisticated, self-propelling gun of which the British Army has ordered 170, could be the first VSEL product under threat if, as many expect, cuts are made in the British Army of the Rhine as part of an agreed scale-down by NATO countries. One defence expert in the International Institute for Strategic Studies suggests that two out of the three British divisions in West Germany could be pulled back, along with their hardware. Total manpower in BAOR at present is 50,000–55,000 men, supported by around 1200 tanks, 1500 armoured personnel carriers, 250 guns of various kinds, 150 Sam missile launchers, 130 aircraft and sixty armed helicopters.

Although one theory is that reductions in Europe could be countered to some extent by a build-up in specialist forces suitable for long-range deploy-ment, the Institute of Strategic Studies points out that there are not many places left where colonial-style military operations are likely to be needed.

VSEL's armaments prospects – it has also developed an ultra-lightweight howitzer capable of being slung under a conventional helicopter – might be helped by more active export marketing, and the US army is currently testing the lightweight gun.

Overall, however, diversification certainly has a key place in the strategy currently being worked out, possibly through acquisition or partnerships with other companies. By the end of the century, VSEL needs to free itself from the umbilical cord of MoD contracts and become a 'multi-customer, multi-product company,' marketing itself to buyers at home and abroad. The new strategy, says Chalfont, needs to be in place within five years.

In a way, it is a bit like a nationalized industry being thrown into the pit of free-enterprise competition, with the additional challenge of finding new products and new markets and applying all the management disciplines that go with that culture change. VSEL went through the first stage of that process in 1986, when a management consortium bought out Vickers Shipbuilding and Engineering from state-owned British Shipbuilders, beating off a higher bid from Sir Nigel Broackes' Trafalgar House to secure the business for £60m.

(Prior to that, shipbuilding had been one division of the mighty Vickers group based on steel, ships, aircraft and engineering. The present Vickers plc, chaired by Sir David Plastow, is a front-runner to build the new Challenger 2 tank for the British army, but its diverse operations include that jewel of civilian industry, Rolls-Royce Motors.)

At the time of the VSEL buyout, the extraordinarily high ratio of worker-shareholders (82 per cent) was hailed as a landmark in British industrial relations. Within a year, however, most had taken their sixfold profits on a soaring share price (though 3000 of the 14,000 workforce still hold their favourable share options, due in 1991), and two years after privatization there was a damaging three-month strike.

Today, with a comparatively new chief executive, much respected in the industry, and a hard-nosed new finance director implementing cost controls unheard of in a business geared to assured MoD contracts, VSEL has a streamlined, reorganized divisional structure that effectively creates five autonomous business units; shipbuilding, armaments, engineering products, combat systems and fleet support, plus a couple of ancillary businesses.

Each division has its own board, setting its own financial targets and managing its own marketing under a 'dotted line' of responsibility to the pared-down central board (Chalfont reduced it from twelve to six, three executive directors and three non-executives). The central board's primary duty is setting the new strategic agenda but it also controls functions such as personnel and operates a system of 'audit panels' for capital investment, the review of tenders, and quality control.

The new structure was put in place in the spring and in late May a basic review of the company's goals began, prior to formulating a five-year plan by the spring of 1991. Chief executive Noel Davies is adamant on the need for that preliminary process: in his experience, he says, 'the weakness of so many British companies is that they go straight to the numbers without first thinking "where are we going, what is the market, what is the competition, what do we need to do to improve our products to beat the competition, what resources do we need to make the product"?'

A fundamental culture change is going on in Barrow-in-Furness, the remote Lancashire peninsula where the original Vickers company built the Royal Navy's first submarine in 1901 and where a truly 'company town' has depended for 90 years on naval defence contracts – until recently on a cosy cost-plus basis.

The Barrow workforce – 14,000 work for VSEL out of the town's total 60,000 population, and the company employs a further 2000 at its Cammell Laird shipyard in Birkenhead – boasts a high and adaptable degree of technical skills, but, as VSEL senior management ruefully admits, has been 'cushioned' from the cost-cutting hurricane that devastated British heavy industry in the early 1980s. It is by no means solely a blue-collar problem; indeed, finance director Norman Broadhurst suspects that though workers as a whole 'have not been stretched in terms of productivity,' he could encounter his stickiest resistance to change in the ranks of middle management.

A veteran of the battered but surviving Sheffield steel industry and, earlier, of China Light and Power in Hong Kong, Broadhurst likes to quote a Hong Kong Chinese maxim that 'you do not break anyone else's rice bowl.' That protective principle, he argues, can apply just as easily to British middle management, particularly in a company town like Barrow, resulting in weaknesses being bolstered rather than exposed. Middle managers at Barrow may need to fasten their seat belts for a bumpy induction into 'business awareness'.

Despite its dependence on massive defence contracts, VSEL is as well placed as any company to tackle the challenge of the 'peace dividend'. Chairman Lord Chalfont, whose seventy years bely a sprightly and energetic personality, was a former foreign office minister under Harold Wilson – when he was nicknamed 'the minister for disarmament'. Before that, as Alun Gwynne Jones, he was a regular army officer and, later, defence correspondent for *The Times*. Among a diversity of roles, including chairmanship of the forthcoming Radio Authority, Chalfont sits on the Lords defence committee and knows the political ropes of defence inside out.

Chief executive Davies, headhunted last September from the 600 Group, is steeped in Barrow shipbuilding, having spent twenty-two years of his career there, until Vickers was sucked into British Shipbuilders. At the dawn of the nuclear submarine age, he was chief engineer at Dounreay in

1956, working on the prototype for the Royal Navy's first nuclear-armed submarine, *HMS Dreadnought*.

Neither of them is convinced that defence cuts will force radical changes in VSEL's core business. 'I expect the core to continue,' says Davies, boarding one of the company's two Beechcraft executive planes for the fifty-minute flight from RAF Northolt to Barrow, where he currently works three midweek days, spending Mondays and Fridays in the London office. His view is that, beyond Trident, non-missile nuclear submarines will still have a defensive role to play. Davies believes the Navy will stay nuclear, and Barrow is the UK's only nuclear-capable yard.

Other types of ships could be built at Barrow, though the massive Devonshire Dock Hall, the size of three football pitches and equipped with an ingenious ship-lift that does away with slipway launches, was designed specifically for submarine construction. (The depreciation on its £220m capital cost is a major challenge for the finance director.) In the 1950s and 1960s, Barrow even built passenger liners for P & O and though the need for those has virtually gone, Lord Chalfont does not rule out other forms of maritime construction; ferries, say, or oil-exploration equipment.

Davies is fond of saying that whatever can be made in the engineering line, Barrow can make it – though, he adds ruefully, not always at the right price. In its time, the heavy engineering department at Barrow, housed in a Victorian redbrick listed building, has turned out such diverse civilian products as cement plants, pumps, and diesel engines for British Rail.

Options for future diversification in engineering could involve a link-up with other companies, either as licensees or partners, to provide equipment for the single European market (shipping it out directly on barges) and possibly also for Far Eastern markets.

The development of non-military, non-maritime products is certainly possible, says Chalfont, provided that the manufacturing process is 'synergistic with the skills and culture of our company. To acquire, say, a completely different kind of company in a different part of the country might be fine for the future of the group and the shareholders, but we have also got to be thinking about those 16,000 people up at Barrow and Birkenhead. We have got to bear the interests of both in mind.'

There seems little doubt that, even if the Trident programme survives unscathed, that level of labour cannot continue if the group is to compete more sharply. Chief executive Davies expects a return to 'historical' levels of 10,000–12,000 by the time the fourth Trident goes on her sea trials around 1994. Given that normal wastage averages 1000 a year, that looks a manageable target, but the seventeen unions involved in VSEL's two shipyards have already had to bite on an unexpected redundancy bullet. Five hundred jobs, one-fifth of the workforce, were axed from Cammell Laird after the

Birkenhead yard lost out to Swan Hunter for a recent Navy order for Type 23 frigates.

Tenders will be going out later this year for another four Type 23 frigates, but it seems unlikely that, however finely VSEL sharpens its pencil, it can narrow the competitive gap in time. On some engineering and commercial products, that gap has sometimes been as far as 30–35 per cent from the competition. Reductions in overheads, which account for a third of the finished product's cost, are among finance director Broadhurst's top priorities.

There are 'big numbers' to soak out in terms of costs, Broadhurst indicates. He expects the MoD under Treasury prodding, to move ever faster away from the old 'cost-plus' culture and become a lot tougher on its suppliers, possibly bringing in value-for-money audits. Saving taxpayers' money this way would be Secretary of State King's easiest option. 'It will soon be up to management to manage costs in new MoD contracts as they would in a normal business,' predicts Broadhurst.

In the red sandstone terraced streets of Barrow, remote on its peninsula west of the Lake District, the fate of Trident will loom large, at least until the next election. Within the massive bulk of Devonshire Dock Hall, a strictly classified area, the first Trident is already recognizably in place; the second is partly assembled and 'long lead' work has begun on the third, although the formal contract has yet to be signed. The last of the Trafalgar class nuclear-powered submarines is also being finished, due for launching later this year.

Some take the view that there are limits to what the most enterprising defence company can do to convert to civilian production, though Racal has succeeded spectacularly with market leader Vodafone. Britain's track-record of transferring advanced military technology to civilian products has not been encouraging, but the MoD's deep pockets have scarcely provided an incentive. As Harvard's Michael Porter pointed out in his new book, *The Competitive Advantage of Nations*, fully half Britain's government R & D has gone into defence.

Now, at the eleventh hour, efforts are being made to co-ordinate research on 'conversion'. Brigadier Tony Cranstoun, assistant director of marketing and development at the Defence Manufacturers' Association, is organizing a seminar on the future of the defence industries in mid-July.

'Because so many of our members are in subcontracting, they need to take a view of what their niche markets are, if any, and what they are going to do about their marketing strategy,' explains Cranstoun. 'We have been trying to tell them for a long time that there are too many companies chasing too small a slice of the cake: this will force them to diversify.'

Three unions in the defence industry are also reported to be working on conversion research.

Lord Chalfont does not believe the difficulties in converting military to civilian production are insuperable – though there can be problems of differing quality control if both are attempted at the same time.

'You have only got to look at the spin-off from the US space programme – an enormous spin-off into the civilian economy,' he points out. 'I think the problem can be solved, provided there is a high degree of strategic planning and thinking.'

Chalfont is critical, however, of Britain's lack of attention to non-military R & D. 'That is now beginning to hit us very hard, and it is something we in this company are thinking about very much. It is the business of business to get its R & D right. There is a general tendency, when companies come under constraints and reductions, as the defence industry is doing now, for R & D to be the first thing that is cut. I believe you ought almost to increase your R & D proportionately as you come under constraints.

'We do need the encouragement of government – perhaps even some government initiatives – but in the long run I think the real responsibility does lie with industry.'

# 21

# The great attraction of staying small

July 1990

Sara Jackson

It is a glorious summer day in a picture-postcard Buckinghamshire village. Andrew McNaughton and his wife, Anne, are standing in their garden. The skies are azure, the cherry blossom is out, bird-song fills the air. It is 11 a.m. on a Monday. 'Tell me this,' McNaughton asks, 'what are we in now? Business time or leisure time?' It is hard to answer.

McNaughton Dynamics is run from the McNaughtons' home. Founded in 1987, it is an aerospace and defence ground equipment consultancy. It also has a small manufacturing capacity – in the back garage. It has three directors (Andrew, Anne and Andrew's father), and no other employees despite the fact its turnover has grown by £25,000 in two years and is now at £100,000.

The McNaughtons are not alone in deliberately resisting growth. Bill Sargent runs a family ice-cream manufacturing company based in Hibaldstow, South Humberside. W Sargent & Son was founded by his father in 1922. Sargent now has a turnover of £250,000, a permanent staff of six and a summertime staff of twelve. He does not want to grow his company – pride in the product and the family name forbid it.

Bill Sargent senior started making ice-cream in 1922. The first batches were made by the gallon, boiled on the kitchen fire, cooled in a hand freezer and sold from a pony and trap. Today, the boiling, freezing and selling mechanisms may be more sophisticated, but the ingredients remain unchanged. No preservatives are added to the product; it is made and sold fresh daily. Modern ice-cream machinery blows air into the product, Sargent's does not, so the ice-cream is more solid – and it cannot be deep frozen. The ice-cream is produced in the dairy next to the family home, with an average output of about 250 gallons a day.

Sargent's ice-cream is a legend in Lincolnshire. On a summer Sunday, the queues outside its Hibaldstow kiosk stretch further than the eye can see. But the business has only three kiosks and six ice-cream vans and it sells no further than Lincoln, twenty miles away.

Derek Dishman set up his company in 1987 after he and co-director

Susan Hawkins were made redundant from the credit department of the video company for which they worked. 'I would sell my business and walk away when it got to the size beyond which personal relationships were no longer possible,' he insists.

Credit Limits is a debt collecting agency. It also runs the entire sales ledger for companies generally too small to afford a computer themselves or with insufficient time or office space to run it themselves. For the first year he worked from home. He has now acquired premises in Barnet, Hertfordshire. In 1989 the turnover was £54,000. For 1990 Dishman anticipates it will be £125,000.

All three companies are examples of Britain's three million small firms. All three have in common a strong desire to resist growth. 'Small' refers not to turnover but to management structure. A small firm has a limited number of managers within the company, generally the boss(es) and some delegated jobs. A medium-sized company, on the other hand, will have developed a full board and a tier of directors. Of Britain's small firms 96 per cent employ fewer than twenty individuals; over 66 per cent consist of only one or two people.

Paul Burns, professor of small business development at Cranfield School of Management considers that the vast majority of UK companies are life-style businesses, set up by their manager not to achieve riches but a way of life. McNaughton is a champion of this concept. 'My goal is to enjoy the one life we have been given,' he says. 'Owning your own company, your own small company, is about the total integration of your personal and your professional life.' The size of his company, he feels, gives him this quality of life, something he believes would be more elusive if the company grew too big.

Although not established with this objective, W Sargent and Son also provides a life-style for the family, one where personal interest, hobby and work all become inseparable. Behind Sargent's home and dairy stand the stables. Sargent not only owns eight horses, including two greys, he also owns carriages collected by his father: two landaus, a station cab, a brougham and a gypsy caravan. A keen horseman, he has also started a business driving couples to their weddings in a horse and carriage. Last year he drove thirty-five couples to church.

A crucial facet of Dishman's job satisfaction lies in having a close working relationship with his employees. Dishman currently employs six people. 'I do far more hours now than I ever did,' he says. 'Not only Monday to Friday but often weekends as well.' A self-confessed workaholic, Dishman now takes no holiday either. Yet he sees the personal advantage in running his own company to be freedom. Yes, he does work much more than he ever did. 'But I do not have to,' he insists, 'I choose to.' But to maintain close links with employees he considers it necessary to remain small. It is this factor that determines just how large he will let his company grow.

'I want to be in a position to know all my employees' names and their spouses' names,' Dishman avers. 'And for them to come to mind instantly when I bump into them in the street.' He has introduced a profit-share whereby 20 per cent of profits at the year end are paid out to staff. 'I can only make £40,000 a year on my own, but the business will ultimately make much more than that. We also do very small things which I think count largely. For example, all our staff get a present on their birthday.'

For Dishman this limit would be fifty employees, for McNaughton 100. 'I cannot see an instance where I would ever employ over 100 people,' says McNaughton. 'I think that when companies get beyond that size they lose their identity, their family image. What I would like to generate is a company that cares for its employees, that does not get bought and sold, where everyone thinks of their job as something they enjoy going to.' To motivate future employees McNaughton sees profit-share as essential.

McNaughton's sentiments reflect his experience. In 1987 he was working as director of aerospace for Lear Siegler's UK office. He left when the company was being taken over 'yet again' by another organization. 'It struck me that there were people who had worked within the company for thirty years who were likely to be kicked out,' he explains. 'It made me realize that corporate loyalty is a vague will o' the wisp that disappears as soon as ownership of the company changes. I felt I was not prepared to give my loyalty for many years to have it thrown back at me by a group of faceless people that took over the company.' McNaughton set up on his own and took many of its clients with him.

For Sargent, the governing factor in the desire to remain small is reputation. 'When people compliment me and say your ice-cream is still as good as when your dad made it, I feel as proud as punch about it,' he says. It also means that he is not prepared to expand because to do so would require using a different process and introducing additives and stabilizers. The business sells retail only. 'We could go a hell of a lot bigger,' says Sargent. 'We've had the chance to supply shops and have been approached by hotels all around the area. But to expand any bigger would mean altering the product altogether.'

Sargent knows because he tried it. And he kept it up for just one day. Three years ago constant appeals for the company to sell wholesale led the family to install different machinery capable of producing ice-cream on the required scale. 'I had that many complaints, people ringing me up and saying "if this is Sargent's we want no more of it", that we scrapped the new machinery and reverted to the old process,' he recalls.

Sargent's current business is the result of his reputation and he will not jeopardize it. He concedes that he could set up another small dairy elsewhere in the country that produces the ice-cream in the traditional way, but he would only do so if one of his sons was there to oversee the operation. He would on no account install a manager.

The experts have their own views on why some companies resist growth, an unwillingness to delegate being one of them. Catherine Gurling, director of the programme for enterprise at the London Business School, considers that the prime motivation for a manager in keeping his company small is an unwillingness to extend the span of control. Sargent freely admits he wants to keep his hands on all aspects of his business. His customers get a product that is available nowhere else, the quality of which he zealously guards. 'A manager would soon run the name down,' he says, 'because he just would not have the same interest.' Sargent trusts no one other than the family. But his reasons are other than a reluctance to delegate. 'It is part of the family secret as well,' he says. 'We do not want others to know how to produce the ice-cream. We will tell people the main ingredients, but not the others – because that is where the secret lies.'

Fortunately Sargent has two sons who, like himself, have been born into and immersed in the family business. One is currently studying business studies and management, and another has just joined the marines. Both have the same feel for the company and expect to join it.

McNaughton's business is much newer, but he too is reluctant to bring in a non-family director and confesses himself to be a bad delegator. 'I would really enjoy bouncing ideas and getting some fresh thoughts in, but I fear falling out with someone having shared your life's work with them. It happens so often,' he says.

'Family businesses are terribly difficult,' concedes McNaughton, 'because at the end of the day it is the people who started the business whose child it is. Our company is the product of our work. It is like bringing another person into the world, going through the back-breaking tasks of getting VAT approval, phones in, dealing with the tax man, accountant, company cars . . . all the myriad of things that have to be done. Now I do not want it to turn into some monster and beat me.'

Gurling also believes that the fear of taking risks, of over-expanding on staff and on debt is a factor behind many small businesses staying small.

Dishman admits his company has taken no risk at all since opening. The company is currently turning business away. He wants to grow to achieve critical mass, but slowly. He is concerned not only to recruit precisely the right person but also not to incur debt. 'We presently run without borrowings,' he says, 'which is untypical of small companies. We have got money in the bank and if we had no turnover for two months I could still pay all salaries. I would like to be certain that anyone I take on has got a job as far as I can see into the future. Otherwise we could be temporarily short of work and I would not feel comfortable,' he says.

But when asked whether greater risk for potentially higher returns is attractive, both Dishman and McNaughton look slightly amused. 'Uhm, I think that is called greed,' ponders McNaughton. 'If you are after a crock of gold after five years then you have got to take risks to get it. I am not.' Dishman echoes his words. 'I am not greedy,' he says. 'I actually don't pay myself much more than Viv (who runs the office). We need to reinvest in the company, and I don't think my basic attitude to that will change. I can live on what I pay myself now.'

London Business School's Gurling, however, admits that growth is not necessarily a good thing. 'Growth has been made into something of a holy grail,' she says. 'This is because people make money out of companies growing. It is just not true that growth is universally good. A merchant banker or venture capitalist will, of course, want a company to grow but it might not be in its own interest to do so.'

McNaughton feels confident he can control the size of the company and that diversification of his operations is the key to control of growth of the business. Any of the areas can be expanded or contracted and the company is relieved from over-dependence on one service. 'Why should a company always grow?' he insists. 'Why not take on a unit, expand to twenty people then 100 people, contract again to twenty, expand to fifty then down again to two? Why not? Why should a company always be something that grows bigger and bigger until it falls over?'

Nonetheless, small firms that want to remain small walk a tightrope, balanced between the Scylla of collapse and the Charybdis of inevitable growth. Some companies do not have any choice about growth. 'For some businesses the option is to go bust,' says Cranfield's Paul Burns. 'You don't know the scale of demand and if you don't grow to meet it you are out of business. The problem is finding a market niche which allows them to remain small. The businessman must match his aspirations with the marketplace.'

Some firms need to stay small to remain successful. Sargent's is one of them, where the nature of the product is dependent on perpetuating a non-commercialized manufacturing process and using relatively costly ingredients. Credit Limits, however, is not. Dishman admits that growth will eventually probably run out of his control.

'We will have a sales team, administrative department, half a dozen consultants, and they will all be going hell for leather for growth, because that is what companies always go for, or they will just be going at normal speed but the salesman will still tend to get new customers and you will not be able to stop it. If you do, half a dozen clients will suddenly get taken over and we will end up short. There is always natural wastage.'

Dishman considers his current size to carry too much risk, and he does want too achieve some further growth. 'We are still delicate, there is no critical mass,' he admits. 'I think you need ten or twelve employees before you are really safe from losing big clients. Normally with a small business 20 per cent of clients are worth 80 per cent of your income. We were suffering from that when at one stage one client was 80 per cent of our income. Now probably four big clients represent that figure.'

'I see problems in doing what I enjoy doing,' says McNaughton, 'which is working as a manufacturer of aerospace and defence equipment while being small. There is an absolute built-in bias against small businesses. I have been to MoD offices and people have said "why have you put a private address here? Why not the address of your solicitor"?'

McNaughton currently has the possibility of manufacturing an airconditioning unit for a new version of the Harrier. He designs in his upstairs office and builds in his garage. Before he gets the contract, British Aerospace's quality team wants to vet his own quality organization. 'I am a small business operating out of a garage and British Aerospace would not like that tag,' he says. 'If I want to keep this contract I will probably have to take on premises. Again, I will have to balance that contract against quality of life and decide whether I want to take it.'

Nonetheless, these companies are not short on new ideas for future business. McNaughton and his wife have expanded their consultancy and manufacturing business to include a data processing service, using their Apple Macintosh computer. Not only this, they are developing the export of spare parts for British equipment in undeveloped countries. 'But if it ever looks as if the tail is going to wag the dog,' McNaughton says, 'I will bring that area down.'

Sargent considers the future of his company to lie in ice-cream parlours. Located in an area where the bulk of the population is employed by the steel industry, his company felt the pinch when redundancies happened. 'In the early 1980s we really saw sales decrease from the vans,' he says. 'The steelworks in Scunthorpe went from 28,000 men to 8000. This was a big blow for people and money became tight. People could go into a super-market and buy a four or five-litre tub of ice-cream for £2. It costs me £2 for a gallon of milk.' He noticed that the kiosks still pulled in business, so he developed the Hibaldstow kiosk into an 'ice-cream parlour' and made it worth a trip out.

Sargent is looking for a site in Grimsby to build another parlour. He can see the family firm expanding 'in a limited sort of way, within a fifty-mile radius. It is no good putting too many sales outlets too near because they will cut one another,' he says.

Dishman wants to expand into cash-flow related services. 'We are looking at "rent an expert",' he says. 'Many companies cannot afford a credit manager full-time; by using me one day a week they are ensuring them-selves against catastrophe. Nothing major will go wrong. A few minor things might, but they would not bankrupt them.' It also means that the company gets an annual contract. 'Debt collecting is very much up and down,' he continues. 'We get new clients, sort out the mess and then the job is done. This requires a constant source of new clients.'

All three companies consider there are real advantages for clients in dealing with them as small operations. 'We have picked up a number of customers off Dun and Bradstreet, who are the biggest in the business,' says Dishman. 'That is because their clients never talk to the same person for two days running. People come to us because they know they will be talking to Viv or Maggie and they will still be here next week. They are receiving a personal service. At the moment we are more interested in giving service and trying to get in every penny that is recoverable rather than maximizing our own profit on the debt-collecting side. But I think that will maximize our profit in the long term.'

McNaughton agrees. 'The reality is that you are much more likely to get both good terms and good products from a sole proprietor than from a big organization. Someone running their own business is proud of their products and will do anything to make sure everything is all right.'

Like McNaughton Dynamics, Sargent's appears to be the sort of company that is fortunate to operate in a market which enables its directors to control its size. Dishman, however, is resigned to eventual growth beyond this control.

Running a small company is similar to riding a bicycle: it is necessary to go forward to retain stability. For Credit Limits the analogy is particularly apt.

'If you sit still, you will go backward,' Dishman says. 'If you want to grow, you will grow, there is no easy way of staying the same size. A very mature business could. But when it gets bigger than I enjoy working with, that is when it gets flogged.'

# 22

# Doing it MI way

October 1990

Sara Jackson

'I walked into that building and I was so overcome by the black leather loungers, by the switchboard – man, you should see that switchboard – by the televised screens, by the men walking around in designer suits. It was so glamorous. You think "Wow! This place is making money." And I was sold.'

To illustrate the point, Stephanie Barker taps her forehead, slapping an imaginary 'sold' sticker on to it. She is describing the west end office of the MI Group, the life assurance sales company previously known as the Porchester Group. And she was there not as a potential client but as a potential employee.

'Who do you know who earns 100 grand a year?' they asked. 'Nobody,' I said. 'Well look around,' they told me. 'You can write your own pay cheque. You can go right through the structure in nine years or in nine months.'

And some people do. Stephanie Barker did not. Twenty-one years old and straight out of university, she was, she now admits, naïve. With £800 'twenty-first' money in the bank, she joined MI Group on commission only, and left three months later – £1,700 in debt.

Many members of the public, so irritated by cold calls from the MI Group salesforce attempting to entice them into their offices in order to sell them savings plans, pension plans, life assurance or general insurance, are so anti-MI they would have little sympathy for Barker's plight. She was, after all, one of the plague of telephone irritants.

Tony Peck, chairman of London-based PR consultancy Infopress, says the company was overwhelmed with persistent telephone calls from various MI Group representatives. 'I knew exactly what they were going to say each time they rang. Some of them were clearly reading from a script and I knew it better than they did!' he says. 'They caused so much irritation and took up so much of mine and my employees' time that I eventually sought legal advice.' Infopress threatened that not only would it seek an injunction but it would also issue a press release revealing its actions. The calls abated for a couple of years, but Peck says they are again on the increase.

MI Group is certainly creating a high public profile for itself. But for a company that evokes so much popular hostility it is doing remarkably well. Indeed, a company which had captured the hearts of the masses could hardly hope for faster growth. It is one of the fastest-growing life assurance companies in the business. In 1981 sole proprietor Trevor Deaves, then twenty-seven, started up the Porchester Group employing roughly forty people. In 1987, keeping on all Porchester staff, Deaves bought Merchant Investors and launched the MI Group. Now the MI Group employs over 3000 people and claims it sells on average 15,000 policies monthly. Total funds under management have nearly doubled in three years, from £228m in 1987 to over £450m today. It has still some way to go to catch up with such long-established market leaders as the Prudential and Standard Life, but it is growing fast.

MI is no stranger to controversy. Back in 1981 when the Porchester Group was formed, a legal wrangle immediately erupted between Porchester and Berkeley Walbrook, for which Deaves had formerly worked. Then, in 1985, a series of *Daily Mail* articles claimed that Porchester, in its chase for sales and commission had been selling without proper information and had mistreated junior salesmen. With no concrete evidence nothing was ever substantiated.

To meet Trevor Deaves is to discover the force behind all of MI's paradoxes. Deaves, to coin a new phrase, exuberates energy. He is all dynamism and no pretension. Outside the Wimbledon office a Rolls-Royce Silver Cloud draws up. Deaves is at the steering wheel. The Silver Cloud convertible is, I discover on further enquiry, a 'drop-head coupé by Mulliner Park Ward. Particularly notable for its Chinese headlights. Quite rare.' Deaves loves cars and at any one time has between fifteen and twenty on the go. 'The number changes. It is a hobby. I had a Corvette Stingray, for example, which I swapped recently for an XK120. I don't go out actively looking for cars but people tend to come to me and there they are, and I like them.' Deaves, 'not yet institutionalized' and proud of it, wears his thick ginger hair most definitely on the long side.

Deaves has not simply an answer for every question about MI, but a torrent of assertions delivered with humour but absolute conviction.

Questioned on the morality of taking on people like Stephanie Barker, who end up less than penniless; on the morality of the pressure applied to sales reps; and, moreover, on the morality of cold calling, Deaves is incorrigible. Cold calling is acceptable under LAUTRO (the life assurance industry regulatory body regulations. 'And,' he asks, 'if it is immoral to allow you to run your life commission only at twenty-one, I give you a question. Should we be allowed to vote at eighteen?

'If you are talking about controversy, I will tell you what makes MI controversial,' Deaves continues. 'Number one, it is new. There are many new insurance or financial concerns that have really got going. That in itself makes it controversial. People want to know what on earth did *that* come from. Number two, I am not an actuary or an accountant or a lawyer. They always are. Look at Sir Mark Weinberg of Allied Dunbar; a lawyer. I am a *salesman* (here he contorts his face with incredulity). *That* makes it controversial. Number three. I'm young. And you have got to remember something else, the others are employees. I am a proprietor. These insurance companies, they are either public or a mutual. This is a very large, privately owned insurance company. Now that is strange.'

He admits that cold calling means the group has 'a good name among our clients but a bad name among people who have had a number of calls.' Nonetheless he supports differentiating between cold calling and cold selling (of which he does not approve). Our calls account for only 10 per cent of MI business, the rest comes from referrals and existing clients. 'That is why you are right,' Deaves admits, 'because for less than 10 per cent of the business we get a lot of aggro. But I'm a purist. If I were to say to a new recruit, "you cannot cold call because we don't want people thinking MI is bad news," I have reduced one of their areas of activity. At the end of the day I am in this business as a result of a cold call and I am very, very pleased that somebody rang me and sold me a policy for £15 and then recruited me.'

Deaves moves on to a more serious justification. It is the belief that MI has a genuine service to offer the public. 'I don't think one should underestimate the importance of the product,' he says. 'Therefore while it is legal we should continue to use it. With an ever-increasing older generation and less and less money in the purse to keep them, people have to become self-supporting. It is not a matter of ideology, it is a matter of mathematics. Therefore if all these young people start long-term savings and pensions it is decreasing the inevitable burden on the state. Life assurance diminishes the number of widows and children who must go to the state for support. But,' he continues, 'having said all that, we may well move to a situation where we voluntarily cut down or eradicate cold calling.'

Under LAUTRO regulations all representatives have to have a background of 'requisite competence.' Only those with this level of competence can make cold calls. MI Group makes an estimated 30,000 a day. LAUTRO regulations require that cold callers immediately identify whom they are, whom they represent, and state the genuine reason for the call. If the person called wants to hear nothing of it, then the caller must immediately terminate the call. Michael Abrahams, chief enforcement officer of LAUTRO, says that most complaints from the public are not, in fact, about cold calls and those that are, are generally within the rules. Apparently, the greatest sources of irritation from life assurance salesmen are their attempts to switch existing policies (for example, mortgages). There are no plans to restrict cold calling in relation to life assurance and unit trusts.

Nonetheless, a report by Dr Oonagh McDonald, published earlier this year and commissioned by the Securities Investment Board (SIB), found the methods of training and follow-up by life assurance firms somewhat patchy. Training and competence are currently a matter for members; LAUTRO requires only that sales representatives should be 'suitable and competent'. In the wake of the McDonald report, LAUTRO intends to set down standards, approved by the SIB, that members will be required to maintain. 'The standards imposed will be much higher than those currently observed by some firms,' says Jebens.

On the subject of failed MI representatives, Deaves puts it down to a matter of ensuring good recruitment in the first place. 'I have to discount the people who leave MI,' he says. A visit to an MI office reveals why. The visitor steps into a low hum of activity. But it is not the carefully co-ordinated decor of black and chrome office furniture and venetian blinds that provide the initial impact. It is the dozens of young men sitting or standing behind those desks hanging eagerly on to their telephone receivers.

The individuals behind the desks are far from the disgruntled and once impoverished ex-employees now working in other professions. It is hard to believe that this sleek sales machinery can produce the sort of irritation so often encountered among the general public.

And yes, they are motivated. Catherine Hold graduated from university in 1985 and went on to design equipment for handicapped people. She has now been with MI for one year and five months and is already earning double her last salary. The previous month she grossed £3,600. By the same time next year, she anticipates an annual salary of between £50,000 and £60,000. But Hold insists that she is not just working for the money: 'I am determined and ambitious and I wanted to get to the top in whatever I did. Clichéd as it sounds I wanted job satisfaction.' She takes no holidays; she has no desire to. For the first four months or so she cold called and picked up about twelve clients. She now has about eighty, all of them referrals derived from those original twelve.

The pressure is definitely on. On the walls of the sales room are boards. On the boards are the names of every sales rep; next to their names are the number of new policies they have won that month. Those (new recruits) that have none are visible for all to see. 'The sort of person who works here would not be daunted by that board,' says Hold. 'You have got to want to prove yourself publicly.'

Still, not everyone can achieve the riches that MI offers. Andrew Thompson, twenty-eight years old, worked at MI for over a year; he has now returned to a career in civil engineering. He, too, had wanted to make 'some serious money', but found himself struggling to stay afloat. 'There are lots of other people struggling,' he says. 'But not that many leave. They stick at it, even though they are not getting anywhere.'

Growth (and a salesforce making 'serious money') is one thing, perform-ance is another. MI apparently has them both. 'Their growth has been phenomenal,' says a city analyst. 'One of their main attractions is their product. They act as middlemen and not many insurance companies offer that form of contract.' Most sell their own product only. MI Group has reciprocal arrangements with individual fund management businesses and MI's name lies adjacent to theirs when the funds line up on the performance charts.

Deaves digs around for a copy of *Money Marketing*. According to an August issue, MI Group ranks number eight in the top ten UK insurance companies over every fund listed, and also ranks in every one of the individual funds. 'I defy you to show me any company that is featured as much as us. In fact, not even that. Even if you added two together they would not occur as frequently as MI,' says Deaves, triumphant. 'There is no other insurance company in the UK, according to this, that performs as well as MI.'

Apart from performance, why has MI seen this amazing growth? Deaves sees 'three or four main reasons, probably 100 small ones.' The central factor is the fact that MI reps do not go out and see potential clients – rather, they come into MI offices. And why is this so important? 'Why?' demands an incredulous Deaves. 'Why do you think it is so important you go and see a barrister rather than he pops around to your house in the evening to discuss a brief? The answer is, because professionals tend to sit and people come to them. When you go out you are selling; as soon as people come in they are buying.

'We are successful because we offer a service rather than a product,' he adds. 'A client, before he bought a policy' (MI calls them programmes), 'would meet me twice if not three times. Then when he became a client he would come back every six months, just like he would to his dentist, for a check-up. He would remain my client for, let us say, over fifteen years. As he gets older, he takes out a pension, or maybe even has his own company, all doing business with me. Why? Because of this constant ongoing service. Most people will buy a policy from someone and never see them again.'

The crucial factor is, however, motivation. 'We are a very mo-ti-va-ted company,' he says, dissecting and stressing each syllable as he speaks. 'Motivation is the thing that gets you to go from A to B quicker.'

But what is this motivation that drives sales reps to bludgeon their friends and relatives for business, to make forty cold calls a day in a desperate bid to make a sale, and which drives some reps into debt? The company provides no financial support whatsoever for a new recruit. Telephone calls are paid for and that is it. All new reps must attend a three-day training course held in Bristol. Although the training itself is 'free', all transport and accommo-dation is self-funded. They have even to buy their own stamps to send out correspondence to clients, their own coffee from vending machines installed in the offices. MI may give its new recruits the moral support of an office environment, but it gives them little else.

Such a policy exists, not, Deaves insists, to bolster company cash flow but to enhance that moti-va-tion. 'Life is about choices,' he says. 'If you can close down the number of areas and choices which send people off the wrong way, then the better it is. So, I am delighted that they have to pay for coffee, because they will sit there and think I don't want another cup of coffee and instead of walking away and getting one will pick up the phone and do some business instead.'

For those recruits who do find themselves four months down the line and totally broke, succour is discretionary. 'If you had done some business, I might advance you against that business done. However, if you had not done any business then I probably would not advance you a penny. Because I think it would make you weaker,' says Deaves.

MI does not recruit from within the industry: 'That would be like teaching an old dog new tricks.' Those it recruits are given no assistance at all in building a client base. Here, the harshness of Deaves' regime contrasts with many of MI's competitors. Alan Spriggs, chief sales manager at Colonial Mutual explains that 60 per cent of the people Colonial Mutual recruits already have experience. 'They are unlikely to need to fall back on cold calling,' he says. 'And most of our inexperienced recruits are given a list of clients who have already approached us.' Colonial Mutual salesmen receive non-returnable finance for the first five months after which they are on commission only. Many of Allied Dunbar's recruits, being older, bring a client base with them. But public affairs director Bob Gill explains that a manager is able to introduce a younger, perhaps graduate recruit to some existing clients.

The company that Deaves has created has a culture unique in the life assurance industry. Quite simply, it is younger. MI's sales force has an average age of twenty-seven years. Allied Dunbar's is forty-one. The result is a very young client profile. 'Often a client reflects the salesman,' explains Deaves. 'You can generally give or take three years either side.'

But Deaves believes there is more to MI's culture than youthful energy. 'You have got to be somebody who has been disillusioned in a normal career to appreciate what an opportunity this is,' he says. 'The majority of our sales people are graduates. They have been conned into believing that if they get their degree they would go off into the big wide world and be successful. Now they cannot afford to buy a new property or pay the mortgage they have got, and they would not want their boss's boss's boss's job. Right? They are on – I don't know, what do people earn out there – fifteen grand a year? They are recruitable. We bring them in, train them up and they can soon be earning £20,000 to £50,000 a year.'

'I think growth is all down to culture,' says Allied Dunbar's Gill. 'It is not easy to be successful in this business. But the test of any company is whether in twenty years' time it is a major player. It is easy to be young and aggressive when you are young and still small. It is much harder when you are employing 10,000 people.'

'You may think I am biased,' Deaves says, 'but MI is good news. It is a bit like the Olympics: great if you win golds, nothing if you come fourth. It is a winner's company. I have stood up publicly and said MI's going to be the best. Over my dead body.' He pauses a moment in reflection. 'You know I was a winner and yet nobody ever gave me the opportunity. As soon as somebody gave me the opportunity I loved it. I have a little mission in life and it is not religious. I would like to be the bloke who created a genuine opportunity for people like me.' If Deaves himself is around, mo-ti-va-ted and at the helm for the next twenty years, MI is likely to continue doing just that.

In February 1991 Trevor Deaves left the MI Group.

# Section Five

## Ethics and Values

# 23

# The way we live now: have British values changed?

December 1988

## Carol Kennedy

'What kind of a people do they think we are?' asked Winston Churchill in December 1941, denouncing the Japanese attack on Pearl Harbor in a speech to the US Congress. Today, there seems to be a new, reflective spirit abroad in Britain in which one might turn the phrase around and ask: 'What kind of a people do we think we are?'

Suddenly, 'values' have become a national talking-point, a focus for the disquiet many people feel about certain behavioural trends in the Britain of the late 1980s.

Opinion polls reveal a widespread concern, particularly among women, that people are more selfish than they were ten years ago. Yet paradoxes abound: charitable giving is said to be a third greater in real terms than ten years ago.

Home Secretary Douglas Hurd feels compelled to urge the teaching of 'personal responsibility, self-discipline and civic duty' in the national schools curriculum. He has condemned the 'casual brutalism' purveyed by youths with 'too much money in their pockets and too many pints in their stomachs' – a phenomenon no longer restricted to weekend pub brawls, but which has now spread to young men in city pinstripes on London railway stations.

Other social factors play a part in the general unease. For a government so committed to family values and public thrift, it is supremely ironic that the divorce rate is at its highest ever level (168,000 in 1987 compared with 27,000 in 1961); that over one-fifth of all live births in 1987 were to single parents; and that the personal borrowings of the British people stand at an astronomical £36bn – more than £1000 for every family, excluding mortgage credit.

Predictably, 'values' have become a political anvil on which the Government's opponents are hammering 'Thatcherism' as responsible for every unlovely aspect of late-1980s Britain, from lager louts to insider trading.

Interviewed on television in the summer, Lord Jenkins of Hillhead, chancellor of Oxford University and the former Labour cabinet minister who helped found the original SDP, said bleakly: 'The obtaining and spending of money have become the absolutely dominant values in society, and this will be damaging.'

At the Labour Party's autumn conference, leader Neil Kinnock signalled his intention to shift the political battle to the theme of selfish materialism – 'No number other than one, no time other than now, just me and now!'

Political rhetoric apart, has society really changed that much in forty years, beyond the inevitable differences wrought by industrial and economic change, wider social mobility and such factors as the youth culture and the greater economic independence of women and young people? Have we abandoned what some like to think of as the old values in Britain, such as willingness to judge a person by other measures than visible success; the philanthropic, voluntary impulse to serve without counting the salary first; decency in public behaviour and integrity in business dealings?

Some survivors of the postwar era might add to that the desire for 'one nation' and the social cohesiveness which many remember – perhaps through rose-tinted glasses – as the legacy of shared hardship in the Second World War and after.

To find out some answers to these large questions, *Director* interviewed more than a dozen men and women eminent in the law, public service, business enterprise, education and academic life, authorship and politics. They were of varied political persuasions and religious faiths and all able, from long experience of Britain in the last forty years, to give a considered view on how far society has changed and the debits or credits of that change.

Revealingly, hardly anyone turned down the invitation to participate: clearly, social values and all the ramifications of social behaviour associated with them evidently strike a common chord. (One of the few who did decline was the man theoretically in charge of the nation's broadcasting values, the recently ennobled Lord Rees-Mogg.)

It was a distinguished roll-call: Lord Devlin, the retired law lord; former Ulster Unionist and erstwhile Conservative MP Enoch Powell; Lord Quinton, chairman of the British Library; Dame Cicely Saunders, founder of the modern hospice movement; new TSB chairman Sir Nicholas Goodison, lately chairman of the Stock Exchange; Professor Ralf Dahrendorf, former head of the London School of Economics and now Warden of St· Antony's College, Oxford; human rights lawyer Paul Sieghart; Dame Mary Warnock, philosopher, educationist and Mistress of Girton College, Cambridge; former ICI chairman Sir John Harvey-Jones; Professor Peter Townsend of Bristol University; historian Elizabeth Longford; former Bowater chairman and Macmillan cabinet minister Lord Erroll of Hale; WH Smith chairman Sir Simon Hornby and financier/businessman Sir Sigmund Sternberg, a founder-member of the Institute of Business Ethics.

Every viewpoint differed distinctively – at least one chose to play devil's advocate and take a 'what is wrong with making money?' line, as well as severely questioning the received wisdom about social solidarity forty years ago – but a majority were disturbed about at least some current trends.

Ralf Dahrendorf, indeed, regards British society as in many ways 'more precarious today' than at any time since he came here from Germany to teach economics in 1952. Dame Cicely Saunders thinks society has become 'extremely materialistic' – but adds that if she were starting up her hospice movement today she would find no more shortage of willing helpers than in the late 1940s when she first conceived the idea.

Sir John Harvey-Jones, who now combines a number of directorships with an academic role as chancellor of Bradford University, fears that there is 'less respect for individuals for the sort of people they are and more belief that money is a sort of marker.' And he also believes that the 'value that people are now putting on material things' may be adversely affecting the way some managers run their businesses.

Dame Mary Warnock thinks 'people have always been self-seeking, but now it has become respectable.' In her high-windowed, book-lined office in Girton (now 50 per cent male students), she sees fewer of her undergraduates going into teaching and public service, 'enormous numbers into accountancy and law.' (Many will choose that route as a way into industry.)

As a comforting fire crackles in the grate on a crisp Cambridge morning, she deplores the 'disintegration' of the public service ethos and reflects that, although it is natural to aspire to better material conditions, 'we are gradually sinking back into the nineteenth-century attitude that you must always succeed at the expense of somebody else.'

Virtually all those interviewed believe that there has been a serious loss of discipline and self-discipline which needs to be restored if society is to feel happier with itself.

WH Smith chairman Sir Simon Hornby says flatly: 'The great change is that people have not been brought up as well. Both at home and in schools, discipline has deteriorated quite enormously.... The key to happiness in life is self-discipline, I am sure of that, and you cannot be self-disciplined unless you have been taught discipline.'

While most feel that changes in society were inevitable as a result of the huge social and economic revolution since 1945, Ralf Dahrendorf puts the watershed much more recently, at the start of Mrs Thatcher's second term in 1983. Dahrendorf is a committed Anglophile who feels that some of the cosy old values of the 1950s had to go if Britain were not to miss irrevocably the chance of economic regeneration. Yet he wonders if, in some areas, the price has not been too high.

'I do not think many countries have ever seen as dramatic a change in apparent prevailing values as Britain has seen in the last six years,' he says.

'The only other examples I can think of are Germany at the time of Ludwig Erhard and maybe what Gorbachev is trying to do in the Soviet Union.'

Six years ago, he recalls, he wrote that Britain had four major strengths which were also weaknesses:

'First, continuity and tradition. Second, extraordinary excellence at the frontiers which was never translated into ordinary activity; Nobel prize-winning without technology and management. Third, the existence of autonomous institutions, the balance of British civil society. Fourth, a sense of solidarity in groups, of cohesion.

'Now all four have been attacked quite significantly in the last decade. I argued at the time that these four virtues were at the same time responsible for Britain's poor economic performance, so maybe the virtues had to be destroyed, painful though that is.'

In the 1950s, he recalls, when he came to teach at LSE, 'one of the many distinctive characteristics of Britain was the sense of belonging, not necessarily to the host society but to one's group, often to one's class. This was more important than individual achievement, individul success. Indeed, you tried to hide your achievement because it was not really 'done' to be different from others. And that made life very pleasant, but not very efficient. It made life very, very agreeable and it is one of the reasons why many people, including myself, liked this country – but it is one of the reasons why Britain all but missed out on the economic miracle of the 1950s and 1960s, at least why we fell so far behind some comparable countries.'

The price paid, though, he thinks is 'very high, notably in the field of civil society.' He is worried by application of marketplace philosophy to institutions like the universities and broadcasting – 'not, to me, related directly to the main economic objective' – and by what he perceives as 'an attack on the climate of excellence.... Now I think Britain is likely to be more interested in licensing than in inventing.'

Many thinkers, including himself, were urging change in the 1970s but the astonishing thing, he says, is that no one 'had any real idea about the corner from which those changes would come. Most of the talk about changes at that time, including my own, was actually rather corporatist. It was really extrapolation, change in line with the British tradition rather than a break with it, which Mrs Thatcher has done.'

Is it, in his view, a permanent revolution? 'Clearly, you do not turn a society upside down in six years,' he replies thoughtfully. 'But at the same time I am quite sure that it is more than an episode: it is not an individual's whim, it must have responded to some frustration that was there, some desire to see something totally different.'

He sees great significance in the fact that the opposition parties are tacitly accepting – 'or not attacking' – the main economic effect of Thatcherism.

'That means you cannot go back to old values, you have to find some new synthesis.'

One recent event, however, he believes will leave its mark on history as a point when the pendulum of concern about values began to swing back. That was Nigel Lawson's tax-cutting Budget of 1988, which proportionately benefited high earners to an unprecedented degree. Many beneficiaries did not like it, he believes. 'They had a feeling it was going over the top. That Budget might well have rather an important place if we look back on this period in five years' time.'

On the wider subject of business ethics, Dahrendorf feels that 'the emphasis on extreme individualism and individual success has given an air of legitimacy to business practices which are sharp, and to breaches of ethics like gazumping.' And he adds with the sadness of a true Anglophile: 'People tell me that a gentleman's agreement no longer exists; you can shake hands and get a telex an hour and a half later saying, Sorry, it's off.'

Dahrendorf is even prepared to consider, with due caution ('the links are very complicated'), the possibility that 'there may be a connection between the changes of the last decade and the new expressions of violence', in the sense of the individualist ethic run riot.

'I would regard British society as more precarious today, in terms of political freedoms, in terms of giving people a sense of basic security from which they can operate, and in the most obvious sense of personal safety and integrity. If pushed, I would probably say that quite important things have been – if not destroyed, at any rate dented, half-broken.'

Sir Nicholas Goodison, chairman of the Stock Exchange from 1976 until last month (November), when he assumed the chairmanship of TSB, takes a robustly opposing view. He has small patience with the argument that business ethics are deteriorating – at least in the City. Nor does he think we are getting nastier as a result of getting richer, or wanting to get rich. 'I have not noticed that the Swiss are more unpleasant, or the people of Hong Kong or Germany,' he observes tartly.

(Lord Quinton seconds this view, asserting that 'the American example shows that increasing wealth does not necessarily coarsen people or make them more awful. There is a lot of crime in the US, but the actual texture of everyday life between neighbours in most of the US is more amiable than it is in this country.')

The Stock Exchange, Goodison maintains, has always had a code of strict ethical rules and it is a strength for the financial sector in general that similar rules are now being applied on a wider stage. 'You could argue that ethical standards are probably higher today than they were,' he says.

'The change in the City is in scale, not in ethical standards. Competition is intense, and competition in any normal world might lead people to cut corners. That does not mean to say that everybody cuts corners because of competition, but some will. There is a naive belief in some quarters that you can in some way abolish crookery. Well, you can't. Human society is such that there will always be some crooks, there will always be some dishonest people, there will always be some who will cut corners. But proportionally, there are no more than there have ever been.

'Although you will get isolated examples of bad, immoral or illegal behaviour in the City, it is well known throughout the world that the City of London has a code of behaviour second to none, and it is one of the reasons that the City attracts the business that it does.'

Yes, he agrees, the young are richer than when he was starting in the city in the early 1960s, but 'I don't think that is a particularly immoral thing and I don't think it leads to any worse society than existed in my youth. Ruminating for a moment on earlier periods of history when decadence undeniably ruled, he adds: 'No one is eating pies out of which blackbirds fly, or going in for absurd extravagances at their dinner parties.

'I think the fact that there are a number of well publicized cases of people blueing money in ways that the British did not blue money thirty or forty years ago is misleading. The positive side is that in the past ten years the British have been encouraged to trade in a more entrepreneurial manner than in the previous forty years, and that is good for Britain, because if you don't create the wealth, you haven't got the wealth to spend on society.

'I think the years up to the late 1970s were dreary, governments were pursuing dreary policies of equality, the effect of which was to drag everybody down to the same level. If you don't give people the incentive to pursue their natural human ambition to be slightly better and better off than others, you will end up with a grey society of the sort we see in Eastern Europe.

'I personally come down on the side that says you have to accept that some people will show off extravagant wealth in ways that you or I might consider rather unacceptable, as the price you pay for the general wellbeing of society. And to balance those rather unpleasant people, you have extremely pleasant people who give away enormous amounts of wealth to endow hospitals and colleges and major charities.

'I think Mrs Thatcher has improved society because she has made it possible for people to improve themselves.'

Lord Erroll of Hale, former chairman of Bowater and president of the board of trade 1961–63 in Harold Macmillan's Government, is another robust defender of so-called materialism. 'There is nothing wrong with trying to get money,' he maintains roundly. 'Money does make the world go round and don't let us be ashamed of it. The British have always been very money-conscious. When the rich reach a plateau of their own desires, they are rather scornful of those who are not as well off and fussing about a bargain. . . . We all want financial security.'

Erroll, who began his working life in the 1930s as an engineering apprentice following education at Oundle public school and Cambridge, says it is 'a fairytale' that society was more united during and after the war. There were strikes and political divisions and by no means all the British public wanted the war, he recalls, 'but they never got a chance to say whether they wanted to go to war or not.' As for society's present problems having a moral dimension, he snorts: 'Some people see every little upset as a symptom of Britain's moral decline. Nonsense, we are all right.'

Sir John Harvey-Jones is a good deal less sanguine about the acquisitive tendency and its effects on values. His best selling book *Making It Happen* devoted much space to the importance of developing and communicating values within companies, and he wonders: 'Are companies in the City worrying about their values when people are given an hour to clear their desks?' For all that, he believes more companies than in the 1970s are 'making a conscious effort' to think seriously about their values.

'There was a tremendous belief in the 1970s that everything was measurable, that if you just crunched the numbers out everything would happen, and of course it didn't, so there was a reaction which said, it's not just numbers, it's at least as much hearts and minds stuff. I have always been a hearts and minds man rather than a numbers man.'

Corporate values, he believes, are much more than just behaving honestly: 'if one has to take pleasure in the fact that one operates honestly, then we are in a hell of a bloody mess.' They are 'how you deal with people, the degree to which you involve them and listen to them, how you reward them, whether you believe in just throwing money at them and then getting rid of them at the drop of a hat. . . .'

What concerns him is the evidence he perceives that the higher value people are putting on material things is affecting the management of companies. 'Every businessman I know is watching his share price like a hawk,' with all the attendant pressures that puts on a company, not merely to perform to the best of its ability. 'More of us are now pretty disenchanted with the view that just performing in a company will give you a good share price. As people get more and more money tied up in their own companies, in options and so on, people actually now think of putting their companies into play in ways I have never, ever met before.'

The old belief that if you increased your profits by a sustainable 10 per cent a year you would have a good share price has proved, he says, to be 'ill-founded.' One company he knows increased its profits by 30 per cent last year, yet its price had drifted down and continues to do so, while the firm is 'doing better and better.'

'Now that situation would change instantly if there was a buzz in the City that the firm was going to be the subject of a takeover.'

Like Dahrendorf, Harvey-Jones dates a change in social ethos to around six years ago – the start of Mrs Thatcher's second term. 'It was fuelled by the ability of quite large numbers of people suddenly to acquire very, very large sums of money.'

Part of the result, he believes, has been a new tendency to judge people in material terms, by how many 'K' they earn. 'It seems to me now there are very few bastions of society which a lot of money will not breach.' On the other hand, he concedes, the old lack of admiration for possession of money may have been a bad thing in terms of social mobility.

'But I think there is less respect now for individuals in terms of the people they are, and more belief that money is a sort of marker of what sort of person you are. The fact that an awful lot of people who are money-obsessed are absolute four-letter words whom one would not cross the street for does not seem to matter any more.'

'I am not comfortable with a socially divisive Britain. As a businessman I think that anything that increases envy and divisiveness in our society makes it that much more difficult to run successful businesses.

'But I suppose the good thing that a pushy, aggressive young person who wants to can go the whole way now and get more or less whatever they want. . . .'

Dame Cicely Saunders is in a unique position to perceive both the mean streaks and vast generosity in British society. After wartime nursing service and through the experience of nursing a dying patient to whom she became very close, she conceived the idea of reviving in secular terms the old religious hospice movement. She subsequently qualified as a doctor and set up St Christopher's Hospice in Sydenham, south London, in 1967 – the first of a network now exceeding 100 around the country.

A tall, imposing but warmly humorous woman, she grows sharp when reflecting on the difficulty of getting more government funding (a third of the hospice financing comes from the NHS, two-thirds from donations).

'I think the way the Conservative philosophy comes across is to go for yourself and the devil take the hindmost, and why should it be the voluntary sector that is always picking up the hindmost?'

Yet the hospice has no shortage of willing staff, at NHS rates, and she says if she were starting out again today, 'I don't think I would have any more difficulty than when I started in getting people who were interested in this field.'

There is 'a remarkable amount of caring around,' she says, and it is wrong to think people no longer care for their elderly relatives. Only 10 per cent are in institutional care, though many live outside their families.

'I have always been an optimist,' she smiles. 'If I hadn't been, I would not have built this place. I would not have believed that it would have gone on running on faith and an overdraft twenty-one years later.'

A good deal less optimistic – indeed, profoundly pessimistic for the future – is Professor Peter Townsend, head of the sociology department at Bristol University. A lean, tired-looking man in a starkly functional office heaped with books and papers, Townsend speaks from an avowed socialist viewpoint. 'This government has been more radical than any in my lifetime, probably in the last 200 years,' he argues. 'It has been changing the structure of society very rapidly, generating a growing divide which is very serious not only for the future of social relations, but frankly for the future of productivity and production.

'I don't think it is so much that there has been a change in emphasis on individual achievement as on *what* individuals are encouraged to achieve, and crucial to this is that public service has gone out of the window. . . . The assumption is that business takes the lead in providing the caring society and there is no real appreciation of the different ways that people can serve the public.'

Townsend has first-hand experience of observing the underside of the enterprise culture. He is working on an update of the nineteenth century classic by social reformer Charles Booth – *Life Amid the Labouring Poor* – and has spent seven months living in London's Brixton and Bristol's St Paul's districts. Family and neighbourly values, he says, simply cannot withstand the intense pressures of economic struggle and pockets of high unemployment. 'In a sense,' he maintains, 'we are seeing the wheel turn full circle to the kind of desperate conditions in the inner cities that we have not experienced for 100 years.'

Townsend claims he perceives signs among some high earners of a 'kind of social schizophrenia' – even to the extent of willingness to forgo tax cuts to benefit poorer people. But he also maintains 'there are those who are contemptuous of the poor, and their numbers are very serious.'

A less pessimistic socialist view comes from Elizabeth Longford, the distinguished historian and matriarch of the Longford literary tribe.

Lady Longford speaks with the perspective of age (she is 82 but recognizably the Oxford beauty of sixty years ago described as the 'idol of Isis') and the experience of bringing up one of the most gifted families in England. There are seven surviving children headed by Lady Antonia Fraser (Catherine Pakenham, the eighth child was killed in a car crash in 1969), and at last count twenty-five grandchildren including a fresh crop of authors.

In her cosy Chelsea sitting-room, with a portable typewriter perched on a stool, the author of *Victoria RI* and *Wellington* muses on how much better life is in many ways than when she was lecturing to the Workers' Education Association before the Second World War or campaigning for Labour in the 1945 election.

'People do feel the dignity of their own nature and position as human beings much more than they did. The change came in the war, when, for all the horrors that brought, society did feel welded together by common endeavours and common suffering.' She regrets the passing of 'the principle of one-ness' in the setting up of the health service and family allowances paid to all, regardless of means, but is certain Mrs Thatcher was right to correct some of the things that 'began to go wrong' – notably in the field of organized labour. 'Certain actions of the trade unions would never have been tolerated by Attlee or Hugh Gaitskell,' she says with conviction.

She believes the pendulum of opinion has begun to swing 'very gently' against the materialist ethos. 'The intense admiration for the yuppies has begun to ebb, and it is helped by seeing these TV reports of Saturday night drunkenness.'

And she adds, emphatically: 'I don't think there is any lack of people with social consciences in this country, but they are only aroused now by a kind of freak genius like Bob Geldof. They are sheep without a shepherd.'

This could, she suggests, be more constructively tapped by government than it is. National pride can be evoked in many ways; not only in winning the Falklands War, but in helping other countries 'where there is terrible debt or disease.'

'But the last ten years seems to have established a moral that such things are nothing to do with us as a nation. If we care to contribute as individuals, that is OK.'

Nationhood, in a different context, runs like a threnody through Enoch Powell's conversation when he considers questions about social values. Now seventy-four, and out of the parliamentary arena for the first time since becoming a Conservative MP in 1950, he confesses that 'the great dis-illusionment of my adult life' has been the diminishing of Britain's historic parliamentary autonomy with accession to the Treaty of Rome in 1972.

'I would never, in 1950, have supposed that in 1972 the House of Commons would be allowed by the public to pass a bill which stripped the House of Commons of all its historical authority and powers – legislative, political, and ultimately judicial, as well as fiscal.'

In the small, spartanly furnished front study of his Belgravia home, Powell is reluctant to be drawn on personal observations of changing social values, distrusting the illusory powers of memory. But it is clear that, to this lifelong parliamentarian and historian of parliament, something of the soul of the nation disappeared in 1972.

Asked if he does see a connection between that event and the nation's idea of itself today, he ruminates: 'A nation which is prepared to give up its characteristic self-government would be prepared to give many other things up. It would be surprising if there were not some consequential change in the self-respect of a people who . . . would contemplate the bargain of giving up a self-government which historically was inseparable from who and what they were.'

'For parliament is part of what the British are, in the sense that the Assemblée Nationale is certainly not part of what the French were, and the Bundesrat is certainly not part of what the Germans are,' he continues.

Choosing his words with microscopic care, he adds: 'I don't think you can do more than say that it looks probable there may be some sort of link between a society's political character and its social behaviour. It seems *a priori* not an absurd assumption. But then if I am invited to pick out symptoms and evaluate them, I begin to remind myself that I am an old man. . . .'

Others were willing enough to identify symptoms of social behaviour that disturbed them, from random, casual violence to what Professor Peter Townsend, professor of sociology at Bristol University, calls the 'contemptuous attitude' to the poor that he detects in many well-off people. A number expressed firm belief that resumption of national service in some form – not necessarily military – would provide a salutary outlet for undisciplined energies.

Lord Devlin, the retired judge, casts a generally benevolent eye over the current troubles of society from the idyllic setting of his Georgian family home in a lush fold of Wiltshire. He puts them down to a period of 'unexpected turbulence, like in the weather. I don't think we know much more about the collective mind of people in a community than we did about the weather in the days before scientific forecasting. You just have to wait for change.

'But there is going to be a time when I think we really will have to face up to the fact that we have got to teach young people how to use their time between school and university, or find something to interest them if they are not of university standard.'

Does that mean national service? Devlin concurs, with the qualification: 'It has got to be made attractive. You can't do it by compulsion. You couldn't have something like Ernie Bevin's mine boys: that won't work in peacetime. I think you could do it in the country, but of course it is not in the country that the main problem is. You do, however, have to teach people of eighteen who are not going to university what to do with their time.'

Support for the idea of some form of national service is also voiced by Dame Mary Warnock and lawyer Paul Sieghart, one of Britain's leading experts on human rights. 'There is an argument for conscription,' says Sieghart, 'but it needs to be highly disciplined and to have some ritualized violence in it which does nobody any harm.'

Yet Sieghart is convinced that the 40-year march of British society away from one that was 'basically authoritarian, paternalistic and blinkered, to one that is much more self-determining' has been a beneficial process.

'I came to the conclusion that the kind of disorder, amorality, immorality and all the rest which we have in our society is the price you pay for a self-determined society rather than an authoritarian one – and that the price is not too high.'

Wreathed in cigarette smoke in his paper-crowded, eighteenth-century legal chambers in Gray's Inn Square, he recalls: 'Before the war, if you wanted to know the answer to a moral problem, somebody would tell you with absolute certainty what it was; your parents, or priest, or doctor, or teacher, or, indeed, your newspaper editor.... The notion that it might actually be excusable to take something from a very rich supermarket to stop your children from starving was not discussable. It simply did not exist. There was no kind of what is technically known as situational ethics, no kind of moral relativism. Things were black and white.

'My generation fought viciously against this in the second half of the 1940s – an incredibly liberated period when everything was questioned, no value was sacrosanct.

'I still think it inherently wrong and dangerous to accept the authority of anyone for any moral proposition,' he adds, citing the dreadful example of Nazism. But the corollary of self-determination, he insists, must be self-discipline – 'and unfortunately there are a great many people who can't do that and don't know how.'

Sieghart is strongly in favour of moral education being part of the curriculum, 'starting in primary schools.' It should, in his view, 'not be telling the kids what is right and wrong, but enabling them to work out for themselves what is right and wrong, how to marshal moral arguments and test them for their validity.'

Dame Mary Warnock would not agree. 'I certainly think teachers and schools as a whole have an enormous responsibility for moral education, but not as a slot in the timetable. I think it is part of the atmosphere of a good school, it is a matter of endless conversation. The good schools are doing it, the bad schools are not. It is easier for smaller schools, of course.'

Something many schools clearly are not doing, she feels, is evident from the behaviour of the City louts in their pinstripe suits. 'What has gone is the assumption that if you wear a pinstripe suit you behave properly, not like a yobbo. That assumption went all through the private schools, the grammar schools, the direct grant schools, but it has all gone.'

One theme running strongly through the discussions was the effects of postwar child-rearing on the family and its values. Lord Quinton, genially brandishing a Churchillian-sized cigar in his British Library office ˙on London's Wardour Street – in a building that once housed Ivor Novello's family music business – says Freudian influence has been 'enormous, from the top to the bottom of society. No doubt a lot of good has been achieved by the diminution of repression, but I think it seems to allow more aggression to flow outwards than it used to.'

Mischievously, he adds. 'We are a curious people. We don't like food and we don't like sensuality and we don't like children. We like animals and drink and fighting. I am not speaking personally!'

The family theme struck a decisive note with many. Lord Devlin, who at eighty-two is surrounded by a large and close-knit Catholic family, has sharp views on what he sees as the virtual destruction of the family by socialism. 'The theory of socialism ignores the family, it is the state that is important; not the state acting through the family but the state acting directly.' As examples, he cites the role of social workers going into a family, as at Cleveland, and removing children into care. 'They never seem to reflect on the price they have to exact. The cure is worse than the disease, I should say.'

Historian Elizabeth Longford fervently disagrees with the proposition that socialism attacks family values. 'Absolute nonsense. Families need help, they always have. When I was young, families were cast on the dust heap if they hadn't got money. Often it was only the daughter who was able to find work, the father was humiliated and the family broke up. People don't need to have social workers in their homes if they don't want them.'

Mary Warnock agrees with Quinton that the 'non-authoritarian idea of bringing up children probably had a considerable effect. But I don't think we could go back to having a kind of close-knit, authoritarian family, and personally I would be deeply against it if we did, because of the position of women in such families. The whole family ethos depended crucially on the woman being at home, and I really think that we have gone beyond that.'

So to the $64,000 question: do we have to accept that a price we may not like has to be paid for the economic and social freeing-up of the last forty years? Or can we regain some of the old values while keeping the best of the new? Can we, in short, put the genie of unpleasantness – new–rich vulgarity, the 'I want it now' ethos, the new brutalism of some sections of society, and the rest – back in the bottle?

Philosopher and sage Lord Quinton speaks for many when he says it certainly cannot be done by some sort of government campaign for the moral improvement of society. 'If anything is going to be done, it will be done by discussion, by communication of thoughts and by a mild change in the direction of public opinion about things like child-rearing and what you expect from education.

'There clearly is not any necessary connection between being better off and being coarser or more violent or more unpleasant. There are a lot of very unpleasant poor countries.'

# 24

# In search of social excellence

April 1989

## Carol Kennedy

The office of the Chief Rabbi, spiritual leader of British and Common-wealth Jews for the last twenty-two years, is austere in the extreme, a forbidding maze of concrete corridors and bare staircases, housed in a shabbily anonymous building in London's Bloomsbury.

But Lord Jakobovits – the only rabbi ever to have been honoured with a peerage – is a far from austere figure. A large, impressive man with the face of an Old Testament prophet and a rich, rolling voice, he has a warmth, humour and almost theatrical charisma about him that enlist admirers far beyond the limits of his own congregations.

Not least among those admirers is Prime Minister Margaret Thatcher, who bestowed the unprecedented peerage last year (following an equally unique knighthood in 1981) as a personal award to the man rather than the office. Thatcher is known to respect the trenchantly expressed views of Immanuel Jakobovits on social and individual values.

Those views are among the most conservative – unpolitically speaking – and forceful of any religious leader in Britain. Yet Jakobovits does not subscribe to the fashionable notion of 'Victorian values', once indelibly endorsed by Thatcher in a TV interview with Brian Walden.

'I hate the expression "return to Victorian values",' says Jakobovits with feeling. 'The values were not all that high in Victorian times. The values I speak of are not 100 years old, but 2000 or 3000 years old. They have stood the test of time, and I think we have to rediscover them and apply them to *our* time.'

Such values, Jakobovits explains, have to do with setting social and individual objectives that go beyond material betterment. Ernest Bevin once lamented the poverty of the British people's aspirations; Jakobovits believes we are not ambitious enough in a wider sense.

'The visions are far too low,' he argues. We ought to say that our society will be a better society – not merely when the economic order is stable or when the standard of living has improved or the trade gap has been filled. It is not as simplistic or as materialistic as that to find the keys to a better society, a more resilient society – possibly, even, a more enterprising society.

'Every person should feel that he or she is called upon to make a mark in the world, to make a difference to the world.'

Jakobovits, now sixty-eight and with just two more years to serve as Chief Rabbi, believes that not enough is done to search out and publicly recognize examples of excellence in British life. He was a moving spirit behind the foundation of the Institute for Business Ethics, which is backed by all the major religious leaders, but he would like to take the concept further.

'Just as we give Queen's Awards to firms that excel in exports, so we should give awards to firms that excel in business ethics; that treat their employees in an exemplary way; that care more for the customer than the profits. If a firm has established a norm to which business ethics ought to be held up, give a Queen's Award for that,' he exclaims, embracing the air in a characteristically expansive gesture.

'We ought to highlight in the media and in public recognition excellence in virtue, just as much as excellence in economic endeavour and success. It can be done; after all, we have awards for bravery.

'You can go to any school class and find youngsters who excel in caring for others; doing voluntary work, or joining a choir to entertain in old people's homes. There is some wonderful work being done, but we do not highlight it enough.'

When we spoke, Jakobovits had not long returned from the traumatic task of helping to comfort the townspeople of Lockerbie and those who lost relatives and friends in the Pan Am air disaster. In the town he had heard of a supermarket owner who gave the keys of his shop (closed for a public holiday) to volunteer workers with the rescue services, telling them to take all the supplies they needed and return the keys when they had finished.

'There is still an enormous fund of nobility left in everyone's heart. But do we have to go through tragedies to bring this out?' he asks, raising his hands.

Jakobovits, as a German-born Jew who came to Britain as a sixteen-year-old refugee from the Nazis, has seen enough of real brutality and decadence to view any lesser ills in society with equanimity.

He is, however, severely condemnatory of the permissive revolution of the 1960s, which he believes is now passing into history.

'It was a pernicious philosophy; that as long as you have a good time and enjoy yourself that is all that matters,' he growls. 'It was not only amoral, but immoral. And it led to incalculable misery, because people discovered that if all you pursue is happiness, it will elude you. A sense of disillusionment set in, which led, in part, to the drug culture.

'People sought escapism from a world that had betrayed them; marriages became subverted and exploded with incalculable consequences for the stability of society. Children are often now brought up in a no-man's-land, perhaps with no identifiable father or mother, no love in the home. Obviously they become misfits in society. We pay an enormous price for having allowed this erosion of the family.'

Jewish life has not been immune from the infection, Jakobovits says. 'If we take it that every third marriage today breaks down, with us it would be every eighth marriage, which is bad enough. These were unheard-of statistics in Jewish life. The breakup of the family threatens us just as much as it does society in general, and we have to be on our guard. The shoring up of family bonds is one of my major targets in my inter-community relations.'

In other respects, however, Judaism has kept the onslaught of modern secular values at bay better than some Christian churches. The Chief Rabbi talks of 'an enormous upsurge' in synagogue attendance among young people, directly attributable to the intensification of Jewish religious education, which in turn was fed by the move towards larger families to replace the tragic population loss of the Second World War.

'We now have proportionately twice as many children of our community attending Jewish day schools than we did twenty years ago,' says Jakobovits. 'We have an enormously growing minority who are far more committed, more knowledgeable and more observant than their parents and grandparents ever were.'

Central to the Jakobovits philosophy, and deeply rooted in Hebrew tradition, is the conviction that modern society suffers from an emphasis on rights rather than duties. He cites the difference beween the US Bill of Rights and the Jewish concept, where 'there are no rights whatever. There are no rights mentioned in the Bible; it only has the Ten Commandments – duties, obligations, do's and dont's.'

Loss of certain 'family virtues' and 'what one might call neighbourhood morality,' with individuals caring for each other on a local basis, would be on the debit side of any postwar social balance sheet, believes Jakobovits. But high on the credit side, he stresses, is the willingness of people now to care about the sufferings of humanity in obscure corners of the world and to raise millions to relieve famine in Ethiopia or the Sudan.

'That is a new feature in the brotherhood of man,' says the Chief Rabbi emphatically. 'Nobody ever cared on that scale before for people who were out of sight. And the media have helped in this, for all the blame we may attach to them in other areas.

'The very concept of the Third World, that we should care for other nations with loans, credits and so on for their self-sufficiency, is a new idea. That is an enormous advance that is not sufficiently credited.'

Inescapably, Jakobovits is drawn to compare today's international awareness and co-operation with the outside world's reaction to the onset of the Holocaust in Nazi Germany fifty years ago.

'We lost one-third of our people, and the world stood by idly and in silence, wrung its hands and allowed it to happen,' Jakobovits says with quiet intensity. 'This would be inconceivable today, that brutality should take place on such a scale while the world stands by and does not protest.

'We no longer allow governments to get away with wickedness on a national scale without an attempt to arouse public opinion and use international pressure to put it right.'

Related to this is the 'revolution' in Christian-Jewish relations, started by the man whom Jakobovits calls 'the saintly Pope John XXIII.' The Vatican Council instigated by Pope John resulted in new guidelines being issued to Roman Catholics and revisions of the liturgy to help rapprochement between Catholics and Jews. Protestant churches have followed.

'For many centuries we were at the receiving end of a great deal of bitterness and hatred, rejection and persecution, and are now not only on speaking terms but on very friendly terms and co-operate at many levels,' says Jakobovits, who enjoys a warm personal friendship with the Archbishop of Canterbury, Most Reverend Robert Runcie, and Cardinal Basil Hume, Roman Catholic Archbishop of Westminster.

A measure of his own sensitivity to ecumenical relations is that, when he was told of the proposed peerage – controversial to some in the Orthodox Jewish community – he worried that it might appear to intrude on the constitutional place of Anglican prelates in the Upper House. He was touched when the archbishops of Canterbury and York left a Synod meeting in order to give him support on his formal induction into the Lords.

Jakobovits is anxious not to be perceived as 'an alternative moral voice' to the bench of bishops. 'I want to strengthen them rather than challenge them,' he says.

But he pulls no punches when he does speak. He has attended the Lords about nine times and spoken in five debates, taking a somewhat tougher line than the government on the matter of banning Sinn Fein and other members of proscribed organizations from the airwaves. Jakobovits believes that anyone should be banned who utters anything remotely advocating or justifying violence, particularly against innocent civilians.

'I would like to extend the ban to voices of sedition that advocate violence in breach of the law,' he states unequivocally. 'Not only the speaker but the media also should be covered by criminal legislation to ensure that nothing ever encourages or excuses terrorism.'

On the wider moral battlefield, moves towards bringing some kind of moral education into the national curriculum are welcome in his view, though he questions how soon or how far it will become practicable. 'Values, commitments and attitudes take a long time to shape and cannot be taught in the same way that you teach a language or a science,' he says.

Apart from his views on 'the voices of sedition,' the Chief Rabbi clearly feels television must take some of the blame for society's growing indifference to the rise in violent crime on the streets of Britain. 'The cheapening of life' is a phrase he uses often, and he believes this is an inescapable consequence of the 'surfeit of violence being fed into the means of communication.'

'By highlighting violence, television creates a certain immunity to the horror of crime,' Jakobovits believes.

He was appalled once to hear a police chief on radio say: 'We'll have to learn to live with crime.'

'That is a counsel of despair,' he insists. 'We have to learn the opposite, *not* to live with crime. We all have a part to play here; we must not accept it. People talk of deterrents and punishment as if these two were the only defences against crime, and that we ought to increase them. I think the main thing is that we should train people to have values, not to think of crime as a possible option. Then you do not need deterrents and you do not need punishment.'

The increase in casual violence is not the only social ill for which Jakobovits would bring TV to book, at least in part. He sees it as part of the general 'dehumanizing' and 'mechanization' of life over the last forty years, in which individuals simply have less physical and verbal contact with one another and 'social graces' have suffered. Conversation with the corner shopkeeper has given way to the solitary loading of a supermarket trolley; fixation on TV programmes is 'in tremendous competition with family bonds.'

Jakobovits would like to see fewer rather than more hours of TV, to encourage children to read, converse and think and to strengthen family relationships. For these 'educational' reasons, none of the huge Jakobovits family – six children, one of them a rabbi, and at latest count thirty-three grandchildren – have a television set in their homes. 'If they want to see something, they have to come to the grandparents!' chuckles Jakobovits. Then, more seriously, he adds: 'It needs an enormous amount of self-discipline to swim against the stream, to live this kind of self-controlled life. But it *can* be done; it *is* being done.'

The acceleration of life caused by the communications revolution and the demand for 'instant answers,' in Jakobovits' view, place additional burdens of decision making on individuals. He once told the prime minister: 'We are expected to make ever more fateful decisions in ever less time. And the result is that many of the decisions are bound to be wrong.'

But surely the speed of late-twentieth century life cannot be put into reverse? Jakobovits argues that its effects could be mitigated 'if we were bold enough and resolute enough.' On a business trip, for example, 'you cannot slow a jet plane down, but what you can do is not to go into your conference or meeting straight away; keep one day open and do a bit of reading.

'We save an enormous amount of time with all our gadgets, but what do we do with the saved time? The more life speeds up, the less time we have for life itself.

'That, I think, is the great challenge: how do we arrange our lives to have more leisure for the things that really matter – to cultivate friendships, the arts, sciences, literature; broaden our interests, or do more learning and study, develop our tastes?'

In two years the Chief Rabbi will himself be released from his own 'enormous time pressures,' though he appears to thrive on the challenges of managing his widespread flock, along with a weighty agenda of writing and lecturing.

Besides 200-odd congregations in Britain (not all of them strictly under his formal jurisdiction) he has pastoral duties in Australia and New Zealand and is president of the Conference of European Rabbis.

The arcane processes are already beginning that will, in due course, elect his successor as Chief Rabbi. Those who work with him – and many outside his faith – are in no doubt that Baron Jakobovits of Regent's Park in Greater London will be an exceedingly hard act to follow.

# 25

# Can Britain achieve a moral consensus?

September 1989

## Carol Kennedy

Meeting Cardinal Basil Hume for the first time is something of an eye-opener.

The Archbishop of Westminster, Britain's leading Roman Catholic prelate, often appears in photographs as a slight, even frail figure with the ascetic, other-worldly look of a medieval monk. He does have a monastic background, having been Abbot of Ampleforth, the Benedictine monastery responsible for the famous Catholic public school, before Pope Paul VI chose him as successor to the late Cardinal Heenan in 1976. But there is nothing frail, ascetic or other-worldly about the tall, powerfully built man in clerical black suit – no scarlet-trimmed robe or cardinal's red cap on this occasion – who steers you with a strong handshake into the sitting-room of Archbishop's House behind Westminster Cathedral.

Only a slight stiffness in the walk, the result of a hip operation, betrays the wear of his sixty-six years, thirty-nine of them spent in the service of the church as priest, theology teacher, monk and cardinal. In his youth, he was formidable on the rugby field. The eyes are blue and shrewd, and there are frequent ripples of laughter, often at his own expense.

In conversation, he will switch from talking almost lyrically about the church to acerbic observations on the status of teachers and the tangled historical mess of Northern Ireland – which among many other comments he observes tartly is 'not a good advertisement for religion.'

Hume has periodic encounters with the world of business and finance, giving talks to the Stock Exchange, leading companies and gatherings of businessmen. They are memorable occasions, according to one Catholic director who has attended several. 'He stands up in front of these bankers and businessmen and talks about God,' he says wonderingly. Hume says of these meetings that he is constantly struck by 'something deep in people making them feel they need something to give them a real sense of the ultimate purpose in life.

'People may be doing a very secular job in a very secular society, but it does not follow that everything in their makeup is secular,' he says. Hume sees the late 1980s as a period of great contradictions, with heavy materialistic pressures on individuals, set against examples of self-denial and even heroism in everyday life. He finds young people now more interested in religious belief, and more prepared to discuss the issues, than in the 1950s and 1960s, when 'I couldn't talk to them at all,' he recalls with a touch of sadness.

Then, brightening, he adds: 'I am beginning to think that the 1980s could turn out to be quite full of hope and promise after all.'

Sometimes, he finds, a family crisis will act as a catalyst, pulling an individual sharply back to deeper things than getting and spending. A businessman whose wife developed cancer admitted to the Cardinal that he had shocked himself by realizing his business preoccupations were more important to him than his wife's illness or his daughter's education.

Hume is seen as very different from his predecessor, the impulsive, outspoken former archbishop of Liverpool, Cardinal John Heenan. Where Heenan had a populist touch but could not get on with the Catholic intelligentsia, Hume is an academic and thinker, much respected by Catholic opinion-formers. Heenan was conservative by temperament, though he identified strongly with the poor and saw himself as a people's priest: Hume, for all his establishment family background, has 'quite a radical edge,' says one leading lay Catholic.

The son of a distinguished physician, Sir William Hume, and a French mother, Hume speaks French fluently and sometimes converses in that language with Pope John Paul II. In 'business' terms, Hume is regarded as a better organizer and delegator than Heenan; altogether a more 'laid back' personality. His relationship with the Catholic bishops and archbishops of England and Wales is more of a partnership than a hierarchy, though he presides over their conferences and his influence in practice runs much wider than the diocese of Westminster.

A deeply reflective man – Benedictines have a gentler, more contemplative tradition than the worldly, cerebral Jesuits – Hume's published works have tackled some of the problems of leading a spiritual life amid secular pressures. But he would be reluctant to condemn current British society for lack of moral values. 'I tend to think that no age is more virtuous, or less virtuous, than any other. I think fallen man is a constant throughout history,' he observes.

On one aspect of current morality, however, he has emphatic views.

'One of our problems is that we have no real moral consensus. I think a lot of people basically agree on certain things – that we should be decent to one another, must not be cruel to one another – but on certain important issues a consensus is not so clear.' Such issues he defines as those of 'life,' among

them abortion, euthanasia, protecting the environment, and those of 'love' –
preparation for marriage, stability of marital bonds, homelessness.

'To talk of life and love issues may sound wishy-washy, but when you
come to think of it they are the two things fundamental to everyone,' he
continues. 'Unless you protect life and protect love, I think society is in a
very poor way.

'One of the very bad things about the permissiveness of the 1960s was the
sexual revolution, which I don't think did anyone any good.'

How to achieve a moral consensus in current British society is obviously a
task of enormous difficulty. Hume believes it can only begin to progress
through discussion among people in all walks of life and differing faiths. He
has been involved in such discussions with trade union leaders, among
others.

'You don't come to any conclusion, but you heighten people's awareness
that there is something important here, and people talk to each other, and
once that happens, you begin to discover where the consensus might be. It
is going to be a long process,' he comments.

Does he think Kenneth Baker's proposals for including moral education
in a national curriculum would help?

'Obviously schools have a role to play,' Hume replies, then, with growing
emphasis, he adds: 'But the urgent thing in education today is not theories
of education but the value you give to teachers.

'One of the most important things we need to do in our society is to restore
the morale of the teaching profession,' he insists. 'Its status has got to be
recognized. It is lower in this country than it used to be.'

Many parents would doubtless argue that teachers themselves were more
than a little to blame for that situation, all the way from the anarchic
'child-centred' theories of the 1960s to the readiness of large sections of the
profession to walk out on strike like any industrial worker. But Hume is not
deflected. The role of the teacher is a vital key, he argues.

'The teacher has such a tremendous power. The kind of philosophy of life
a teacher has will communicate itself willy-nilly – sometimes more in
off-the-record remarks and attitudes than in what you say in the classroom.'

The multi-culturalism of modern society presents special difficulties in
reaching any kind of moral consensus, Hume agrees.

'As far as I am concerned, morality has to flow from religious belief, and
the morality of the Commandments is given, and unchanging. So I don't
think morality can stand on its own. It won't happen tomorrow, but I think
long, long-term that our inter-faith dialogue – as opposed to our ecumenical
dialogue among Christians – will have to prepare for our ultimate moral
consensus.

'We have still scarcely begun to have contact of minds with other re-
ligions. The most remarkable thing in my time here has been our growing

relationships with the Jewish community. This is very, very important. When I sit down with the Chief Rabbi, we often find we are talking the same language about issues. After all, Christianity and Judaism are more than cousins, so some consensus is already there, and the inter-faith dialogue is growing in this area, largely through people like the Council for Christians and Jews. But I believe it also has to grow with the Hindu community and the Islamic community. That is beginning to happen, slowly.

'Once one begins to appreciate how other people think and what determines their faith, then through that inter-faith dialogue we ought to be able to see not only where we differ, but also where we agree.'

Yet how much real influence can a church leader hope to exert on social values, or on the search for a moral consensus, in these days of declining congregations and widespread indifference to authority?

Hume admits his main preoccupation is to find ways in which the church can contact 'those thousands of people who have never in their lives been touched by the church.' He believes the solution may lie in greater use of TV and radio.

'Christian values cannot just be communicated by the churches. I think the only way to communicate them more widely is through the media. I spent eight minutes on breakfast television on Good Friday, speaking to some three million people. Then on Easter Sunday night I was on "*Songs of Praise*," watched by twelve million people. My Good Friday broadcast brought me within two days a letter from a man in the north of England. He told me: "I have been lapsed for years, and the moment you stopped speaking I rang up my local priest, and now I am back in church." That was the most marvellous thing.

'So I think we can still touch people when we get the opportunity through TV and radio to actually speak to their hearts and minds.'

Like all church leaders, Hume is continually being called on to make public statements on social or political issues, or matters of human rights. From time to time he will do so, but from long experience he has learned that 'personal contact with a minister is the most effective way of making a point, and often a better way than putting public figures on the spot in public.'

One recent issue on which Hume quietly tackled a minister behind the scenes was the effect that cutting back social security benefits was having on homeless sixteen and seventeen-year-olds unable to get either a job or a place in a Youth Training Scheme because of their lack of abode. The government had argued that young people often bring hardship on themselves by leaving home, but the new rules were bearing harshly on those who had been forced to leave their parents for good reason. Hume discussed the human problems with Nicholas Scott, the minister responsible, who proved 'sympathetic and understanding, and did what he could,' says the cardinal.

Last February, Hume wrote to Margaret Thatcher protesting at a bill then going through the South African parliament which aimed at restricting the ability of organizations, including churches, to distribute funds sent to them for the welfare of black people. An earlier bill had been dumped after international protests, only to be replaced by a remodelled version.

Thatcher's reply assured Hume that such legislation was of an 'unacceptable nature' and that diplomatic pressure from Britain would continue to be exerted.

'I wouldn't like to overstate the kind of influence there is nationwide from this house,' says Hume. 'Our contributions are modest, but sometimes effective,' he adds with a quiet chuckle.

Hume's highest-profile public intervention in recent years – apart from contesting the terms of Kenneth Baker's Education Reform Act over Catholic schools opting out of local authority control – was to lead a campaign for re-examination of the trial evidence on which the so-called 'Guildford Four' were sentenced to life imprisonment for a pub bombing in Guildford in 1974. He had become seriously concerned about a possible miscarriage of justice after meeting a man convicted on a related charge of bomb-manufacturing. Together with two former home secretaries (Merlyn Rees and Lord Jenkins) and two lords of appeal (Devlin and Scarman), he asked home secretary Douglas Hurd to have the case reopened.

Hurd eventually announced last January that the case would be re-examined by the Court of Appeal, singling out Hume's role in his statement to the Commons.

Any talk of church leaders influencing events, especially Protestant and Catholic leaders in these islands, cannot avoid confronting the dread subject of Northern Ireland and the seemingly insoluble conflict in which two professing Christian communities are locked there. How is the church, on either side of the sectarian divide, to meet this overwhelming challenge?

Hume picks his words carefully, prefacing them with the caution that 'one can never talk about Northern Ireland without upsetting somebody.

'The difficulty in Northern Ireland, which is a complete tragedy, is that it is always seen as somebody else's problem, somebody else's responsibility. There is too much "they", not enough "we",' he says sharply. Then, warming to a deeply felt theme, he quotes Cardinal Newman: 'The trouble with the English is that they can never remember history; the trouble with the Irish is that they can never forget it.'

'I think we are very insensitive as English people to exactly what we did to Ireland, historically, with the plantations and Cromwell – and I think we need to acknowledge that. To think it is just a religious squabble is not to have understood Northern Ireland.

'I sometimes feel,' he adds crisply, 'that if this were happening in Cornwall or Devon, we might well have resolved it by now.

'It is not a great advertisement for religion. But one of the aims of religion is to make saints – and to make saints out of sinners, so the raw material of the church is always going to come from the fallen people.

'One of my fundamental beliefs is that the church as an institution is an earthenware vessel scarcely able to carry the wonderful and holy and sacred things which are entrusted to it. The institutional church we see and talk about never is the ideal we would like it to be; never has been and never will be. The trouble is that public perception of the church is just that earthenware vessel: one has to look beyond to the mysteries and sacred realities it is trying to contain.

'The church is peopled not by saints but by sinners trying to be saints, and an historical church is always going to get tangled up with other issues. Religious controversy on the battlefield is not a pretty advertisement for the church, but it is reality, it has happened, and you cannot defend it.'

Hume has been to Northern Ireland twice during his tenure as Archbishop of Westminster. 'My impression is that it is the extremists on both sides who make the news, but there is a very large community there that is tired of all the violence and trying hard to live together,' he observes.

'But remember, it was comparatively recently that the Catholic community felt much discriminated against. As a minority it had to suffer adverse conditions, economically, politically and in employment. Catholics had a grouse we should have heeded years ago in this country.'

'Obviously, there is a whole Catholic community there whose sympathies are more with the Republic than with us,' continues Hume. 'They have the same faith, the same background, the same culture. After all, geographically that is where they belong. But we can never defend violence under any circumstances,' he concludes sharply.

The conversation moves on to falling church attendances – in 1967 half the registered Catholics of England and Wales went regularly to Sunday mass: by 1987 the Catholic population was broadly the same, but churchgoing had dropped to about a third. Was there any evidence that abandoning the Latin rite for the vernacular version initiated by the Second Vatican Council of 1963 had turned people away?

'It is very difficult to judge,' Hume remarks. 'There are those who say they ceased going to Mass once the Latin Mass ceased; others who tell you they keep going because it has changed.

'I think great changes occurred in the church before Vatican II. In fact, I believe the world changed in 1961. At that time I was teaching theology in a monastery, and a group came into my theology class who could not accept the kind of things I was teaching. This group had all been to universities at the end of the 1950s and it seems to have started then: I think the origins were in the war.'

This new mood among his theological students – hard, questioning, sceptical – had troubled Hume enormously. 'I went to the Abbot and said I could not teach any further. He said I must go back and do it – that is the way things happen in monasteries!' Hume laughs his deep, amused chuckle. 'I was released two years later, when I became Abbot myself in 1963.'

His face grows serious again as he contemplates the 'obstacles' that have slowed the once accelerating momentum of the ecumenical movement – paramount among them, the issue of ordaining women.

'Dialogues go on between different denominations, and have to go on, but we keep on creating problems, and one has to say quite clearly that the ordination of women to the priesthood by a part of the Anglican communion has complicated matters enormously,' Hume says with deliberation. 'Paul VI writing to Archbishop Coggan, and now this Pope writing to Archbishop Runcie, have both said that the ordination of women constitutes a very great obstacle to church union.

'Now, we have to leave it at that. But the dialogues have to continue, the prayer and the effort for Christian unity have to continue. Ours is to work and pray, and whatever is achieved will be done in the Lord's time. But we've got to stop putting obstacles in the way.'

# 26

# The archbishop and the wealth ethic

October 1989

## Carol Kennedy

'I believe of course in wealth creation – that is necessary if we are going to do all the things that we ought to be doing for our society in our privileged position in the world. It enables us also to give leadership in other parts of the world for good causes. But there is no *automatic* connection between wealth creation and a happy society.'

Late summer sun is spilling into a quiet panelled room in Lambeth Palace and Robert Alexander Kennedy Runcie, 102nd Archbishop of Canterbury in the line begun by St Augustine in the sixth century, is speaking softly but with measured conviction about the stresses that a headlong pursuit of economic success can inflict on people, whether as individuals or as a community.

He sees a risk of the successful becoming like the Pharisees, self-righteous and 'judgemental' in their attitudes to the unsuccessful. The 'obsession' of many young people with making money quickly leaves him uneasy, along with the fear that a generation of hard-edged achievers may prove less sympathetic than present business leaders to what he calls 'the left-behinds, the casualties of success.'

'I resist the idea,' Runcie says with feeling, 'that the only driving dynamic of society is self-interest.' At a later stage in the conversation he speaks of the strain on community structures when 'we put our competitive demands before the needs of others.'

It does not show in his relaxed and attentive demeanour, but Runcie has been under considerable strain himself this day, with headlines and radio reports blaring the rumour – fortunately unfounded – that his kidnapped envoy, Terry Waite, has been put to death in the Lebanon following the hanging of US kidnap victim Colonel William Higgins. The unsubstantiated reports anger him for the distress to Waite's family, whom he has telephoned reassuringly, but there is always an element of fearful uncertainty; one more twist to the stabbing anxiety he has lived with since Waite was abducted in January 1987. He prays for him every day in his private chapel where a candle burns in perpetuity.

Runcie's decade in Lambeth Palace has been marked by stresses unknown to his immediate predecessors. Controversies have crowded in on him; some personally wounding, like the attack on his leadership in *Crockford's* by Canon Gareth Bennett, who subsequently committed suicide; others threatening the very fabric of Anglican unity, such as the rows over women priests.

There have been political rumblings too, and even murmurs of disestablishment. Runcie has been in office almost as long as the woman who recommended his appointment has been in 10 Downing Street, but it is popularly supposed that Margaret Thatcher and Runcie's Church of England are now frostily divorced on many issues.

He was much criticized by right-wingers after the Falklands war for calling for compassion towards Argentine losses, and the maverick Bishop David Jenkins of Durham – another Thatcher-era appointee – enraged government ministers by using the word 'wicked' about the results of some social policies.

Runcie is tough enough, however, to shrug such attacks off his broad shoulders. Even his sharpest critics credit him with resilience and consummate diplomacy. Where the future of Anglicanism is concerned, one of the younger bishops believes that Runcie will be seen as having saved the Church of England from 'falling over the cliff' of disestablishment.

A tall man of soldierly bearing – he had a gallant war in the Scots Guards, winning the Military Cross for a tank action in the Netherlands in early 1945 – Runcie's private personality has a robust warmth and directness that sometimes gets lost under his archbishop's robes. At sixty-eight (this month), his hair is still tinged with Celtic red – his family roots are in Ayrshire – and the blue eyes can turn disconcertingly penetrating. Off duty, he relaxes by swimming in the sea off Kent and by reading novels and Mediterranean history, on which he is a noted scholar: as Bishop of St Albans, he spent holidays lecturing with stirring eloquence on classical sites visited by Swan-Hellenic cruise liners, and in his 'geriatric years,' he laughs, hopes to return to them.

He has learned to be wary of tabloid headlines suggesting church and government are in perpetual disagreement, but he does not deny that there are differences with the Thatcher administration's view of society. This is partly the result, he suggests, of the political polarization that has taken place in Britain between the largely Conservative, prosperous centre and south and the poorer areas in the north and in Wales, where government support is low.

'This is a major change in the last generation,' he says. 'By contrast, the Church of England maintains its presence and ministry in every parish in the land. It continues to be in daily contact with those areas in which the Conservative Party has little support. This makes the Church sensitive to the needs of those areas and that section of the population which has not benefited from the last ten years of Conservative government.

'The tensions which you speak of between Church and government are never as evident to me as they seem to be to the popular press. Relationships between Lambeth Palace and government departments are friendly and co-operative. My own meetings with Mrs Thatcher and her ministers do not betray the sort of suspicion which is often spoken of.

'Of course there are some differences between us. The present government supports a view of society in which an individual's rights and duties are enhanced. That is part of the Christian ethic, but the Church always balances this with its understanding of Christians belonging to one another and making up the body of Christ. That gives us a corporate dimension to our faith and ethics, which is bound sometimes to be at variance with a highly individualistic approach.

'We *are* individuals but together we go to make up a community – whether it be a family, town or church – and it is when we put our competitive demands before the needs of others that the structures of community life break up. The Church puts much of its energies and resources into building community life. It does so in its life of worship but also in its service, social and practical, to parishes, institutions and organizations throughout the country.'

On some aspects of current individualistic mores, Runcie speaks out with unmistakable concern. This is where he senses the danger of Pharisee attitudes towards the unsuccessful.

'One of the challenges sometimes presented to the churches – and particularly to the Church of England – comes from the section of our political and commercial leadership which says, "We have made the people wealthy; it is the Church's job to make them good." That is *not* the Church's view of its task. It wants to make people godly. Godliness and goodness are not the same thing.

'Jesus reserved his most astringent criticism for the Pharisees. We tend to think that the Pharisees were unscrupulous, double-dealing, untrustworthy. That was not the case. Most of them led lives of exemplary moral rectitude. That did not cause them to escape the sharp edge of Jesus' tongue. He disliked their self-righteousness and their judgemental attitudes.

'Those are the real dangers in our society today. I sense that they are both increasing. The successful are always tempted to regard their success as a sort of blessing or reward for righteousness. This can lead to judgements being made about the unsuccessful, the unemployed, the poor and the unintelligent which are both uncharitable and untrue.

'I am thinking of the sort of attitude that suggests that the unemployed do too little to help themselves, that if only you have determination and drive you can get on in the world. Those attitudes lead people to be dismissive of the value of their fellow human beings. Those attitudes reduce human dignity. Those attitudes harden our hearts. They create barriers between us and God.'

Runcie is not criticizing the desire for business success, he emphasizes. 'If you go into business you must aim for success, but success in business doesn't necessarily prove that you have made a success of life,' he observes. It is at this point that he makes his comment about believing in wealth creation, but not as a goal to be achieved before any other goals can be considered. 'There is no *automatic* connection between wealth creation and a happy society.'

He readily acknowledges that in his time as Archbishop of Canterbury Britain's economic performance has 'not only created greater prosperity in the country as a whole but has also given people in other parts of the world more confidence in our country as a place for investment.

'Now, along with this I would like to see more awareness that we are using this greater wealth more responsibly to deal with the left-behinds, to deal with the casualties of success, to deal with issues that cannot simply be left to the wealth trickling down – issues like housing, homelessness and the mentally handicapped.'

Plainly, in Runcie's view, it is not enough simply to enable more people to get rich and then rely on private largesse to help plug the holes in society. And he credits many of his contemporaries in the City and the business world with this understanding.

'A number of them do believe that we have a responsibility to the left-behinds in our society, not a simple responsibility of patronage,' he says. 'But I just wonder whether, with the pressures and the push that are being demanded of the younger generation coming up – the man who is on top salary at thirty – they are going to have these sentiments.'

The Church Urban Fund, born out of the famous report *Faith in the City* (Runcie recalls 'it was not greeted with much enthusiasm by some government ministers, but it did have its effect – not long afterwards, the government put inner cities towards the top of its agenda'), has been powerfully supported by the likes of BP's Sir Peter Walters and United Biscuits' Sir Hector Laing.

'It has not been difficult for me to talk to such people about business ethics, moral leadership, the need for a world vision,' says the archbishop. But he is concerned that tomorrow's business leadership – today's high-pressured yuppies – may feel less committed to community help.

'I hope I am wrong,' he adds fervently. But he does feel that the ties that existed between an older generation of achievers and the church have been weakened.

'The Church's strength is not so much in the Archbishop of Canterbury

in Lambeth Palace, but in the parishes of England,' he ruminates. 'Someone once said of the Church that its centre is in the circumference. Many of
the people I know who are in positions of significance in the country have
done their stint as churchwardens in their parishes, and the weakening of
those ties between Church and business success is something I watch
carefully.'

Runcie speaks often of the 'pressures' affecting today's young achievers,
pressures to perform that sometimes lead to corner-cutting and rule-bend-
ing, as seems evident in the unhappy saga of County Natwest and Blue
Arrow. (His own son and daughter are in media businesses, respectively a
BBC producer and PR executive.) Does he feel there is an unhealthy
amount talked about money in the upwardly mobile, credit-burdened
Britain of 1989?

'There is much more obsession with incomes and targets and promotion
prospects and how soon you can get your mortgage after you leave university, and what you will be "on" after five years as a graduate,' he remarks.
'But I have to put alongside that the enormous proliferation of voluntary
groups and activities which have released an amazing amount of altruism.
So I am rather chary of grandiose solutions or grandiose judgements. I
think we have to create conditions in our society in which people can grow in
reverence and respect and good aspirations.'

And what of society as it is? Are we in danger of becoming uncaring about
those who can't keep up?

'Sometimes people looking in on us from outside think we project an
uncaring image,' Runcie replies. 'There is a lot of mockery of the language
of compassion and caring, and it is implied that what we need is less talk
about a caring society and more efficiency in public spending and freedom
in creating the money to do the good works. There is a belief that if we
talked a little less about caring and more about efficiency, more people
would be benefited.

'Now, I am aware of this and try to pay attention to it. I was at an
international gathering the other day and I said I can't put my signature to
this document because it is all about the creation of a caring and compas-
sionate community and in the first three paragraphs the word "concern"
occurs four times. I said people in my country regard that as typical of the
jargon of the woolly do-gooder. Two people at the table looked at each other
and one, a Canadian, said rather bravely: "Yes, and that is why some of us
are worried about your society".

'I can see both sides of the argument, but I think perhaps we have to learn
a new vocabulary that will better balance the undoubted need for efficiency
in the running of the economy and the creation of wealth with that
traditional valuing of each other which has been the best in our past.'

When addressing private gatherings, Runcie sometimes quotes US

President George Bush's declared aim of a 'gentler, kinder America.' Does he feel the success ethic is inevitably at odds with such a goal in Britain?

'Experience has taught me,' he replies, 'that everyone needs to be needed. If a company does not feel deeply that it is performing a service, or if directors and others have no outlet for suppressed altruism, morale will suffer.

'These are days when the simple dictates of profit and self-interest are recognized as the dynamics of industrial success – but to regard these as the sole dynamics of society or an organization is fatal.

'I resist the idea that the only driving dynamic of society is self-interest. It has been described as the necessary dynamic of a capitalist society, but that is all the more reason why it should not be regarded as the overall dynamic.'

The business community, he believes, is 'becoming increasingly aware of the importance of doing more than just running a business. And statements about "a healthy society being vital for a healthy economy" are being increasingly backed up by action.'

He is heartened by many aspects of the enterprise movement, especially those encouraging young and unemployed people to set up their own businesses.

'There are also the moves towards policies for local purchasing by the major companies to help small businesses. The City is making finance available on special terms for community enterprises, and there are imaginative educational ideas such as the "Compact" schemes and some good training programmes.

'I think the new atmosphere between local authorities and private enterprise is a positive factor, as is the way some developers are increasingly taking account of local needs. . . .

'But all of this, though most welcome, only goes part of the way towards meeting the needs of the really deprived areas. It hardly touches on the problems of poor housing, lack of amenities, and continuing unemployment, particularly on some of the large housing estates.

'These problems are what lead to that sense of being left out, of isolation and despair, which in turn can lead to the symptoms we are familiar with – drug and alcohol abuse, crime and vandalism, debt and family break-up. It is very difficult for companies to have a direct impact in this area.'

Many, however, are already helping through the Church Urban Fund, set up in 1987 to channel financial and advisory help to local problems. Although the money raised so far is not enormous – about £2.5m so far from companies and trusts – it is cost-effective, says Runcie, because it uses the Church's resources of buildings and people throughout the country.

But what of the Church's impact on matters, not necessarily economic in origin, that desperately concern many families – the rise in child abuse cases, for example? In the wake of one recent appalling sexual killing of a teenager, several commentators suggested it was the Church leaders' responsibility now to speak out in outright condemnation of such practices. Where were the old-fashioned concepts of sin and evil?

Runcie's reply betrays an edge of irritation. 'I dislike the term "outright condemnation",' he says. 'It is all too easy to slip from condemning the sin to condemning the sinner. The Church has always attempted to hate the sin but love the sinner.' Jesus, he points out, 'did not speak out much about sin. Instead, he suffered and died for sinners on the cross.'

He questions whether child abuse ('a very great sin') is actually growing as much as people think, or just becoming more visible. 'It is simply that an age-old problem is surfacing and, I believe, being confronted. And why is it surfacing? Because those liberal values now often under attack have helped people draw a distinction between the unacceptability of a practice and the unacceptability of speaking about it.'

Runcie suggests there are other areas of exploitation that receive less concern. 'What is our response, for example, to the importing of shoes made by child labour, with appalling pay and lethal conditions, and sold to us unwittingly? This is a sin of the marketplace and not a sexual crime, and so goes largely unnoticed. Sin is not a matter only of individual bad behaviour.'

Would he include City malpractices as 'sins of the marketplace'?

'They can be,' he replies cautiously, weighing the fairness of his words and again stressing how the pressures of a performance-orientated society can distort moral judgements.

'There is a danger of pace and pressure neutralizing the activities of the market rather than letting them be the subject of value judgements. I am not in a position to talk about regulatory mechanisms, but the very fact that there is a greater demand for them I think is significant. It may show a breakdown of the kind of face-to-face culture which existed in the City and in commercial deals in past days.

'I am aware that people criticize City dinners and lunches and so on, and no doubt some of that may have had its day, but I would be sorry if the culture it represented of friendship and trust between individuals doing business together and knowing each other was lost.'

A few weeks earlier, Runcie had made an unusually sharp speech on the dangers of fundamentalism – a speech some thought weakened by his subsequent protest at a BBC TV programme satirizing aspects of the Salman Rushdie affair. Runcie defends that protest on the pragmatic grounds of needing to encourage moderate Muslim opinion in Britain and thereby help douse the hotheads. But he is concerned that fundamentalist attitudes are spreading in many basic ways.

'I recognize that fundamentalism is a word that can be used in different senses,' he explains. 'I was using it in the sense of people being intransigent about their own opinions and unable to listen or think there may be illumination from elsewhere which God has to give. I find that a distressing tendency in the world, and you can discover it in politics as well as in religion.

'Getting places quickly by not listening is a dangerous policy for churchmen, or politicians or diplomats.'

Then, laughter breaking in, he adds: 'You can be an intransigent liberal too. I have been told that I might be judged by some people to be a liberal fundamentalist.'

As he walks the wide corridors of Lambeth Palace, with the portraits of some forty of his predecessors gazing down at him, Runcie must occasionally feel the breath of fundamentalist passions in England's own past. There, for example, are the aquiline, inscrutable features of martyred Thomas Cranmer, burned at the stake by a bigoted regime in 1556. In the long eye of history, 1556 is only a blink away.

But there have always been those to strike a balance against the intransigent. Runcie quotes Oliver Cromwell's famous appeal to the Great Assembly of the Church of Scotland: 'I beseech you in the bowels of Christ, think it possible you may be mistaken.'

'I hope that spirit, which recognizes difference, dissent, the readiness to admit you may be mistaken, will always be part of the British character and will have a part in our public life, because that makes for a richer, more healthy society in the broadest sense,' he says thoughtfully.

'I was talking some time ago to a Hungarian who came here as a Jewish refugee after the war, and he said Britain then might not have been as efficient as it is now, but it was a less abrasive place in which to live. That is why he came here. That is why a lot of people came here, and why I hope they will continue to come here, because it is a place that reckons respect and tolerance and spiritual values equally important with material success.'

And can we still say that about ourselves?

Runcie pauses for a second, considering. 'I hope so. I think so. But we must not say it with any sense of complacency or superiority.'

# Section Six

## The City Effect

# 27

# Dealing with the fund managers

May 1988
Stuart Rock

There has been a shift of power in the City since 'Big Bang', with the chief beneficiaries being the fund managers.

'Enjoy it while it lasts' they were told at the National Association of Pension Fund managers conference earlier this year. If that sounds a note of urgency, it is misleading. The investment community's grasp on the financial markets is in no immediate state of weakening.

The total sum of money invested in funds and trusts at the end of 1987 was estimated to be £198bn, according to Phillips and Drew research. Nearly a third of the total UK equity market is in the hands of the fund managers.

An increasing share of that money is being placed in the hands of external fund managers – the merchant banks, the insurance companies and independent operators.

The increased sums have brought increased activity. Research shows that the funds turn over their investments at a much faster rate than twenty years ago. In the seventies it was typical for a fund to hold a UK equity for an average of sixteen years. Now it is more like two or three – a climate fostered by the lower commissions payable to brokers since Big Bang and also by cuts in stamp duty. (According to Bank of England research, in 1986–87 turnover varied greatly between an insurance fund and a unit trust. An equity in the former might still only be traded once every five years, in the latter probably every two.)

Behind the statistics and the occasional controversy over a takeover bid, though, are a number of personable, articulate and usually undemonstrative people, who lay emphasis on the long term and who have an ability to say that they have been wrong.

'I think that one of the principal qualities that a fund manager needs is a sense of humility,' says Keith Niven, a thirty-nine-year-old Scottish director at Schroders Investment Management, the fund management arm of the merchant bank.

The foremost thing a fund manager must bear in mind, he says, is that 'you will always make a lot of mistakes. If you get 60 per cent of your decisions right, then you are doing well.

'I came from a background of pure mathematics and actuarial work, so I believed that everything could be put into a formula. It was something of a shock to learn that it did not work like that. Some new people expect, not unreasonably, that they will achieve a high level of success all the time. Coming to terms with the fact that they will not, yet maintaining self-confidence, is often the toughest part of the job.'

Nigel Beidas, head of the UK equity group at insurance company Confederation Life, goes along with that.

'You have got to be able to live with your decisions if they go wrong,' he says. 'A successful fund manager will only get 65 per cent right.'

If a sense of personal fallibility is well developed, so is the need to maintain an independent stance. You would be hard-pressed to find a single fund manager who admitted to following the recommendations of the brokers' analysts.

At Schroders, Niven and his fund managers tap into an in-house reservoir of investment analysis that provides a training ground for future fund managers and also acts as a distillation point for the reams of brokers' reports that flood in each week.

'Less, or at least more aware, brokers would be a good thing,' reckons Chris Rodgers, a courteous Oxford graduate who deals with UK equities as one of Schroders' fund managers. 'I might hear the same message five times in a day.'

As at Schroders, Confederation Life has its own research desk. It is seen as a necessary first step. ('You cannot be a good fund manager unless you are a good analyst,' says Beidas.) Research from the outside brokers goes first to Beidas, then to UK equity manager Jan Etherden and then to the analysts – the reverse of Schroders' process.

'We use them as information sources,' says Beidas, 'as they are usually closer to managements than we are. But we pick the stocks ourselves – their recommendations are too short term.'

'The most common phrase you will hear in this office is "yes, OK, we will have a look at it",' says Confederation's UK equity manager Etherden. 'That enables me to make a better-informed decision so that I can sleep at night. I have a handful of regular contacts at the brokers, and they will all try a number of ideas on me each day.'

Confederation's small team works in relatively spacious offices in Chancery Lane. The atmosphere is conducive to decision making (although the actual number of firm buy or sell decisions can vary widely day to day; often it can be none at all). A bit more edge can be felt on the eighth floor of 8 Devonshire Square, close by Liverpool Street Station, where GT Management – a quoted independent fund management company – is based.

Stephen Hazell-Smith's desk is more like a dealer's than a fund director's in size; and there is no internal research department for back-up, merely a background hubbub from the open-plan floor. His opinions, though, are similar.

'A good broker's analyst will tell me what is going on,' he says. 'After that I will make my own mind up. You cannot rely on analysts to be consistent. They don't necessarily need to be. You do have to be consistent when you are managing a fund.'

All of them believe that the brokers have become too short term in their analyses and that it is the investment managers who are taking a longer view.

'We will tend to stick with stocks for three to five years,' says Confederation's Beidas. 'We start on the basis of buying stocks that are undervalued – for example, a cyclical industry at the bottom of its cycle. The research that we do will make projections of the sustainable growth rate for the next five to ten years. We take the view that we cannot assess when a company will outperform; but if we bought it depressed, we will sell it when it is going well.'

'We try to take a long-term view,' says Schroders' Rodgers. 'The brokers can tell us where a company is going in the next few months. We ask ourselves where it is going in the next three to four years.'

Taking the long view must not strangle 'flexibility,' though, according to Hazell-Smith. He uses that word a lot. 'The market is constantly evolving. You are dealing with shifting targets, subject to human ebbs and flows. You cannot be too fixed in your views.'

Sounds great. But though Hazell-Smith and the rest may preach 'long-termism,' the fact is that the funds are under increased pressure to 'perform' according to the sophisticated measurement criteria established by consultants such as Noble Lowndes or the WM Company. Certainly, fund trustees are more aware of performance – and they are much more willing to change their fund managers.

Those subjected to these pressures are ambivalent. All would welcome the demise of the quarterly league tables, first introduced to guide trustees towards the best long-term performing funds. On the other hand, none would really want to be measured less aggressively.

'It is harder to take a divergent line,' says Niven. 'If you do, then your performance may be much better or much worse. It may turn out to be much better – in three years' time. But if it goes wrong in the first year, will you still have the client there when the results eventually vindicate your decision? Probably not.'

GT's Hazell-Smith says he senses 'an increasing sense of rebellion' against the quarterly tables. 'I would be delighted to get away from them.' That said, he acknowledges them as a discipline as well as a pressure, part of the rules of the game. In the faster game of unit trust management

(Hazell-Smith runs one), 'loads of magazines provide weekly unit trust performance tables for their readers, who are our customers. If you believe the customer is always right, then you have to heed their demands.'

Giving the punters what they want means that the institutions differ in their methods of administration. The 150 or so clients that have entrusted a cool £8bn to Schroders Investment Management are, in effect, buying the Schroders' brand. Oxford man Rodgers is not just a fund manager – he is an account representative into the bargain.

Schroders' investment policy is determined top down. A macroeconomic perspective is obtained by general consensus; targets and ranges for each stock sector are decided. Within that framework Rodgers acts as a UK equity stock picker. So, for example, Schroders' policy is to hold ICI. It is up to Rodgers to determine quite how much ICI he will have in his particular portfolios. He reckons about half of each of his portfolios is thus loosely prescribed; the other half will be his own decisions. His performance is monitored once a quarter against in-house models.

At Confederation Life, the approach is bottom up. The fund managers look for undervalued stock. Portfolios are structured in the style of the individual manager. Beidas, for example, likes to hold a high number of stocks (up to 160) at any one time.

GT sits somewhere in between. The UK equities desk has a number of common stocks as a core portfolio across the group's funds. Hazell-Smith has a responsibility to collate information about certain sectors – electronics, television networks, office equipment, gold and mining, lifes and composites. He also runs a small companies fund. On the typed piece of paper outlining this information is scribbled "these allocations are not set in stone." '

The working style of the investment house is clearly of great importance. 'Individual flair must be given its head,' says Schroders' Niven. It is one of the hardest balancing acts to achieve – letting the fund manager have room to breathe, and thereby keep him or her interested, while keeping the corporate culture pre-eminent. 'People either stay here for fewer than two years or up to 20,' Niven remarks.

Etherden at Confederation probably could not manage without a lot of personal scope. 'Theoretically, I could totally disagree with Nigel (Beidas) and it would not pose too much of a problem,' she says. It is fairly unlikely it would happen, though – both she and Beidas started as analysts with Confederation in 1980 and 1983 respectively and have yet to work elsewhere.

It was third time lucky for Hazell-Smith at GT; he had tried two other investment houses in search of a style that would suit his temperament.

Whatever the background, a similar cast of mind is evident, however. Both Beidas at Confederation and Rodgers at Schroders admit to having been fascinated with the workings of the stock market from early teens, for example.

'I had a strong idea that this was what I wanted to do,' says Rodgers. 'I was interested in how money worked. Perhaps I am too enthusiastic, but I can't understand why I am paid to do this. It is like getting a salary for your favourite hobby.'

Beidas just wanted 'to go into something in the stock market. I have not regretted not going into stockbroking, especially since Big Bang.'

The fund managers' world is relatively stable and perhaps more reflective than other areas of the City. The enjoyment of the job stems, it seems, from the freedom to be intellectually quizzical.

'I am fascinated how industries change,' says Beidas. 'Look at the way UK store groups have generally failed to expand in the US while building groups have made it work. Why is this? These kinds of issues are very interesting.' He cites curiosity, an interest in and a knowledge about how companies operate and work as a chief ingredient in making a good fund manager.

'I most enjoy small companies,' says Hazell-Smith. 'They tend to value their shareholders more, and therefore you develop better relationships. You will meet some rogues and you will lose out once in a while, but that is part of the game. Footsie (FT-SE 100) companies tend to be blander in their approach.'

Etherden also runs a small companies unit trust. 'What interests me about small companies,' she says, 'is what presses a particular guy's button, why they go into the office each morning and whether they will continue to do so.'

'I think it is a privilege working in a job where world affairs are important, says Niven. 'Your opinion can be asked about ICI's profits or the price of gold or the American elections. It makes you a great bore at dinner parties, though. My wife complains that I always have the definitive answer to everything.'

The jokes, the clear-headedness, the positive curiosity – these are qualities that do not fit with the 'gnomes of EC4' image. 'I suppose that the financial community will never be popular,' says Niven. 'We are a secondary industry. But unless you have this fluid market many companies could not operate. Perhaps we have more respect for industry than the other way around.'

# 28

# The men from M & A

November 1988

## Stuart Rock

Mergers and acquisitions (M & A) is the most profitable part of corporate finance work. According to *Financial Times* research, over £70bn worth of M & A work was handled by the top ten merchant banks in this field in 1986. The volume dropped in 1987 but the top ten still handled over £50bn. The fees, based on the value and the success of the deals, are large.

Along with the rewards comes a reputation. Fired by the Guinness affair and stoked thereafter by revelations of insider trading, a presumption exists among many outside the business that this is a field strictly for the piratical, requiring aggressiveness and a thrill for hostile, expensive combat.

Nicholas Aylwin, managing director of corporate finance at the London office of US investment bank Paine Webber, furrows his brow as he ponders this picture. He hardly conforms to the villain image. Indeed, he looks perplexed at any suggestion that the work he conducts is deemed in any way dubious. In his eighteen years of M & A work, he cannot remember an occasion when he was involved in a genuinely hostile bid. 'My work is about the initiation and negotiation of friendly transactions,' he says. 'Hostility can often just be a substitute for a negotiating position.'

In essence, M & A work is not about swashbuckling. It is more about chess. The work of the M & A departments is about the researching, initiating and executing of transactions.

Analysts will study and explore possibilities, particularly by valuing company assets and studying their corporate strategy. Contact is then made with potential purchasers. This is often the so-called 'cold call'.

It is only in this decade that M & A departments have started to generate business. 'When I joined here in 1982 the way in which we operated was totally different,' says Michael Martin, a tall thin Irishman who heads the M & A team at merchant bank Kleinwort Benson. 'The City had tended to be more reactive. I realized that we had to push our ideas more. We were producing research tomes that had no added value. It was backroom research and was not being taken forward. We are now more opportunity driven, suggesting ten or so ideas on a reasonable day.'

Martin's team of twelve is separate from the corporate finance department. 'Basically, our job is to come up with ideas.' They may or may not be involved in the execution of deals. So, while the corporate finance department would defend a Kleinwort client in the face of a bid, the M & A team would handle sales of subsidiary companies if that was part of the defensive strategy. 'It would be up to us to identify who would be interested in buying a particular business and who would pay the best price,' says Martin.

Being such a lucrative market, M & A is no longer the preserve of the established merchant banks. One of the new generation of competitors is Wasserstein Perella, a specialist M & A firm established in New York earlier this year. Currently its European operation is small (just five in an office in London's Curzon Street) but its aspirations are high. It is headed by Jean-Luc Biamonti, a citizen of Monaco who worked with Nestlé and First Boston before joining Wasserstein Perella soon after its formation.

His research is done principally by Paul Aylieff, a Cambridge-educated economist. 'My job centres on valuations work,' Aylieff explains. 'I have to spot undervalued assets and work out how best to exploit them. The reason the market undervalues companies is because institutional investors do not always have the time to go into detailed analysis, especially when they are looking at companies with a diverse range of interests. I will look at those division by division and see whether the sum of the parts is worth more than the total.'

Occasionally, though, an M & A deal is just a reasonably astute hunch. For example, Paine Webber's Aylwin was flying across the Atlantic when he thought of Gerald Ratner. It was no original thought – just that Ratner was already the biggest retail jeweller in the UK and that perhaps he might be considering expansion in the US. Once in New York, he asked a colleague to identify some likely acquisition targets. He then telephoned Ratner – 'who did not know me from Adam' – with his idea. Two days later, Ratner was in New York and the acquisition of Sterling Inc was under way.

'You have to conceive of opportunities by thinking laterally,' says Aylwin, 'so that the client and your competitors have not thought of it. So you need to know a lot about the people and their strategies. There is no substitute for experience in this game.'

That experience also helps to temper the blow of having an idea rejected. There is a high failure rate. 'Failures are endemic,' says Aylwin, 'so you just have to be prolific in your development of ideas.' Kleinwort's Martin puts a figure to it. 'I suppose that it may be only four or five ideas out of 100 that will be accepted. You have to be pretty resilient.'

Martin believes that this high rate of rejection puts paid to criticism that M & A teams, who have to set up deals in order to make their profit, are promoting short-term ideas rather than thinking long-term. 'We are not peddling things with superior salesmanship,' he says. 'On the contrary, companies are well practised at making up their own minds. They have the luxury of rejecting our ideas. And, what is more, they do not have to pay for them.'

'By and large, M & A people do think long-term,' assents Aylwin. Interest in acquisition is fermenting in the marketplace and not just in the minds of the dealmakers. 'For every company wishing to be sold there are fifteen potential acquirers.'

Creation, though, is only part of the story. 'I would like to divide the job 50:50 between the research and initiation stage and the actual implementation,' says Biamonti, 'but it never is.' Aylwin, too, finds that the balance is difficult to keep. 'In the last few weeks we have been wildly busy finishing transactions. Therefore you lose out on creating new business. I like to spend half my time creating, the other half concluding.'

Once an idea has been converted into action, negotiating skills come into play. Negotiation is the art form of the M & A expert. They all refer to it as the cut and thrust. 'I enjoy the cut and thrust of it,' says Aylwin. 'However friendly a negotiation there are always going to be tensions, whether it is over the chairman's car or last year's dividend. I just enjoy negotiating.'

'It is not just bargaining hard,' says Biamonti. 'It is more complex than that. It is understanding the risks, the personalities and the constraints under which one side might be operating that are not understood by the other. A lot of people tell me that they have good negotiating skills. It is easy to say but hard to prove. It develops with experience. You can learn the technicalities. It is more difficult to define how you learn negotiation. It just comes from being there. Certainly, I look at myself now and there are things that I do that I would not have done five years ago.'

That reflects the growing complexity of M & A work. The basic materials – cash or shares – remain the same. The instruments by which they are used are becoming ever more intricate. 'You can get some frightfully complicated arithmetic,' says Aylwin. Both he and Martin trained as accountants. The fine eye for detail is invaluable.

Yet Aylwin believes that 'imagination is more important than technical knowledge. You need to have a perception of the client's strategy and why they should want to acquire a particular business. You will then need to know the technical structures necessary to get the deal done.' He sees the level of computer literacy in US investment banks being much higher than in traditional British merchant banks. It will, he believes, prove to be a key competitive advantage.

The eponymous founders of Wasserstein Perella have been at the forefront of Wall Street innovation for some time. Here Biamonti bides his time. 'The European markets are not as similar to the US as we would like,' he says. 'But the trend is there, particularly with leveraged buy-outs. In continental Europe there are no such things as junk bonds. Not yet, anyway. But they will come. M & A will be a global market.'

One of the more controversial aspects of M & A tactics has been the use of debt. In the US, corporations are willing to burden themselves with colossal amounts of debt in order to acquire or avoid being acquired. The first signs of this occurring in the UK were there prior to the 1987 crash, notably with Barker & Dobson's abortive bid for the Dee Corporation. Although the crash has switched the emphasis onto companies who have cash, the faith in debt is gaining ground.

'The first thing to remember is that the stock market is not always available to issue equity,' says Martin. 'While UK companies are more likely to raise equity rather than debt, equity is in the long term the most expensive form of finance. It also dilutes existing shareholdings.

'One should not be opposed to debt, if you want an array of financial instruments from which to choose. There may be occasions when there is no point in putting in any more capital outlay; in other situations debt would be totally unsuitable.'

All three agree that the use of debt or equity operates in cycles. 'Within bounds, debt is not unhealthy,' says Aylwin. 'The debt to equity ratio in the UK at the moment is at a low point in the cycle. Are you really saying that professional bankers are not able to assess credit-worthiness and the debt-servicing abilities of companies?'

Biamonti takes a more radical view. His toughness is hidden by his relaxed and amiable manner and the twinkle of humour in his eyes. 'Debt forces and accelerates necessary restructuring,' he says. He argues that the possibility of selling companies to financiers creates more liquidity in the marketplace than if there were only other industrial companies prepared to be purchasers. The leveraged buy-out is a principal tool. 'Debt gets us back to a more entrepreneurial environment by enabling managers to purchase their own companies,' he adds. 'If European companies are going to compete against the Americans and the Japanese they will have to be more dynamic. Debt will assist this.'

While they reject the image of debt-peddlers firmly, other slurs have been more insidious. The Guinness affair still touches a nerve. 'It has had an adverse effect,' says Martin. 'So have the reported incidents of insider trading. But they were one or two instances in the context of thousands of transactions. It is hard to eliminate those who bust the rules in what is a lucrative market. The rewards are such that it will attract those who operate on the fringe. But it does get disproportionate coverage.'

'Yes, there have been some bad stories,' says Biamonti. For once, his face sets a little grimmer. 'Any industry has its good and bad people, and there are no more bad people in ours than in any other. But I have a lot of respect for people in this business. Considering the stakes, people are extremely honest.'

Since the days of Roger Seelig at Morgan Grenfell, the business has shied away from the 'star'. Anonymous teams working behind the strength of the corporate name are in. (Two prestigious merchant banks did not want to be featured in this article because they thought that it might be promoting unduly one particular member of a team.)

'There are people within the business with big egos,' says Martin. He dismisses himself as 'just another boring accountant.' He recognizes that M & A work does need 'a bit of razzamatazz', but it will not come from Kleinwort's. 'It is a strong belief here that it is the client who should appear in the newspapers and not the dealmaker. The concept of the star has worked against the City.'

Their job has to some extent been over-glamourized. 'There is a lot of hard graft,' says Aylwin. Nonetheless, if somebody like Aylwin turns up at a company, it means that something is cooking. In that way, they are exotic.

There are side-effects. 'There are too many people trying to get into M & A,' says Martin. 'That means a lot more work weeding out those who are not suitable.'

Prospective candidates have to match a demanding shopping list of qualities. Aylwin cites, in no particular order: 'someone who is stimulated by the strategic thinking that goes into shaping companies. They need to be tenacious, numerate, energetic, discreet and informative. They need first class communication skills and, increasingly, linguistic ability.'

'The basics of a good M & A operator are sound technical knowledge of accountancy and finance plus a preparedness to work very long hours,' says Biamonti. ('You can forget about your private life. I took twenty-six flights in August and had one day's holiday. You just have to make sacrifices.' Biamonti's schedule is unusual. Because he is in charge of Wasserstein Perella's European operations, most of his meetings are in continental Europe. But Kleinwort's Martin also spends only one third of his time in his office.)

On top of that, Biamonti adds 'an ability to get to the essentials. It is easy to lose track with all the details that are involved. As the Americans say, you have to be able to cut through the bullshit.'

'You can easily assess a lawyer or accountant who wants to get into corporate finance work,' says Martin. 'They have to be steady, effective and conscientious. But we are looking for creativity, which is harder to demonstrate, particularly if you are a newly qualified accountant. Curiosity – someone who questions what is going on around him – is the first thing that I look for.'

They enthuse about their job. 'It is the excitement of being in the middle of things,' says Biamonti, who, among other deals, was involved in the sale of Buitoni to Nestlé. 'You then read about what you have been doing in the pages of the *Financial Times*.' He cites variety: 'When I was with Nestlé I had a lot of money to look after. You were a little king and bankers invited you to lunch. But it gets repetitive. Here it is never boring. You can never apply the same recipe to two deals.' The money is not bad. 'It compensates to some degree if I have to cancel the family vacation at the last minute,' Biamonti says wryly.

Competition is a prime motivator, whether it lies in the ingenuity of the idea or extracting the best settlement for a client. And the competitive instinct is going to command a higher premium as the marketplace becomes more crowded. 'You only get a short innings,' says Martin. 'In the US you might not be able to get back into deals if you are ill for three months. The pace of change is that quick.'

Aylwin sees this as being good for businesses. 'There will be a greater variety of transactions and mediums through which they can be achieved,' he says. 'This means richer opportunities for business, both for acquirors and vendors. The more fluid the market, the better its operation.'

It is difficult to define just to what extent the men from M & A are driving the process of change and how much they are just the medium through which corporate desires are projected. 'It is probably companies that lead,' says Biamonti. 'But once that trend has been established, then to a certain extent – but not 50 per cent – we are generating the ideas. In the 1970s we were selling unprofitable companies, dispensing with dogs. Today you see companies evaluating their portfolio of assets and divesting successful operations because they do not fit in. People are realizing that others could use an asset better than they themselves can. That is a positive trend.'

# 29

# Knight errantry and the round table

February 1990

Mihir Bose

Somewhere in an office in London's Holborn is a small round table that played a historic role in the country's largest leveraged buy-out. It was at this table, one day in the middle of 1988, that David Smith sat with his colleague Liz Hignell and decided it was time that Gateway, the supermarket chain, should be broken up. Just over a year later Gateway was indeed broken up in a £2.13bn deal that provided one of the most exciting, complicated and talked-about bids for years.

A freelance management consultant, Smith had given up his job with Arthur Young (as it then was) to do something different. Liz Hignell, also from Arthur Young, was the only person he employed. The round table was no more than a temporary parking space; it belonged to a friend who had loaned it to Smith when he left Arthur Young – 'I have got a spare desk in my office. Park yourself there while you sort things out.'

But if he had no track record in retailing, Smith had been building up a steady reputation as a deal-maker. And in many ways his takeover of Gateway has a Shakespearian ring to it. For almost everything he had done in the three years preceding it had involved Gateway. Very often Smith would plan a bid for a company only to see Gateway intervene and ruin everything: the bid has turned out to be his complete revenge.

These thoughts were far from his mind when he left Arthur Young in 1986, after twenty years, feeling that 'consultancy had got very defensive. It was going down the route of auditing.'

Even before he left the accountants this philosophy had brought him into contact with John Fletcher, who had been sacked by Asda and then made an unsuccessful bid for Cullens. It was some time after this bid failed that one of Smith's Arther Young colleagues suggested he should meet Fletcher. The two struck up an instant rapport and decided to put together an offer for Fine Fare. But Garry Weston of Associated British Foods, who owned Fine Fare, rejected the bid and Fine Fare was eventualy sold to the Dee Corporation, as Gateway was then known.

This was no deterrent to Smith or Fletcher. They were convinced that there were bargains in the high-street supermarkets and they focused their attentions on Budgens. Booker, which owned it, seemed prepared to sell it and a deal seemed close. But the day after they talked, the Dee Corporation made a bid for Booker and so the plan had to be shelved.

Meanwhile Fletcher, with Smith's help, had got involved with Barker & Dobson and was trying to make it a top confectioner. About a year later, in 1986, the Budgens plan was taken off the back burner. Booker had fought off the Dee Corporation and now accepted a £90m, offer by Barker & Dobson for Budgens.

Just as this deal was going through, a paragraph in a US newspaper caught Smith's eye. This said that the Dart Corporation of the US was buying a stake in Safeway. Smith immediately made the connection. Dart might make a bid for Safeway (US), or Safeway might take steps to protect itself. Either way the Safeway stores in the UK would be put up for sale. This was also the time he was leaving Arthur Young so, joined by Liz Hignell, he started putting together a bid for Safeway.

Smith was by now a consummate deal-maker with vast experience and his sharp Scottish accounting skills were in great demand. While he was still at Arthur Young he had helped in the defence of Bell against Guinness. In the course of the bid he had had a fair amount of contact with S G Warburg and while Smith's accounting expertise was not enough to save Bell, he got to know people in Warburgs quite well.

He had heard that Jim Millar, who runs the Scottish supermarket chain William Low, was interested in bidding for Safeway. Smith suggested to him that he should make the deal through Warburgs. As it happens, Low's bid for Safeway did not get very far. It did not even become public knowledge as James Gulliver's Argyll Group scooped up the stores. But the meetings in connection with the bid had put Smith in touch with Robin Binks, director of Warburgs' corporate finance department.

It was the middle of 1987 when Gateway came into view as a possible bid target. So far Gateway or Dee had thwarted Smith's plans. Now as Fletcher and Smith sat 'musing' they decided to turn the tables. Gateway had to be a target: it was not performing and something had to be done.

By December 1987 they were ready with a £2bn bid. But the stock market crash had intervened in October and Smith found that 'the institutions were a bit funny. They wanted a parachute and we were offering them a ladder.' In other words, the offer of Barker & Dobson shares plus cash in a post-crash market, where the preference was for cash only, was not attractive.

But if Smith had failed to kill Gateway the bid had wounded the company and while the management of the holding company in Milton Keynes exuded confidence, the managers who ran the food stores from Bristol were getting restive.

One of the Gateway men who had actively opposed Smith was Bob

Willett, the trading director of Gateway food markets. It was only six months since he had joined Gateway from Owen Owen. 'I knew things were wrong with the company but that was the reason I had joined and I was confident they would be put right,' he says.

Once the bid was defeated Willett looked forward to the changes that had to be made. Gateway had acquired all the trimmings that flabby corporations do: an expensive London flat next to the Ritz for entertainment by its executives, a cumbersome board structure and wretched performance.

'As you get bigger, sales per square foot go up,' says Willett. 'Ours was just the reverse: our sales per square foot were higher in our smaller stores than in our bigger ones. We were attempting to be all things to all men. We were trying to run superstores, big food markets, medium-sized food markets and small ones. We presented a disparate picture to the customer and he was confused. We needed to focus, get a grip on the major business. The company was rudderless. We had some good stores, some marvellous people, hardworking. Companies don't go wrong with bad soldiers. They only go wrong with bad officers.'

But after the Smith–Fletcher bid had been beaten, Willett waited in vain for the officers to change their habits. The Gateway Foodmarkets board, which was unwieldly enough as it was with sixteen directors, was made even more cumbersome. It acquired another tier, an executive board, with four managing directors.

Ian Wolseley who had joined Gateway a month before Willett as marketing director was the first to feel fed up and left in the summer of 1988. Through a mutual friend he arranged to meet Smith. The meeting confirmed for Smith what he already knew: Gateway was unhealthy and there were people running it who admitted that. The first bid may have failed but there was a chance for a second strike.

Wolseley now started acting as the bridge between Smith, Willett and the other directors of the food stores: Richard Quinton, the finance director, Peter Fisher, personnel director, Roger Reason, operations director, all of whom felt just as dissatisfied.

Some time in September or October 1988 a dinner was arranged in London between Smith, Willett and the others. 'It was just a conversation over a bite to eat,' recalls Willett. 'It was nothing clandestine or anything. As directors of Gateway we could not talk of anything. It was more a conversation of "what are you chaps thinking of doing"? It was by now common knowledge that things were not going well at Gateway with main board directors of the holding company leaving. We felt powerless. If these main board directors can't make changes then we can't.'

Willett came away from the dinner thinking things would remain the same. 'I didn't think for the world that within months David Smith would be sitting there as my chairman. At that stage I thought "nice chap, interesting meeting but nothing is going to come of it". So we got on with the job.'

Smith, however, left the dinner encouraged. 'It validated our conceptions about Gateway. It encouraged us to pursue the matter.' The discussions had confirmed what Smith had long suspected: Gateway had made one acquisition too many. The Fine Fare acquisition, which had thwarted Smith's own plans two years ago, had taken much longer to integrate than people expected. 'If you have got a solid infrastructure inside the company, you can take on anything. But don't forget the company had been going through a series of acquisitions,' explains Willett. 'It had come to the stage when all it was doing was harmonizing the business, not developing the future of the business.'

Smith and Liz Hignell were now joined by the man who Smith sees as the most crucial player in this story: Alastair Dickson, a Scots lawyer in his late 1930s who heads the firm Dickson-Minto with offices in Edinburgh and London. 'Without Alastair,' says Smith 'the bid for Gateway just would not have happened.'

When the history of buy-outs is eventually written, Dickson may well figure as the most important person. Smith calls him the 'leading commercial lawyer in relation to leveraged buy-outs.' Almost all the major buy-outs like Premium Brands, Magnet, have been through companies set up by Dickson that bear the initials DMWSL: Dickson Minto Writers to the Signet London.

The company that was now formed for the Gateway bid was DMWSL 32. Dickson called the bid 'project triangle', as the symbol of Gateway was a triangle. Hignell idly sitting round the table suggested that, in that case, the company making the bid should be called Isosceles and the name stuck. With Dickson providing all the support staff necessary – administrative, legal, secretarial – Isosceles, as a subsidiary of DMWSL 32, got ready to make a bid for Gateway.

Smith's first thought was to turn to KKR – the great buy-out specialists in America. Smith and Hignell spent several weekends in the US but in the end KKR felt it could not do it. The bid was to be a hostile one and it would not own 100 per cent. In the middle of all this came the RJR Nabisco deal and KKR's entire resources were concentrated on that.

So it was back to the round table to discuss alternatives. One was to approach the innovative US investment bank Wasserstein Perella. But as Smith, Hignell and Dickson argued about approaching them, Warburgs' Binks called. He had been thinking about Gateway. It was in a poor shape, the institutional investors were unhappy, but how could change be effected?

One way of effecting change is through strong non-executive directors. At Beecham and STL non-executive directors intervened and changed the executive heads running the company. But Gateway did not have such strong non-executive directors. Unabashed, Smith told Binks: 'we have got a plan'.

The approach from Warburgs was doubly welcome from Smith because in his talks with KKR it had been decided to use Warburgs. So began the exercise of funding it. In a sense this was a re-run of the exercise that had been undertaken with Barker & Dobson the year before. 'Many of the financiers still had our old projections. They dusted them down and compared how accurate we had been and how far we had progressed. They were impressed.'

Negotiations with Asda for the sale of the superstores were begun and the gang of four, as Smith had begun to call Willett and his fellow directors, were told that a bid was coming.

While Smith was planning his move things were happening at Gateway. Towards the autumn of 1988 it was announced that there was to be a new chairman and chief executive for the foodstores. But Willett's optimism turned to dismay when contradictory announcements were made: the new man would arrive soon, he would not arrive till the New Year. Then suddenly in November he was there in the form of Louis Sherwood.

Sherwood, who had worked with James Goldsmith in his days as a food retailer, almost fifteen years earlier, promised the changes that Willett and others were looking for.

Soon after his arrival, Willett was promoted to marketing director and took an instant shine to him. 'I liked the man. But it became painfully obvious by January 1989 that there was not going to be any major change.' There was a fundamental difference in philosophy and approach. Willett thought Gateway needed a revolution in management styles and strategy, Sherwood preached 'the gospel of evolution. But the business needed a radical change, a radical re-positioning. We were being criticized by our customers for our standards. The customer was saying we were not regarded as having clean stores. All the research was showing we were underperforming in the growth areas, overperforming in nil growth areas.' The die was cast.

Some time in March 1989 Smith gave Willett and the others a presentation of his plans. 'But we didn't know the bid details. David's presentation had no numbers. He told us what he was going to do, like the disposing of the superstores and the financing for the bid. We said we supported the rationale behind the bid but could not comment on the figures.'

Twenty-four hours before the bid was announced, with the market already sensing something was afoot, the deal with Asda on the disposal of stores was concluded and the gang of four were given full details. And on that Monday in April last year, as Warburgs made the announcement,

Willett and his fellow directors went to Sherwood and told him they supported the bid. 'He asked us to sit down. He was pleased we didn't resign. He listened to us. Then he phoned Mr Monk and two hours later, three hours later, we were suspended.'

This did not surprise the gang of four, who had consulted their lawyers beforehand and were warned they would be suspended. 'But the alternative was leaving the company and running away. I would not be doing my duty as director of the company if I ran away. We had done nothing wrong. We had fulfilled our fiduciary duties as directors. We had said this bid is right for the staff and the shareholders of Gateway.'

Although they were suspended with full pay they found the period very difficult. Before the bid they knew something was happening but not quite what. Now they had to follow it in the papers where there were many attacks on them. Alec Monk had said what they had done was despicable. There was an injunction by Gateway stopping Willett and the other defectors from talking to anybody. The injunction was lifted but personal undertakings were given by the gang of four that they would not communicate with Isosceles and only communicate with the press through lawyers.

'There was nothing to do,' recalls Willett. 'We are not golfers. I had my second game of golf ever. All we could really do, apart from gardening and walking the dog, was talk a great deal.'

By now, in April 1989, Smith and Hignell had moved to Warburgs' corporate finance offices. The round table had served its purpose and Smith felt confident about the opening bid of 195p in cash. But late in the game there was a sudden change. Wasserstein Perella, the firm Smith had thought of asking before Binks rang, teamed up with the American supermarket chain A & P and created a white knight: Newgateway, headed by a genuine retailer, Jim Wood.

The emergence of the white knight had two dramatic consequences. After the Newgateway counter bid the gang of four was sacked. 'Now,' recalls Willett, 'we hadn't got any income coming in. We went to our bank managers and asked them to stay with us.'

Smith and Binks also had to rethink their strategy hurriedly. What had looked like a simple fight was now awfully complicated. They finally came up with a novel offer. Isosceles offered cash as well as what became known as the 'stub', a mixture of preference shares and equity to counter the higher cash offer from the Americans.

But the Americans kept offering more cash and when they finally came up with 242p in cash, Smith and Binks decided that the 'stub' should be valued. Salomon Brothers was called in and valued it at between 30 and 35p. So Isosceles' offer of 215p in cash plus stub was just that bit better than the Americans'. There was not much in it and it was still desperately close. Every move by Smith and Isosceles was being matched by the Americans.

Garry Weston of ABF sold his 15 per cent stake and Hignell thought it would take Isosceles over the crucial 50 per cent mark but Newgateway continued to buy.

Finally it all rested on the Prudential. Its vote would decide the winner.

Mick Newmarch, the Pru chief and his team had grilled Smith, Binks and the Isosceles team. In the last days of the bid in July 1989, he rang Smith to say: 'I just thought I would let you know we have made our decision.' There was a pause. Smith held his breath. 'Pru has decided to accept the Isosceles bid and we wish you the best.' Then he added an important rider, 'we would like the market to know.' The Pru knew its decision would influence the waverers and Smith, aware of the publicity coup, made the most of it. Over the next twenty-four hours a huge operation of gathering up the share certificates began, to have them delivered to the Bank of Scotland to make sure the 50 per cent target had been reached.

The gang of four had developed the habit of watching Channel Four's *Business Programme*. 'We used to take turns to gather in each other's homes. It was meant to give us confidence. We were round at Richard Quinton's house when we saw on television we had won. We jumped for joy. It was sheer relief. No, we did not drink champagne – Sainsbury's or whatever – we were pleased we could now get on with the job.'

But Newgateway did not give up. It continued buying even after it lost and ended up with 40 per cent. Two days after the bid Smith met Monk for the first time in the flat next to the Ritz where Monk had so often entertained. Now he was handing over the keys.

Since then much has happened. The bid cost Isosceles nearly £100m, a good bit of this is going to Warburgs, which made between £20m and £25m and saw first half pre-tax profits jump from £47.8m to £102.5m. However, the flat is for sale and the proceeds should refit six stores. Newgateway has been neutralized, having accepted the offer and got board representation, and Smith has gone ahead with his disposals. The Milton Keynes headquarters has gone. Medicare has been sold and more supermarkets are due for disposal.

David Smith may well be somebody who has turned out to be lucky. That is, to an extent, the view taken by city analysts. 'It is a weird coincidence that most of the leveraged buy-outs in the UK have come in the non-food retailing sector,' says Andy Brown, food retailing analyst with Morgan Stanley. 'These are businesses that are cyclical and very dependent on interest rates. If interest rates go up then this has two consequences on a leveraged buy-out: one, it affects consumer spending and therefore the performance of the stores and, two, it means that the cost of the floating loan they have taken to engineer the buy-out goes up. But Gateway on the other hand is a food retailing business, which is a fairly stable business.'

In other words, even if we have a recession we will still have to eat. In addition, food retailing, unless you are building big stores, does not require a lot of capital. Gateway is getting rid of its superstores to add others. It is also pretty dominant in small towns up and down the country. The one-horse small town may be an attractive fiction of the wild west but the two-store small town of Britain where both the stores happen to be Gateway Food Markets is not all that uncommon and, as Brown says: 'if Gateway is better run under the new management and it sells off some of its other stores then there is a potential for their smaller stores.'

During the bid Smith was worried that Gateway would be bottom of the food retailing league. Willett, now chief executive of the food stores, with Wolseley and the others back as directors, accepts that Sainsbury and Tesco are in a super league of their own but is seeking to position Gateway in the big league.

Smith, confident he got interest rates right, swapped loans into dollars or capped them at the right rate, feels that while other buy-outs go sour, 'we can sit pretty.' So much so that Smith, himself, has acquired new offices even if there is still a feel of living out of suitcases. When I visited him the office was indicated by a handwritten sign, the wrappings had yet to be removed from the sofa and the boardroom was full of Topolski prints. But there is one piece of furniture missing which suggests that, for the moment, Smith's days as a nomadic deal-maker may be over. The board table is a large rectangular one and there is not a round table in sight.

# 30

# Bitter sweet: Rowntree after Nestlé

April 1990

## Sara Jackson

On a Wednesday morning in the spring of 1988, 11,000 men and women suddenly found their jobs, their community, and for many the economic stability of the city in which they lived, declared as threatened. Everything had been put on the line by a mechanism over which they had no control and about which they had little knowledge.

For at 8.30 a.m. on April 13, stockbroker S G Warburg, acting on behalf of the Swiss company Suchard, started buying up Rowntree shares. It was under instructions to acquire 14.9 per cent of Rowntree and was paying 630p for shares that had closed the previous day at 483p. Suddenly, after the quiet since October 1987, here was money in the city. There was the chance to earn big commissions, meet targets, make money. Lots of money.

Within thirty-five minutes it was mission accomplished. And, as the fund managers and stockbrokers might have added, Rowntree was into play.

Nothing unusual in this: it is after all how the City makes its living. But the Rowntree takeover was to prove one of the most bitterly contested and emotive in corporate history. The man in the street knew this company, and he cared. Rowntree was proud of its company, and it cared. Moreover, the bid and eventual acquisition introduced burning issues regarding Britain's merger and acquisition policy that had long laid dormant.

It awakened the country to the disparity between Britain's open policy on foreign takeovers of British companies and the barriers on the continent. A universal cry went out that the playing field was not level. 'Competition must be fair,' announced Michael Heseltine. For although Suchard and later, mega-giant Nestlé, could bid for Rowntree, British companies were prevented from bidding for Swiss concerns.

'Rowntree is one more example of a major British company with its roots and headquarters in provincial Britain faced with effective termination of local autonomy,' Heseltine said.

'That would be regional assassination,' agreed Conal Gregory, MP for York. John Marshall, MP for Hendon South, announced 'if the Rowntree takeover is allowed to go ahead Britain will end up a branch factory economy.'

'The Swiss are using financial muscle where marketing strategies have failed,' argued Edward McMillan-Scott, MEP for York. 'The Swiss strategy to ride piggy-back on established EC companies all the way to 1992 is clear.'

Tesco and Argyll both backed Rowntree. Sir Adrian Cadbury added his voice in support. Unilever's Mike Angus drily commented that 'takeover used to be the price of bad management. Now it is the price of good.'

*Financial Weekly* produced statistics backing its claim that 'by most criteria Rowntree is a better company than Nestlé.' Sales had grown by 50 per cent between 1983 and 1987 compared with 26 per cent for Nestlé. Trading profits were up 73 per cent compared with 27 per cent; gross margins by 18 per cent contrasted with Nestlé's 1 per cent (although they conceded that at 10.4 per cent Nestlé's were still higher than Rowntree's 9.1 per cent, reflecting the 'lower relative spending of the Swiss company on brand building and brand support'). Finally, earnings per share at Nestlé had risen 23 per cent, compared with Rowntree's 37 per cent.

In 1988 Kit Kat, Aero, Break Away and Toffee Crisp hit record sales levels. In 1986 Kit Kat became the UK's biggest selling 'counter line', a position it retains.

It was not only Rowntree's record as a successful company that made the country baulk. It was its history as a caring one. York's largest employer, the company perpetuated its founding policy of employee care and community support. Each day up to 300 Rowntree pensioners used the company restaurant where for 85p they took lunch. The company ran Old Time dancing for the pensioners. There was a billiards room, a TV room, clubs, trips to the sea-side. Employees visited pensioners on their birthdays.

On June 23, Nestlé upped its offer to an irrefusable £2.55bn and Rowntree's board, after extensive discussions with both Suchard and Nestlé, recommended the latter's offer. People wanted to know what was going to happen to York.

Two years on and, according to Rowntree chairman Peter Blackburn, nothing has happened. The directors are enthusiastic about a situation and a company that only twenty-four months ago they fought so hard against. 'All the promises that were made by Nestlé at the time have been more than kept. Not only that, there has been a great preparedness to invest some very substantial sums of money in the UK business,' says Blackburn.

Managing director Graham Millar gives examples. 'Last year £35m went on expansion. That is more than we have ever spent in any year. This coming year it will be over £50m. There is a new cocoa processing factory being built in York for £13m and a new Polo mint factory at £15m; £6m is going to extend our existing research laboratory to transform it to the principal Nestlé R & D confectionery centre in the world. That will bring some new good level jobs to York.'

In the run up to the acquisition Nestlé had argued that the two companies' markets complemented one another, that Nestlé had the marketing and distribution skills to make Rowntree's brands grow faster overseas. In 1988 Ken Dixon, then Rowntree chairman, was unwavering in his insistence. The bid was unwelcome; Rowntree was developing its brands successfully by itself; it was determined to remain independent.

In 1990, Rowntree's managing director echoes Nestlé's arguments. 'Geographically Rowntree and Nestlé are well suited. Nestlé is strong in the US and the Far East where we hardly existed. Growth does not happen overnight – but it will.'

Blackburn is positive about the developments that have been made in Rowntree's overseas markets. 'To date, a new joint venture has been created in Japan called N-Mackintosh KK, in which Nestlé holds a two-thirds shareholding. The venture is with Fujiya, a Japanese company that had the licence for certain Rowntree products prior to the acquisition. The aim is to introduce Nestlé brands into the Japanese market and former Rowntree brands will be very high on the list. That has happened since the acquisition – we could not have done it before.'

Nonetheless, Rowntree, although keeping its UK autonomy, has lost control over its many overseas subsidiaries. 'We had subsidiary companies in the major markets of the EC,' explains Blackburn, 'some of them with manufacturing facilities. Rowntree had, over a period of twenty or more years, been building up a European business, initially based on small acquisitions in Germany, France, and later in the Netherlands. We were very much at the forefront in thinking about the business on a European scale and at the time of the acquisition our continental business was turning over £300m.'

'Nestlé operates across the world on a market by market basis so each country is headed up by what Nestlé call a market head and he is responsible for all the business within that country. He reports into Vevey, the world headquarters of Nestlé. Here in York we have a direct responsibility for the UK chocolate business, but not for any former Rowntree chocolate businesses outside the UK.'

Blackburn minimizes the changes that have occurred within Rowntree UK as a direct result of the acquisition. 'In the UK there were certain businesses Nestlé decided not to keep and those were sold. There was a transfer of responsibilities. The Rowntree grocery business went to Croydon (Nestlé's UK headquarters), Rowntree took responsibility for Nestlé's UK chocolate business.'

'We have lost, as a result of the acquisition, between 60 to 80 jobs in the UK. We used to run an international company from here and the people responsible for that, including many friends I have worked with for a quarter of a century, have gone.'

Blackburn and Millar insist these are the only cuts that have been made, and that Nestlé's promise to keep the UK management intact has been honoured. 'Absolutely so,' says Blackburn. 'Nothing has changed. The UK business is run by the same people as it was before. Indeed the role has been enhanced as Graham and his team now have commercial responsibility for Nestlé's UK chocolate business.'

A confectionery buyer for Amalgamated Foods sees no change in the service provided by Rowntree. 'Nestlé has left it to get on with itself,' he says. 'However, it usually takes Nestlé about two years to start making changes.' A City analyst believes that, as Nestlé promised, Rowntree is 'definitely becoming the European centre for Nestlé's confectionery industry.'

Peter Blackburn, in conjunction with various market heads and local managers is responsible for developing Nestlé's world-wide 'chocolate strategy'. 'The chocolate strategy group is a small body of people who cover both the commercial areas and the technical (production and R & D) to develop confectionery strategies to drive the now considerably enlarged Nestlé chocolate and confectionery business forward, and to realize the full potential of the investments in confectionery Nestlé has made,' explains Blackburn.

The directors, unsurprisingly, have nothing but praise for Nestlé. But Ian MacLaurin, chairman of Tesco, reflected a large body of public opinion when he said, in a letter to Lord Young: 'the Rowntree organization for many years has dedicated itself to serving major multiples and the British public at large. The same cannot be said of Nestlé, whose reputation to the trade in no way approaches that of the Rowntree company.'

Nestlé's image was marred by encouraging the sale of powdered milk for babies in third world countries and for using unwarranted additives in its apple juice in the US. Many feared that it would be inevitable that over a period of time Rowntree's company ethos would be infiltrated by Nestlé's.

Millar considers the Nestlé baby milk scandal to be 'totally unfair'. Blackburn insists that 'having worked with the senior people in Nestlé, they seem very straight and honest and quite genuinely people with whom I feel very comfortable. If it was not like that, I for one, would not be here.' Millar interrupts. 'I was going to say exactly that. If I felt uncomfortable, I would not stay. Honestly.'

And what of the budget Rowntree set aside for investments in the community at large and the welfare of its workers? Rowntree was renowned at the time of the takeover for its employee welfare programme. The company provided a sports ground and two gymnasiums at a time when there were no similar facilities. It was one of the first companies to establish medical and dental care and affordable homes for its workers.

A library was built in 1928. The timber-framed red brick building still has its original leaded windows intact. Employees may borrow tapes, videos, records (even books) – all at minimal prices. The Joseph Rowntree theatre remains very heavily subsidized by the company. For a nominal charge local amateur and professional groups (including the Rowntree players) have the use of the full services of a professional theatre.

Rowntree pensioners continue to be cared for by the company. 'Pensioners are still part of the Rowntree family,' says Michael Blackburn, the company's PR manager. 'Even today, once here you tend to stay. Each year we have a long-service party for those with over twenty-five years of service.' In 1989 700 such employees attended the party with their partners. Between them, they clocked up 11,370 years of service.

But also, Rowntree was and is York's largest employer. The *Yorkshire Evening Press* declared that 'the acquisition of Rowntree by Suchard or Nestlé would pose a serious threat to the way of life of a whole community'. Has it? Has the budget Rowntree set aside for investment in the community at large and the welfare of its workers been cut?

'Not one bit,' Millar emphatically states. 'We are encouraged to keep doing the Rowntree thing. Our values remain the same,' says Peter Blackburn.

But not everyone agrees. Conal Gregory, MP for York, says that the picture is not as rosy as Blackburn and Millar would paint it. 'Our fears on point after point have come home to roost,' he says.

'Rowntree was planning a major confectionery museum in York. It was to be the number one in the UK and Europe, showing the history and manufacturing process of confectionery, all in an old property in York. It has been totally stopped. All the work, and the research and investment already made is wasted.'

'Since the takeover there have been no new community initiatives from Rowntree. No innovation there. They have been careful to continue, to carry out a holding process so as not to alienate the local community more.' Gregory believes a reduction in their current support is inevitable. 'I see them as trying to keep the status quo for two or three years before they start to retract,' he says.

Gregory is insistent that any representations that redundancies since the acquisition have been limited only to those employed in Rowntree's international division are untrue. 'That is just not honest,' he says. 'Confectionery buyers have been made redundant. Senior middle management have been paid off – I am sure on good terms, but it has been very traumatic. For many it is too early to retire and they are in north Yorkshire as, say, forty-five-year-old specialists in confectionery. Where do they go? I do not doubt that top management who were forced to retire were able to look after themselves.'

Gregory considers that Rowntree is not prepared to confront Nestlé on contentious issues. 'The present management does not seem to stand up to the Swiss management, he says. 'There were many employees who had built a loyalty to the company through shared ownership. They were of course forced to sell their shares. I was surprised that Nestlé did not offer a trade-in. The employee share participation at Rowntree put the company at the forefront of British industry. Now, with their non-EC masters, they are very regressive; they have moved to a forties position. We used to look to Rowntree for enlightened management, but now we must look to other companies.'

Giving another example of what he perceives as Rowntree's willingness to bow before the Swiss, Gregory states it was necessary for him to pressure them to insist that as promised, Nestlé's UK confectionery production was moved to York. 'The York management were so subordinate, fawning to the Swiss, that it took outside pressure to force them to remember the undertakings that were made.'

But for those Rowntree employees on the factory floor, 1000 of whom lobbied Westminster in May 1988, life goes on as it always has. 'The biggest difference since the takeover to Rowntree employees is that they can now buy coffee and yoghurts in the company shop as well as chocolates,' says PR manager Mike Blackburn. 'People are much more relaxed than they were eighteen months ago because they have actually seen signs of willingness to get behind the business and help us attain our objectives. You can see as you go around – morale is high. Their eyes are bright.'

And so indeed they seem to be. Enthusiastic employees seize the visitor and demonstrate the pipe that runs to a vat in which the batter for Kit Kat wafers bubbles. Piped music plays where Dairy Box centres are coated in chocolate. Chatting women in impeccable white caps and coats form a production line where each individual carefully places two sweets in the tray. Each day the women move down a place – for some chocolates are harder to get in than others.

It is one of the women's last day. She is leaving to have a baby. As is traditional, a long table commands one side of the Dairy Box production line. On it are decked out hand-knitted baby clothes, cuddly toys and cards, all gifts for the mother-to-be and her child.

Blackburn and Millar consider themelves fortunate. 'We believed in everything we fought for at the time,' says Blackburn. 'Rowntree was one of the biggest and most successful chocolate companies in the world. We were very content and we really believed in what we were saying. But Nestlé has been extremely sensitive and wise in the way it has handled the acquisition. It has been true to the promises it has made, and it is turning out very well.

But that is not to say there were not very real issues at the time. Rowntree's case was the first involving all the European acquisition issues and the valuation of brands, and those issues have not changed.'

One of those issues was the speed with which some fund managers sold out 14.9 per cent of the company within thirty-five minutes, and for what proved to be a grossly undervalued price.

'I do not think the City had a sense of the value of this business and the brands when this whole thing started,' says Blackburn. He firmly rejects accusations that Rowntree had failed to woo the City. 'Our stockbrokers told us we were upper quartile in terms of the frequency with which we contacted our shareholders. For years we talked about Europe, how long returns there would take and what investment was necessary. For years we talked about brands and the values of brands. I can show you supplements to our accounts which are ten years old and are about brand strength. I think half the thing was that people did not actually listen until it became a big issue.

'We are one of only seven of the top 200 companies to run a business in this part of the UK. Everything is down in the south-east. I think that automatically there is the idea that we are a bit provincial, that we are country boys. I understand that. But a lot of effort was put into the City.'

Blackburn continues. 'But what happened one morning? After a stock market crash the previous October, with people under pressure to meet their targets, someone comes in offering substantially more than yesterday's price.'

'And 15 per cent of the company went in 35 minutes.'

Millar interjects. 'I also think, to be absolutely honest, that £10.75 was a very compelling argument. God knows the pressure anybody's under to refuse £10.75.'

But what of those that sold out at £6.30? Here Millar is less understanding. 'I think those people who sold out at the dawn raid knew jolly well what they were doing, that they were in effect putting a company up for auction. I think they were into it for short-term gain. And I think that whatever they say they are economic with the truth. They don't look long term and don't think long term.'

'A lot of these people are fairly young,' adds Blackburn. 'They have got monthly or quarterly targets, and suddenly after a bad period, £6.30 is on the table for a substantial holding in a company where the previous day it was £4.70. That looks very attractive.'

'The fact was, however, that in half an hour a company that employs 30,000 people around the world, that has been going for 200 years, is out like that.' He snaps his fingers. 'Thirty-five minutes.'

'I don't know how you resolve these differences. But you can imagine how certain people felt here.'

Blackburn and Millar do not accept that the takeover could have been forestalled had they only been more receptive to the approaches of interested parties at an earlier date. Ken Dixon had met Nestlé chairman. Helmut Maucher, in November 1987. Maucher had suggested a 25 per cent stake in the business. 'But who is going to sit on a 25 per cent for years and years and years? It is deferred rape,' says Millar. 'Then again, had Nestlé taken a 25 per cent stake we would not have had Suchard making a counterbid.'

Fortunately, Nestlé, for the time being at least, appears prepared to let Rowntree continue to run itself. But for many, the real tragedy of Rowntree remains unchanged and unresolved. It was that government policy meant that a Rowntree merger with a British competitor was impossible.

'I would be surprised if you did not see more famous British names acquired by foreign companies wanting an increased foothold in Europe,' says Peter Blackburn. 'Many of them will not be so fortunate as we have been.'

# 31

# When breaking up is hard to do

June 1990

Mihir Bose

In April, as England finally gave up in the West Indies in the last test in Antigua, one fanatical English supporter was missing: the island's most famous corporate raider. In his diary in New York he had pencilled in April 18 as the start of the test when it was actually the day England's battered cricketers flew home.

But the oversight does not much matter for, in the last six months, there is little else that Roland Franklin has missed. In that time, he has led a masterly campaign to take over DRG, the Basildon Bond to Sellotape paper and packaging group, and is now busy doing what he always said he would: selling all its businesses, except a certain core.

The bid brought to the City the blunt Wall Street tactics of a raid declaring beforehand that he wants to dismember his prey. Franklin did not take over DRG claiming he could run it better. He argued that as a conglomerate it was fatally flawed and it was best disposed-of to various buyers with the profits going to Franklin, his fellow investors and the banks that had funded the purchase.

Franklin's Pembridge Investments, the Bermuda-based company, was set up for the sole purpose of taking over DRG. Funded by an international cast of investors, many of whom also funded Sir James Goldsmith's attempt to do a similar unbundling of BAT, the bid went against all normal takeover arguments. DRG had made record profits the previous year and most analysts gave Moger Woolley, its chief executive, great credit. As one BZW analyst puts it, DRG had a 'record of uninterrupted earnings per share growth since 1984, in mature and cyclical business' – better than its rivals in the UK, US, Canada and Europe.

In contrast, the City remembered Franklin and recoiled. He was the banker behind the collapse of Keyser Ullmann, the fringe bank headed by Edward Du Cann. In 1979 the DTI report had criticized Franklin and his co-directors for incompetence and accused him of giving evidence that conflicted materially with the facts.

But all this cut little ice with Franklin. In a business world that is rather fond of double speak Franklin is almost intimidatingly direct. During the bid, in a sort of modern version of a medieval baron besieging a city, he set himself up in a suite at the Savoy, and dressed often in an orange shirt and purple slacks (something that was almost as shocking to the City as his bid), would start meetings by saying 'right then, let us discuss my Keyser Ullman days.' He would go on to give his own, highly plausible history, part myth, all overlaid with the disarming Franklin charm.

This was allied to the Franklin record in the US where his image was far removed from the Keyser Ullmann débâcle. In the years since the secondary banking crisis of the 1970s, Franklin had been schooling himself in deals similar to the DRG one, acting as Goldsmith's assistant in the US and earning respect as a man of impeccable British charm who packed a very un-British punch.

Like all successful generals, he was lucky as well. In mid-October 1989 just days before the DRG offer closed, the market crashed, raising fears of a repeat of 1987. It turned out to be a grey Monday rather than a black one, but it made the Franklin offer of 590p a share for DRG irresistible. In the early 1980s, before the Woolley era started, DRG had once cut its dividend. This had led to an exodus of income funds, which tend to be long-term holders, and their replacement by institutions which market growth funds. Although analysts advised DRG was worth 700p, these institutions, frightened by the fall, took the cash. A few resisted even after Franklin got over 50 per cent but they eventually caved in.

That Friday evening, barely twenty-four hours after Nigel Lawson had resigned, Woolley, in a less sensational style, did the same. Along with non-executive chairman Sir John Milne, he called on Franklin at the Savoy. Both Woolley and Franklin, the expat and the home-grown man, were, in Woolley's words, 'terribly civilized and English' about it. Franklin offered a cup of tea and Woolley arranged that when Franklin arrived at DRG's headquarters in Bristol the following Monday he would be received with 'due courtesy'.

But now more than six months later, Franklin's unbundling does not look quite as spectacular as the bid suggested. DRG the conglomerate, with its famous brand names, still remains. Franklin has sold just three businesses: an envelope manufacturer in France, Spectral Technology Group, the ultra-violet lamp and print drying specialist, and DRG cartons, very much fringe DRG business. DRG may be dead but will it, like Banquo's ghost, haunt Franklin?

City analysts are convinced he is finding it difficult to sell. 'It is not a seller's market. The price he paid for DRG means he is having to ask for some very high multiples which you cannot really get in this climate', says Stephen Weller of UBS Phillips & Drew.

Weller's argument is that Franklin has made a fundamental mistake with

DRG. DRG is not the hated conglomerate, whose various parts can be profitably lopped off, leaving behind a core business, he has made it out to be. 'A lot of DRG's value,' says Weller, 'is in its structure. Once you start breaking it up, a lot of it evaporates. It is not like a company making one product in three places which you can sell off. Each division comprises a range of things, they complement each other. It is like trying to sell pieces of a jigsaw.'

Franklin is dismissive of such criticism. 'Analysts have a record of talking unmitigated nonsense from start to finish on this bid,' he says. He admits, though, that high interest rates and the slip in the market have worked both for and against him. 'My timing was poor in one respect. The profits of DRG were less than I thought they were going to be, less than DRG thought they were going to be. I got caught on the wrong part of the cycle. I was somewhat compensated by paying less than I might have had to pay if the cycle hadn't gone wrong,' he says.

And the moment of his triumph, that very civilized tea party with Woolley, also marked a defeat. Franklin wanted to keep Woolley. 'In Crown Zellerback and Diamond International [*the two US paper companies where Franklin practised his unbundling skills*] the chairman and chief executive stayed with us. I think it is a pity Moger Woolley did not stay and has led a campaign against us. He is a man who knew a great deal about the business and could have helped in pursuing the policies we have decided to pursue. He had a lot of qualities. It is just that our philosophies were different.'

For Woolley, the idea of joining Franklin was anathema. 'I am a long-term builder of business. He is a breaker-up. He is no different from an asset stripper. There was no way I could work with him,' he says.

This means Franklin was left with the task of learning about DRG. He had never claimed any expertise in running the company and, while other businessmen glory in the title industrialist, he abhors it: 'industrialist is the last thing I would like to describe myself as. I am an in-house merchant banker.' What he brought to DRG was a simple, if brutal, idea: the concept that conglomerates do not work. 'Conglomerates are positively harmful in a fairly massive way', he says. 'It always surprises me I have such difficulty in persuading other people. It seems to be common sense. If you focus on a particular thing you are likely to do better than if you focus on several things.'

One of the first things Franklin had to focus on when he got to DRG headquarters was defining the core business he wanted to retain. 'I had a sort of plan. I knew we were going to have a core business. I thought it would be packaging but I left it open, thinking it might be something else. You cannot really tell with an unfriendly public company,' he recalls.

A hostile bidder is, to an extent, like an opposition party coming to power after a hard-fought campaign. It is never quite sure what it will find.

Franklin saw the essence of his first ever UK unbundling to be very like the successful ones he had done in the US, but each unbundling has its own characteristics.

Crown had been very different from Diamond. 'I did not pre-sell anything in Crown. But I was on the board of Diamond along with Goldsmith for about eighteen months. We had 25 per cent, which was built up to 40 per cent, and they more or less asked us to take them over. We sold things with the agreement of the board.'

There was no question about pre-selling any of the various bits of DRG. 'We didn't know what they had got. If you don't know what you are selling it is difficult to negotiate the price. I don't think we had enough information before we got inside DRG to create a concrete transaction with anybody.'

But perhaps the biggest problem posed by DRG was that for Franklin's purpose it was so elusive. He was confronted with brand names and a lot of small operating units; a stationery division (about 60 per cent), a packaging division (about 35 per cent), and other bits and pieces. DRG was one company, it was a giant labyrinth, inside which was a lot of interaction. It did not have subsidiaries but divisions.

For Martin Franklin, Roland's twenty-five-year-old son, who went to school in Clifton College in Bristol, before completing his studies in the US, the structure was most unnatural. 'A corporate structure is always better with subsidiaries. The way DRG structures itself made for its own vulnerability. It had divisions which meant its profits were not reported to companies house, so it could hide from shareholders exactly what it earned and how it was doing. We restructured it into limited companies,' he says.

Of course, the restructuring is not quite as altruistic as this would suggest. 'We did it for tax reasons,' says Roland with customary candour. 'You are allowed to do so under English tax law. You allocate to the shares of the subsidiaries you create, a proportion of the purchase price, so in aggregate they acquire a tax base equivalent to your total purchase price of the company. Thus, when you sell the shares you are only paying tax on the profit you are making.'

So DRG, a company full of brand names but no subsidiaries, now found itself parcelled into twenty subsidiaries. But did this not prove Woolley right that DRG was not a conglomerate at all and therefore more difficult to sell? No, says Franklin the younger: 'DRG is far more of a conglomerate than we ever imagined it to be. We are involved in more asset sales than we ever thought we would be. I would have been delighted if there was a synergy, in fact there is none. Dickinson and Robinson merged in 1969 to form DRG. But for people who work there, in their minds no merger took place. Dickinson people feel they are part of Dickinson; Robinson people feel they are part of Robinson; nobody feels they are part of DRG.'

And although the structural reorganization took time, DRG has confirmed Roland in his opinion that all conglomerates are the same. 'Inside DRG I found a mixture of good things and bad things, slightly more so in DRG than most. Where they had a problem they left it alone and went on to buy something else. This is one of the fundamental problems with all conglomerates.'

The most vivid illustration of this came with flexible packaging. 'Flexible packaging in the UK was in a very poor state. Five factories in the neighbourhood of Bristol employing 3500 people which made no money at all. This is another rule about conglomerates; the nearer you are to headquarters, the more mess you are in because everyone belongs to the same golf club and nobody likes to take the radical measures which are necessary to do the right things.'

Yet, for all the fire that the Franklins gave forth on conglomerates, those who ran DRG were not badly burnt – except, perhaps, for the headquarters staff. 'I did not go in and chop heads off. Everybody had three-year service agreements which I cheerfully honoured,' says Roland. 'But in my philosophy the headquarters has no function, therefore the people who operate out of it are without a job.'

'There has not,' says Martin, 'been one management change at the operating level. The head office yes, but I do not call that staff. No operations took place at head office. Sixty people were employed there at the high point. When we took over DRG the head office was on three floors. Now it is on half a floor and we will end up with about seven people. In a conglomerate the skills are at the operating level.'

But the operating units did not emerge unscathed. Woolley had left with the non-executive directors. Three crucial main board directors – Barry Stevenson, in charge of finance, Tony Clarke, in charge of packaging and Hans Jorgenson, who succeeded Woolley as chief executive in November, stayed on. Some operating directors were sacked. Francis Harris, who ran the Fife-based Transcript group being a notable casualty.

The story, as Harris tells it, was pretty brutal. He had opposed the bid. On the Monday, following Franklin's victory, he received a two-line fax saying all capital expenditure was reduced to £1,000. With a budget of £1.7m, half of which was committed, this meant fairly hefty cutbacks including the staff Christmas party which was cancelled. 'After the memo,' recalls Harris, 'I heard nothing at all. There was an extraordinary period of silence.'

Harris tried to organize a buy-out for his plant but was told by Clarke that it was not on. The Franklins are not keen on buy-outs. ('Managers are not wealthy people,' says Martin.) On the company's bush telegraph Harris heard about head office staff being made redundant. On January 9 he was asked to go to Edinburgh airport to meet Clarke, whom he had known for twenty years, and Jim Foulds, the personnel director.

The three men walked across the road to the Norton House hotel. Clarke obtained a room and ordered coffee. 'You have probably guessed why I have come here,' he said to Harris as soon as the waiter had gone. Harris replied that he did not know. 'Your services are not required. Don't bother to go back to your office,' said Clarke. Harris asked for an explanation but Clarke refused to give one. Harris had a three-year contract, was paid for one year and when he protested was told he could sue. 'I was,' said Harris, 'an obstacle.'

But it is too simple to see Harris as a victim of unbundling. He never met the Franklins and they have little recollection of him. 'Oh, that Francis Harris, he was not doing very well,' recalls Roland, somewhere from the depths of his memory. 'It was a management team decision,' says Martin. Transcript's 1989 performance had sharply deteriorated: in 1988 it made £5m, in 1989 it made under £2m and Woolley, who is surprisingly free of rancour about Franklin, says he would not dispute Franklin's word that it was a management decision.

Jeff Penna's departure after thirty-six years with DRG, during which time he had built up the plastics business pretty much from zero, was more of an indication of the Franklin desire to remove what are seen as useless layers of conglomerate management. Penna was chief executive of plastics, reporting to Clarke, the main board director, but with an operating managing director under him. Again Clarke made him an offer he could not refuse and though he felt 'pretty sick' at the time, there is no bitterness. 'I was in a layer which they wanted to take out,' he says. Roland recalls: 'there were several chains of command and he was therefore surplus to requirements.'

Other operating managers were quickly invited to meet Martin and Roland. This was part of a philosophy to isolate the operating units. 'The ones we keep will report direct to a very small staff which we have and whose purpose is not to intervene and control but to know what is going on and to monitor,' says Martin.

The meetings impressed Martin. 'The quality of the managing directors at the operating levels has been marvellous. Very good. When you get down to the silent level, the managing director of the operating company, he is one of fifty-seven other operating managing directors. Once a year he meets the chief executive to beg for capital expenditure. That is all the contact he has with the chief executive of a conglomerate.'

The Franklins claim they are working to liberate this silent majority, so much so that instead of the selling of the business being a trauma for them it becomes a joy. 'We come along, and we say, "I have got here a list of ten people, all of whom have expressed interest in your business." We ask them "who do you feel comfortable with, who would you like to work for and work with?" We have the final say but they have a strong input in the decision-making process. We put them in homes they feel most comfortable with,' says Martin, making it sound as if selling a business is like fostering a child.

As a child draws warmth and sustenance from a good home, so the manager gets financial gain. 'We have generous incentives for managers when we sell businesses. If we sell the business at what we consider a good price we will share a proportion with the manager. That is, a multiple of what a manager will see with his income. The result is that the management is pleased, the buyer is pleased, everybody ends up a winner, except the chief executive of the conglomerate.'

But it will be sometime before all DRG operating managers feel like winners. The Franklins have done just three deals, worth about £100m. It was the end of March, almost five months after the takeover, when the third sale, that of the carton business took place.

DRG had two businesses in the cartons factory. 'One,' says Roland, 'was not bad business potentially, but so undercapitalized it needed £7m spending on it. So they were trying to sell it to someone in a similar line of business relatively locally. It would have meant putting 370 people out of work, literally. We explored that avenue ourselves, then I was delighted to be able to do what I had spelt out in my offer, the sort of thing we could bring to the table.'

The deal was done by Martin. 'The only people who should own carton manufacturing businesses are carton manufacturers, not paper business or distribution business. It fits in with our philosophy. We know a lot of industries. We happen to know Tom Johnson who is the president of Manville Forest Products Corporation, a billion dollar carton manufacturing business in the US. The deal was done in three weeks.'

The unions were delighted with the deal. Manville wants to use the factory as its base for its operations in Europe. 'Manville is going to invest a large sum of money, certainly in excess of £10m over the next five years, more money than DRG has spent on it in the last decade. There will not be a cut in employment, if anything there will be an increase,' says Martin. And, of course, it was good money for the Franklins since they sold to Manville because, as Martin admits – it was the highest bidder.

The Franklins intend pursuing similar 'everyone is a winner' unbundling until they unravel it all down to the core business which is medical packaging and rigid plastics. 'We shall keep that,' says Roland, 'float, sell it to somebody else, but that is the core of the business which is worth preserving and the rest is better in other people's hands.'

But the selling process is not easy. 'You can go for several weeks when nothing happens,' says Roland, 'then you can sell four businesses in one week, or get agreement to sell.'

This fact of life is unlikely to satisfy the sceptics. Weller of UBS Phillips and Drew, for example, feels that 'the consortium, if the interest rate scenario and the economic climate does not lift in the remainder of the year, could lose £100m. Mr Franklin is looking at the end of 1991 for completion. That dictates against him making profits.'

Such a viewpoint does not faze the Franklins. The interest burden is £1.6m a week. But the company's cash flow is £82m a year. 'When you take into account,' says Martin, 'that we have sold £100m of business, I am at rather a comfortable level. The more I do, the more comfortable it becomes, until you get down to the profit level. But you do not get down to the profit until all you are left with is the core business.'

'As far as our banking liabilities are concerned £180m is all we had to sell in our first year,' says Roland. 'We are not under pressure. I would like to go faster but it does not go much faster.'

'When you have companies with high market shares in niche markets whether you are in a good economy or a poor economy, there are always industrial buyers available to purchase the business,' continues Martin.

Yet, in a curious way Weller and the Franklins are closer in their estimation of where DRG will be by the end of the year than might first appear. Weller envisages that 'by the end of 1990 no more than a third or half of the business is to be sold.' Martin says: 'by the end of the year half of the business will have gone.' He thinks that by then they may be down to the core but that 'this will not be a quick operation. We will be running the DRG business for another couple of years at least, absolutely.'

Already Martin admits that he has 'had a steep learning curve' and at the end of those two years he might have learnt that, while all conglomerates may be evil as his father says, they do not all unbundle in the same way.

# Section Seven

## Employment Issues

# 32

# Age: discrimination's last frontier?

September 1987

Stuart Rock

British business is discriminating against the executive over forty, and this in spite of a working population that is growing older.

Recent surveys of recruitment advertising reveal that while discrimination on grounds of sex and race may be out, your age can easily lose you the chance of a job. One survey by consultants MSL found that of 928 advertised posts that specified an age 88.5 per cent stipulated an age limit of forty.

A three-week survey of national newspapers by *Director* found that approximately 15 per cent of jobs advertised in *The Times* specified an age; nearly 25 per cent did so in the *Daily Telegraph*; and well over 40 per cent in the *Financial Times* (in fact, a whopping 214 out of 457).

The age limits paralleled the MSL findings. For example, one issue of the *Daily Telegraph* carried well over 400 senior posts but only two asked for someone aged 45-plus – the jobs were a golf club secretary and the chapter clerk for Salisbury Cathedral.

Public advertising is, of course, the most overt form of executive recruitment. But even in other fields, such as executive search, the message is little different. Patrick Andrew, executive chairman of head-hunters David Stevens International, says that it is frequently the case that 'we cannot search for anyone over thirty-two.' Indeed, he adds, 'in many instances, I have seen the best candidate turned down before an interview because of age.'

Bob Whitney, director of MSL and the man who instituted the company's research into age discrimination, says that 'client companies often specify age as the first thing, and they can be very specific. Yet it is the worst criterion by which you judge a person.'

At an Institute of Personnel Management conference to take place next month, the issue will be put firmly on management's agenda. Peter Naylor, chairman of the IPM's standing committee on equal opportunities, has prepared a discussion paper on the subject, an advance copy of which has been obtained by *Director*.

In the paper Naylor argues that the IPM should endeavour to create 'a climate in which more is done to reduce the reliance placed by employers in using age as a sole criterion in employment decisions.'

Yet that fairer climate does not seem destined to be achieved with the help of legislation. In 1983 a Private Member's Bill on the issue of age discrimination failed; last year Welsh MP Ann Clwyd sponsored a similar bill that suffered the same fate. The Department of Employment does not have a view on the subject; it is not an issue, and legislation would create extra red tape, the department says.

There are signs, though, that it is *becoming* an issue. At a recent conference on the future of executive recruiting, Sir Monty Finniston – a still active 75-year-old – told one delegate: 'It is rather ridiculous, this consideration of age as a major criterion: I really do not understand it . . . I think it is a sin.' Finniston was not alone in condemning the practice.

The roots of age discrimination lie in stereotyping. Older people are too often lumped together as being weaker of health, lower in productivity, slow to adapt and resistant to learning new skills. Naylor of the IPM says: 'These beliefs may, and probably do, influence employers. It is disturbing in as much as such beliefs are, at present, not supported by any objective evidence.'

On top of these time-honoured unproven assumptions, recent circumstances have compounded the problem.

Educational norms have changed radically in the past twenty years. The first generation of business school graduates has fed through the system, adding a new qualification – and, by implication, a disqualification for the rest – into the selection of procedure of senior personnel. The rise in graduate traineeships has sounded the death-knell of the earlier attitude that automatically equated experience with ability.

Such shifts are not bad in themselves. What they do contribute to, though, is a lowering of the acceptable age threshold for a particular job. The perception that youth equals energy equals output becomes even more blinkered.

Unemployment is not just a problem of the steel worker and the docker. The restructuring of British industry in the late 1970s and early 1980s haemorrhaged middle and senior management as well as blue-collar workers. Since then, the sharp rise in takeovers and subsequent rationalization programmes have ousted more. The boardroom putsch may make for enthralling reading, but little attention is ever given to the consequent fate of those who lost.

Pension and salary structures have changed, once again disadvantaging the older businessman. Directors' pay has increased dramatically. Firms are willing to pay large sums to get the twenty-eight to forty-year-old they want, especially in the boom areas of data processing, advertising and marketing, and financial services. This generation, who from next year can also look at the option of a portable pension, may both want to, and have the freedom to, retire at fifty. The previous industry-based, lower-salaried, pension-frozen breed does not have such luxuries.

Employer interests have moved away from those who have worked with one company all their lives – the 'womb-to-tomb' type as they are known to outplacement consultants – to those who have proof of a reasonable degree of job mobility. Once more, a generation is rejected, despite the fact that the number of jobs carried out within one company may be as varied as those experienced by more restless spirits.

Opinions differ as to the nature of the crisis. Consultant and headhunter Andrew believes that 'a very serious experience gap is building up in some of our major industries. People who performed, went through a period of growth and then lost their job, not necessarily through any fault of their own, are not finding jobs that utilize their talents properly. The rot has got to stop.'

Derek Edwards, director of outplacement consultancy Sanders & Sidney, admits that there is a problem but does not see it in quite such dramatic terms.

'Fear of age is in the businessman's mind,' he says. 'People can be almost paranoid. They ask me "who wants a fifty-year-old?" with despair in their voice.' He believes that much of this fear is unfounded, created only by the attitudes of others – the 'what are you going to do now?' questioning.

That said, Edwards recognizes that companies have a pride about the age of their workforce. (This is illustrated by one job advertisement which reads: 'firm of three partners of average age under forty years (just!) . . .'). Edwards also notes that if a company is faced with two equal candidates, it will choose the younger.

As much as anything, the solution to the problem lies in the hands of the employer. The IPM's Naylor sees an unquestioning acceptance of stereotype, which reinforces the belief that the older person is not up to the job, and thus leads to self-fulfilling prophesies. 'Such beliefs become enshrined as received wisdom. Worse than that they become part of business or institutional policy.' It is a vicious cycle, which he says must be broken.

Age discrimination is also based on convenience. Faced with 150 CVs, a personnel director uses 'date of birth' as a convenient means of initial selection. Companies to which *Director* spoke that had specified an age in their advertisements said that they had no aversion to employing someone older, but the age limit indicated their preference. In other words, they were happy to look at anyone, but would try to dissuade some.

(This line of thinking can lead to some intriguing copy: 'Personal qualities of drive, initiative and imagination will be important. Age indicator twenty-eight to thirty-five, though pertinent candidates outside this range will certainly be considered' or 'age is entirely secondary to ability, but you must have the correct blend of experience and enthusiasm.')

It is the inability to get over the first hurdle that most infuriates people. Once at an interview, the chance is there; to get to the interview is very difficult. What is doubly irritating is that if a company actually does get around to seeing the forty-five-plus candidate, he or she is quite often the right person.

'Employers grouse initially,' comments Sanders & Sidney's Edwards, 'but if the chemistry is there, age is often the first thing to go.'

It might be thought that examples would have produced a more flexible approach. After all, a woman in her late fifties appointed a man in his seventies to run Britain's coal industry not so long ago. At a recent executive recruitment conference, Donald Young, director of personnel and organization development at Thorn-EMI, cited the case of its semiconductor subsidiary Inmos as one where age was certainly no barrier to effective management.

'The turnround of Inmos has been one of the most heroic and effective pieces of management leadership I have ever seen, and that was done by a man called Douglas Stevenson who was sixty-three,' he said. 'I have never seen such phenomenal skill, wisdom and energy applied to a very knotty international business problem by anybody.'

In his discussion paper, the IPM's Naylor makes a number of recommendations as to how the problems of age discrimination can be overcome.

'Hiring decisions about people over fifty should be made in terms of personnel practices that were formerly applied to people at the age of forty,' he says. He wants to encourage organizations 'to confront directly the issue of whether or not older applicants *can* do the job' and he suggests companies enshrine their employment policies in a statement such as 'age is not an acceptable primary or sole criterion for hiring, firing, lay-offs or redundancy.'

Naylor also urges companies to make a wide range of career counselling and planning facilities available, as well as retraining and a willingness to give older workers a wider range of responsibilities. A greater degree of flexibility in designing remuneration packages, and the possibility of tax exemptions for the contributions of older employees are also suggested.

Ultimately, though, there are two key areas to be addressed: legislation and the development of second career opportunities.

Naylor believes that it may be necessary 'to have some form of legislation to proscribe discrimination in employment on the grounds of age alone.' But as MP Clwyd was to discover, it is not something that has attracted government support. The argument is that it would be difficult to identify whether discrimination was taking place. A company could easily say that it was vital for its management development programme that it employ a thirty-five-year-old, which would be difficult to disprove in a court of law.

'Not putting the date of birth on a CV would be an attempt to solve discrimination, but in practice it would not work,' says Edwards of Sanders & Sidney.

The US and Canada are the only developed Western nations to have such legislation. The American Age Discrimination in Employment Act (ADEA) was passed in 1967, and has been regularly amended ever since. Recent changes have meant that there is no mandatory retirement age for many categories of worker. And now the Equal Employment Opportunity Commission has told its officers to be on the look-out for 'age harassment'. (Possible grounds for a lawsuit include jokes made about an employee's age, and the failure of management to halt the same.) Paradoxically, though, the average age at which retirement is taken in the US is actually dropping.

In an assessment of the ADEA conducted by the Department of Employment's Unit of Manpower Studies, it was concluded that employers and employees had lived with the legislation without much difficulty. The report noted that 'Congress would seem to regard the certain guarantee of employment rights as being more important than possible additional unemployment.'

US legislation has spawned a pressure group – the 50,000-strong Gray Panthers – which monitors 'ageism' in both the workplace and as it affects the elderly as consumers. The Panthers' Jean Hopper says that law cases have been successfully contested; only recently one successful prosecution under the Act won $48,000 from a Calfornian federal agency.

The Gray Panthers is now embarking on a major 'work project', in which it is analysing how older people can, by dint of arranging more flexible hours, fit into the workplace at their greater convenience. This will need a sympathetic corporation with whom to arrange a model programme, says Hopper.

Another objective the Gray Panthers has is the promotion of 'intergenerationalism'.

'When the economy is not growing there tends to be increased divisiveness between the generations – particularly at work,' says Hopper.

Indeed, acting as a father figure to a team of young Turks is seen as a sound second career by outplacement consultant Edwards. If, as he says, performance is not often a reason for firing executives ('the face does not fit' is the usual one), then there should be enough demand among young firms for a bit of managerial nous. 'There are lots of holes in project management', notes Edwards.

This view is echoed by Andrew, but he also has seen instances of a young entrepreneur frightened by the suggestion, thinking that the older man would tie him down. Once more the stereotype works its influence.

A non-executive role would appear to offer fresh pastures but Sanders & Sidney say that there are currently more people than vacancies in this area. Besides, it would take more than a non-executive post or two to meet the financial demands of a mortgage, a car and the well-being of a family.

There are, it seems, no firm solutions to age discrimination. What is required is far-reaching cultural change; business needs to take a more flexible and often more imaginative approach.

The older generation have to think of themselves more positively. They may have to adjust to the ideas of aggregating their income from a variety of sources rather than from just one job. Current management incumbents should be looking now at what pre-retirement services are being offered by their company, and what training programmes are open to the over-forties. The corporate personnel structure and its age profile need to be analysed, especially in the light of a particular forthcoming vacancy.

'Old age hath yet his honour,' write the poet Tennyson, and 'something ere the end, some work of noble note, may yet be done.' Perhaps that message still needs to be reinforced. As Hopper of the US Gray Panthers says, reacting to the fact that the UK has no age discrimination legislations, 'You are just penalizing yourselves.'

# 33

# Who are the unemployed?

November 1987

## Carol Kennedy

Well, who *are* the unemployed? The short answer is that no one seems to know. The Department of Employment keeps no data on what skills unemployed people have, or what industries they have worked in; the kind of basic information that could begin to explain the skills gap in areas where there are both jobless and job vacancies.

Of 25,336 vacancies at Jobcentres recorded in March as remaining un-filled for more than eight weeks, 5404 were identified as due to skills shortages. (Jobcentres are notified of only about a third of total vacancies in their areas.) In 75 per cent of cases, the local labour supply was unsuitably qualified.

Labour shortages are most acute in the building industry, especially in the south east and along the south coast, where employers cannot keep pace with the construction boom for lack of plasterers, carpenters, plumbers and, particularly, bricklayers.

A survey by the Building Employers' Confederation in the first quarter of this year disclosed that two-thirds of its respondents found it difficult to hire bricklayers; nearly a quarter found such labour 'virtually unavail-able'.

Shortages also exist in microelectronic technology, computer staff, trained clerical staff, professional engineers and engineering craftsmen, accountants and nurses. Yet no reliable information exists on who among the unemployed is qualified to do what, and in which areas.

The lack of raw data on Britain's most contentious and intractable domestic problem is a constant source of frustration to anyone working on the subject, from university academics through privately funded study units like the Employment Institute to researchers in the government's Manpower Services Commission.

The explanation lies in cost reductions. Until 1982, people registering as unemployed were asked to state their last job. But as part of the drive for cost-effectiveness in the civil service, Jobcentre and DHSS functions were separated and registration became voluntary. If such information-gathering were to be reintroduced, an unofficial estimate has worked out that even a brief interview of two to five minutes could require up to 300 extra staff.

Some independent progress is being made in building up a profile of the long-term unemployed. The Employment Institute, a charitable organization working in cramped offices off the Albert Embankment and headed by former Treasury civil servant Jon Shields, is compiling a study in conjunction with a researcher in Southampton University, due for publication later this year.

Meanwhile, the MSC's Skills Monitoring Unit in Sheffield provides a broad picture on a regional basis of the qualifications existing among the employed and unemployed, and this comes as close as anything to defining the intractable core of Britain's unemployment problem.

'Qualifications' in this context means anything from CSE to higher degrees and includes completed trade apprenticeships. Even on this broad definition, fully half the unemployed of Britain have no qualifications at all, and more than a third (36 per cent) of those in work are also totally without formal qualifications. Regionally, the best-qualified workforces are, not surprisingly, in the south east and south west; the worst qualified in the west midlands. The same regional pattern applies to those out of work, with only 43 per cent of job-seekers in the west midlands holding formal qualifications from CSE upwards.

Put bluntly, we are an unskilled nation, sharing the plight of Eric Fletcher of Cleveland, who confronted Mrs Thatcher on her autumn visit to the area with a sheaf of 1000 unsuccessful job applications. Training was not for him, he said, he was 'just a labouring man'.

'Employers are not going to find the skills they need because from time immemorial we have under-invested in the skills and development of people,' says MSC director Geoffrey Holland. The labour shortages that *Director* interviews with employers round the regions have pinpointed are, says Holland, 'the tip of an iceberg of lack of skills and adaptability.'

Historian Correlli Barnett, in his chilling book *The Audit of War*, reveals that poorly trained, shoddy workmanship damaged Britain's war effort in the factories and laid the foundations for postwar decline. The failure of generations of employers to provide proper skills training and the low priority given to higher technical education means that even in the eighties, up to 70 per cent of school-leavers are 'only equipped to be coolies, like their fathers and grandfathers, but in a technological world that had little need of coolies.'

Professor Charles Handy of the London Business School, author of an influential book called *The Future of Work*, is deeply concerned with Britain's lack of 'brain skills'. Now working on a sequel to the book, he produces a statistic from McKinsey in Amsterdam that by the end of the century 70 per cent of all jobs in Northern Europe will require brain skills.

'At a very crude guess, about half of those brain skills will be tuned to a higher degree,' says Handy. 'That means by the end of the century about 35 per cent of the new workforce should have been to university.

By that yardstick, Handy adds, all European countries are 'grossly under educated'. Only the US and Japan qualify. The UK claims about 18 per cent; but about 40 per cent of British school-leavers lack even one O-level or CSE, Handy says.

Handy, author of the much-quoted recent report *The Making of Managers*, takes a swipe in passing at Britain's poor record in this area, too. Seventy-nine per cent of British managers have no qualifications beyond O-level. (Incidentally, one of the hardest unemployment nuts to crack is that of redundant managers aged forty to forty-five and over.)

On prospects for long-term unemployment, Handy says: 'We are going to be stuck for a long time with a lot of people who have been badly educated and have no kind of vocational credential. They are the lost generation. The twelve-year-olds will probably be OK; there are fewer of them and they are going to get a better education.'

Indeed, the good news is that youth unemployment, on present demographic trends, looks like being greatly diminished, if not a thing of the past, by the mid-1990s. The bad news is that whatever educational reforms take place to improve basic skills, they are not going to affect the quality of the workforce until after 2000.

MSC director Holland cites his 'rule of three sevens': seven out of ten of those who will be in the workforce by 2000 are already in the workforce; seven out of ten of those left at the minimum school-leaving age, many with very few qualifications; and seven out of ten of *that* segment have had no systematic training since leaving school. That is the 'iceberg' underlying the skills shortage and the more than one million long-term unemployed who have been out of work for a year or more.

The latest age breakdown available for the long-term unemployed is based on the April 1987 figures, when total unemployment was 3,107,000. It runs as follows:

- Under-25s: total unemployment 1,026,000: long-term 286,000
- 25–54: total unemployed 1,708,000: long-term 797,000
- 55 plus: total unemployed 373,000: long term 212,000

There is a tendency, says Holland, to believe that getting the schools right will solve the problem, but the nub of the training challenge applies most acutely to those of working age now.

What all the pointers indicate is that Britain's mass of unqualified people will find it progressively more difficult to find work. As more jobs require sophisticated technology and manual work becomes increasingly mechanized, the future looks bleak for anyone who describes himself as 'just a labouring man'.

'I don't see many unskilled jobs around in the next century,' says Handy.

Among jobs lost in public sector employment alone since 1980, the unqualified and low-skilled have been hard hit, though manpower cuts by local authorities have applied virtually across the board, with only social services, housing and police showing increases. Sizeable falls are recorded in education services, construction, transport and refuse collection.

Manufacturing industry lost just over two million jobs between March 1979 and March 1987, while the service sector gained 1.2 million – not as many as were lost in metal goods, engineering and vehicles. The Institute of Manpower Studies has predicted a growth of 500,000 service-sector jobs between 1985 and 1990 but a loss of 650,000 manufacturing jobs in the same period.

Many of the new service jobs are in traditionally low-paid industries such as catering and retailing, or in areas such as financial services requiring quite different skills from manufacturing.

As Dave Taylor of the Unemployment Unit, a part-voluntary research body backed by the Leverhulme Trust and some local government grants, points out: 'Vacancies for bar staff in East Anglia or accountants in London are not a great deal of use to unemployed fitters in Sheffield.'

The Unemployment Unit has detected a further worrying trend towards loss of skills among those who formerly filled competent technical jobs in industries that have suffered shake-outs.

'A de-skilling process goes on when people are intermittently employed,' says Taylor. He cites the example of a redundant textile worker who has been forced to take less skilled work elsewhere. If he loses that in turn, his skills have gone down a notch on his CV.

What all the employment research bodies agree on, however, is that the work ethic is still alive and well in Britain despite pockets in Scotland and other areas where a subculture has grown up of dependence on the dole, born of almost three jobless generations. (This is quite distinct from exploitation of 'the system' of unemployment benefits within the black economy.)

The MSC's Holland says there is a 'high willingness' among the unemployed to embark on Job Training Schemes, which offer on-the-job experience for the equivalent of unemployment benefit plus travelling expenses. Seventy per cent of those on Youth Training Schemes find jobs, he says, and two-thirds of those who use the MSC's 'Jobclubs' (centres providing job information, stationery, stamps and phones for those out of work for six months or more) find work within four weeks, even in areas of high unemployment.

'There are more jobs around than meet the eye,' Holland maintains, pointing out that seven million jobs change hands every year.

Holland does not accept that there has to be a hard core of semi-permanent unemployment. Unemployability, he points out, is a moving frontier. As a young man with the Ministry of Labour in the early 1960s he took part in a survey to establish an 'irreducible minimum' of unemployment at a time when the total without work was 250,000. The 'irreducible minimum' turned out to be 100,000. The concept then of three million unemployed would have been unthinkable.

The lurking danger, in Holland's view, is that the frontier is moving in skill terms as well, so that the distance is widening between available jobs and available workers. 'What is going to determine unemployment is international competitiveness.'

Employers, says Holland, must take a positive approach to training their existing workforce in new skills. To nudge them more in this direction, he hints that the MSC 'might be more skilful in using leverage' where training grants are concerned; moving more to a 'conditional' partnership with employers.

At least one industry suffering skill shortages – construction – is now making more training places available, including apprenticeships.

Looking to the long-term future of employment, Professor Handy sees more of the manual trades becoming self-employed (he thinks government should encourage the trend to self-employment by a 'negative income tax') and most people's working lives being half as long as the traditional 100,000 hours (forty-seven hours a week, forty-seven weeks a year, forty-seven years). Only half the working population will be in full-time jobs by the end of the century, he says, citing a study by the Warwick Institute. The others will be part-time, temporary or self-employed. At managerial level, he sees people retiring at forty or forty-five like army officers and, with a secure pension, embarking on part-voluntary work involving some social fulfilment, such as 'para-doctors, para-teachers or para-priests'.

But what of the short to medium term? The Employment Institute's Shields tends to a bleak view. The former Treasury official expects some 'choking off' to take place in the economy next year if the government's inflation targets look like facing trouble. The international economy will slow down, he predicts, and special measures like the YTS will stop having their effect on the rate of change. But given what he calls 'legitimate' government pump-priming on selected regional projects, he sees 'quite a good chance' of full employment by 1995.

On the future of brain skills, Handy thinks the government's proposed educational reforms will be beneficial if they can be made to work. He points out that Britain has more Nobel Prizewinners per 1000 head of population than any other country. 'I don't believe that 40 per cent of our kids are incapable of getting one O-level or CSE,' he concludes. 'I don't believe we are a stupid nation.'

# 34

# Addicts in the workplace

September 1989

Tom Nash

Ask UK chief executives about the problems their businesses are facing and the responses may range from high interest rates to strikes. One problem that is unlikely to be recognized, however, is addiction among management and staff.

But the major forms of addiction – drugs, alcohol, tobacco and solvents – are a serious business problem. An estimated 40 per cent of the UK population are affected by at least one of them – the majority in full-time jobs.

Leaving aside the human cost, the cost to business in financial terms is staggering. Alcohol-related problems alone cost more than £700m a year in sickness absence. Illnesses related to nicotine addiction lead to the annual loss of some 50 million working days. 'At a guess I would say that not less than 100 million days a year are lost because of addiction in its various forms,' says Professor Griffith Edwards, director of the Institute of Psychiatry's addiction research unit. 'That is the equivalent of a fair sized general strike – every year.'

And there are huge unquantifiable costs to industry caused by adverse effects on safety, performance and productivity.

Traditionally, addiction has been underestimated and ignored by the business community. But the problem is getting worse and demanding attention. In the UK 30 per cent of the population is addicted to nicotine; 700,000 people have a dependence upon alcohol; 100,000 people are taking heroin. In addition, approximately one million people suffer from long-term dependence on drugs such as sedatives and tranquillizers that were originally supplied as short-term solutions.

Practical answers do exist. An employee developing problems can be recognized and the problem tackled before the person concerned loses his or her job. Against a background of worsening skills and labour shortages, companies are starting to realize that it is not only humane for them to encourage employees to seek treatment, but also cost-effective.

Drug and alcohol abuse has far reaching effects in the workplace. It impairs judgement and blunts reactions, increasing the risk of physical danger if machinery is being used. It damages job performance, leading to lower productivity and lost orders. It attacks health, with long-term effects ranging from lack of concentration and short-term memory loss to complete physical and psychological collapse. And it can manifest itself in erratic and aggressive behaviour – even violence.

At management level, in particular, the effects of mind-influencing substances can be disastrous. Professor Edwards cites the true case of a finance director with a drinking problem. It was eventually taken seriously only when he insulted a trade union official at a company party, but the problem had existed for twenty years and may have inflicted substantial damage to the company in areas as diverse as accounting and industrial relations.

Addiction can also strike indirectly at individuals, destroying their careers and damaging their companies' efficiency. 'Take the genuine case of the blue-chip high flier whose wife drinks heavily and disgraces him in public,' says Professor Edwards. 'Or the company doctor whose son is addicted to heroin. Can either be expected to perform to their full potential at work?'

Employers have three options if they are faced with an employee whose work is suffering because of drink or drug abuse. The first is to do nothing. While this is a natural reaction for someone faced with a problem he does not know how to tackle, it is not really a practical option at all. The likelihood is that the employee's problem, and the damage it is causing to his employer's business, will get worse.

The second is to sack the person concerned. This may seem an easy way out, but it ignores the investment that has been made in the employee and the cost of finding, recruiting and training a replacement. There are also the possible costs of an industrial tribunal. From a human rather than a business perspective, like the first option, dismissal does nothing to help the individual himself.

The third option is to be prepared for problems of alcohol and drug abuse to arise and to have a company policy for dealing with them.

'Many companies simply have no policy for dealing with addiction,' says Professor Edwards. 'They often take the attitude: "we are a nice blue-chip British company and it cannot happen to us".'

The TUC agrees that an alcohol policy is necessary. 'Good intentions are unlikely to have much effect,' says Peter Jacques, head of the TUC's social insurance and industrial welfare department. 'But there is no model policy. Each company needs to develop an approach that suits its particular place of work.'

While every company's circumstances are different and there is no universal, off-the-shelf solution to the problem of drug and alcohol abuse, guidance on the sort of policy companies should consider implementing is available from the Department of Employment and the Health and Safety Executive. It can be split into five main areas.

The first is prevention. It may be a cliché, but the fact remains that prevention is better than cure. More specifically, it is both cheaper and more effective. It is important to remember that the work environment itself can sometimes encourage employees to misuse alcohol or drugs. They may be worried by their job or they may be bored at work. (Alternatively, they may in some organizations be encouraged to think of alcohol as a necessary part of corporate entertaining, as a 'social oil.')

Employers may be able to do something about irregular working hours, too much or too little work, inadequate supervision. Other measures they should consider include setting an example themselves, making sure that alternatives to alcohol are available, gaining acceptance of a no-smoking policy and using health promotion booklets and posters to get the message across.

The second issue is recognizing the problem when it arises. This should be based on monitoring job performance, behaviour, accidents and attendance. Early recognition and early action are vital if a potentially serious problem is to be dealt with quickly and efficiently.

The third issue is giving help. There may be times when dismissal is required for safety reasons, but in the vast majority of cases, employers should encourage employees to seek confidential help and treatment. Addicts must be given the same protection and employment rights as any other employees with medical problems.

The fourth important issue is to make sure that the company policy on drug and alcohol misuse is properly applied. It is no good having a policy tucked away in a staff handbook that is not put into practice. Managers must be made aware of the policy so that they and the staff working under them know whom they can go to for help and advice within an organization, or outside it if the company does not have its own occupational health staff.

Companies should make sure that all staff know that they are expected to take a sensible attitude to drinking, that drug misuse will not be tolerated, and that they understand the standards of work required from them.

The fifth issue is monitoring the application of the policy. Procedures need to be reviewed regularly to ensure that they are effective and still meet the needs of the company.

The TUC's Jacques stresses that it may be specific features of the workplace, such as poor working conditions, low pay, excessive overtime or inordinate shiftwork that create stress – from which temporary relief may be sought through alcohol or drugs.

'We ask all employers to think of the social problems that can be caused when the production line is speeded up or when employers fail to provide a decent working environment in the pursuit of profits.'

Jacques also complains that all too often companies operate double standards. 'Over-indulgence in the boardroom is accepted as an excusable part of the job,' he says. 'After all, it is claimed, customers must be offered hospitality. But in the same company, the shopfloor worker who arrives the worse for wear may face instant dismissal.'

Jacques says that double standards also apply in attitudes towards male and female drinkers. The man who has had too much to drink is often looked upon as 'a bit of a lad,' whereas a woman in a similar condition is considered to be 'showing herself up'.

Above all, the TUC maintains that alcohol and drug abuse is not a disciplinary matter but a health problem and should be seen as a health problem, for which employers themselves should take some of the responsibility and try to relieve some of the underlying causes.

'Both trade unionists and employers need to develop a new level of awareness so that they can agree on effective policies for dealing with alcohol and drug abuse,' says Jacques.

GEC is one UK company that has implemented just such a policy. Concentrating principally on alcohol problems, it has set up an advisory service that enables the company to rehabilitate sufferers, who are considered to have a medical rather than a disciplinary disorder. Many participating GEC companies have extended the service to include close relatives who live with employees.

GEC subsidiaries are fairly autonomous, so they have not been forced to adopt the advisory services. The aim has been to persuade each management that it is in its enlightened self-interest.

'From a business point of view the policy is aimed at increasing efficiency and profitability,' says Bob Randall, co-ordinator of GEC's alcohol advisory service. 'From the drinker's point of view there is a humanitarian need to avert the natural, almost inevitable deterioration which will involve pain and embarrassment.

'The biggest pitfall has been management's perception of what alcoholism really is. People are inured by the comforting stereotype of the skid row derelict. They fail to realize that before problem drinkers reach that stage they have to drink excessively for a considerable number of years.'

Similarly, the image of the drug abuser is that of a junkie 'shooting up' heroin in a slum or a public convenience. It is a seedy and criminalized image and, while it does occur, it is not the norm. Like the majority of problem drinkers, the UK's million tranquillizer addicts are not criminals, but ordinary people who have a dependency that needs to be treated as a health issue.

According to Randall, once senior managers realize that alcoholism usually starts with social drinking and develops very gradually over a long period of time, they begin to accept the widespread existence of problem drinking.

Because referral and treatment are confidential, it is difficult to compile statistics on the effectiveness of GEC's advisory service. However, Randall believes the policy is working increasingly well as attitudinal barriers are broken down, even though some people remain unable to accept that others may have a drinking problem. 'Sometimes even those whose responsibilities include the care and well-being of employees are indifferent,' he says.

The belief that management can make a considerable impact on the problem of drug and alcohol abuse is shared by the Institute of Directors and the Confederation of British Industry. Research by the CBI shows that similar companies in the same industry, in the same locality and with equivalent workforces can have astonishingly different levels of absenteeism.

The employers' organizations agree that companies should introduce policies on drugs and alcohol. Without ignoring the disciplinary aspects of the problem, they urge the provision of wider counselling services and employee assistance programmes (EAPs). EAPs are commonly used in US companies to provide support and advice to employees on matters ranging from legal and financial difficulties to marital breakdown – all of which could be symptoms of the problem of addiction.

A recent study of 100 US companies by the Commission for Economic Development found that more than a third had some kind of formal health promotion programme for their employees. The incentive is obvious: US companies are much more likely than their UK counterparts to be financing healthcare and therefore need to control the spiralling costs involved. However, the aim has also been to control the cost of absenteeism.

Toiletries group Johnson and Johnson, for example, has introduced a 'Live for Life' programme to promote employee health by achieving specific improvements in areas such as nutrition, weight control, physical fitness, stopping smoking, and managing stress. The programme consists of health screening, seminars and individual consultations and there are non-financial incentives, such as small gifts, for success in reaching various goals.

The results of this and other US EAPs are impressive. Johnson and Johnson has noted a 15 per cent fall in sickness absence since the 'Live for Life' programme was introduced. At Du Pont the figure is 25 per cent and at Canada Life it is a remarkable 42 per cent. Johnson and Johnson also found that hospitalization costs increased at only about one third of the rate of subsidiaries not participating in the scheme.

Interest in EAPs is growing among UK companies. Polaroid, for example, has set up a 'wellness' programme at its Dumbarton factory. All employees receive cholesterol level checks and fitness tests, with additional carbon monoxide checks for smokers. Staff are also asked to complete a detailed questionnaire on their lifestyle and dietary habits.

Based on the data gathered from the health screening, each employee is given recommendations about the changes in diet and lifestyle necessary for healthier living. Those who are keen to make improvements are supported. For example, they can have individual exercise programmes designed for them to be used in the company's gym, while healthier dietary habits are encouraged by indicating which dishes in the canteen have high fat or low fibre content.

Another initiative is the Hampstead-based Capital Recovery Centre. This is the first clinic in the UK to work hand-in-hand with industry and EAPs on the problem of alcohol and chemical dependency. A feature of the centre is that it offers a thirteen-week evening treatment programme geared specifically towards employees in employment and, because the cost can be less than a third of in-patient treatment, it may provide a model for other centres to follow.

Companies considering setting up an EAP specifically on alcohol and drug-related problems can get professional consultancy advice from Turning Point, the largest national voluntary organization helping people with drink, drugs and mental health problems. Founded in 1964, Turning Point now has forty centres throughout the country, employing more than 160 staff. Last year it helped 5000 new people and continued to support thousands of existing clients.

Specifically, Turning Point helps companies in three main ways: by setting up an effective written policy on managing drink and drug problems; by training senior executives, occupational health advisers, personnel and welfare managers on the range of problems and how to identify and respond to them; by researching companies' individual needs.

Action on Addiction is another charity launched in an effort to harness the financial muscle of big business in the fight against drug and alcohol abuse. Chaired by Michael Ashcroft, head of services conglomerate ADT, the charity's initial task is to raise £6m towards the establishment of a national addiction centre.

Ashcroft says that while many professional organizations already operate very successfully in the field of addiction, there is a serious need for a central focus – a 'centre of excellence' that can correlate treatment, training and research across the total spectrum of mind altering substances.

'I do not think business in the UK has fully addressed itself to its social responsibilities,' says Ashcroft. 'Addiction is a business problem because it affects the whole of society. No business is immune to it, but this has not been perceived yet in many UK company boardrooms.'

Ashcroft believes that much can be learned from the US where addicts find it easier to admit their problems in the knowledge that their employer will not fire them, but help to rehabilitate them.

'British companies cannot take too much credit so far,' says Ashcroft. 'But it is not all gloom and doom. Alcohol on Addiction intends to make the problem a popular cause. After all, addiction is about people we know.'

The Institute of Psychiatry's Edwards has the last word: 'Addiction is the biggest socio-medical problem of our time,' he says. 'Ignoring it does not make sense. There is no magic formula, so we must make a positive effort to get to the root cause. In the meantime, every firm should have facilities for its employees.'

# 35

# When theft is worse than murder: employing ex-offenders

June 1990

Sara Jackson

In England and Wales, twenty crimes are committed a minute; 1208 every hour; ten million a year. The annual loss to business in time taken off work by employees who are victims of crime is estimated at £140m. Tax sustains expenditure of £250 a week to keep the average inmate in jail, £15m a week to maintain the prison service. Then there is the cost of supporting the judicial system and of supporting families dependent on a spouse in jail.

Two-thirds of men and four-fifths of young people will re-offend within two years of their release from prison. But those who are unemployed are three to five times more likely to reoffend than those in work.

Breaking the crime – unemployment – crime cycle is seen as essential to reduce re-offending. And the task of charity organizations, National Association for the Care and Resettlement of Offenders (NACRO) and the Apex Trust is to do their utmost to ensure that employers help them do so.

But this is no easy task. Employers are not going to offer an ex-offender a job simply on the basis that he is an ex-offender, even if they have recognized the cycle. They want the best person for the job, and ex-offenders are largely unskilled with little work experience.

Disadvantage and discrimination are reflected in the unemployment statistics. In 1987 the North East Probation Service found the rate of unemployment for its clients to stand at 72 per cent, compared to a total unemployment rate of 13 per cent.

Parliament, in an effort to ease the burden of bias suffered by those with a criminal record, passed the Rehabilitation of Offenders Act in 1974. The Gardiner Committee, which researched the circumstances giving rise to the Act, found one million people in England and Wales who had a criminal record but had been free of convictions for the last ten years.

The Act accordingly aimed to rehabilitate offenders 'who have not been reconvicted of any serious offence for periods of years and to penalize the unauthorized disclosure of their previous convictions.' By easing the re-employment of ex-offenders, the hope was that re-offending could be reduced. A connection still recognized in 1988 by the then Home Secretary Douglas Hurd when he stated that 'a suitable ex-offender employed today could be one crime prevented tomorrow.'

The idea of a 'spent' conviction was introduced. After serving a prison sentence between six and thirty months an offender became rehabilitated after ten years. Under six months and the rehabilitation period dropped to seven years. Serve over thirty months and a conviction could never become spent.

The Act made it unlawful for an employer to refuse to employ a 'rehabilitated offender' solely on the grounds of a spent conviction. There is no need for an ex-offender to disclose his spent conviction in applying for a job (except in professions such as medicine, law, teaching, accountancy, and of course, the police force), joining an organization, or taking out insurance.

But the Act has not had the desired effect. Difficulty in finding a job remains the biggest problem faced by ex-offenders. The Apex Trust estimates that four in ten people in custody are excluded from rehabilitation by serving sentences over thirty months. Over 90 per cent of the Trust's clients have no knowledge of the Act or its terms. And the majority of employers are in the same boat.

A survey commissioned by the Apex Trust's Employers Advisory Group (EAG) for its 1989 report *Breaking the Cycle*, revealed worse. Many employers in professions exempt from the Act regarded their exemption as meaning they did not have to employ ex-offenders at all, when it only gave them the right to have a spent conviction declared.

Changing the situation is no small job. Few employers will admit to discrimination against ex-offenders. The personnel director at Procter and Gamble echoes the official recruitment policy of many companies. 'We look at every candidate for suitability for the job on offer, and being an ex-offender in itself is not a barrier. However, it may indicate something about the interviewee which is important in relation to the job and we have to take it into consideration along with the many other aspects of the application.'

A personnel manager outlines BT's policy on this area. 'Basically we recruit people who are suitable for the job. We do employ ex-offenders, but obviously we would not take someone with a history of embezzlement into the finance department. We do try to be as fair and open minded as we can. We are one of the country's biggest employers and feel we have a community role to play.'

But large companies are less receptive to the employment of ex-offenders than they would have us believe. 'In our experience it is the smaller companies that are more considerate and willing to take the chance and employ those with a criminal record,' says Michael Quill, employment officer for the West Midlands Probation Service. 'Big companies often practise blanket discrimination policies. Smaller companies tend to be more helpful and many ask less questions.'

And the fact remains that few companies will disclose the number of ex-offenders they employ, even those that the Apex Trust can identify as being sympathetic to them. Such information splashed over the media does not make good PR.

Discrimination aside, to improve their chances in the job market, ex-offenders are in desperate need of training. Established twenty-five years ago by Neville Vincent, the philanthropic chairman of Bovis (the building company), the Apex Trust works with all types of ex-offenders and people at risk of offending and focuses on improving their employment prospects. Its core funding comes from the Home Office, Department of Employment and the private sector.

The Trust's Employers Advisory Group is a committee of representatives from various British companies including British Telecom, BP, British Rail and Northern Foods. Noel Finnegan, from BT, explains its function. 'We aim to give to Apex the benefit of our industrial experience and the viewpoint of employers who have recruitment responsibilities. BT is co-operating with Apex in the southern London district, allowing it to carry out an audit of the skills required by BT there and then to train up ex-offenders to make them more attractive as employees.'

The EAG considers that pretty soon companies are going to be forced to turn to previously untapped sources of labour, and assisting in the training of one such source, ex-offenders, is in their own best interests.

One quarter of all vacancies which remain unfilled for more than eight weeks do so because of skill shortages. In three-quarters of cases the local labour supply is just not suitably qualified. The situation is expected to get worse. The Department of Employment forecasts that the number of sixteen to seventeen-year-olds in the population will fall by 25 per cent between 1987 and 1995.

'Ex-offenders must now be considered as a source of labour,' states the EAG in *Breaking the Cycle*. 'As pressures on output increase, so too will employers increasingly have incentives to invest time and money in training.'

Offenders do receive some training in vocational skills in prison. The Prison Service Industries and Farms Division operates in all prisons, but the work involved depends on whether the jail is a long-term training prison where inmates are trained for release, or a short-term local or allocation prison where inmates await removal to a training or top security prison.

Keith Gerard, national development officer for prisons, explains the differences in training. 'When people stay for a long time they are able to acquire more demanding skills. Contrast Winston Green prison in Birmingham, a short stay "local" prison, where the main industry is the sewing of post bags for the Royal Mail. At the other end of the scale is Kingston Prison in Portsmouth where they do printing work to a very high standard and produce 80 to 90 per cent of the internal work for the prison department. They also have a vocational training section. The computer skills people are acquiring are very saleable.'

'But,' says Peter Chapman, regional director with Apex, 'the vocational training schemes in prisons are nowhere near big enough or adequate. Although having said that, I know the circumstances under which they are labouring: the restrictions imposed by space, finance and overcrowding.'

'When people move from one prison to another, no account is made of skills already acquired,' adds Gerard. 'In some prisons, some inmates would not be employed at all. There just are not the staff or facilities to guard them.'

Chapman suggests that we could improve our prison system by taking a few hints from abroad. 'In the US, employment is actually taken into prisons,' he says. 'There are more private prisons and they therefore look to be cost-effective. The working prisoner will earn a salary commensurate with the outside, and deducted from it will be their upkeep. Some spending money is given to them, and the rest is put away in trust. There needs to be a greater awareness in the UK that there are these opportunities.'

But why would an employer want to take on a prison inmate? 'Because he cannot get a draughtsman outside,' is Chapman's reply.

The skills shortage factor is a major incentive behind giving prisoners employment opportunities.

Gerard cites the example of Costain, which has been developing opportunities for inmates to be released and work on company building sites. 'Precision engineering companies are also interested,' he continues. 'Basically because of the skills shortages and demographic trough of young people. The whole idea is we are saying, "Look, we have a whole pool of people here".'

Chapman has the same message: 'we don't say, "here is an ex-offender, please show your charity and employ him". We say, "here is an individual with certain skills you require. The disadvantages you are concerned about no longer apply".'

For those offenders who nonetheless join the ranks of the long-term unemployed, the private sector has co-operated with the government in the launch of Employment Training. Set up in September 1988, the scheme provides up to twelve months training and work experience for 600,000 people at an annual cost of £1.4bn.

In 1986 the Apex Trust started a programme in Seacroft in Leeds. It aims, as in other schemes it runs, to rehabilitate the inner city area by training the local community in those skills local business needs. Seacroft, a rundown housing estate, where houses, stripped of copper piping and water tanks, stand empty, their windows boarded up, was top of the crime league table for Leeds.

The Trust set up an employment training programme that includes not only vocational but educational training. 'Many people here have immense problems which start way back in basic skills,' explains Chapman. 'They lack literacy, numeracy, communication and behavioural skills.'

The Trust asked the local community what it wanted. The answer was a re-upholstery service and a twice weekly luncheon club for pensioners. Workshops were set up teaching not only re-upholstery, but also catering and office skills.

Now, in the limited space of Apex's Seacroft premises, men of all ages from eighteen to sixty learn not only a trade, but the disciplines necessary to hold down a job. Most after six to nine months will go on a placement with a Leeds firm, in the hope that from there they can get a job. Nor is the outlook totally bleak for those who do not.

'After a year people have been used to being out of the house and do not want to go back to it,' says Janet Harsley, a basic skills trainer. 'So the men go on to do a lot of charity and voluntary work. Even if they do not go into the business they are trained in, we give them a reference and they have acquired a willingness to work and time keep.'

Skills shortages in some areas taught are so acute that the cream of the trainees is scooped up immediately. 'The demand for placements from companies is now greater than the rate at which we can train people to the appropriate level,' says Chapman. 'The problem is, of course, finance.'

The project receives less than 5 per cent of its sponsorship from private enterprise. 'They don't see the problem we are tackling as being part of their problem,' shrugs Chapman. 'But our work is in their interest, because we are increasing the pool of trained potential employees and are also reducing the number of people likely to offend against what might be their business.'

It seems a valid point. In the four months following the project's establishment, Seacroft's crime rate dropped by an average of 33 per cent a month.

On the day of my visit, a portakabin had been delivered to provide new space for teaching office skills. The portakabin was sponsored by two or three private sector clients, the bulk of the funding made up with an £8,000 grant from the City Action Team. 'Marks & Spencer, and the Yorkshire, Barclays and National Westminster banks are the biggest corporate sponsors in the Leeds region,' says Chapman. 'Small companies tend to donate in kind – a new carpet or office desk.'

But even when ex-offenders are trained in marketable skills, discrimination against them still thrives. Employers who have proved willing to take ex-offenders on have increasingly found themselves disadvantaged by the growing use of fidelity bonding and, in particular, block bonding insurance schemes.

Aiming to safeguard an employer against theft or financial loss resulting from the actions of an employee, an individual bond is used to insure a particular job, and a block bond to insure every employee, whether or not he or she represents an identified risk.

However, many insurance companies refuse to bond all those with a criminal record. The Prudential admits 'we normally would not look to insure an ex-offender unless their conviction is spent under the Rehabilitation Act, when we are duty bound to ignore it. If a client was keen to take someone with a criminal record on to a trusted position and wanted us to insure them, we would politely decline.'

To combat this discrimination, the Apex Trust and Lloyd's Underwriters have introduced the Apex Fidelity Bond, which provides cover for loss of up to £6,000 each employee. The cost is currently £30 each person, but the Trust is negotiating with the Department of Employment in an effort to persuade it to pay half for each employee who was previously registered as unemployed. The project waits only for government money.

'We intend it to be available for everyone coming out of prison,' says David Owen, director of the marketing and technical division of Sedgwick James London, Lloyd's largest broker. 'It is planned to be an automatic process for those who want to access it and who have been carefully screened by the probation service.'

The offenders hardest to insure, reflect the offences employers are least likely to brook. 'It probably has been easier for an honest-to-goodness murderer to get insurance,' says Owen. 'For a pilferer it is almost impossible.' Chapman agrees: 'offences against an employer are the ones hardest to accept.'

The nature of the offence committed is, according to research by the Apex Trust and Institute of Criminology, the crucial factor influencing the recruitment decision. Ninety per cent of companies interviewed gave most weight to this, rather than to the sentence served or the frequency of the offending behaviour. Stealing from customers, embezzlement from employers and sex offences were most likely to deter employers.

'But the 1 per cent re-offending rate of Apex Trust clients against employers is much lower than the general rate among the population at large,' reminds Chapman. This fact and the many initiatives under way to encourage employers to play their vital role in breaking the cycle should at least provide businesses with food for thought. But recruitment personnel have yet another cause to reassess their recruitment strategies. The ex-offender is not quite the minority group many of us believe.

Ten per cent of the population of the UK is registered with a criminal record at the Criminal Records Office; one in every three men will have at least one serious conviction (and that is excluding motoring offences and drunkenness) by the time they are thirty. The demographic change of the 1990s will bring a serious skills shortage indeed if that kind of percentage of the population is considered unworthy of employment.

# Hong Kong: The Ultimate Enterprise Culture

# 36

# Lydia Dunn: tough charmer facing China

January 1988

## Carol Kennedy and Adam Baillie

Forget the Joan Collins model of 'power woman', *Dynasty* style, outrageously designer-clad and brandishing her sexuality like a blunt instrument. Lydia Dunn of Hong Kong is the real thing, one of the world's most influential women in her unique combination of business and political activity. The soap opera characters could take lessons from her in just about everything except how to ham it up: she has the real-life edge in talent, charm and glamour.

The influence she wields in Hong Kong, both onstage and backstage, is immense. As the senior member of Hong Kong's Legislative Council and one of the most senior on the Executive (cabinet) Council (Legco and Exco), she occupies a central position in the current intense debate in Hong Kong over its political future under the Chinese flag. As head of the Hong Kong Trade Development Council, she is in charge of the territory's international economic lifeline. And as a director on the boards of John Swire and Sons, the Hongkong and Shanghai Bank and Cathay Pacific Airways, she is squarely at the heart of the decision-making process in Hong Kong's key international trading businesses.

At this most political of times for Hong Kong, the one question which cannot yet be answered is the true extent of China's commitment to honour the Sino-British Joint Declaration, under which Hong Kong will become a Special Autonomous Region within China with its freewheeling capitalist system guaranteed for fifty years after 1997. This is necessarily an act of faith – but Lydia Dunn believes it.

'The Joint Declaration is very detailed in that all the existing rights and freedoms we now enjoy will be preserved,' she says. 'Now, either you take that promise and accept it, or you do not. I accept it.

'Apart from everything else, why should China spend two years – *two years* – negotiating this document when all they had to do was sit back and in 1997 Hong Kong would be theirs? Why would they want to make that kind of commitment unless they are sincere about giving Hong Kong these freedoms?'

For her, Hong Kong is its own guarantor for its current way of life.

'China did not devise this "one country, two systems" formula for altruistic reasons,' she goes on. 'They have made this unique formula for Hong Kong and have entered into this unique agreement for self-interested reasons. China needs Hong Kong's managers, Hong Kong's technology. They need Hong Kong's economic success. So if we destroy that, then we destroy the main reason why we have one country, two systems. The key to all this is that we must preserve Hong Kong's economic success.'

Despite the crash in Hong Kong's stock market in October – an inevitable reaction to the international financial collapse – Lydia Dunn is bullish about Hong Kong's export-led boom, now in its third year. The only problem she identifies is one she reckons the rest of the world would envy. 'It would love to have that kind of problem – our shortage of labour because of the boom in our economy,' she says.

Yet she is acutely aware of Hong Kong's nervous business disposition and its tendency to panic attacks in times of crisis. 'Hong Kong is a very small place; it is also a very sensitive place,' she says. 'Confidence is very fragile in Hong Kong in the best of times.'

For that reason she is vigorous in defence of the controversial Public Order Amendment Bill, passed in March last year, which made it an offence to publish or speak 'false news' capable of causing public alarm or disturbance. Critics have suggested that it hands Beijing a 'blunt instrument' to crack down on freedom of expression after 1997. Lydia Dunn strongly refutes this.

'We cannot have rumour-mongering going on in Hong Kong that could damage confidence,' she argues. 'In Britain if someone says something that is false it will take a long time for it to get around the country. In Hong Kong it takes hours, with all sorts of consequences. It could mean a collapse in the stock market; it could mean a flight of capital; it could mean a flight of people.

'I don't think we can risk any of that. It would not be good for stability or for Hong Kong's economic success. The law is there to protect the stability of Hong Kong, and the reasons for it are sound. They are sound today and they will be equally sound after 1997.'

Born in Hong Kong in 1940 (in Chinese astrology a 'Year of the Dragon') into a prosperous Cantonese merchant family, Lydia Dunn, for all her prominence on the public stage and her high social visibility in Hong Kong, remains a somewhat enigmatic personality. In interviews she rarely talks about herself or her background. Her father, Yenchuen Yeh Dunn, ran a trading business in Shanghai in the 1930s, and Lydia speaks fluent Mandarin and Shanghainese as well as Cantonese.

She was educated first at St Paul's Convent School in Hong Kong and later at the University of California at Berkeley, where she took a Bachelor of Science degree. Her business career began at twenty-three as an executive trainee at Swire and Maclean, a subsidiary of John Swire, the blue-chip, blue-blood British "hong."

By 1978 she was on Swire's main board, subsequently becoming executive director of Swire Pacific and chairman of two Swire subsidiaries. In 1981 she became a director of the immensely powerful Hongkong and Shanghai Banking Corporation and in 1985 joined the board of Cathay Pacific Airways, Hong Kong's flag carrier.

She regards herself first as a business woman.

'I never think of myself as a politician, I am a businesswoman who happens to be highly involved in public affairs, and that is how in Hong Kong one got involved in politics. I did not "go into politics" – I was headhunted,' she says with a laugh.

Progressing through a series of advisory posts on government and industry committees, she was made an 'unofficial' (that is, government-appointed) member of Legco in 1976 and six years later became an unofficial member of Exco. Her role in recent years has been aimed at avoiding any damaging splits among Hong Kong legislators that might polarize public opinion and upset the delicate political balance within Hong Kong and in its relations with China.

'The most important thing of all in the years up to 1997 is the question of the future government structure,' she says. 'We want a smooth transfer of sovereignty so that come July 1 1997, we do not have a disruptive change but a smooth crossing, so that all that it brings is a change of flag and nothing else.

'That means when we are close to 1997 we must have a government structure that will on the one hand give us the high degree of autonomy promised in the Joint Declaration and on the other will be acceptable to China. There is no sense having something the Chinese will be uncomfortable about.'

Questioned about issues on which, as one prominent Hong Kong businessman has said, Hong Kong could 'shoot itself in the foot,' in particular that of an elected legislature (as promised in the Joint Declaration) Lydia Dunn says: 'Elections... yes, I think that Hong Kong people are very pragmatic and realistic people and very sensible people. We have shown this really throughout our short history. The population in Hong Kong, largely Chinese, understands the constraints – the political constraints – within which they can move. Those constraints are not very tight but they are there nonetheless.

'It is no different under British sovereignty. There are certain things we cannot do. There are always constraints – the constraints being that Hong

Kong must never think that a high degree of autonomy equals independence. It does not mean that.'

Like every other pillar of the business and political elite in Hong Kong, she argues that the territory's colonial system of government has worked well in the past.

'Politics,' she says, 'has arrived in Hong Kong after 100 years.' But she maintains that the government already has a unique system of consultation through a network of advisory boards and committees.

'We get their advice and input before proposals are given to the Executive Council to consider,' she points out. 'And even after Exco has looked at it, if it is something that we think is even slightly controversial we would then issue a consultative document so that everybody can comment on that. In my opinion there is a great deal of merit in that system of consultation.'

The need for harmony has been a constant theme throughout her recent speeches. 'She is trying to put a message across that consensus politics are best for Hong Kong,' says Exco colleague and industrialist Allen Lee. He considers this her principal achievement.

Without her influence, he says, the last few crucial years in Hong Kong might have been very different.

'We would not have had such cohesion, and issues might have been handled differently,' he says. 'There might have been a lot more public confrontation.'

Stephen Cheong, another colleague on Legco, says her views on consensus have developed over the years. 'She is good at putting opposing views together and working out an acceptable compromise, even if it is not totally agreeable to either side,' he comments.

Both men admire her style in pursuit of this goal. Lee says her 'patience barometer is very high,' while Cheong confesses that at times he has been 'astonished at the cool and the patience she is able to muster when she needs to. She has great determination, a clear mind, and above all persistence and the ability to learn from people.'

In her early days on Legco, colleagues remember, her main concern was the need for a more efficient and publicly accountable civil service. 'She was insistent that the government review this, but she was ignored,' says Lee. 'Her proposals on this have now been accepted, after eight years.'

In short, like every successful politician anywhere in the world, she has the essential qualities of staying-power, stamina and resilience. She has taken some fairly hard knocks in Hong Kong over the last few years, especially during the nervous days of negotiation leading up to the Joint Declaration, during which she was publicly snubbed by China's veteran leader Deng Xiaoping and was accused in Hong Kong and Beijing of not being representative of the Hong Kong people.

More recently, during the Daya Bay incident, when over a million Hong

Kong residents signed a petition protesting against the nuclear power station on Hong Kong's border with China, she came under some fierce criticism for not breaking her holiday to return to a Legco in uproar.

She weathered the storm with her usual resilience. Admiring colleagues say she has 'grace under pressure' and is not affected by criticism. When she feels frustration and anxiety, she does not show it. 'She does not get emotional,' says one long-time associate.

This does not mean she is uncaring or any kind of an 'iron lady'. Personally, she has extreme warmth and an acute sense of humour. To watch her in action at a grand Hong Kong official function is a lesson in the art of charming birds out of the proverbial tree. Hardened international businessmen find her style irresistible.

Under the Hong Kong system, of course, she has no elected constituency, and in the past has been viewed by the general public as a somewhat distant, if well-respected figure. But the impression of aloofness is changing. She is meeting the public more, speaking more openly and becoming more accessible to the press.

Since becoming chairman of the Hong Kong Trade Development Council in 1983, her international exposure has been heightened. Lee, a colleague on the council as well as on Legco, who has travelled with her on many trade missions, says: 'She does a fantastic job in promoting Hong Kong.'

Given her apparently boundless energy and shrewd business track record, it is surprising that Lydia Dunn has not joined the ranks of Hong Kong's immensely wealthy entrepreneurs. Was she ever tempted to go into business for herself?

'Oh yes,' she says, 'One is always tempted, and of course, when one was younger. . . . But I never did, for two reasons. First, in my firm, the working environment is such that I don't think I could do any better outside on my own. I can do all the things I could do if I ran my own business, and the team is very supportive. The returns and rewards are very satisfactory.

'Second, there is my public life. Because I became involved in public affairs at an early stage, over ten years ago, that really did limit the time that I could go out and start a business on my own. So I never did.'

She runs her busy and complex life – with at least two formal Exco and Legco meetings each week, around which are slotted board meetings and a wide range of charitable and educational committees – from her Swire office on Hong Kong's waterfront.

'One just somehow manages,' she says. 'I think it is a characteristic of Hong Kong. It is a very efficient place where one is able to accomplish a lot in a much shorter time than, say, New York or London. The physical size of the city has something to do with this – the fact that one can go to five or six different meetings in one day.'

Lydia Dunn does not believe that the essential, entrepreneurial, character of Hong Kong will change when the new era begins in 1997.

'Over the years, we have seen many changes in Hong Kong, from physical appearance to the way we do things,' she says.

'But the basic character of Hong Kong is that we have a very hardworking people who believe in rewards from their own hard work rather than relying on the state, and who believe in educating their children so that they can move up the social ladder; who are basically more interested in advancing their own economic wellbeing rather than taking part in politics. I think that character will never change.'

Lydia Dunn herself with her understated elegance epitomizes the new sophistication of Hong Kong, a world away from the rather outworn image of pink Rolls-Royces and ostentatious display associated with an earlier business generation. Her twelve-hour days and weekends loaded with work lead some to see her as a slightly lonely figure. In leisure moments she likes to potter among Hong Kong's antique shops.

The next decade will test and challenge her political skills and determination to the full in getting her message across on the uncertain road to 1997. Few who know and work with Lydia Dunn doubt her capabilities to win through. Indeed, the one fault most commonly ascribed to her may prove her greatest asset.

'Like any woman, however capable, she nags,' says a male colleague, who regards her with the greatest affection.

'Her expectation is probably a little bit too high – it is not her fault.'

# 37

# Living with a new head office

May 1988

## Carol Kennedy and Adam Baillie

The mood of Hong Kong today, nine years before its return to Chinese sovereignty, could be described as a triumph of hope over faith. Under the glittering surface of an economic boom scarcely dented by the world stock-market crash of October 1987, the territory's 5.5 million inhabitants are taking stock of their prospects in the run-up to July 1997 and beyond.

The nervous years of negotiations over Hong Kong's future and their aftermath have given way, over the past year, to a new realism. February's white paper on the development of representative government finally laid the ghost of immediate direct elections and confirmed that China is already, as a Chinese director of one of the British-owned 'hongs' put it, the new 'head office'.

The issue of direct elections, however, is still highly charged. Indeed, if Beijing had not agreed to them, there would have been no prospect of them despite the Hong Kong government's green paper of March 1987 – as the governor, Sir David Wilson, inadvertently let slip to a local journalist late last year.

Yet many Hong Kong Chinese believe that the promise of direct elections was implicit in the Sino-British Joint Declaration of 1984 and that they would be held before the Basic Law (Hong Kong's mini-constitution after 1997) was promulgated by Beijing in 1990.

The white paper of February 1988 killed that hope: elections will not take place until 1991, when the Basic Law is a *fait accompli*.

Lawyer and legislative councillor Martin Lee lost an eyeball-to-eyeball duel with British foreign secretary and fellow lawyer Sir Geoffrey Howe over the semantics of the Joint Declaration, which was diplomatically vague on the form of elections and their timing. Lee is not alone in Hong Kong in believing that the opportunity to vote before the Basic Law might have stemmed Hong Kong's brain drain – a matter of increasing concern to all sectors of government and business. Shortly before the white paper revealed that the date would in fact be 1991, Lee told *Director*: 'We could turn the tide of emigration if Britain would agree to elections in 1988.'

The true dimensions of the brain drain are unknown, but statistics confirm an accelerating outflow of the trained talent that underpins Hong Kong's current boom. Requests for the 'Certificate of No Criminal Conviction' (CNCC), essential for obtaining overseas visas and work permits, have more than doubled since 1982 (the year the negotiations with Beijing started) and rose by more than 50 per cent between 1985 and 1986.

The majority of visa applications were for Canada, the US and Australia in that order, and in 1987 (January to September), total immigration visas to Canada doubled from 1986 to reach almost 17,000. In all, Hong Kong is losing some 30,000 people a year at all levels, from managerial and professional down to those with basic clerical skills. The principal area of loss is computing, accounting and middle management – the life-blood of an economy increasingly dependent on sophisticated services.

Until recently, the official line from the upper echelons of Hong Kong's government was that emigration moved in an ebb and flow, with as many people returning as leaving. Chief Secretary Sir David Ford told *Director* in May 1987 that 'Hong Kong is seeing a brain drain in reverse: people are coming back from Canada and the US armed with degrees and work experience. They have helped promote Hong Kong as an international city.'

To a large extent this is still happening, and those Hong Kong Chinese who return, having secured their 'insurance policy' – a US or Canadian passport – along with international business experience, are being avidly wooed and well rewarded – the new phenomenon of the 'Chinese expatriate'. But, as Simon Murray, managing director of the giant trading conglomerate Hutchison Whampoa, put it: 'Salary is not an issue. This is not about dollars and cents.'

TL Tsim, director of the Chinese University Press of Hong Kong and a leading historian of China, spells out his uncompromising view of the issue. 'The Joint Declaration is an act of faith – but if you have a choice, then why accept it? You are risking all that you have.'

Tsim, whose parents came to Hong Kong as refugees from the 1949 communist revolution in China, is one of the most forthright voices of the generation that, without direct experience of the revolution, cannot accept that philosophy has changed in Beijing. China has always believed in central control – in imperial as much as in communist times – and it regards concepts such as democracy and human rights as Western inventions. His parents' generation, Tsim points out, were the *crème de la crème* of China, and he fears a repetition of that loss in the current exodus from Hong Kong.

In his office in the university in the New Territories, which run up to the Chinese border, Tsim says: 'I am a seasoned risk-taker but what are our chances – 0.5 per cent; five million for Hong Kong, one billion against. I do not believe in the Joint Declaration because the Chinese have never stuck to paper.'

Tsim can afford to be critical. He is one of those who admit they do not plan to stay in Hong Kong after 1997. But the essentials of what he calls 'the fear syndrome' are shared privately by many leading figures in Hong Kong, and by most of the citizens who responded to a pre-white paper official survey. This revealed that, if offered the choice, an overwhelming majority would opt for preserving Hong Kong's old status under the British flag.

Politics, as leading Hong Kong politician and businesswoman Lydia Dunn (now married to Hong Kong Attorney-General Michael Thomas) frequently points out, is comparatively new to the territory, but the pressure cooker of current events has built up an enormous head of steam over the best means of preserving Hong Kong's 'high degree of autonomy' promised under the Joint Declaration.

Politicians such as Lee and Dunn have crossed swords publicly – Dunn believing that Hong Kong's best strength lies in consensus, which elections would not necessarily help. But the distance between the opposing viewpoints may be less than it seems. The diagnosis of the problem with China is the same though the prescribed treatments differ: historian Tsim believes in surgery, politician Dunn in medicine and lawyer Lee, as one wit put it, 'in exorcism'.

Do Hong Kong people feel that Britain has sold them down the river? The answer is probably yes, in a resigned, faintly cynical way, though as one middle-aged professional Chinese woman comments: 'What more could you do? China is the big one.' But the issue has gone beyond that.

The question now is the extent to which the UK will fight Hong Kong's corner in the years in which it still has influence.

The omens here are not particularly reassuring to the nervous. Almost weekly, pronouncements come winging down from Beijing that seem designed to assert that China is now the master. On one recent occasion, Li Hou, secretary-general of the Basic Law Drafting Committee, declared that it was not the business of the British Parliament to debate the terms of the Basic Law. Earlier, he said Beijing would not give any more weight to the views of the Hong Kong government on the Basic Law than to any other section of the Hong Kong community.

Yet the Chinese cannot want to shake confidence in Hong Kong. 'China has tremendously good intentions towards Hong Kong, but whether or not they will tinker with it; whether they grasp how Hong Kong works – that is the question,' says Hutchison Whamapoa's Murray. Behind that question lies another, as historian Tsim points out. 'It is against the Chinese character to own something and not run it. Just look at Chinese entrepreneurs,' he says.

Chinese management, however, has a basic weakness when it comes to long-term strategic thinking. In many of Hong Kong's famous Chinese-run companies the strength of management is only skin-deep, with little in the way of management development below the family at the top.

The present generation of Beijing leaders appears committed to preserving the golden goose at the tip of south China. But what of the generation after? Memories of 1949 and the political upheavals of communist rule, especially the Cultural Revolution of the late 1960s, die hard. Few Hong Kong Chinese believe that history could not repeat itself, however unlikely it may seem now. Hong Kong has a written guarantee that its capitalist way of life will remain unchanged for fifty years after 1997 – but there are no guarantees that China itself will remain unchanged.

'We are all talking up the confidence – we have to do that,' says one eminent Chinese businessman. Hope, then, rather than faith. But the prospects for Hong Kong are economically dazzling, and that itself is the best guarantee that the golden goose will be kept alive and allowed free range.

# 38

# The quick-buck economy goes for the long term

May 1988

Carol Kennedy and Adam Baillie

Hong Kong's hyperactive economy is still riding high after two years of double digit growth. The pace is expected to slow down in 1988, but only to levels that would break records in most free-enterprise countries.

In 1987 Hong Kong's GDP grew by 13 per cent and its corporate profits by 30 per cent: this year the official forecast is for 8 per cent GDP, and analysts are projecting 15 to 20 per cent growth in corporate profits. Given Hong Kong's export-dependent economy, this is still remarkable.

The sheer scale of current investment in Hong Kong is the best measure of continuing local and international confidence in the territory's buoyant economic prospects, whatever doubts and fears exist about the '1997 syndrome' and the future under Beijing's rule. Billions of dollars are being poured into huge new property and infrastructure developments, construction work is everywhere (mostly under the signboards of Japan's Kumagai Gumi and Hong Kong's native Shui On), and ambitious new schemes are expected to be launched soon that will entirely alter Hong Kong's physical appearance, including the world-famous view of its island waterfront.

Land reclamation is adding valuable new real estate to the western end of Hong Kong island, and plans are being drawn up for the shoreline to be pushed out further in order to accommodate a six-lane highway to run the length of the island and link up with the new eastern harbour tunnel now being built.

That will mean the famous Star Ferry pier being relocated some three ferry-lengths nearer Kowloon, cutting down the crossing time by a minute or so and creating more land for a new generation of spectacular skyscrapers to tower over the harbour.

Northwards to the New Territories, a new motorway scheme is being planned to link up with the highway being built to Guangzhou and the southern part of Guangdong province, upon which Hong Kong's industry is increasingly dependent as a secondary manufacturing base and, along which the enormous volume of exports to and from China will travel.

Hong Kong's container port at Kwaichung, which in January this year overtook Rotterdam to become the biggest and busiest in the world, is set to expand again. The only problem for the government is deciding how much bigger it will need to be to cope with the expected increase in container traffic.

As Graham Barnes, the territory's secretary of lands and works, explains: 'Kwaichung was built when the government did not know enough about it, but it is not only used by Hong Kong and south China but is the main port for exporters deep into China. As China itself does not deal in standard containers, everything comes down to Hong Kong as break bulk, to be stuffed into containers.'

The decision about whether the port will be three-berth or seven-berth will be made in December. 'It would be nice to have a breathing space in which to decide, but time is not on our side,' says Barnes. If Hong Kong's current growth continues at its present rate, he points out, restraints will have to apply to cargo traffic using the airport. Port expansion is therefore top of the agenda.

A bigger project still, however, is Hong Kong's new airport, the need for which is now accepted by the government – if somewhat belatedly from the viewpoint of Gordon Wu of Hopewell Holdings, the mastermind behind the scheme most likely to be chosen.

There has been talk of a new airport for years, and the government spent HKS$200m on feasibility studies for one to be sited on the island of Chek Lap Kok in the early 1980s, when it became clear that Kai Tak's existing single runway would no longer be adequate for Hong Kong's needs in the 1990s. But the plans were shelved in 1983.

Since then, the use of air cargo for exports has mushroomed to the point where 28 per cent of exports, 19 per cent of re-exports and 21 per cent of imports – by value – transit through Kai Tak.

Wu's Hopewell Holdings, together with a consortium of companies that include several mainland Chinese corporations such as the Bank of China and the Guangdong provincial government, has submitted plans for the new airport to be built off Lantau island to the west of Hong Kong island and the harbour.

The airport would be built on reclaimed land – the water off Lantau is only 3.5 metres deep – and be linked to both Hong Kong island, Kowloon and the New Territories by highways that would connect with the new road system in the New Territories.

The HK$25bn development would not only provide an airport but an overall infrastructure scheme that would solve Hong Kong's chronic congestion in both traffic and cargo movements. Rush-hour either side of the harbour at present makes central London's traffic look positively free-flowing.

Wu, a stocky, ebullient engineer, is confident his plans will be accepted. As for the cost of the airport, he claims 'money is the least of my problems' and says the project could be completed in just under three years from start to finish. The governor has said he would like to see any such project completed by 1997. 'This infrastructure is Hong Kong's future,' insisted Wu. 'Otherwise how can 5.5m people hope to compete with Taiwan (19m), Korea (40m) or Japan (100m)?'

'The danger of developments on this scale is of overheating the economy,' says land and works secretary Barnes. But the necessity for Hong Kong literally to build its own future with some such scheme is widely accepted. As one local businessman after another tirelessly reiterates, unless Hong Kong continues to keep its customers' goods (both domestic and international) on the move, the economy has no future. The territory has no natural resources and no domestic market of a size to sustain its economy and its standard of living – the second highest in Asia after Japan.

Over the last few years, China has proved to be a major factor in Hong Kong's stunning economic growth. Not only is Hong Kong the principal port for southern China, but cheap Chinese labour has enabled Hong Kong manufacturers to keep their costs down by subcontracting work to Hong Kong-financed factories all over southern Guangdong province, which adjoins Hong Kong's New Territories.

Jack So, executive director of the Hong Kong Trade Development Council, estimates that up to one million mainland Chinese now work indirectly for Hong Kong manufacturers, which in effect has almost doubled the available workforce.

That, as director of industry K Y Yeung points out, has both positive and negative aspects. Hong Kong manufacturers' investment in manufacturing facilities in Guangdong has prolonged the product life of goods that are no longer economic to make in Hong Kong – such as toys – by using cheaper Chinese labour, but it has also diverted attention from upgrading factories and their output in Hong Kong itself.

The textile industry in Hong Kong has gone notably upmarket in recent years, but the need now is to do likewise in electronics and hi-tech products. The government is now attempting to encourage Hong Kong industrialists to make longer-term investments in more sophisticated manufacturing processes that can compete effectively with South Korea and Taiwan. In those countries, investment in hi-tech industries (dependent on a high degree of automation, training and quality assurance) is much greater than in Hong Kong.

'Hong Kong manufacturing has got to move upmarket in design and quality in its high technology,' says textile industrialist and legislative councillor Allen Lee. 'Fashion has moved but technology lags behind.' Lee – incidentally, one leading local businessman who is content not to own a

British or North American passport but merely the Hong Kong Certificate of Identity – has submitted models of a proposed science park along the lines of London's South Bank Polytechnic, and says the government is now willing to put resources into such a scheme and attract people in.

'Up to now we have relied on the quick response of a customer-designed product,' says Lee. 'This strategy is not going to survive in the longer term.'

The Hong Kong industry department has launched a raft of schemes to encourage the upgrading of manufacturing processes, including setting up technology centres, releasing more land for industrial estates and finding ways to train technocrats and implant more professional qualifications. One scheme under consideration would enable trainees to be sent abroad on sponsored scholarships, an area in which – as industry director Yeng explains, Hong Kong needs British expertise, especially in design management and quality control.

Such schemes fall a long way short of any planned 'industrial policy,' but the government is nevertheless becoming increasingly involved in the economy as Hong Kong businessmen themselves begin to think less in terms of investment for the quick buck, the fast turnover, and more towards longer-term planning and greater emphasis on managerial professionalism.

It is a mark of Hong Kong's maturing economy that many of its major local companies like Hutchison Whampoa are starting to diversify overseas, or to look for opportunities to do so. This is no longer seen as simply a pre-1997 ploy to move assets out of the territory. As one investment banker puts it, 'Hong Kong is simply too small a place now for cash-rich, big players to invest all their eggs.'

Conversely, the opportunities for overseas investment in Hong Kong are getting larger, and not just because of China's economic *perestroika* and Hong Kong's unique position as its tradesmen's entrance.

Britain, although trailing fourth in investment in Hong Kong manufacturing, after the US, Japan and Germany, has traditionally had a strong stake in services in the territory. In its combined interests the UK is one of the four top overseas investors along with the US, China and Japan. British consultancy firms with offices in Hong Kong now outnumber British banks and financial services: it is Japan that now has the biggest foreign banking presence.

Indeed, Japan may soon become the top overseas investor in Hong Kong. Japanese retailers dominate the Hong Kong department store business (though Marks & Spencer is soon to open a Hong Kong store), and Japanese construction companies find the permanently rebuilding skyline of Hong Kong a highly lucrative field.

Kumagai Gumi, whose signs are ubiquitous, is one of the principal contractors for the new Bank of China building, which is designed to overtop the spectacularly eccentric Hongkong and Shanghai Bank headquarters. It is also in partnership with the Cheung Kong property firm for development of a multibillion dollar housing and industrial complex near the airport, and another on the south side of Hong Kong island.

Britain does, however, appear to be waking up to the new opportunities after a decade that saw a gradual decline of UK commercial interest in its booming colony. British exports to Hong Kong topped the £1bn mark for the first time last year (and that did not include British capital equipment for the giant Castle Peak power station). At last, as British trade commissioner Reg Holloway delightedly proclaims: 'Britain is catching up on its competitors in bread and butter goods.'

About thirty UK trade missions visited Hong Kong in 1987, and Holloway detects a new attitude on the part of British exporters. We are getting a new sort of people coming out here,' he notes. 'They are keener, much more enterprising and tenacious – no more dozing on sofas after a boozy lunch.'

Geoffrey Taylor, director of Hong Kong's newly established British Chamber of Commerce, also finds that 'British companies are improving their performance in Hong Kong and in China.' The Chamber, together with the British Trade Commission, hosts a number of exhibitions of British goods and has an ambitious programme of seminars to advise would-be exporters on how to gain more advantage in trade with the region.

Hong Kong businessmen take a slightly less roseate view of Britain's commercial acumen in the territory. Says textile boss and legislative councillor Stephen Cheong: 'For God's sake, take note of that market of one billion people in China – do not let the Japanese wrap it up.'

'Britain is Hong Kong's traditional partner,' says trade director Jack So. 'Now is the time for Britain to reaffirm this commitment and take advantage of Hong Kong as a market in its own right and as a re-export market to China.'

'It is not so much that Britain is falling behind, as that it is not really doing as much as the Americans, the Japanese and even the Germans are doing in the Hong Kong market.'

# 39

# Who will manage Hong Kong?

May 1988

## Carol Kennedy and Adam Baillie

Hong Kong will be a goldmine over the next decade for those with management skills to sell – consultants or executives who can help fill the gap left by retiring expatriates and the growing brain drain of qualified Chinese.

International consultancies are already doing a thriving business in the territory. 'This place is ripe for a systematic approach to management,' says Barry Curnow, chairman of executive recruitment consultants MSL International, who visits the territory about every eight weeks. 'It will be a management development crucible over the next ten years. Every rising international executive should come here for a bit. It is multicultural; it is where the systems meet.'

There is likely to be a boom in short-term expatriates both before and after 1997, and executive search consultants will be kept busy as more Hong Kong-based companies realize they are increasingly competing with multinationals.

Most big international companies in Hong Kong are actively seeking to bring on local management talent. Dual management is not uncommon in both the private and public sector, with Chinese managers shadowing *gweilos* (expatriates) and vice versa.

In Chinese family-run firms, however, it is a different matter. They are notoriously weak on management development, and there is often only a vulnerable line structure beneath the powerful family at the top. Chinese line managers in western firms, too, are often reluctant to embark on management development programmes or to take an aggressively ambitious approach to career progression. Their skills are often seen to lie in implementation rather than in taking initiatives.

'There may be a cultural factor here,' says one senior and much-travelled Chinese executive in a UK-owned firm. 'Traditionally we are brought up never to challenge our parents, even if we think they are wrong. The Chinese family structure values obedience, whereas in the western culture you challenge and you are taught to be independent at a very young age and, if you do not understand something, to speak up.

'A lot of my western friends say: "How can I get my Chinese executives to speak up at meetings?" They are afraid they will say the wrong thing or lose face, and if they are challenged on a point in front of everyone they feel it makes them look bad – they would rather it was dealt with outside the meeting.'

Chinese management style, he explains, is basically that of 'a relative surrounded by relatives. The Japanese are much more institutional in their thinking and that is why you see so many large Japanese companies. It will be a very long time before Chinese companies really practise management development.'

Merchants above all, the Chinese like to feel they 'own the shop'. Their favoured businesses are those that require a comparatively small operational management. Even Sir Y K Pao's shipping and property empire is essentially run by him and his two sons-in-law. Li Ka-shing has two trusted lieutenants in Simon Murray and K S Lee to help him run the overall strategy of Hutchison Whampoa's far-reaching operations, but even so, says one local management consultant, 'there is no doubt where the power lies.'

Hutchinson Whampoa – now the only Hong Kong-based hong, since Jardine Matheson moved its head office to Bermuda – is in fact a western-structured company with an oriental layer on top. Half the eight divisional managers are British, with two Chinese and two Canadian, but there is a rising generation of talent among the 236 Chinese managers in Hutchison Whampoa, which employs 3000 people.

Vincent Lo, chairman of the construction-to-finance conglomerate Shui On, agrees that the Chinese like to see a family name at the top of a company, but says that family-owned businesses are now bringing in more outside management – if not at top levels. 'There has always been a problem in management in Hong Kong, but now there is a great deal more interest in professional management,' asserts Lo.

Paul Cheng of Inchcape Pacific is right at the sharp end of planning a new age of management development. He is that rarity in Hong Kong, a Chinese executive director on the board of a 'hong' – one of those grand old trading companies founded in the heyday of British colonial rule. Inchcape's global operations, ranging from automotive and shipping services to buying for major retailers around the world and marketing and distribution of a vast range of products, are still run from St Mary Axe in the City of London, but the far eastern region, managed from Hong Kong, is second in sales to the UK, producing £289m out of a total of £1bn in the first six months of 1987.

Cheng is a genuine rising star among the ranks of local management. Search consultants see him headed for the top, and he is one of five line directors reporting to Inchcape Pacific Chairman and Chief executive Charles Mackay.

An affable, American-accented man just past fifty but looking a decade younger, Cheng was born in Xiamen in south China and brought to Hong Kong at the age of two when the Japanese invaded Manchuria in the late 1930s. University-educated in the US, with an MBA from Wharton, he had nearly thirty years' experience working for US corporations, mainly in pharmaceuticals, before joining Inchcape in 1987 as director responsible for corporate development.

Cheng has since taken over one of Inchcape's five business streams in the region – marketing and distribution – and has tucked a further business, wines and spirits, under his wing until it grows big enough to warrant a board director of its own. Meanwhile he continues to assist with senior appointments in the region and is drawing up a blueprint for a whole new management culture at Inchcape Pacific.

Looking relaxed in sports shirt and polished loafers in his elegant forty-ninth floor harbourside office – executives in leisure clothes are the only sign that it is Saturday morning in this business-obsessed city – Cheng is seizing a few hours' quiet work amid a whirlwind schedule typical of a multinational director's life in the territory.

As retiring president of the American Chamber of Commerce in Hong Kong (a remarkable 'first' for a Chinese businessman), he has had to forgo a trip to Beijing with chairman Mackay and Inchcape group chairman George Turnbull, in order to hand over formally to his successor at Amcham's inaugural ball that evening. On Monday he will be jetting off to Tokyo on Inchcape business. He is the very model of the modern Chinese manager, projecting international *savoir-faire*.

International is a word that looms large in Cheng's conversation, as it does with most leading industrialists and politicians when discussing Hong Kong's future. 'To me, one of the key things in ensuring the continuity of Hong Kong's prosperity after 1997 is that we must maintain an international community here,' he says. 'We cannot turn into a Chinese city overnight.'

He made that point strongly to leaders in Beijing recently, as a member of a group invited north from Hong Kong's international community to exchange views on the future constitution. The Chinese appeared to accept the principle that a legislative council under Hong Kong's special autonomous status should be international in nature.

'I think it is absolutely critical that you have 20 to 30 per cent of the seats filled by members of the international community,' says Cheng. But at the same time he acknowledges, in a revealing phrase, that China is 'head office,' and says: 'I do not think people should be unrealistic in their expectations.'

Pursuing the analogy, he argues that it is one thing for head office to leave the subsidiary alone 'as long as it is making money and running a good operation – but it is still head office, and I don't think people should forget that.'

As he prepares Inchape's management development plans for the 1990s (some are already in operation, ranging from graduate entry to quite senior levels), Cheng has to think hard and long about the implications of the outflow of Chinese managerial skills. He reckons that, on balance, the exodus is probably more than the inflow of those who have secured their 'insurance policy'.

Many of those who have gone will return – one management consultant believes nine out of ten will come back. The men are usually eager to return to the excitements of Hong Kong business, but their families are sometimes reluctant, once the children have become established in North American schools. (Improving educational standards in the critical ten to fourteen-year-old age bracket is a matter the government may have to tackle if valuable managerial talent is to be wooed back.)

Inchcape has done its own internal survey on brain drain intentions. The company has not yet seen a significant impact – 'out of 5000 people we may have lost a dozen executives, of whom maybe a third will come back,' says Cheng. But people planning to go may not want to signal their intentions until nearer the time, and timing becomes more significant the longer the decision is left. Managers may continue to return while there are still several years of the status quo left. But anyone planning to leave in three or four years, after the Basic Law is promulgated in Beijing, probably will not come back.

Cheng intends to start hiring Chinese with foreign passports: 'at least you know you can run with them a little bit longer, whereas someone who is still looking for that parachute may decide in two or three years that he wants to move.' He takes a detached view of the government's policy of 'localization' – replacing expatriates with Chinese as soon as posts fall vacant. 'I don't believe in localization for its own sake,' he says; a view which Hutchison Whampoa's Murray would endorse.

'We don't care very much where our senior guys come from as long as they are competent,' says Murray.

Localization is a sensitive issue in Hong Kong. The private sector is under no pressure to adopt it, and there are many who feel the government is pursuing it too fast, with a resulting, just-perceptible, decline in operational efficiency and decision making, like a speck of grit in normally well-oiled machinery.

It is accepted, however, that localization will be much longer term in some areas; half the police officers after 1997, for example, will continue to be British, and at least half the judges will be expatriate (from the Commonwealth at large, not necessarily Britain). There were no law graduates in Hong Kong until 1972. At present only 15 per cent of judges are Chinese:

the official view is that Beijing will be quite happy if the ratio reaches 50:50 by 1997.

Like most of Hong Kong's international companies, Inchcape has a fairly weighty proportion of expatriate managers – seventy out of 180 executives – and most of them populate the top three of the company's six grades of management. In five years, Cheng would like to see the ratio closer to 50:50, though the mix will be rather more subtle than that suggests.

'In the next two or three years we will be changing our culture,' he explains. 'Inchcape wants to become a very aggressive, international marketing services group rather than having this overseas trader image – I feel we should be building an international management team.'

Like MSL's Curnow, he sees a future for international managers working in Hong Kong on short-term contracts, but he wants to create a standard set of terms and conditions of employment. This would abolish the old expatriate privileges (some of which are now applying to returning Chinese managers) but allow remuneration to take account of specialist skills, regardless of origin. 'We are going to stop using the terms "expatriate" and "local",' he explains. 'Reward will be simply on merit.'

Such a programme entails changing a lot of attitudes, he indicates. 'It is like turning a big oil tanker around; people who came out from the UK at nineteen and are now in their fifties are not going to change. But when they go back to the UK, in their place you are going to see a new group of modern, specialized expatriates coming here for a shorter period, a mixture of that and local talent. There will be a natural evolution.'

The key question arrives. 'What would drive you to leave after 1997?'

Cheng pauses and replies candidly: 'Well, I have a US passport, so I can stay or move out as I like at any time. If I didn't, I might feel a lot less bullish. I think the answer is, if they started to put too many restrictions on comings and goings, or on financial movements. We are so used to things being wide open, you can have an account in any currency you want, you can move your money in and out. Communications are fantastic, you can pick up a phone and talk to anybody in the world, get on a plane and go anywhere.

'If they started to put bureaucratic meshes in and damp the free-flowing style of Hong Kong, then I think a lot of us would find it hard to adjust.'

# 40

# Coining it in the countdown

May 1989

Carol Kennedy

The 100-degree view from the opulently panelled executive suite on the forty-seventh floor of the Bond Centre is probably the finest in all Hong Kong, a city where spectacular views come ten to the dollar. To your right rise the thickly wooded slopes of The Peak, where the Governor and the 'old money' live; spread around and below are the crowded towers and shimmering harbour; away left, to the north, beyond Kowloon and the New Territories, loom the misty mountains guarding China.

The building itself, an elongated silver hexagon that resembles a partially twisted Rubik's Cube, is the headquarters of the Asia-Pacific operations of Australian tycoon Alan Bond and a visible expression of the soaring property values that are fuelling Hong Kong's jet-propelled economy. Bought in late 1986 for HK$1.9bn, its asset book value just two years later was put at HK$4.5bn, and rentals per square foot have more than doubled. In that time, too, Bond Corporation International Ltd (BCIL) picked up a HK$128m profit by selling a half-share in the building to a Japanese corporation. (And the Bond Centre is not even regarded as a premium location – in the dazzling waterfront stock exchange building, rents have multiplied over four times in three years.)

Like every other big corporate investor in Hong Kong, a place of notoriously volatile nerves in the countdown to Chinese sovereignty, BCIL is apt to have its every movement scrutinized for portents as avidly as entrails were studied by soothsayers in ancient Rome.

When billionaire Bond, whose global investment strategy took a recent knock over Lonrho, earlier tried unsuccessfully to regain private control of the listed 25 per cent of his Hong Kong corporation, local pundits were agog; was Bond preparing the ground to pull out his assets if the Hong Kong bubble burst?

BCIL managing director Peter Lucas waves that one away with Australian insouciance. 'Sure,' he agrees, 'if BCIL had gained sole control of its assets we would have been able to move wherever and whenever we wanted. But that was never the point of the privatization. We said when we came, and have said *ad nauseam*, that we are in Hong Kong to stay, privatization or no.' The object, he explains, in a company often accused of over-gearing, was to unlock some of the assets tied up in a then sluggish stock market. In the event, after shareholders snubbed Bond's offer, the market perked up and unlocked that value by its own force.

Bond's Hong Kong strategy in his drive to 'globalize' is essentially that of most other outside investors in the territory (with the noticeable exception of the British); not merely to exploit opportunities through the celebrated 'gateway to China', although BCIL has a number of joint ventures cooking in the People's Republic (PRC), but to use Hong Kong as a springboard for the whole booming Asia-Pacific region.

'Joint ventures in the region generally, not only in the PRC, loom high in our expectations for growth,' says Lucas. The Australian-based group, reaching saturation point domestically with its brewing and media interests, has judged that 'Australia's future lies in Asia'.

As delegates from thirty-four countries, including Bond himself, were told in February at Hong Kong's 'PacRim 89' conference (the second international symposium on finance, trade and investment in the Pacific Rim countries), the region offers stunning market opportunities – two billion potential consumers aged eighteen or under, for a start.

'I think the Asia Pacific region is on the verge of a tremendous explosion,' says Lucas. 'The base from which these economies are commencing present huge opportunities.'

Around 10 per cent of the Bond group's Aus$10bn assets is invested in Hong Kong and, says Lucas, 'I am sure that will grow.' BCIL's strategy for China, where it is pursuing a number of its core interests including 'ideas on media and communication', is for joint ventures to be established not later than 1992, the midway point to the Hong Kong/China 'deadline' of 1997.

The glittering prizes to be won from the developing Pacific Rim economies – what leading Hong Kong trade official Jack So calls 'the Chopstick Belt' – are dazzling enough, given Hong Kong's key geopolitical setting, to insulate fears of a US recession and to deflect at least some of the underlying uncertainties about 1997. Taiwan, for example, where foreign exchange controls were relaxed last year, releasing a flood of tourists into Hong Kong, is already the target of a determined drive by Hong Kong traders.

But China's recent behaviour in Tibet – once also the subject of a Chinese promise to maintain autonomy, human rights and freedom of religious belief – is certain to send shivers through Hong Kong as the final draft of the Basic Law, Beijing's mini-constitution for the territory, is hammered out this year.

Anything that shakes the confidence of the Hong Kong Chinese and aggravates the brain drain is particularly sensitive in the present state of Hong Kong's economy. Founded on simple manufacturing and assembly techniques performed by a cheap and plentiful workforce, it is now rapidly moving to a service economy (more than 400 financial institutions including seventy-five international banks are crammed into the serried towers of Hong Kong Island), and battling with a severe shortage of labour in all sectors.

The government is under strong pressure from employers to bring in short-term contract labour from China and – for the service industries – from the Philippines. Many building sites are bereft of workers and projects are running late; the Hongkong and Shanghai Bank alone was short of 200–300 tellers earlier this year; the new Marriott hotel management angered rivals by importing the five-day week concept to lure scarce staff.

Hotels are poaching from retailers, retailers poaching from banks, and banks poaching from other banks. In consequence, earnings are being ratcheted up to unheard-of levels: in the past year, manual wages have risen by 20 per cent; those of office workers by 15 per cent. In a classic economic Catch-22, rising standards of living lead to rising aspirations and fewer Chinese are likely in future to be willing to spend their working lives inserting teddy bears' eyes, shifting bricks or scrubbing floors in the tourist hotels.

Many manufacturing operations have been moved across the Chinese border, where labour is still plentiful. It is said that more people work in China manufacturing for Hong Kong than in Hong Kong itself, though the territory's chief export industry, textiles and garments, is strictly bound by international quotas to manufacture within Hong Kong.

Jack So, executive director of the energetic Hong Kong Trade Development Council, which is chasing market opportunities around the 'Chopstick Belt' as well as in Mexico, Portugal and Spain, says as a result of processing in the Pearl River Delta, Hong Kong's re-export figures have shown phenomenal growth, up by 43 per cent over the same period of 1988. So, who is marked by many in Hong Kong as a high-flyer destined for political eminence, sees Hong Kong becoming the added-value service centre for Chinese-made goods, deploying its brilliant marketing and negotiating skills and its new-found expertise in quality control.

But if Hong Kong is to fulfil a role as 'China's university', as one bullish expatriate property developer dubs it, there is much to be done in upgrading its technology and R & D base. 'Hong Kong has never had the capability of producing original design and high-quality equipment for markets 10,000 miles away as the Japanese did,' says Jimmy McGregor, former director of the Hong Kong General Chamber of Commerce and now an elected member of the colony's 'lower house' Legislative Council. 'Our products have gone upmarket, but our designs are still culled from a book.'

The Hong Kong government has an ambitious programme of technology colleges and training schemes, and money is not short. With one or two exceptions, Hong Kong has run a budget surplus for nearly twenty years, and in the 1989 budget financial secretary Piers Jacob produced a bumper harvest of HK$14b, though, like Chancellor Lawson, he dare not inject too much into the economy for fear of fuelling inflation.

This year the economy is widely expected to slow down, to around 6 per cent, but over the long term, business leaders believe Hong Kong's spectacular track record in growth (10 per cent compound over the last ten years) can be maintained. In construction alone, huge reclamation and infrastructure projects – including the new airport that Governor Sir David Wilson has pledged to announce this year – will be worth at least HK$60b in contracts. People in prime-rent harbourside offices joke wryly about losing their views as the bursting financial district is set to edge still farther into the sea.

The chief executive or 'taipan' of Jardine Matheson, by long tradition one of Hong Kong's most influential businessmen, is in little doubt that the boom can continue. 'I think in ten years' time we will look back and still see a 10-per-cent growth rate, though short-term it may slow down somewhat,' says Nigel Rich, who took over Jardine's top seat in January after a fifteen-year career with the worldwide trading group. Only forty-four and with the kind of saturnine good looks that might have cast him for taipan in the TV serial of James Clavell's *Noble House* (based on Jardines), Rich believes that even a US recession would now have less impact on the sensitive Hong Kong dollar, thanks to the new 'financial muscle' in south east Asia.

Jardines, Hong Kong's oldest trading group, which fluttered Hong Kong nerves a few years back when it moved its registered office to Bermuda (for reasons largely involving the captive insurance market), still derives the bulk of its considerable profits in Hong Kong. Its six recently restructured and highly autonomous divisions embrace interests as diverse as Mandarin Oriental Hotels and Pizza Hut franchises, Mercedes Benz distribution, shipping, insurance, and a growing number of supermarkets in Australia and the UK. Most future acquisition strategy, indicates Rich, will be focused on 'the region', and the new taipan will spend a lot of his first year out of his porthole-windowed office overlooking Hong Kong harbour.

Hong Kong's growing internationalism, however, extends well beyond the massive new markets burgeoning on its doorstep. More and more investment by the big locally-controlled companies is going into Canada, Australia and the US (in that order, the preferred destinations for managers and skilled workers seeking foreign passports), particularly into real-estate and hotels.

Merchant bankers confirm that the wealthiest Chinese have steadily been moving private assets offshore for years – Hong Kong money is said to be behind the massive jump in Toronto real-estate values in the last year – and that some corporate assets are following.

This can, of course, be read as an insurance policy against 1997, but there are sound business reasons for Hong Kong corporations to spread their activities abroad. A community of 5.5 million in a single town, even on the tip of a market 200 times bigger, just does not offer the necessary room for expansion.

Li Ka-shing, the dynamic sixty-year-old entrepreneur who built up Hong Kong's biggest personal fortune from a humble but cash-generating business in plastic flowers in the 1950s, is a classic example of what every Hong Kong Chinese would do if he could. Apart from corporate investment overseas, Li has gone into Canada in a big way on his own account, joining two other Chinese tycoons in an ambitious redevelopment of Vancouver's old Expo site.

Li's Hong Kong flagship, the British-founded transport, trading and property-based 'hong' Hutchison Whampoa, has significant investments in Canada and the UK, with a 43-per-cent stake in Husky Oil and Gas worth Can$4b and the largest (£3m) single shareholding in Britain's Cable and Wireless. Priority investment areas for the group, says joint managing director Simon Murray, are Canada, Europe via the UK and the US, as well as expansion in Asia-Pacific.

But Murray, an effervescent forty-seven-year-old whose colourful career started at sixteen with a spell in the French Foreign Legion, emphasizes that 85 per cent of Hutchison's assets are in Hong Kong and that over the next decade this is unlikely to be diluted by more than 10 per cent.

'I think it possible that over the next decade we could end up with a spread of 75 per cent of our assets and business in Hong Kong and 25 per cent outside,' says Murray. 'It is simply difficult to find new things to do in Hong Kong.'

Hutchison is already the largest retailer in Hong Kong with some 250 supermarkets, drugstores and specialist shops; it is massively involved in the colony's infrastructure, building 25 per cent of its roads and handling half the throughput in the world's busiest container port. Its presence is everywhere from soft drinks to electricity supply to mobile phones to the property that forms a key component in any Chinese-owned business. Over the next five years Hutchison plans to build and sell some 50,000 apartments, its usual strategy being to put them on top of commercial property, which is retained for long-term income.

Asked the inevitable question about prospects after 1997, Murray replies crisply: 'The answer is HK$33bn. That is what we have just committed in Hong Kong; $14bn into a power station, $10bn into expanding the container terminal.... If we were not positive about the 1997 scenario we would not be putting big money into these very long-term projects.'

The group, he adds, is also seeking (against tough competition) the franchise to operate cable TV in Hong Kong. 'Whoever does that will probably have the largest cable TV operation in the world – one operator, over five million people. That is a programme in which it takes seven years to get your money back. A container terminal takes three or four years to build and four to five years to get your money back. These are all ten-year timeframes we are talking about.'

Murray and other business leaders see 1997 as something of an anti-climax. It will be 'business as usual,' they assert, with a few cosmetic changes to flag and letter-heading – at least for the first few years. After that, Murray speculates, 'the Chinese may want to tinker a little bit with the system. But I think they have the good sense to realize that if they put a finger in the wheel and a spoke breaks, that is a good time to take it out again.'

Until Tibet, the 'confidence' issue was largely on the back burner in Hong Kong, certainly among the business community. This spring, however, members of Britain's Parliamentary Select Committee visiting the territory to examine the way in which Sino-British agreements are being translated into the Basic Law will have had an earful from legislators concerned about protecting human rights and about the pace of progress towards a demo-cratically elected parliament. (The 'democracy' issue was one on which the Sino-British Joint Declaration remained curiously vague.)

Can the Chinese be trusted to deliver? Most business leaders, both Chinese and expatriate, take a severely pragmatic view, believing China's self-interest in Hong Kong to be too deep to risk damage by the sort of clumsy gut reaction it displayed in Tibet. (Importantly, China will want to run Hong Kong well as a key to the eventual regaining of Taiwan.)

Ultimately, however, it is in the lap of the gods. As Hutchison's Murray breezily puts it: 'You either believe in this thing or you don't believe in it. Nobody has the answer, certainly not the Chinese. We all have the intention of making it a success. The problems will arise in people's methods of making it a success.

'There will be a little bit of jostling and manoeuvring,' concludes Murray, 'but China needs Hong Kong and Hong Kong needs China. That is where our long-term trading growth is going to be. (China is Hong Kong's second biggest market after the US, and Hutchison is one of the biggest day-to-day traders with China, doing an average HK$1bn business a year.)

Certainly one potent indicator of business confidence is the high-flying property market and the related boom in equities with a property element. Although much of the rise in property values come from sheer demand and supply, squeezed by the labour shortage, the fact remains that buildings, unlike other assets, cannot be moved offshore.

David S. Davies, who came to Hong Kong with a construction company fifteen years ago and built up his own property development agency, now ranked third in the territory and grandly called First Pacific Davies since it was taken over by a banking–property–trading conglomerate called First Pacific Group, believes the market is much more mature than it was. 'People are prepared to buy on a 5 or 6 per cent yield, which means you have got to look long-term for your capital growth,' he says.

Davies – not to be confused with the David J. Davies who formerly ran Hong Kong Land, though the two are fellow directors of First Pacific – also believes the Hong Kong property market is much more solidly based that in its previous, heavily leveraged boom period just before the 1983 collapse. 'At the time the banks were heavily involved in lending: this time round there is a lot of equity in the developments themselves,' says Davies. 'Our only problem is, there is so much money around and just not enough product.'

Hong Kong has been good to Davies, who enjoys all the trappings of success including a yacht. Like most other expatriates who run prosperous businesses in the territory and who see Japanese, Australian and US money pouring in (not to mention mainland Chinese money, estimated at around HK$700bn through the state investment arm Citic), he cannot understand the British reluctance to capitalize on the investment returns in its last colony. Only one British property development company, London and Edinburgh Trust (LET), appears to be seriously involved in Hong Kong.

The whole consumer market is awash with the surge in disposable income and the Japanese are moving forcefully into retailing, building on a well-established base of department stores. Britain's Marks & Spencer has just opened its first store in the territory, the only UK chain as yet to do so.

'Britain needs to take a much more conscious look at Hong Kong,' insists First Pacific's Davies. 'It is no good waiting until 1998 to see what it is like before entering the market. The Chinese respect longevity, and you have got to put your time in.

'That is why companies like Hutchison have done so well, because they take a long-term view.'

'After 1997,' says Jardine Matheson's Rich, 'the rules may change, it may be a different environment, but I think the change will be progressive rather than sharp. . . . We have tended to focus on a countdown to 1997, but I think we would do better to think of it as a "count-up" to a whole host of new opportunities.

'I think people will be making money in Hong Kong for a long time to come.'

# 41

# When assets walk away

May 1989

## Carol Kennedy

Some unusual advice columns are appearing in the *South China Morning Post* these days – such as how to keep warm in the Canadian winter. It is a sign of the times; a recent poll revealed that nearly a third of Hong Kong families are interested in emigrating or have members with residency rights abroad. Canada remains the top choice; Toronto with its harsh winters now rivalling mild Vancouver, the traditional Pacific landfall. It is followed by Australia and the US, and these three account for 95 per cent of Hong Kong's current outflow of skills and talent.

The brain drain, heavy with Chinese managers and professionals anxious to obtain a foreign passport before China regains control of Hong Kong in 1997, more than doubled in numbers between 1986 and 1988. This may have been as much due to increased US quotas for Hong Kong people as to worries about the Basic Law, but the government's carefully cultivated insouciance, dismissing the problem as part of Hong Kong's history of transients, only put a match to the rumours of a huge and damaging exodus. At one point a respected US news agency put the outflow as high as 70,000 a year.

Last year the government finally came out of the closet on emigration and appointed a task force of statisticians to investigate. It now reports that the actual figure in 1988 was 45,800, up from 20,000 a year in the five years before 1986. The figure, however, looks worse than it is in terms of skills, because at least half represents non-working dependants. Of the working skills that are leaving Hong Kong, it is now calculated that only about 10,000–11,000 fall into a managerial or professional category – half the level most of Hong Kong still believes it to be.

Government officials now cautiously think the worst may be over; that the outflow has reached a plateau and will begin to decline in 1989, perhaps to around 42,000. But in the boardrooms of the major Hong Kong companies, in the banks and hotels, there is still watchful concern.

'We have seen an alarming exodus at upper and middle management level,' says Simon Murray, joint managing director of leading conglomerate

Hutchison Whampoa. He is referring to Hong Kong at large rather than his own four-division group, which employs 480 managers, 400 of them Chinese, and has lost perhaps ten this year to the brain drain. 'It is of concern – or should be – to every Hong Kong company,' adds Murray, who sees it as a prime responsibility of management to ensure talented people are induced to stay.

Companies like Hutchison or Jardine Matheson with international operations are at an advantage here, because they can deploy people abroad – in Hutchison's case, for example, to Husky Oil in Canada – long enough for them to obtain the coveted passport. The problem is more acute for the small to medium-sized Chinese company, which has come late to management development and lacks the resources, both human and financial, to put golden handcuffs on its top talents.

The man who sees the daily wear-and-tear of emigration on local companies across the board is John R. Hung, joint executive director of the Hong Kong Management Association.

The story he tells is one of increasing strain as management teams have to be rebuilt, often with less than adequate material, placing additional burdens on already hard-worked senior managers.

'What has happened is that those who remain have doubled up,' says Hung, a quiet, contained man who runs his self-financing, HK$35m-budget association mainly on fees from management programmes and a miserly HK$100,000 government grant.

'They have taken on the responsibilities of those who have left – at no extra remuneration,' explains Hung. But he warns: 'This situation can't go on forever. Companies can cope for a year or two, but they can't expand.'

Hung admits there is a growing feeling that 'the experience gap is widening, that the quality of management is not as good as it was four or five years ago.' Chinese graduates coming into management now tend to come from a less well educated background than the professional families that used to provide candidates for Hong Kong's two universities.

'Perhaps the cream has decided that an overseas education is better,' says Hung ruefully. The government is pumping resources into higher education: 'we are growing at the tertiary level as fast as we can,' says Michael Rowse, who heads the emigration task force. The territory's output of graduates is forecast to quintuple by the end of the century. In the short term, the Management Association's answer is to concentrate its courses, to 'expose younger people to the sort of problems they would normally encounter over a longer period,' Hung explains.

In 1988, 95 per cent of managers attending the association's 4600 different programmes came from small to medium-sized businesses. Many were owner-managers running enterprises with fewer than ten workers, and quite a few came from mainland China on specially tailored courses to familiarize them with the pace and business methods of Hong Kong.

Some Hong Kongers believe that the hidden effects of emigration may be felt more in the second generation. A toy manufacturer, returning from European and US trade fairs on the Cathay Pacific nonstop service, cites a Chinese industrialist of his acquaintance whose son and daughter are both carving new lives in Australia. The daughter went into hotel management in Melbourne and is now engaged to a Chinese-Australian; the son went to Sydney with Price Waterhouse.

'No way are they coming back to Hong Kong,' says the toy manufacturer, sipping his champagne. 'They will be Australians. It is not so much the current crop of managers we need to worry about as the children of the middle class.'

Families are undergoing huge strains as a result of the anxiety to establish residency rights and gain foreign educations. Flights to and from Australia and Canada are full of tired Hong Kong managers trying to keep a foot in both camps; retaining their congenial, low-tax jobs in Hong Kong while their wives look after the children in Sydney or Vancouver.

It is hard to assess the current state of confidence among the Hong Kong middle class. Polls indicate a reasonably high degree of optimism, but there remain serious doubts about China's long-term intentions.

Hong Kong's free-range capitalist prosperity, after all, was founded on refugees from Chinese communism. Memories are particularly long among the Shanghainese families who built up most of Hong Kong's business fortunes.

The Chinese leadership succession after Deng Xiaoping is seen as less of a question mark than it was. 'I think Deng has set the platform for the future reasonably well,' says Hutchison's Murray. Management consultant Robert Friend of MSL Group agrees: 'The succession is as secure as it can be, and more so than we could have dreamed of ten years ago.'

But there are likely to be years ahead when the constant temperature-taking of Hong Kong will show sudden feverish rises. Opinions differ about the crunch dates, but those most often cited are between 1992 and 1994. 'If we get through 1993–94, we'll sail through 1997,' predicts Hutchison's Murray.

The key to everything is the passport issue. Everyone tells you that if by some magical change of heart Britain offered the right of abode to the 3.5 million Hong Kong citizens who qualify as British nationals, comparatively few would take the option. But the knowledge that the door was open could solve the brain drain 'at the stroke of a pen,' as Hutchison's Murray says, while acknowledging that the very thought is 'electorally impossible' for Margaret Thatcher.

Hong Kong citizens have never had an automatic right of entry to Britain, but their position has been made even more equivocal over a period of some eighteen years. Plainly, fears of being seen to discriminate positively in the dread area of immigration in favour of skilled, industrious Hong Kong Chinese make Whitehall blanch, since Britain has never operated the 'points' system that works so efficiently for countries like Canada. The argument was also reiterated recently by foreign secretary Sir Geoffrey Howe that it would be seen by Beijing as undermining China's credibility.

But the passport issue will not go away. Portugal, perhaps the poorest country in the EC, is granting passport rights to 100,000 inhabitants of Hong Kong's Portuguese-controlled neighbour Macau, also due to revert to Chinese sovereignty. Many of these, through the single market, would eventually be able to reside and work in Britain.

Hong Kong Law Society president Simon Ip dismisses the argument that a British reversal on passports would be a slap in the face for China. Rather, he argues, it would be seen as an act of confidence in the Sino-British treaty. 'People who live in Hong Kong are loathe to leave and do so only as a matter of last resort,' insists Ip.

Stories of returning emigrants support that view. Hong Kong, as Hutchison's Murray points out, is one of the few places in the world where an enterprising person can acquire capital.

In the big corporations, too, opportunities for Chinese promotion have never been better. Jardine Matheson chief executive or 'taipan' Nigel Rich says when he first came to Hong Kong in the 1970s 'the majority of our businesses were managed to two or three levels by expatriates. Today many are run by Chinese, and that will continue to happen.'

The Chinese authorities have not yet expressed formal fears about the outflow of talent, although if it were to increase they might well feel it reflected badly on their own credibility. Privately, even some senior Hong Kong civil servants concede that Britain shows up poorly on the passport issue against little Portugal, which 'did the honourable thing.'

There is a palpable sense of betrayal about Britain's laid-back attitude since the signing of the Joint Declaration, though the local Chinese, great gamblers, know well enough that China, as Legco's Jimmy McGregor puts it, 'holds all the kings and aces.' A recent poll indicates that only 30 per cent of Hong Kong Chinese trust Britain, just ten points above the percentage that trusts China. A case, perhaps, of 'a plague on both your houses.'

# 42

# Seven years to high noon

May 1990

## Carol Kennedy and Adam Baillie

In the crush of humanity struggling through the frontier checkpoint where southern China meets Hong Kong's New Territories at Shenzhen railway station, a flurry of blue passports is thrust in the air. Improbably, their gilt lettering proclaims their Chinese owners as citizens of Jamaica, Surinam and half a dozen other small and distant countries.

There is no more graphic illustration of the obsession that has gripped the Hong Kong Chinese – 98 per cent of the territory's population – ever since the tanks rolled and the guns opened fire in Beijing's Tiananmen Square last 4 June. Seven years away from Chinese rule, the professional and managerial people of Hong Kong are now desperate to insure themselves and their families against a 'worst scenario' after 1997. At the very least, the shock of Tiananmen has led many to question Beijing's commitment to keep Hong Kong a free and open society for fifty years.

Emigration, which before June 1989 had appeared to be stabilizing at around 40,000 a year – about a third being 'key' managerial and professional people – is likely to approach 60,000 in 1990. (Disturbingly, more than half of those who already have second passports still intend to leave before 1997, according to a survey for the Hong Kong Institute of Personnel Management.)

Foreign Secretary Douglas Hurd's proposed package for 50,000 'key' families – up to 225,000 passports in all – is regarded as the very minimum Britain could honourably do, and the heads of Hong Kong's largest international businesses have been outspoken on the necessity to be generous.

'We must get the passports, that is absolutely vital – and we must get more from other countries – to persuade people to stay,' says Sir George Turnbull, chairman and chief executive of the Inchcape Group, which derives the second largest chunk of its earnings and profits from the region run from its Hong Kong office. Simon Murray, managing director of Hutchison Whampoa, one of Hong Kong's largest trading conglomerates, heads a group of influential Hong Kong businessmen lobbying for the maximum number of British passports and says vehemently: 'the moral issue simply cannot be swept off the table.'

Hong Kong has weathered crises of confidence before, the sharpest just before the Sino-British agreement was signed in 1984, but this is different. After Tiananmen, as Yeats wrote in another context, 'all is changed, changed utterly' – the difference being that this time, no terrible beauty is born for anyone.

A Cambridge-educated Chinese lawyer, in her forties, talks over a traditional dim sum lunch of the 'deadening of hope' among her contemporaries, and of the 'lost generation' in their twenties who had shed their refugee parents' suspicions of China and had welcomed the prospect of rejoining the motherland. Now they, too, are looking for passports.

The mood is noticeably more sombre than a year ago. Economic performance is down – Hong Kong's once-miraculous growth, averaging 8.8 per cent over the last decade with two years in double digits, slumped in 1989 to 2.5 per cent and financial secretary Sir Piers Jacobs' best expectation is for 3 per cent in 1990. The Hong Kong economy catches influenza at the least sneeze of a US recession but, more seriously, China's austerity programme, initiated before Tiananmen, has taken a toll. The 4 June effect, Jacobs believes, accounted for at least one or two points in the decline.

Hong Kong's trade with mainland China showed comparatively little reaction to the Tiananmen trauma: the Special Economic Zones (SEZs) where Hong Kong manufacturers employ at least two million Chinese were largely unaffected by the events in Beijing, 1000 miles to the north. But China's continuing economic difficulties are causing a massive drop in Hong Kong's re-exports growth: from 45 per cent in 1988 to 26 per cent in 1989 and a likely 10 per cent in 1990.

Some factors, however, were directly attributable to Tiananmen: Bank of China felt a sharp draught in its reserves as billions of US dollars were withdrawn in protest following 4 June. The authoritative Moody's Investor Services estimate of US$4bn is regarded as a conservative figure by the Hongkong and Shanghai Bank, and over US$1bn was withdrawn in Hong Kong alone.

('4 June', indeed, has become something of a Hong Kong code for a depressed market: residential property offered at a snip is described as 'a 4 June price', as were the discounts on hotel rooms that followed the collapse in tourism to China.)

Almost a year after the massacre, Hong Kong is still perceptibly stunned and no one can predict how long it will take to regain confidence in working with Beijing. Dame Lydia Dunn, senior executive council member and a director of the huge trading 'hong', John Swire, says coolly: 'there are no guarantees for the future. Our job is to increase the odds of the chances of it working.'

Inchcape's Sir George Turnbull and other leading British industrialists with huge stakes in the region still cleave to the hopeful belief that China's economic self-interest will reassert itself. 'I am less pessimistic now than I was several months ago,' says Turnbull.

'We are not sure how long Hong Kong will take to regain fully the confidence level it had before, but we think it will eventually, and it will be a good investment for us and a good market for the future – and of course, when China does become the big market we think it is going to be, it is the obvious entry point.

'I am absolutely certain that the PRC stance on Hong Kong has not changed,' he adds, citing as an example the huge investments being made on Beijing's behalf. 'You don't put billions of hard-earned currency into a community if you are going to snatch it in 1997.'

Earlier this year, Inchcape bought further into the Hong Kong economy with the HK$700m (£56.5m) purchase of marketing, trading and distribution services from Hutchison Whampoa. Trade and Industry Secretary John Chan wheels out a list of post-4 June investments from US, Japanese and British companies amounting to several hundred million Hong Kong dollars. An Anglo-Japanese consortium including Costain and Mitsui has been set up to bid when the vast HK$127bn (£10bn) airport infrastructure project goes up for tenders next year.

It is noticeable, however, that more Hong Kong companies are re-registering head offices outside the territory; the journal *Asian Business* at the end of 1989 recorded that since 4 June more than fifty-five publicly quoted companies and around fifty private companies had announced a change of domicile. Earlier, Hongkong Land had re-registered in Bermuda, while the big Chinese-owned conglomerates Wing On and Evergo Holdings also moved their brass plates out of Hong Kong.

After 1997, all companies registered in Hong Kong automatically become Chinese companies. The diplomatic response from bankers and legislators is to question the value of a change in domicile – 'Hongkong Land cannot take Exchange Square to Bermuda with them,' observes Chan, referring to the prestigious complex of office towers on the waterfront, housing the Stock Exchange. Paul Selway-Swift, Hong Kong general manager of the Hongkong and Shanghai Bank, says if there were a 'cataclysm' after 1997 and Hong Kong assets were sequestered, all the companies would be left with is 'a brass plate in Bermuda, and that isn't worth much.'

On the other hand, as Hutchison Whampoa's Murray points out when taxed with his group's intentions: 'we do have to think hard about the future. This is not lack of confidence or fear of China, but if Hong Kong is going to be part of a Communist state, even if run as "one nation, two systems", we have got to see how we will look in the international business arena when we are making our acquisitions in the US or London.'

The shoots of new confidence are frail and sensitive to every frosty speech out of Beijing. In a poll, co-sponsored by the *South China Morning Post* last December, more than half the middle and upper-middle class respondents said they did not believe that China would abide by the terms of the Joint Declaration, or could refrain from interfering in Hong Kong's affairs.

This latter conviction is supported by some well-informed Hong Kong sources; control from the centre goes with the grain of Chinese family autocracy as well as with Communist orthodoxy. One very senior official with long experience of working with the Chinese says Beijing's first priority is to control Hong Kong politically. 'China would let Hong Kong go to the dogs if it felt that was necessary to keep political control. China would cut off its economic nose to spite its face.'

China's apparently aggressive stance towards Hong Kong since last June has complicated mainsprings. More even than the emotional street demonstrations in the territory, it was the huge amounts of Hong Kong cash flowing north in support of the pro-democracy students that convinced Beijing's aged rulers that Hong Kong could become a base for subversion.

As a result, they are not only tugging the reins at intervals with belligerent statements, but are, according to one source, 'crawling over every comma' in the various treaties still under negotiation. The collapse of Communism's house of cards in Eastern Europe has affected Deng Xiaoping's regime profoundly but, if anything, China-watchers expect them to tighten central control even further.

People cannot quite put a name to their fears of a 'worst scenario', although few outside the most bullish 'gweilos' (literally, 'foreign devils') expect things after 30 June 1997, to differ only in the change of flag and letterhead and the presence of the People's Liberation Army. Executive headhunter Raymond Tang, his Canadian residence already assured if need be, observes: 'I am not afraid that I will lose my boat and car, just that the place will gradually lose confidence and assurance.'

Others are more pessimistic. The Chinese lawyer who had spoken of the death of hope talked, only half-jokingly, of her name being 'on a list somewhere in Beijing,' and murmured of the midnight knock on the door. Contrasting the austere People's Republic and pampered Hong Kong, she said there was bound to be an element of jealousy in the relationship: 'a street urchin, when he sees a little miss all dressed up sweetly, has an irresistible impulse to pull her hair.' Glancing round the glossy hotel dining-room, she added with a smile: 'we are sitting here waiting for our hair to be torn out.'

It will be a massive task for China to understand Hong Kong, and vice versa, given the vast discrepancies in living standards, communications, education, law and style of governance. In the fast-developing Shenzhen SEZ, Chinese workers and officials earn twice the going rate in Beijing, sometimes more. Yang Chuan Geng, Beijing's senior man in Shenzhen, admits his salary at home would be 200 yuan a month, compared with the 500 a month he is currently earning.

Shenzhen has expectations of equalling Hong Kong's prosperity by the end of the century; of becoming, once the frontier is down, a kind of light industrial suburban hinterland to the glittering financial hub of Hong Kong. Exports from the zone totalled the equivalent of US$2bn in 1989 and are expected to rise by ten per cent in value this year. Chinese officials hint of a tax-free zone in the future, with parity of currency after 1997, when the Hong Kong dollar is unpegged from the US dollar.

Much sooner than that, there may be simplified procedures to setting up Hong Kong and foreign-owned factories in the zone: at the moment, as one Hong Kong trade official sighed: 'it takes them six months to say "no".'

Meanwhile, a taste for the good life is growing fast in Shenzhen. Already, local discos charge more for entrance than the midweek rate at the Grand Hyatt's 'JJ's,' the hottest new attraction for Hong Kong's yuppies. 'The more expensive it is, the more people go,' chuckles Yang. The Chinese characteristic of spending lavishly to impress – you see it in Hong Kong restaurants where bottles of Hennessy XO are drunk through the meal like house wine – clearly knows no frontiers.

Shenzhen may be only the tip of the vast Chinese iceberg, still locked in austerity and backwardness, but China's businessmen in Hong Kong show far more understanding than their political masters in Beijing of how the territory works and, indeed, of its peculiarly nervous business psychology. While hard men like foreign minister Li Hou periodically lambast Hong Kong's 'subversion,' Chinese companies present a much softer face. In the aftermath of 4 June, many companies in the giant Citic group, China's main investment arm, openly supported the pro-democracy demonstrators by taking ads in the local press.

Jin De-Qin, chairman of the Ka Wah Bank and vice-chairman of Citic (China International Trust and Investment Corporation), explains that investment decisions and business strategy generally are centred on four points, in which the 'social effect – the stability and prosperity of Hong Kong' takes precedence over purely commercial considerations such as return on equity.

A similar line is taken by Zhou Zhenxing, board director and senior deputy general manager of the Bank of China. He says that one of the bank's main aims is 'providing finance to support the Hong Kong economy.'

The Chinese banks in Hong Kong – thirteen 'sisters' to the Bank of China – seem more solidly founded than in the mid-1980s when many went to the verge of bankruptcy because of over-lending. Ka Wah was rescued from this fate in 1986 by Citic, which took a massive 92 per cent equity stake, later diluted to 71.5 per cent to meet local regulations. A small number of the remaining shares are traded on the Hong Kong Stock Exchange. Within two years, under Jin – a former president of the Bank of China – and his small management staff from Beijing, Ka Wah was back in profit by more than HK$48m, a figure which rose by 50 per cent to HK$72m in 1989.

'This was not only the first time that Citic took over a publicly quoted company in Hong Kong, but the first time that any PRC (People's Republic of China) company did so,' says the urbane and genial Jin. 'We had to prove that a PRC company could manage a public company and make it profitable. Even though it is not very big, the Ka Wah represents the image of the Chinese company in Hong Kong. Many people have been waiting to see if we can manage it well.'

No one can hang a precise figure on the amount of PRC investment in Hong Kong, but a rough 'guesstimate' puts it at around HK$6bn, half of that in manufacturing and the rest in shipping and real estate, public utilities and, increasingly, transport and communications. China is the third largest overseas investor in Hong Kong manufacturing, with the US leading the field with HK$9bn, Japan following with HK$7bn and Britain ranking fourth with HK$2.5bn.

Japanese investors have also been pouring money into real estate. 'The Japanese haven't made many mistakes over the years,' observes John Kamm, president of the territory's American Chamber of Commerce.

China's recent major investments via Citic include a 38 per cent stake in Dragonair, the domestic airline. Citic is floating a huge bond issue to raise HK$8bn to buy 20 per cent of Hongkong Telecom from Britain's Cable and Wireless – a deal which some see as a shrewd political move by C & W to protect its monopoly in the territory after 1997. China Light and Power, another giant monopoly owned by the immensely wealthy Kadoorie family, is also rumoured to be in Citic's investment sights. The airport and infrastructure are also mentioned by Citic officials.

If and when confidence does return, bolstered by passports on the one hand and perhaps a changing of the guard in Beijing on the other ('age is not on their side,' observes one Hong Kong official), the potential for Hong Kong as a manufacturing, trading and financial services hub for fast-growing Asia Pacific must be almost limitless.

The Hong Kong government, sitting securely on its budget surpluses, has committed itself to a HK$127bn (£10bn) new airport complex, port developments and the longest road bridge in the world, linking the new airport on Lantau island to downtown Hong Kong. Once the airport is operational, the old Kai Tak airport on the Kowloon peninsula will be ripe for redevelopment, and all Kowloon's height restrictions, caused by the flight paths, will be lifted, giving a vision of a new mini-Manhattan rising to face the famous Central skyline.

Increasingly, Hong Kong seems set to become less of a manufacturing and more of a trading and services base: employment now is one third manufacturing to two-thirds services where it used to be the other way round. With inflation now running at ten per cent, coupled with a squeeze on available labour, manufacturing operations are moving out to cheaper bases in southern China, Indonesia, Thailand, Malaysia and the Philippines.

Hong Kong itself, in the words of trade secretary Chan, will act more as 'a sort of regional sourcing centre, managing production activities such as quality control, design and marketing, and packaging it all together.' Jack So, the dapper and energetic executive director of the Hong Kong Trade Development Council (of which Dame Lydia Dunn, political star of the Hong Kong executive council, is chairman), predicts a 'second wave' of factories in the SEZs. He sees a lot of potential still from what he calls the 'chopstick belt' – countries of Chinese culture neighbouring Hong Kong – and pins importance on Hong Kong becoming a key trade fair and exhibition centre.

The city's glittering new convention and exhibition centre, perched high above the harbour in the relatively undeveloped Wanchai district, has bookings up to 1998, and defies the accepted wisdom that exhibitions must have large horizontal, ground-level areas for access: specially designed, gigantic Schindler lifts raise entire container trucks up the tower and enable them to drive out on the exhibition floor.

With more than 200 Asian banks packed into Central's teeming streets – let alone the international banks and financial institutions – Hong Kong's future as a financial and broking hub for the region holds massive promise, particularly since its self-regulatory disciplines were tightened following the stockmarket scandals of a few years ago. The TDC's So is convinced that the switch to services is permanent: 'how can we keep up an average living standard of US$11,000 if people are making plastic flowers? That Asia has gone.'

On the political front with China, So says: 'no one should rule out the possibility of a change for the better. If we lose our nerve, we lose everything.' Hong Kong's hard-driving business community, used to the short-term psychology of 'borrowed time, borrowed space' and a famously effective five-year profit cycle, would certainly endorse that – even if they are hunting for passports, just in case.

Even the Chinese lawyer who fears the midnight knock on the door intends to stay. She has no wish to use her UK passport to join an over-lawyered community in Britain, nor to be smothered by her family in Canada. 'Hong Kong is like a cat,' she says in parting. 'It has nine lives.'

# 43

# Finding the fifty thousand

May 1990

## Carol Kennedy and Adam Baillie

Terence Yu is the epitome of the do-anything, deal-making Hong Kong entrepreneur. He is mid-thirties, sports a well tailored dark suit and a chunky gold Rolex, and drives two large Mercedes cars – one in Hong Kong, the other in the Shenzhen Special Economic Zone of southern China where he owns an industrial chemicals plant. When he came to put up his third share of the equity in a new multi-million-dollar British manufacturing plant in Shenzhen, he did so in cash.

Because he is single, Yu will not be one of Douglas Hurd's 50,000 'key' managers and professionals targeted to receive British passports for themselves and their families. Perhaps also because of his unmarried status, the passport issue is not uppermost in his mind as it is with so many Hong Kong businessmen.

'I haven't got around to it yet; maybe I should,' he says, cheerfully forking up spaghetti in one of Hong Kong's popular Italian restaurants. But Hong Kong entrepreneurs get successful by their 'no-problem' attitude to life, and soon Yu is pouring out a stream of half-humorous ideas for coping if he does not get a passport, one of which would be to buy a house on Macau (which reverts to Chinese rule in 1999, two years after Hong Kong), and commute by hydrofoil. It would be a short-term solution, but he would probably make a profit on the house.

Others are less sanguine. Professor Robert Tricker of the department of management studies at Hong Kong University says he is losing 10 per cent of his MBA students to emigration, 'and at best, one in four will qualify for the Hurd proposals.' Tricker adds that their quality is 'fantastically good,' and, measured by entry qualifications, the Hong Kong students are in 'the top 20 per cent of the world.'

Demand for MBA courses has soared in Hong Kong. Although the principal motivation behind the upsurge is ostensibly to improve job performance and enhance career development, Tricker says an additional factor is 'the belief that possession of an MBA may, with 1997 in mind, enhance the prospects of pursuing an overseas career path.'

Tricker, formerly of Oxford's Nuffield College, reels off a string of alarming statistics. Of just over 1000 accountants who responded to a survey of 4600 conducted by the Hong Kong Society of Accountants, 80 per cent were planning to emigrate before 1997.

The accountants sent a deputation to Tricker to ask what he could do to plug the gaps. He had to tell them, it was 'far too late for tertiary education to do anything.'

Professor Paul Kirkbride, formerly of Hong Kong's City Polytechnic, began to conduct in-depth surveys for the Hong Kong Institute of Personnel Management in 1987. His latest data – gathered before Tiananmen Square – suggests the emigration figure for 1990 will be close to 60,000; that less than 20 per cent of those obtaining visas will return anyway, and that the numbers even of those with foreign passports staying after 1997 will be lower than the government hopes. Well over half – 56 per cent – of those already holding second passports intend to leave before the transition.

Even more worrying is the drain on the managerial, technical and professional sector, 5 per cent of which is leaving every year. Such people were always a scarce resource in Hong Kong, though the government is now pouring funds into new universities.

Kirkbride's studies reveal intentions to leave among just under 50 per cent of all those who responded to his questionnaires, with about 20 per cent still undecided. Post-Tiananmen figures can be expected to show higher levels in favour of departure.

Although the brain drain is said to be affecting professionals more than managers, it is becoming more difficult to recruit locally. Max Lummis, an expatriate from Connecticut, tells of the problems in finding a fifth partner for his consultancy firm.

Scarcely are candidates inside the door, before they are asking such coded questions as 'how many international bases do you have?', and 'what are the opportunities for foreign travel?' It is hard, says Lummis, to find someone without a passport who has 'the necessary commitment to Hong Kong.'

The big international companies are in a more fortunate position. Inchcape, Jardines, Hutchison and the like can move promising local managers to Canada or Australia to enable them to gain residency in the hope that after that, they will return to Hong Kong.

All manner of gossip circulates about the passport black market. Belize, of all places, has become a fashionable source: the going rate for a Belize passport in Hong Kong is said to be US$10,000, and in Beijing – where, curiously, such deals are not yet illegal – it is reputed to be US$30,000. Singapore is experiencing a rush of applications because it allows five years before establishing residency.

Poaching by overseas employers is an occasional phenomenon. Cathay Pacific's maintenance division last year lost 150 of its highly qualified avionics and maintenance engineers to the Australian airline Qantas. The company insists, however, that its active policy of recruiting internationally means that the leavers are being matched.

Regional recruitment is becoming a more important factor for many Hong Kong firms. 'There is a tremendous movement of Asian managers around the region,' says Roger Atkinson, a partner in recruitment consultants LTA Associates. Atkinson believes emigration is 'not yet a major stumbling block at a senior level,' but his associate Tony Tong chips in: 'we are beginning to hear more requests for "an insurance policy" (second passport) from companies hiring managers.'

The partners agree that 'over-promotion' is a growing problem as companies strain to bridge the gaps left by the passport-hunters. Although Hong Kong's graduate supply is higher than ever, the experience gap is the one that shows.

Simon Murray, managing director of Hutchison Whampoa, is the moving force behind the territory's 'Honour Hong Kong' campaign, backed by leading businesses and aimed at securing the best possible deal from Britain on passports. He spends a lot of personal time on it ('it's burning holes in Saturdays and Sundays'), flying to London to lobby recalcitrant anti-immigration MPs ('many of whom haven't been beyond Watford') and industrialists, whose polite but passive support, he insists, is not enough.

'I'd like to see British businessmen who do believe in Hong Kong standing up and saying something. The IOD and the CBI need to be out there giving us support. They are not doing nearly enough to lobby on our behalf. I can't believe that they don't care, or don't see the commercial advantages to their companies.'

Murray estimates that there may be 500,000 foreign passport-holders in Hong Kong. (Ironically, these do not include Hutchison chairman Li Ka-shing, one of the wealthiest men in Asia.) Such numbers would seem reassuring, given Price Waterhouse's 1989 identification of 315,000 key qualified staff who needed the passport reassurance to stay and keep Hong Kong ticking post-1997. However, as Murray points out, if the economy is to grow even at its existing rate, that number will be more like 580,000 by 1997.

The task of identifying the 50,000 heads of families falls to a Hong Kong government committee. Managers may well be determined as passport-worthy on the value attributed to them by their companies. A high salary scores even if professional qualifications do not.

The total envisaged under Hurd's plan is some 225,000 passports, taking into account family dependants – but that itself is a variable factor. Murray thinks it would be better to make it a specific 225,000 now: how otherwise, he asks, do you control the size of families over the next seven years?

'We can't, unfortunately, give a passport to everyone, but we can give a lot more confidence by giving passports to the people who make the place tick and keep the economy humming. That's our best bet,' says Murray.

'I think China dreads two things above all: one, that Hong Kong fails in economic terms and two, that they get blamed for it.

'We don't have any natural resources except our people and if they are leaving town, what have we got?'

# Section Nine

## The European Dimension

# 44

# Unscrambling EEIGs

September 1990

William Pitt

Champagne, haute couture and EEIGs. The world unquestionably stands in France's debt for champagne and haute couture. Whether fellow Europeans should be grateful to France for the inspiration behind European Economic Interest Groupings is less clear.

The humble EEIG carries a heavy burden of expectations, as the 1985 European Council regulation explaining its use makes clear. Among the sonorous 'whereas' clauses in the preamble to the regulation is a reference to the need for 'an appropriate Community legal instrument' to enable 'natural persons, companies, firms and other legal bodies . . . to co-operate effectively across frontiers.'

Such a device is necessary, the regulation argues, in order to 'bring about [the] single market and increase its unity.'

In other words, the single European market is not just about cross-border competition; it is also about cross-border co-operation. And until an 'appropriate . . . legal instrument' to permit such co-operation is created, the single market will not be achieved. Enter the EEIG.

The two great attractions of EEIGs are, theoretically, their simplicity and their flexibility. EEIGs are not joint venture companies; they do not need capital. An EEIG's aim is to 'facilitate or develop the economic activities of its members'. Any debts the EEIG may incur in the process are jointly and severally the liability of its members.

The idea behind the EEIG came from France, where *groupements d'intérêt economique* (GIEs) have been winning converts since 1968. GIEs are simply EEIGs without the extra 'E', trading exclusively in France. There are over 9000 GIEs currently active.

Enabling GIEs to bestride the European stage has not been easy. Agreement was held up until last July, largely because the Germans insisted that the regulations governing EEIGs should provide for worker participation, whereas the British were equally adamant that they need not.

The British won, but at a price. EEIGs may not employ more than 500 people, the point at which worker participation at board level becomes mandatory in West Germany.

This is unlikely to pose much of a problem to companies considering setting up EEIGs. Vision 1250, potentially one of the most exciting projects to adopt the EEIG format, will employ ten full-time staff in Brussels to market high-definition television (HDTV) technology developed by Thomson of France and Philips of the Netherlands. Staff may well increase if the EEIG, which was unveiled on 11 July, takes off; but 500 employees are scarcely likely.

An important reason for this is that the activities of EEIGs must be, in the words of the EC regulation, 'ancillary' to the activities of its members. The work performed by the EEIG 'must be related to the economic activities of its members but not replace them.'

Thus, for example, Vision 1250 may market, and offer access to, HDTV technology to television production companies, as it has already successfully done with the BBC, Thames Television and British Satellite Broadcasting. It may even train cameramen and technicians, but it may not manufacture the technology itself, an activity already performed by Philips and Thomson.

Joint marketing initiatives such as this may well prove the most popular role of EEIGs. Co-operation in research through EEIGs is also likely.

The EC regulation cites another application of the 'ancillary' role which is perhaps more pertinent in the light of the rather exclusive membership of the EEIG 'club' known to the European Commission. An EEIG 'may not itself, with regard to third parties, practise a profession,' the regulation says.

The EEIG structure has proved attractive to members of professions, notably to lawyers, as a means of referring clients to one another. But, as the regulation makes clear, EEIGs set up by lawyers or other professionals may not offer legal advice to clients in their own right.

Such restrictions are probably welcome to most lawyers, and even more so to the insurers. As the members of an EEIG are jointly and severally liable for any debts it may incur, a claim brought against an EEIG for misleading advice could ultimately fall most heavily on the member with the fullest professional indemnity insurance. The 'deep pockets theory' familiar to the US courts, under which plaintiffs seek damages from the richest, or best-insured defendant regardless of fault – could thus gain currency in Europe.

Out of the eighty-five EEIGs known to the European Commission at the end of June this year, nine clearly identify themselves as groupings of lawyers, and doubtless a few others also fall into this category, concealing their identity behind vague 'Euro-' titles and bland statements of purpose. The information held by the European Commission on the membership and objectives of the EEIGs so far set up is not comprehensive. Even the figure of eighty-five may not be the full total because EEIGs are under no obligation to inform the Commission of their existence.

However, quite apart from the specific problems of lawyers and other professions using EEIGs, the European Council of Ministers had good reason to insist that they play an 'ancillary' role to the business of their members. As Richard Grafen at the DTI in the UK puts it: 'No one wants it to become a merger vehicle.'

Grafen, who sits on the Contact Committee set up by the European Commission to explain the functioning of EEIGs, suggests that unfettered, EEIGs might be used by German companies to avoid the worker participation requirements that bind them in their own country. But, since an EEIG may not supplant the activity of its members, this could not happen.

Likewise, EEIGs may not hold shares in any of their member companies, nor exercise any management control over them. EEIGs are designated as servants and may not become masters.

Severine Israël, who chairs the Contact Committee on EEIGs at Directorate General IV (financial institutions and company law) of the European Commission in Brussels, says that EEIGs had to be clearly subordinate to their members because 'otherwise we would have created a kind of company.' She stresses that EEIGs are not intended as a substitute for the EC company, a project the commission has been working on for twenty years.

Israël also admits that the meaning of 'ancillary' may be open to some interpretation. 'It is a new expression we have used,' she explains. In the event of a dispute it would be up to the courts of the EC member state in which the EEIG is domiciled to determine whether this new expression was being adhered to.

Grafen suggests that this is something prospective EEIG members should consider carefully: 'If I were a British lawyer, I would advise you to take this provision fairly seriously because otherwise you would risk having the whole thing wound up.'

One British lawyer more familiar than most with the advantages and drawbacks of EEIGs is Malcolm Keogh, a partner at Manchester solicitors, Pannone Blackburn. His firm has used the EEIG structure to consolidate relationships with other law firms in France, Spain, Italy and Belgium. Notwithstanding Grafen's remarks about not using EEIGs as merger vehicles, Keogh makes it clear that this is precisely what Pannone Blackburn and its European partners envisage.

He describes Pannone De Backer EEIG, which is named after its British and Belgian members, as an 'excellent first step towards full merger.' And he praises the flexibility of the EEIG structure which provides 'a stepping stone [towards merger] for us, but need not be a stepping stone for others.'

Given that Pannone Blackburn plans, as soon as is practicable, to merge with its four European EEIG partners, the current restrictions on what EEIGs may do are rather galling. As Keogh observes: 'We cannot at the moment use a Pannone De Backer letterhead to send written advice to clients. We practise at the moment under our individual names, but we intend to practise as Pannone De Backer as soon as we are able.'

This, presumably, will be when Pannone De Backer has passed the larval EEIG stage and emerged as a pan-European law firm. The prospects of the rules governing EEIGs being changed to allow them to offer legal advice in their own right seem remote.

But a particular attraction of EEIGs to lawyers, and indeed to other professions trading under very different rules in different EC member states, is that members may have widely differing structures and still work together. Thus Pannone De Backer's members include a Belgian limited company, De Backer, a British partnership, Pannone Blackburn, and a French GIE, Groupe Lexel.

The presence of a French GIE, the precursor of the EEIG, as a member of an EEIG in its own right, suggests how the device may be employed to build bridges between companies both nationally and internationally. Severine Israël points out that, following the example set by EEIGs, Belgium has set up a similar mechanism on a purely national basis. Spain and Luxembourg both plan to do the same.

The British seem less enthusiastic. Although Malcolm Keogh at Pannone Blackburn waxes lyrical about the opportunities Pannone De Backer offers its members to 'learn from each other,' the DTI has scarcely trumpeted the EEIG's virtues from the rooftops. 'It is not something we have put a lot of effort into,' concedes Richard Grafen.

He suggests that the attractions of EEIGs may be less evident to British companies than to their continental counterparts: 'A number of UK companies find it easier to set up joint subsidiaries, by contract or in other ways, than companies in other EC member states do.' He cites lawyers as an exception to this generalization.

There are also certain restrictions to the uses of EEIGs likely to prove galling to precisely those companies that might most wish to use them. There is a good reason, for example, why there are no British or German members of Euro Marine Re, a reinsurance EEIG registered in Paris in March this year.

Euro Marine Re proudly proclaimed itself to be the first EEIG established in the insurance or reinsurance business. On the face of it, there would appear to be many attractions in using EEIGs as underwriting agents to write those classes of business not usually underwritten by the member companies.

In the case of Euro Marine Re, the business in question is marine and transport reinsurance. This was ceded to the EEIG by three of its member companies, the Portuguese insurer Bonanca, the Spanish bank, Banco Vitalicio (which is also very active in insurance) and the Italian insurer, SIAT. The business passed on to the EEIG will be managed by its fourth member, the French reinsurer, La Réunion Européenne.

Euro Marine Re has made it clear that it is willing to consider applications from other members. But any German insurance company wishing to join would not be able to because, under German law, insurers may not participate in EEIGs.

The German government has invoked article thirty-eight of the EC regulation governing EEIGs to prevent insurers participating. Article thirty-eight permits governments to prohibit EEIGs from engaging in certain activities on their territory if those activities are deemed to be 'in contravention of that state's public interest.'

The German government takes the view that German insurers underwriting business through the medium of an EEIG are acting against the state's public interest. Clearly the EEIG's inability to pay claims because it has no capital creates the potential for problems in the event of a dispute between the members. But whether this constitutes sufficient grounds to prohibit insurers from joining EEIGs would be a question for the European Court of Justice to decide, should anyone feel strongly enough to sue the German government.

The position of British insurers is rather different, and arises from a procedural muddle rather than an issue of principle. The British statutory instrument of April 1989 which introduces EEIGs into English law does not mesh with the Companies Act and the definition of an 'insurer' under that Act. Whereas an insurer must be a company under the Companies Act, an EEIG is not a company and may therefore not be an insurer.

Any British insurer burning with desire to join an EEIG could doubtless cut its way through this legal thicket, but the process would probably be time-consuming and costly.

Vision 1250, the HDTV project, may in time help to raise the profile of EEIGs and bring pressure on EC member states to allow them to function as freely as possible. Many of the marketing functions to which EEIGs have so far been put are scarcely 'sexy' in public relations terms. The *Association des Producteurs Européens de Bananes*, registered as an EEIG in Brussels earlier this year, is about as exciting as they come.

The chances of HDTV making EEIGs into a household acronym are slim. But if Europe's industrialists find themselves dazzled by the picture quality of the television coverage of the Barcelona Olympics in 1992, they may think again about the uses of the cross-border organization that will have helped to bring it to them.

# 45

# Angst and pygmies in Paris and Frankfurt

January 1990

## Mihir Bose

Consider this paradox. Germany is an industrial and economic giant but a stock market pygmy. Frankfurt, its greatest stock exchange, only conducts business for two hours a day between 11.30 a.m. and 1.30 p.m.

'In financial terms Germany has not reached the same position as it has in exports, for example,' admits Rudiger Von Rosen, executive vice-chairman of the Federation of German Stock Exchanges. 'In relation to GNP the financial market is not as developed as in the UK or Japan or the United States.'

One figure tells the story. The market capitalization of the London stockmarket is 83 per cent of the gross domestic product (GDP); the market capitalization of the Frankfurt exchange is only 21 per cent of the German GDP.

Professor Norbert Walter of the Deutsche Bank puts it very bluntly: 'the stock exchange is next to irrelevant in Germany. We do not have a system to provide equity to companies.' Until the early 1980s when the bull market began to change perspectives, German companies had little need for equities. Interest rates were low, the banks were happy to provide finance and while interest payments could be written off against tax, dividend payments could not. Recently some of the more well-known German companies, such as Nixdorf and Porsche, have been coming on to the market but they generally issue preference shares.

It is a reflection of what Von Rosen calls a certain German patriarchal culture. 'In America young entrepreneurs start companies, work there for three or four years and then they go public. In Germany we have extremely successful firms with about 1000 employees, run by family patriarchs. There are some 378,000 such companies (the exchange lists just 600 companies) and they are the backbone of the German industry. It is not the Siemenses, or the Daimler-Benzes. They may be more spectacular but these patriarch companies lead in production, in the export market. They really dislike the idea of being listed, of publishing figures or letting the outside world know how rich he *[the patriarch]* is. We will never be able to get him into a stock exchange. But perhaps with the new generation, we may be able to reach such companies.'

It is this search for the new generation and the pressure of world markets – if the German patriarch can do without the stock market, the German stock market cannot do without the world markets – that is driving the engine of change. The patriarch may not become an Anglo-Saxon entrepreneur but the German stock market has to come to terms with global trading.

While the English experienced Big Bang, the Germans have gone for what Von Rosen describes as a 'more evolutionary system.'

'In London it was spectacular. We are doing it step by step, hopefully avoiding some of the conflicts,' he says.

The wider world may think of the German stock exchange as the Frankfurt exchange. Frankfurt, it is true, dominates the German financial world. It is the banking capital of the country and has nearly two thirds of the equity turnover, but it is only one of eight exchanges: Dusseldorf, Bremen, Berlin, Munich, Stuttgart, Hamburg and Hanover being the others.

In stock exchange terms Dusseldorf – with about 25 per cent of the trading volume – is the only other one that matters but each of the other exchanges represents a powerful political force: the German länders, the states that the country is divided into. Each länder speaks for the historic and regional diversity of the country and wields great power with its own prime minister and cabinet. In stock exchange terms this can threaten chaos. Last summer a trade in Allianz stock showed a price difference of DM60 between Frankfurt and Munich and closing prices can differ, albeit by smaller amounts.

So the German stock exchange reformer has to tread carefully. It was one topic that even Von Rosen, normally so articulate, wanted to steer clear of. 'No, no it is not a topic I want to talk about. It is a touchy topic. I should not speak about it.' Eventually he did try to answer questions about the undoubted jealousies between the exchanges, but the answer took up almost half an hour and merely underlined how difficult the struggle has been and continues to be. Dusseldorf resents the growing power of Frankfurt; Munich worries if one integrated stock exchange will eliminate its own, negligible, influence.

Von Rosen and his Federation have come under suspicion. When Von Rosen arrived at the Federation, which has only been going for three years, he was also the managing director, without portfolio, of the Frankfurt stock exchange. 'This binding into the Frankfurt stock exchange was to give me more support, but my role in the Frankfurt stock exchange is just a title,' he says. 'The marriage has never been consummated and today after three years I would say this is hurting the effort to integrate. There has been so much suspicion on both sides. Everyone asks who is Von Rosen working for: Frankfurt, or the other exchanges?'

Von Rosen has got the eight exchanges a bit closer. The Federation now issues an annual report on all the stock exchanges, a radical innovation for the Germans and a matter of great pride for Von Rosen. The two data processing centres at Dusseldorf and Frankfurt have been combined; in August a new stock exchange Act came into being and six different central depository institutions, which do the stock exchange paperwork, have been merged into one. This January has seen the mergence of the Deutsche Kassenverein, a classified German central securities depository for the whole clearing settlement. In December the IBIS information system started, which provides computerized price information.

Von Rosen sees the IBIS system, which at the moment is providing information for out of hours trading, as the first step to a fully computerized trading system, similar to the one in London and the other major centres. Such a system is all the more necessary as this month has seen the start of trading in futures and options. 'Two hours trading in shares will not fill the need for our futures and options exchange. Trading in futures needs an underlying cash market, and as the futures market will trade the whole day it means the underlying equity market must offer the same trading facility. IBIS will provide this trading facility.'

But there will have to be a lot more discussions before IBIS attains this status and its launch showed how difficult change can be on the German stock market. The IBIS system was started by six institutions led by the three universal banks, Deutsche, Dresdner and Commerzbank, which account for 4 per cent of the turnover. Frustrated by just two hours' official trading on the floor of the exchange, they went ahead and set up the system and then announced it to the press. The smaller banks and operators were aghast.

Particularly hard hit were the maklers who, in an operation unique to Germany, stand on the floor of the exchange receiving orders from the banks. Each stock has its makler who fixes the price in a sort of street auction matching bids to deals. Maklers call out the prices and the final price will depend on the market reaction to their outcry. This almost medieval system cannot cope with modern trading and over the years a lucrative off-hours trading has started. Half of Frankfurt's equity trading and four-fifths of its bond trading takes place outside the exchange either before 11.30 a.m. or after 1.30 p.m. The trade is mostly in blue chip stocks and IBIS, which will have fourteen stocks, is meant to cater for it. Hence the maklers' fear for their own survival.

Friederich Pfeffer, head of securities trading at Commerzbank, admits: 'it was bad marketing the way we announced IBIS. But I am sure the IBIS system is the way forward to provide a competitive system that can ensure our customers get a good service and good business opportunities for trading.'

Von Rosen can see no alternative to the way the big banks forced the IBIS on everyone. 'Between a big bank and a small bank, between a makler in Bremen and a makler in Frankfurt there are many, many conflicts and many, many different interests. So if you would have a big symposium of 2000 people to discuss these changes you would never be able to change things. I am sure the makler will remain. Trading floor? I don't know. This the market has to decide. We could have a floor, a fully computerized system, or just a screen-based system as in London. There are so many different examples. I don't think anyone in this country knows right now.'

What Von Rosen is confident of is that when the changes come through, 'the question of whether I am the lap dog of Frankfurt or not will not matter. The question is how we can change the institutional, technical and administrative stock exchange framework so that the German markets become competitive as a global market.'

However, not everybody is convinced that the German stock exchanges can change sufficiently for Germany to become a financial centre. Professor Walter, something of a media guru on Germany, is very doubtful. 'I am optimistic on the German economy but I am not optimistic on the financial outlook. As a financial centre we will be lagging for quite a time. There are excellent reasons for Germany to become the leading continental financial centre. But we have a stupid, backward-orientated, narrow-minded people.'

The people who so anger Walter are 'in the Bundesbank. Large parts of the Bundesbank are concerned with how to preserve the autonomy of the Bundesbank. This means being averse to investors, not allowing an offshore market to develop. They want full control of everything. And the ministry of finance and the government are dominated by people who do not understand economics. Our Christian Democrats are not very different from our social democrats. They talk differently; they do not behave differently.'

Walter speaks from a deep sense of personal angst. His own Deutsche Bank has listened politely to his plans to invest in financial studies and done nothing. When he was at the prestigious Kiel Institute of World Economics he was told by his head that he should not be quoted so often in the media. Walter sees in this a certain provincialism. 'The stock exchanges are a typical example of provincialism. They have great difficulty understanding that we have to demonstrate to the world that discussions about making Germany a financial centre are going on. The problem is that we wait till someone else takes the lead then we react. This country praises itself by letting others make the mistake, rather than going first.'

As an example he provides the rise of supply side economics that Margaret Thatcher and Ronald Reagan have used to fashion their political agenda.

'We reinvented supply side economics but we did not sell it internationally. The Americans did. To an extent it had to do with language. German is no longer an important language. But we are no longer architects, we are reactors. It is the legacy of what that damned man Hitler did.'

Hitler's influence has had other stock market effects. The inflation of the 1920s, which helped Hitler's rise, and then the devastation of the Second World War has meant that twice this century Germans have built up wealth and twice seen it destroyed. 'This makes German investors very risk averse,' says Pfeffer. 'They are not used to buying equities in big amounts. It takes us a long time to change the behaviour of our private clients.' The banks are confident that the long bull market of the 1980s did change behaviour, as investors, accumulating wealth for the first time this century, looked to equities. But there is now great fear that the mini crash of October 1989 may have frightened them away.

Curiously, the sheer efficiency of the German settlement system may have been responsible for that. If the German stock-buying system is medieval, the settlement process is ultra-modern, quite the quickest in the world. The computerized clearing and settlement service means you can get your money out in two days – it might take as many as fifteen days or even longer in London. So on Monday 16 October 1989, as Pfeffer recalls, 'the international funds sold big amounts in the German market. They could get their money out in two days but they did not have to pay their clients in two days. Liquidity is the most important feature of our market.' The result was that the market fell like a stone, losing 13 per cent of its value in a day and frightening the small investor.

But Pfeffer is convinced that, in the long run, it will give the German stock markets an edge in the future. 'It can, under certain circumstances, damage us but it is an advantage for all investors. For international customers what matters is liquidity. They want to have a good, quick settlement. If they want to make profits for their portfolios then liquidity is more important than performance which can only be average.'

This suggests a greater appetite for the stock market by the German banks and here they are being pushed by their own clients. 'The pressure for change is coming from industry. When the bull market started the companies rediscovered equities. Between the 1950s and 1982 the number of listed companies actually declined; they started climbing after 1982,' says Hans-Peter Wodnick, head of equity research at James Capel's Frankfurt office. In 1983 only DM7bn was raised through rights issues; by 1986 this had more than doubled to DM16m. And while the crash of October 1987 did slow things down, it is expected to have totalled DM15m for 1989.

'German companies are becoming more and more international and they look at financial ratios and realize they need to show better ratios. Even Daimler-Benz has raised cash,' Wodnick continues. 'This trend of internationalization of companies is continuing and as equity prices continue to rise, equity financing becomes more competitive compared to debt financing.'

But if this Anglo-Saxon practice is catching on, the other one, the hostile takeover, shows no sign of proving popular. The close association of German industry with its bankers – banks hold a large chunk of equity and have a seat on the board – precludes that. Deutsche Bank, for example, has some 28 per cent of Daimler-Benz.

These attitudes are unlikely to be changed by the stock exchange reforms. The worry for the reformers is that if the reforms do not proceed fast enough then, instead of rivalling London, which is what drives Von Rosen and the reformers, Paris may soon catch up with Frankfurt. In some ways Paris is already threatening Frankfurt as the most important of the second division exchanges; London, New York and Tokyo forming the super league.

While this is galling for the Germans, and none of the Germans I spoke to even wanted to admit the possibility, at the end of 1988 Paris' market capitalization was higher than Frankfurt's and Von Rosen himself admits that the 'Paris stock exchange in technique is better than we are.'

Regional differences hardly exist. There is no makler system and while the CAT, the Computer Assisted Trading system purchased from the Toronto Stock Exchange, has to be modified at a cost of $50m, the Paris Bourse is fully automated with both on-screen and floor trading all day long. Yet in some ways the French have the same deep-seated problems with regard to a stock exchange that the Germans have.

Indeed, the French relationship with the stock exchange is also paradoxical. France may not be as renowned an economic giant as Germany but its economy will grow at twice the speed of the UK this year with half the rate of inflation. But in relation to this, the stock exchange remains puny. In 1988 the London market, with a capitalization of £377bn, represented 83 per cent of the gross domestic product. The companies on the Paris Bourse with a £135m capitalization represent just 26 per cent of the GDP.

But if the German reluctance to come to the market represents a certain philosophical attitude, the Paris one is more reflective of the political values that have dominated France since the war. 'I think what a lot of English people do not realize,' says Daniel Pouget, of James Capel 'is that France is not only a centralized political system but a very centralized, controlled economy. Sixty per cent of the French economy is in government hands and the French government does not believe in a free market economy. It says it believes in the stock market but that is a glib statement.'

There was a brief Thatcherite spell of privatization when Chirac was Prime Minister but his defeat at the hands of Mitterrand in the presidential elections and the return of a Socialist Prime Minister has put a stop to that.

Recently there have been attempts at creeping re-nationalization with the government trying to buy back shares in Société Générale, privatized by Chirac.

Mitterrand's latest socialist, Prime Minister Rocard, is considered a pragmatist, a non-ideological man, and the finance minister, Pierre Beregovoy, has taken a keen interest in stock market reform but Gerard de la Martinière, the chief executive of the Bourse, has no illusions about how far the minister will go. 'The finance minister understands the stock exchange but feels there is no contradiction in a strong public sector and the stock exchange. We are not asking for 100 per cent privatization but if we could get some of the French government-owned companies to partially float, say Credit Lyonnais issued 30 per cent of its stock, then this would solve a big problem for us. This market lacks big blue chip companies. There is no lack of medium-sized companies, we have a lot on our Second Marché (the French USM and far more successful than our USM) but our main lack is enough top ten or twenty firms that dominate a market.'

Despite these fundamental problems and a government which, philosophically, cannot concede too many economic powers to the market, the Paris Bourse has modernized itself in a remarkably short time and very successfully. Pouget thinks this is one of the strengths of the centralized French system. 'That is the good side. Once a decision is taken it is taken, be it having a TGV from Paris to Nice or changing stock exchange rules. There is none of the dithering you get in London.'

So the last couple of years have seen hectic changes. In January 1988 the Napoleonic monopoly of stockbroking was broken; this month, January 1990, sees outside institutions, banks, foreign firms, achieve 100 per cent control over French stockbroking firms. The brokers are still the only ones who can deal in shares but anybody can own brokers and several British institutions own French firms. Pouget's own firm Dufour-Koller-Lacarrière, a small broker, found it impossible to survive, so sold itself to James Capel. The ones which are still independent – there are only seven – have gone for a very French solution: a *tour de table* where little parcels of the equity, generally 10 per cent, are sold to various French and overseas institutions.

Last July, 1989, also saw negotiated commissions come in. It has meant higher charges for small investors but then before that a small investor could pay as little as 10 francs for a deal. Now he probably pays about 40 francs, still a lot cheaper than London.

The French have also opened new markets and modernized their dealing systems. The Matif – the futures market started in 1986 – is the second biggest in the world after Chicago and actively used as a hedge by institutions. Share certificates have gone and the whole dealing system has become electronic. Market making was slowly introduced to the Bourse in October.

Not that there have been no problems. The crash of 1987 affected Paris and three brokers have gone to the wall. In nine months to December 1988 the Bourse made a loss of FF120.5m and could make a loss this year as well. And there is the problem of the Guarantee Fund, set up to protect investors. In 1988 speculation on the Matif led to the Guarantee Fund losing FF500m. The Bourse, in a highly unpopular move, had to ask members for FF400m in capital and some FF300m in loans. Now a proper Guarantee Fund has been set up which is separate from the Sociétié des Bourses Françaises – the market's executive body – and funded by fees from brokers.

This has required some persuasion. 'Our brokers want to have the maximum guarantee fund without paying for the guarantee,' says de la Martinière.

What de la Martinière and the French brokers would like is to get rid of the Bourse stamp tax. But the minister, says de la Martinière, 'feels the Bourse is booming so he cannot consider it necessary to sweep away the tax.'

For as long as the stamp tax remains, Paris will fear London. London has 25 per cent of the market in French stocks. Two years ago Morgan Grenfell put through a deal on French stocks, before the Paris Bourse opened, which was worth that day's trading on the Bourse. London has no tax on dealing with foreign shares and this makes it very attractive. 'It does not worry us if the British deal in French stocks for a London firm or a Japanese client,' says de la Martinière. 'Our British friends will then resell it in this market. What is worrying is that our domestic French firms are using London market makers. French operators prefer to use London when dealing with other French operators and they get best execution, lower prices, secrecy – it is difficult for our Commission des Opérations de Bourse, the French SEC, to trace them – and tax exemption.'

The only way de la Martinière can see the tax going is through the EC, the minister is waiting for 1992, but here there is another problem, namely the ideas of Andrew Hugh-Smith, chairman of the London stock exchange.

It would be impossible to have just one European exchange but, as de la Martinière says, 'Hugh-Smith is a clever man. He has proposed that we can get a European exchange if everybody uses SEAQ International. We think it is a bit arrogant, just as it is a bit arrogant to call London the International Stock Exchange. But perhaps the word international is meant to include United Kingdom and Ireland.' With that de la Martinière smiles as if he does not really believe it is all that funny.

The French solution is to select the best European stocks and have them listed on all the European exchanges at the same time. This would be accompanied by linkages between exchanges to make settlement easier. De la Martinière's fear is that 'NASDAQ or the Reuters screen will become the

European stock market. The British have to realize that we want to be part of a common European business, not a London European business.'

By the time all this is resolved both Paris and Frankfurt will be a lot more like the London and New York stock exchanges. However, philosophical differences will remain. It will be 1991 before the Germans get an insider trading law, having preferred to rely on what they call moral persuasion. 'If you have a law against murder does that stop it?' asks Von Rosen and he makes a larger point. 'Why should we change things in this country which are successful but different to other countries? We can do things pretty successfully here.' Nobody can deny that.

The French take a less dogmatic line and if in the end they had to change even more rapidly to survive they would. The fear that they may fall far behind the superleaguers of London, New York and Tokyo haunts them.

# 46

# Perestroika's favoured son

July 1990

Gillian Sandford

Thick Marlboro cigarette smoke billows round Vladimir Svirski. 'I am not a businessman,' he declares. He lounges in a blue open-necked shirt at Moscow's exclusive Octoberskaya hotel. And the disclaimer rings false. Colleagues dub the thirty-eight year-old bachelor 'Mr President.' He heads an umbrella organization to some 5000 subsidiary companies involved in research, development and production. They cut profitable deals with domestic state enterprises or link up with foreign partners in trade and joint ventures. Svirski is a Soviet business success.

Current contracts being fulfilled by his organization amount to 15 billion roubles, he says. It is an impressive figure, yet difficult to evaluate in international terms because of the ideological limits placed on Soviet business operations, the gap between statistics on joint ventures and genuine up-and-running successes, and the non-convertibility of the rouble (the officially agreed rate is 0.6 roubles per US$, but the black market rate is between ten and fifteen roubles).

'Our organization is probably nonsense and the principles of its activity could hardly be understood by foreign businesses. It is a specifically Soviet organization,' explains Svirski. It has a suitably Soviet bureaucratic name: the Centre for Scientific and Technical Activity, Research and Social Initiatives. Broadly speaking, its principle is to enable Soviet entrepreneurs, within the climate of perestroika and through the lure of at least double or triple average wages, to research and develop new products, free from the red tape and supply bottlenecks that previously strangled such innovation at birth.

Companies under the Centre are set up as 'public organizations'. They have their own legal personality, but they bear no resemblance to Western shareholding companies, nor are they co-operatives in the Soviet sense of the word. The form of a public organization offers tax and other advantages over co-operatives, but unlike co-ops, whose founders own the co-op's property – production machinery or computers, for example – public organizations cannot divide up such property among founders because it

belongs to the organization, not to them. This encourages stability, says
Svirski.

Svirski's public organizations are therefore an attractive legal form to
entrepreneurs wanting to make higher than average wages and to develop
and reinvest in new ventures, but not to those wanting to establish a
business, then sell out. Says Svirski: 'the property of our organization is the
property of the legal person which is the organization and cannot be
distributed by people and members of the organization.' This difficult issue
of private property penetrates the heart of Soviet socialist ideology. Thus,
the irony of Svirski's situation is that, using this legal form, he has created a
rich business empire but – even if he wished to – he cannot liquidate its
assets for himself. He sits on a gold mine yet cannot personally make a mint.

So how do Svirski and the Centre benefit from its subsidiaries? The
Centre claims at least 15 per cent of net profit – and a substantially higher
percentage if it has invested capital into their projects or provided certain
equipment, such as computers. The Centre's bank, headed by Svirski,
provides financing. This commercial bank boasts credit capacities of 220m
roubles and nominal capital of 11m roubles. Meanwhile Svirski says he
draws a wage of 1500 roubles a month (up to ten times more than some
Russian citizens).

Svirski, a geophysicist, takes up the narrative: 'it all began well over four
years ago with the idea of taking icebergs from the Antarctic to Egypt. A
Saudi Arabian firm expressed interest. He and several colleagues conducted
preliminary research using their own money, then approached the USSR
Academy of Sciences. They wanted the Academy to set up an organization
capable of implementing the project. The iceberg scheme later died – but
the idea of the Centre was born.

The USSR Academy of Science faces two ways. It is both a government
organization, linked to and receiving funding from the Soviet power structure and a public organization, because it consists of a group of scientists.
Svirski Centre was founded in July 1988, under the Academy of Sciences,
initially to develop and put into practical application the research of the
Academy of Scientists. But the Centre's legal status as a public organization
gives it a wide leeway.

Adopting such a structure was a stroke of genius. It enabled the Centre to
branch out, acting as an umbrella to other public organizations. Such
companies could then carry out research, development and trade, free from
many constraints faced by other new forms of Soviet business – for
example, co-operatives. Radical Soviet legislation has permitted the founding of co-operatives by three or more persons, but co-operatives face higher
financial risks, heavier taxes, and a besmirched reputation because of the
links of some co-operatives with the shadow economy (and even outright
criminality).

The Centre's subsidiaries cover a broad range: an agriculture firm, oil companies, computer software companies, bio-technology and genetic engineering concerns, an alternative medicine clinic, and some social and charitable concerns.

Companies linked to the Centre span most of the republics in the USSR. Many are in Moscow but some are as far off as Siberia. They are serviced by a small regular staff of around thirty people. An executive director heads each subsidiary and takes on additional temporary staff during their project. 'It is the same process as hiring when shooting a film,' explains Albert Beliavskyi, the oldest of the Centre's three executive directors and its legal guru.

But why do Soviet scientists and entrepreneurs need such a Centre? 'Our system which existed before perestroika did not give any opportunity for innovative people to realize themselves,' Svirski explains. 'It prevented people from showing their individual potential, their organizational or creative abilities. They had no place to go to if they wanted to organize something. Before, it was necessary to spend two years setting up a company. It usually failed because it needed the approval of top authorities.'

A measure of this need is the rapid growth of Svirski's organization. Applicants are rigorously scrutinized, says Beliavskyi, and at least half of them are rejected. The Centre has never advertised – preferring people to learn of it through word-of-mouth. Companies under the Centre act independently in almost all respects. They are free to set up their own subsidiaries, so links between the Centre and its subsidiaries' daughter companies are, inevitably, loose. Too loose, maintain critics, for genuine accountability. They hint that some fringe companies may have become involved in the black economy.

Support from liberal politicians and top level contacts enables the Centre to win a reputation for getting things done rapidly. Contacts, particularly within the Russian republics' administrations, help speed through applications for registration of joint ventures. The Centre is also increasingly developing political contacts in the USA, handled, until recently, by Vladimir Korghevsky, the third executive director at the Centre and the man responsible for international relations. (Korghevsky, thirty-three, holds a PhD in philosophy. His thesis was on 'the problem of choice.')

In January the Soviet military top brass joined with Svirski's Centre to organize a conference on the new balance of power between the US and Russia. Key American military figures and foreign policy experts were invited. In the impressive conference hall, amid spanking smart uniforms weighted with medals, sat Svirski, incongruous in his luxuriant dark beard and open-necked shirt. A whisper went round that he was not one of the architects of the unprecedented seminar, but an interloper – the Iranian Foreign Minister.

In the Alice-in-Wonderland world of the Soviet economy, small things often present the biggest hitches. Finding business premises is tough, given the chronic housing shortage. Children play on coloured slides and climbing frames on a patch of grass in front of residential flats in Moscow's Twerskaya-Yamskaya street. Beside the play area a brass plate on a wooden door announces the Centre. At the top of five dusty stairs sits an armed militia guard – the evidence of official approval. A half-landing open to the stairs serves as home to a large desk fax machine and other office equipment. A door on the next landing leads into a generously-sized room: Svirski's inner sanctum.

Svirski picks a graphic example to illustrate the Centre's day-to-day workings: animal dung. Soviet collective farms pitch mountains of the stuff. 'It is a serious environmental hazard,' he says. The Centre thus willingly took aboard five scientists last September keen to devise a machine to process the dung into top quality manure and produce, as a by-product, a chemical which is used, in particular, to make the filament for medical stitches that can be left in the body without harm.

The Centre put up capital investment of 230,000 roubles for western computer equipment, salaries for the scientists and rent for premises. The scientists provided the remainder of the equipment as their investment. The research took three months and sparked other important discoveries. Their wages were 600 roubles per month (almost three times the Soviet average). Now the machinery is ready for use. The Centre is joint owner of the technology because of its initial investment which will continue to yield profit. Hard currency can be gained from export of the chemical.

Svirski was approached by Vital Shelest early last year. Shelest, who is a member of the Ukrainian Academy of Science, founded a company called Eventus under the wing of the Centre. Thirty scientists wanted to research and develop additions to light-sensitivity film, new so-called string sensors and scientific educational computer programmes. They were totally self-financing. 'We were able to sign contracts worth 50,000 roubles with state enterprises. We worked for three months without a salary and then, after the contracts were finished, we received money for wages and to enable us to invest in future activity,' says Shelest.

Most of the scientists continued to work and draw pay from their own Moscow institutes while signing up with Eventus. Top physicists may earn 400 roubles per month. At Eventus they would draw, retrospectively, a further 600 roubles per month. Now short-term projects at Eventus total 3m roubles, while long-term projects amount to 25m roubles. In any given project, up to 70 per cent of income from a contract goes to the scientists and other workers. Shelest currently has 500 employees on his books.

Shelest is fully aware of the contradictions of his position. 'The Soviet Union is now existing in a schizophrenic situation,' he says. 'The old system still remains, but a market system is also now beginning to develop. This co-existence is sometimes very difficult. We need to see a victory over the old regime because the market system is not fully established.

'When I am at the Academy some people do not understand how I can be making more money. But there are many influential scientists who support it. This company, through the Centre, gives enormous freedom to scientists. They just work. They do not have to submit lengthy documents and shuffle paper. For example, in the Academy if they want some equipment, they must submit an application, then they have to wait a year to get it. Here if we want something we just buy it and begin work tomorrow. In the Academy of Scientists you begin not tomorrow – but next year.'

Michael Mogutov's company, Bioprocess, took a hard-headed commercial decision to link with the Centre. His company, previously a co-operative, thus became a public organization with its own legal personality from October 1988.

The new form of company meant that Bioprocess was easy to establish and it offered substantial tax advantages. (The tax on a public organization like Bioprocess is 10 per cent of profit. Co-operatives are taxed on income.) Bioprocess has thrived, developing a wide range of activities – from genetic engineering projects to a joint venture involving the export of Soviet art. Its turnover last year amounted to 3.5m roubles.

The drab, dingy corridors of Moscow's XVth Tagansky district hospital house an example of privatized health care. Dr Anatoly Sitel is a specialist in manual therapy. His centre of alternative medicine, Altermed, was set up under the Centre in September last year. New work includes application of alternative medicine in the treatment of AIDS. He says his team of twenty doctors works six hours a day for the state, six hours for private patients. State enterprises have started employing his chiropractors: the Lada factory on the Volga signed a contract for the treatment of 2000 employees at 154 roubles per person. Foreign contracts are in the offing. His doctors gain around 140 roubles per month from the state and anywhere up to an additional 600 roubles from their work with Altermed.

Svirski speaks with pride of the Centre's development and diversity: 80 per cent of the subsidiaries are scientific and technical in nature, 20 per cent are social or other types of organizations. But in May, after two years passivity, the Academy of Sciences, like a sleeping giant, awoke. It began to baulk at the Centre's activities. Svirski was instructed to terminate all businesses not directly connected with scientific research and to rein in other aspects of the operation. 'The Academy wanted the Centre and our organizations to stay within the very strict management and control of its planning and financial department. It was demanding centralization and this contradicts our interests,' says Svirski.

A face-off ensued and the Centre cut its ties with the Academy. Given the prestige of two years' development and using political contacts, Svirski moved to make the Centre a public organization in its own right. Beliavskyi says dormant legislation from the 1930s provided a sound legal base and the constitution guarantees the right for any group of citizens to unite in a public organization. He cites the principle of the Gorbachev era: 'what is not forbidden is allowed.' Svirski brandishes a thick file of letters, 'these are major public organizations that want to adopt us.'

For all Svirski's bullishness, public opinion in the Soviet Union will be hard to persuade of the virtues of such enterprise. Years of schooling in anti-market demonology has led to a preference for the queue rather than reform.

It was this pressure that forced Mikhail Gorbachev to delay and rework in April his pro-market reform packages. Sergey Krasavchenko, a people's deputy of Russia, says: 'our people have developed bad habits. If a man sees his neighbour lives better than he does, he does not feel inspired to improve his own life – he wants to make his neighbour live as badly as he does. Many people are not ready to accept the market and the reforms, but at the same time people are unable to live as they live now. That is why I think it is a very difficult task to explain it to them and to change their psychology.'

Spring brought internal strains at the Centre. A personality clash with Svirski left Korghevsky plananing to set up alone. By June, he was out. Says Svirski: 'he was expelled for actions injurious to the interests of the Centre. Meanwhile Svirski nurses a new project – founding an international organization with foreign partners. It would claim international status and would be free from many constraints of Soviet law. Svirski and the Centre look set to chart a new route this summer: another chapter in the topsy-turvy world of business in today's Soviet Union.

# Section Ten

## Predictions

# 47

# Four men's future: the road to the new millennium

January 1990

## Carol Kennedy

The last ten years of the twentieth century, according to the best scenarios of business futurology, should be paved with opportunities for new markets, resources and wealth creation undreamed of a decade ago. In some forecasts, too, broad sunlit uplands of leisure beckon for a fortunate body of the middle-aged middle class, through a combination of increased asset worth and changing priorities on the use of time. But, almost certainly, the job of managing companies will be more demanding than ever in a rip-tide of rapidly changing political and technological conditions.

'The complexity of the management task will get more severe,' says Paul Thornton of PA management consultants. 'The number of things firms will have to respond to will increase. The 1990s will be faster than the 1980s. British companies have tended to be weak in responding to change, and rapid response is going to be at the heart of winning.'

Some skill in futurology is required equipment for the chief executives of multinationals. They are constantly having to plan for 'worst-case' scenarios in the context of developments that the most experienced forecasters sometimes cannot see coming. As ICI chairman Sir Denys Henderson observes from hard-won experience: 'No one in the futurology game, and certainly not the professional economists, ever predicts the major discontinuities such as the OPEC crisis.'

With that in mind, and the awareness that 'the only certainty is uncertainty,' in the lugubrious dictum of Italian management guru Alfredo Ambrosetti, we asked Henderson and the heads of three other leading British companies – Sir Peter Walters of BP, Derek Birkin of RTZ and Sir Christopher Hogg of Courtaulds – along with some professional forecasters, what the biggest issues for management are likely to be in the 1990s. Amid all the talk of 'globalization' and 'global brands' – the universally branded product tailored to individual national tastes – we also sought a crystal ball on the prospects for small business.

Only one of the chief executives we talked to – BP chairman Sir Peter

Walters – thinks management has already gone through some of its toughest times and that shrewd use of information technology ought, for most companies, to 'create more mental elbow-room for management.'

As a practical demonstration, he proudly shows off the video-conferencing room in Britannic House, a few steps from the chairman's 31st-floor office. Here, several times a week, BP's head office team talks face to face with colleagues in Aberdeen or Anchorage, Alaska: virtually the whole of BP's global operation can be hooked up on a bilateral basis, saving the company huge amounts in travel costs and executive time; shortening meetings and enabling one person, in Walters' words, to 'do the work of one and a half.'

Looking through the 1990s to the twenty-first century, the basic mood was one of cautious but determined optimism – 'I have got to be optimistic, or I would not be a manager,' says Courtaulds' chairman Sir Christopher Hogg, a noted long-term strategic thinker whose recent announcement of Courtaulds' planned demerger was four years in the hatching.

It was a dramatic time to be reading the future. Suddenly, international management scenarios had been shaken up by the helter-skelter sequence of events in eastern Europe, where forty years of communism seemed on the verge of self-destruction.

Derek Birkin, chief executive of the mining and minerals global giant RTZ – Britain's only leading world player in its field – says the new climate in eastern Europe is 'going to play a major part' in business assumptions over the next decade. 'The question is how the West can help in this process of democracy and improvement of living standards and how particular companies can assist that process while making a sensible return for shareholders.'

With due caution on Soviet President Gorbachev's chances of survival and how far he can 'dismantle the Soviet empire' and meet aspirations for better living standards, Birkin says: 'the longer he carries on, the more irreversible it will be. If Gorbachev can be around for another five years in power, then I think it will be irreversible, and we are talking about a very dynamic situation. It is going to take to the end of the century before all the factors are in play to permit these areas to explode in business terms, though up to then there will be selective opportunities.'

ICI's Henderson concurs: 'I am quite certain the genie's got out of the bottle and that people in eastern Europe want to see their living standards improved. The big question is: will that be achieved, or will we see another Tiananmen Square? But let us take the optimistic scenario.'

Mindful of history's lessons that a country with internal problems is sometimes dangerously led to seek external diversions, Henderson explains the basis on which he looks at global developments.

'I am assuming that whatever happens in the Eastern bloc, it is not going to lead to confrontations with the West – that is a terribly important qualification. So is the assumption that, in business, we manage to skirt around serious trade wars involving the US, Europe and Japan. There are always problems in that particular area, which we somehow manage to tiptoe through.' (Derek Birkin of RTZ seems less sanguine in this area, fearing above all the threat of protectionism from North America which could, in his view, lead to a real risk of world depression.)

With those reservations, Henderson continues, 'the reason I am relatively optimistic is that one hopes we continue to see world peace and that less is spent on defence, and resources are therefore freed up for economic growth. I think the growth will be there, particularly in the eastern bloc and China and LDCs, providing the OECD countries can find a way to make resources available to those in need.

'People now recognize there is a much greater interdependence across world economies and that by co-ordinating in a broad way, you can hope to avoid major disruptions and discontinuities.'

BP's chairman takes the view that the current upheavals in eastern Europe are a supreme example of 'consumerism on the march.' Before the events of late autumn 1989, most forecasters had expected the process to take considerably longer, but in Walters' thinking 'the rise of consumer expectations is inexorable and inevitable.' He sees a much longer timeframe for change in China (we spoke the day before Deng Xaio-ping finally stepped down from his paramount leadership), adding the sombre observation that China's present 800 million population is predicted to explode by another 200 million by the year 2015.

For the energy industry in particular, the prospect of liberalizing business with Russia and eastern Europe glitters with promise. The Soviet Union, Walters points out, has 'almost inexhaustible supplies of natural gas' – maybe 200 years of it. BP and a number of other companies are 'well along the road' to economic conversion of natural gas to gasoline, at present an expensive two-stage process that only New Zealand, with no oil but plenty of gas, finds feasible.

By the end of the century, Walters is confident, fuel from this source will be available at more economic prices than from conventional crude oil, which by then will be scarcer and more costly as accessible reserves dwindle. Fuel from converted gas would also help banish a spectre the BP chief sees looming in the mid-1990s, when the OPEC oil-producing countries, given the rise in the West's consumption and the lack of growth from non-OPEC sources, may well spring another shattering price rise on the world.

Asia Pacific – its threats and opportunities – is another preoccupation for chief executives as they contemplate the coming decade.

'It is going to be a significant opportunity for growth in the next decade, probably for fairly basic chemicals rather than specialities,' says ICI's Henderson. 'But there could be threats, because although local markets will be able to absorb most of the output, some could wash over into Western markets.

'We are pretty well represented in Asia Pacific countries and beginning to put in significant amounts of investment: I think it is the beginning of an exciting growth period there.' Of Japan's own pharmaceuticals industry, Henderson says companies there are spending 'very significant sums on R & D and I would be surprised if they don't grow over the next few years.

'You have to pay heed to what they are doing and face up to that competition. We feel well able to do that because one thing the Japanese have not had much experience in is getting new products through the regulatory agencies in countries outside Japan. But I have no reason to suppose that, if they put their minds to it, they cannot do that.'

Japan Inc is without doubt the biggest single management challenge of the 1990s for the cerebral Sir Christopher Hogg of Courtaulds, the textiles and chemicals giant. He worries what will happen when Japanese companies begin to operate in a truly global fashion instead of, as up to now, mainly building their industrial base in Japan and sending the products all over the world. (The process is already well under way: Sir Douglas Wass, chairman of Nomura International, predicted recently that Japanese direct investment in Europe would rise from its present 17 per cent of Japan's total to around 30 per cent by the year 2000.)

The basic problem, as Hogg sees it, has been growing for two decades but is going to become 'positively acute' in the 1990s.

'We in the West are better at running genuinely international businesses, but what we have not succeeded in doing, with rare exceptions, is building up in the workforce the same commitment to the organization that the Japanese have, and tapping that commitment so that it is reflected in real advances.

'I think that Japanese companies will run into their own problems when they try to cope with organizing on an international scale, as opposed to operating globally from a Japanese base, but we should not draw too much comfort from that because they are so good, so determined, so committed, so effective, that our difficulty in the West is going to be matching them and beating them.'

Both US and UK businesses, however, are likely to be shackled in this, says Hogg, because of the basic short-termism governing the two societies. This runs right through, from the two-party political pendulum on four or five-year horizons ('it is depressing that the centre parties have not succeeded for that reason') to the finance-driven emphasis on company performance, says Hogg.

For those who run publicly quoted companies, he observes, 'a significant amount of time' is spent on concern about the next quarter, half-year or annual figures – how they will be reported, what the effect on the share price will be and who might be eyeing it. In this, Hogg is not so much concerned by M & A predators as by underlying attitudes, 'the relative lack of interest in what makes for good long-term results.' These are not problems that bedevil Japanese industry, he points out.

ICI's Sir Denys Henderson also points to the issue of 'shareholder power' in deciding for the long or short term, and management's responsibility to explain its strategy, essential in the long-term nature of the chemical industry: ICI spends '£1000 a minute' on research and development.

'Increasingly, in the aftermath of what I call the greedy 1980s, shareholders have to make their minds up – is it short-term benefit they want, or long-term growth? This impacts particularly on the chemical industry, where you get the Germans and the Japanese taking the long-term view and the UK and US (which in my view are the only truly open markets), going for instant shareholder value. I think there is a real dilemma here, not only for shareholders but for business in general and in the end I suspect for government too, because it comes back to what sort of economy we think is the right one for this country.'

Hogg is convinced that the short-termism problem is 'much more serious and fundamental than people realize, and that is because practically everyone in a position to do something about it – whether in politics or the financial sector or industry – is caught up in it.'

The Courtaulds chairman's linked views on Japanese long-term thinking and Japanese-style involvement in corporate effort were a driving component behind the planned demerger in 1990 of the textiles and chemicals giant into two separately quoted companies – the test of which will only be apparent ten years from now, he says.

'We are shifting to a management that is younger and therefore has a longer term time-frame; I am taking particular pains now to ensure that what we want to do is thoroughly discussed and thought through. There has to be an enormous proselytizing process in an organization, and the demerger will make this hugely easier.

'I am preoccupied with how to get every bit of a large company thinking like a small company, but you only do that if you are doing the sort of things that the Japanese have done so well.

'I have got to be optimistic or I wouldn't be a manager, but it won't be easy. Big organizations change their habits pretty slowly. But there is nothing much in industry worth anything that is created in under ten or fifteen years – whether it is a brand, a product or a new chemical plant.'

Will we have moved towards the Japanese model by the year 2000? 'We will have moved some way towards it,' says Hogg. 'The question is: how far will the Japanese have moved in the meantime?'

The challenge to management of securing employee commitment goes far beyond the Japanese threat, given the unanimous predictions that Britain and Western Europe are facing a demographic timebomb in the mid-1990s. The heads of large companies are keenly aware, in the words of ICI's Henderson, that managements are 'going to have to work much harder at persuading the bright youngsters of tomorrow that theirs is the business to be in and stay in. Education, the need to improve the skill basis and to attract, motivate and retain top quality employees, is going to be a major challenge.'

Demographics aside, the Henley Centre for Forecasting suggests that managerial and professional skills may be in shorter supply by the end of the century for another reason – the rise in personal asset worth. The middle-aged middle class is increasingly benefiting from inheritance – bequests were running at £10bn in 1988, over half of that going to the 40–50 age bracket, and Henley expects this figure to double by the century's end.

On top of that, says Henley managing director Bob Tyrrell, there is the possibility of people being 'distracted from work' by realizing that their net asset worth offers them the chance of a more leisured and fulfilling way of life. Henley's research suggests that the 'busyness' ethos of the 1980s, when manufacturers waxed profitable on products aimed at managing time, may wane in the 1990s – incidentally forcing a search for new markets for such fashionable adjuncts as personal organizers and mobile phones.

'Priorities in the 1990s will be very different,' says Tyrrell. 'A lot of people have tasted success and found something still lacking. People's attitudes will shift to appreciate the value of time itself.'

Tyrrell sees the 1980s' workaholism as something of an aberration in history, with the well-heeled rising early and working all hours while poorer, less skilled people had time on their hands.

'We are going to see a profound change in symbols and peer groups: if you think of Richard Branson, what is he best known for? Success in activities outside his business,' says Tyrrell.

BP's planning for the skills shortage of the 1990s revolves around two main strategies: better use of information technology and more recruitment of women. BP recruits around 400 graduates a year (80 per cent of them technical graduates) and a quarter are now women.

RTZ's chief executive looks at the recruitment challenge in the context of environmental pressures on his industry, which, like the oil and chemical industries, occupies the front line of 'green' assaults. RTZ's capital spending on the environment, 'always fairly significant, will now intensify,' says Birkin, who has scant sympathy for any company that does not accept its responsibilities in this area. But he warns that if the mining industry does not improve its image on the environment, 'young people will want to go elsewhere.'

Birkin sees it as all part of a growing demand for 'good stewardship in the broadest sense. If the capitalist system is going to survive, and I believe it to be the only proven method of wealth creation, then I think it is going to be even more important that the stewardship is seen to be exemplary, in terms of morals, eschewing greed, while still being hard-nosed and professional. I think there will be an increasing focus on business and businessmen: people are going to have to be seen as effective leaders. Secrecy is just not going to be practical. The younger generation is more sensitive and aware of these issues.'

All the chief executives interviewed anticipated higher expenditure on environmental research, but saw a positive side to the way businesses are being forced to concentrate on environmental matters: not merely in being seen as good corporate citizens but in the scope for new products and services – 'it creates a hell of a lot of new markets,' says Courtaulds' Hogg. But ICI's chairman warns that if consumers demand ever more 'green' products, they will have to pay the cost. 'It can't simply be paid for by the manufacturing industry and will have to be passed on: as yet people have not faced up to that.'

If most of the 1990s' corporate issues – globalization, the ability to exploit new markets from an international base, the ability to invest heavily in environmental R & D – seem to favour the mighty multinational (and BP's Walters believes larger corporate units, by trans-border merger, will be needed in Europe to 'form critical mass and selectively excellent units – my management philosophy'), what does the future hold for the smaller company? Sue Birley, professor of small business studies at Cranfield and a small business practitioner herself who runs a venture capital consultancy, is optimistic on several counts.

She believes there will be 'significant changes in the strategy that large firms will adopt towards smaller suppliers, and more relationships of different natures between them – alliances, licensing arrangements, franchises, joint ventures, investment in R & D, services to suppliers such as management development. Many large firms are already downsizing, going back to their core businesses and strengthening supplier links.'

Birley says the stories of large firms ruthlessly squeezing small suppliers by late paying are largely myth – 'the best propaganda the small firms sector has ever achieved.'

'I run a small firm and I can tell you that our worst payers are other small firms.'

Changing employment patterns will also radically affect the small firm/large firm stereotypes. 'There will be a lot of hiring people on a freelance or project basis, as the media already do.'

Birley is convinced that, despite current handicaps like the steep interest rates, people will continue to take a chance on business start-ups. 'The majority of small start-ups do not borrow heavily anyway. But whatever the complexion of governments in the 1990s, they will continue to encourage enterprise, though the incentives will change.

'It is now very much embedded in people's minds that it is possible to start your own business, and this runs right through from kids at school to executives of large corporations. There are also sufficient role models around for people to feel encouraged. Richard Branson has been very useful here!'

She admits there will be hard challenges in the single market, where it will be difficult for the lone entrepreneur to find out about standards and directives.

'The whole issue of deregulation is in a mess across Europe and it is a huge issue that is going to come thundering down on the small business sector, affecting different parts in different ways. Some sectors, like construction and food, are going to be oppressed by directives. But there are huge opportunities for technology-based industries, which require a bigger market base to take off.'

Will life be tougher in the 1990s, for the small business operator? Birley prefers to think of it as exciting. 'But it's sure as hell going to be different.'